臺灣教會史料論集

王成勉◎主編

中央大學出版中心｜遠流

目　錄

四、個案史料研究

作者簡介
（依筆畫順序排列）

王成勉

美國亞歷桑那大學博士。曾任中央大學歷史研究所所長，現為中央大學歷史研究所特聘教授兼文學院明清研究中心主任。主要著作：《文社的盛衰：二○年代基督徒本色化之個案研究》、《教會、文化與國家：對基督教史研究的思索與案例》，主編 *Contextualization of Christianity in China: An Evaluation in Modern Perspective* 等。

王政文

臺灣師範大學歷史學博士。現職：東海大學歷史學系助理教授。主要著作：《臺灣義勇隊：臺灣抗日團體在大陸的活動（1937-1945）》、〈改宗所引起的家庭與人際衝突：以十九世紀臺灣基督徒為例〉、〈無語問上帝：十九世紀臺灣基督徒的社會處境〉等。

古偉瀛

加拿大不列顛哥倫比亞大學歷史學博士。曾任臺灣大學歷史學系系主任，現為臺灣大學歷史學系教授。主要著作：《臺灣天主教史研究論集》、《戰後台灣的歷史學研究，1945-2000》（合編）、《後現代與歷史學：中西比較》（合著）。

李宜涯

中國文化大學中文研究所博士。曾任中原大學人文與教育學院通識教育中心主任，現為中原大學通識中心教授兼圖書館館長。主要著作：《聖壇前的創作——20年代基督教文學研究》，《晚唐詠史詩與平話演義之關係》。

張妙娟

臺灣師範大學歷史研究所博士。曾任高雄應用科技大學通識教育中心副教授。主要著作：〈日治前期臺灣南部長老教會的主日學教育研究（1895-1926）〉、《開啟心眼──《臺灣府城教會報》與長老教會的基督徒教育》等。

黃子寧

臺灣大學歷史學系碩士，臺灣大學歷史學系博士候選人。主要著作：《天主教在屏東萬金的生根發展（1861-1962）》、〈林獻堂與基督教（1927-1945）〉。

黃淑薇（Irene S. M. Wong）

美國新澤西州立大學圖書館服務學碩士。現職：香港浸會大學圖書館特藏及文獻組主任、資深助理館長。主要著作："The Overseas Chinese Clippings Database at Hong Kong Baptist University Library"; (co-author), "Creating a virtual union catalog for Hong Kong dissertations and theses collections" ; (co-author) , "Applicability of IMLS Framework to Digitization Projects".

鄭睦群

中國文化大學史學研究所博士。現職：馬偕醫護管理專科學校通識中心兼任講師。主要著作：〈淡水基督長老教會對時代的因應──以「二二八事件」與「美援時代」為研究中心〉、〈台灣基督長老教會國家認同與其論述轉換之研究（1970-2000）〉。

Jonathan Benda（班達）

Ph. D., Composition and Cultural Rhetoric, Syracuse University. Lecturer, Department of English, Northeastern University, USA. Major Publications:

"Difficult Writing: Representation and Responsibility in Narratives of Cross-Cultural Encounters"; "Empathy and Its Others: The Voice of Asia, A Pail of Oysters, and the Empathetic Writing of Formosa," in *Concentric: Literary and Cultural Studies.*

Martha Lund Smalley（司馬倫）

M. A. in History, Trinity College, Hartford. Special Collections Librarian and Curator of the Day Missions Collection, Yale Divinity School Library. Major Publications: *An Archival Primer: A practical guide for building and maintaining an archival program;* (ed.), *American missionary eyewitnesses to the Nanking Massacre, 1937-1938.*

Yuki Takai-Heller（高井ヘラー由紀）

Ph. D., International Christian University, Tokyo. Research Fellow at Meiji Gakuin University. Major publications: 〈日本統治下台湾におけるプロテスタント教会史研究 (1895-1945)〉、"Shokuminchi Tochi-Kozo ni okeru Kirisuto-kyo to Sono Ekkyo-sei ni Kansuru Ichi-Kosatsu – 1910 nendai no Taiwan YMCA to K. W. Dowie wo Chuushin ni".

Rolf Gerhard Tiedemann（狄德滿）

Ph. D., School of Oriental and African Studies, University of London. Professorial Research Associate, School of Oriental and African Studies, University of London; Professor, Center for Boxer Movement Studies, Shandong University, China. Major Publications: *Reference Guide to Christian Missionary Societies in China: From the 16th to the 20th Century; Handbook of Christianity in China*, Vol. II.

序

　　史料是史學研究的基礎，而收集史料和了解史料則是進行歷史研究的第一步。「臺灣研究」是近二十多年來在臺灣以及海外發展迅速的新興領域，同時，有關臺灣的史料也不斷被開發出來，在研究上形成更加豐富與多元的現象。

　　然而「臺灣研究」界對於入臺已有數百年的基督教會史料，卻長期存在認識不夠與使用不足的現象，不但影響到對教會歷史的認識，亦形成「臺灣研究」的一項缺憾。臺灣教會史料之所以未被廣泛運用，主要有兩方面的因素。一方面是語言的問題，荷文、西文、葡文以及拉丁文的教會史料，雖然學界多少知道其存在，但是只限於少數學者能夠使用。另一方面是教會界不了解史料的重要性，或是視為私人之物，或是猜忌外來者能否「善用」史料，欠缺積極的開放，故教會界收藏如何，一般學界也了解不多。

　　教會史料是研究臺灣一項頗具特色的史料。教會不但留存自身的歷史，還會因為傳教事工與教會（機構）發展的考量，往往對宣教地區加以記載。至於被差派的宣教士更會詳細向母會報告，從當地宗教的氛圍、教會發展、當地風土人情以迄政治、社會的情況，都會成為他報告或書信的內容。教會機構也會依據地方法令對活動、經費等加以記載。至於神職人員（包括宣教士）和教會信眾亦屢有留下個人資料或傳記。所以幾百年前即開始有相關的教會史料，特別是自晚清起，教會界開始積藏史料，而且呈現越來越豐富的形式。在教會檔案館中，甚至有不少臺灣民俗的收藏。另一個值得注意之處，就是臺灣的教會經歷過被宣教、自主教會、向外宣教等階段，故教會的檔案中，甚至有臺灣教會對海外地區的宣教資料，可以作為了解國外地區與教會之用。更進一步來說，教會史料雖不如官方檔案之系統分明與完整，但是因為信仰的關係，極少有偽造或竄改的情況，故甚有利用與開發的價值。

過去研究臺灣宗教或以基督宗教為主題的會議與論文已經不少，但是對於臺灣教會史料的相關會議卻極為稀少。唯一的一次是筆者在十五年前籌劃的「臺灣基督教史——史料與研究回顧」國際學術研討會，邀請學界與教會人士，就史料與教會史的研究情況加以探討。當時參與者有賴永祥、古偉瀛、鮑曉歐（Jose Eugenio Borao）、郭德士（John E. Geddes）、翁佳音、練馬可（Mark Thelin）、查時傑、鄭仰恩、吳學明等人。研討會中所討論的史料廣及天主教的耶穌會、道明會以及菲律賓、荷蘭、加拿大等地的相關史料。此項會議在筆者籌備完後，由宇宙光機構接手會務和會後論文集的出版。

　　雖然該次會議與出版對教會界與學術界有所貢獻，也常見諸於後來相關的博碩士論文的參考書目，但是由於當時會議能夠含括的教會史料還是有限，同時在近十餘年來教會界史料開放上又有新的進展。如近年來一些在臺的重要宗派（如聚會所、真耶穌教會、聖公會等）都與外界有較多的來往，天主教的輔仁神學院、輔仁大學天主教史料研究中心亦更加開放。另外，在各層級的官方檔案中，亦發現不少與臺灣教會相關的文獻，值得加以分析，供教會界注意和利用。

　　有見於此，筆者遂爭取由中央大學歷史研究所、中原大學通識教育中心與臺灣基督教史學會聯合舉辦學術研討會。在上一次會議的基礎上進一步探討臺灣教會史料，不重複上次已經介紹和討論的教會史料，而在介紹新檔案館與教會相關史料，並注重史料的分析，包括史料的性質為何、史料分布的時間與重點何在、與教會發展的關係，甚至是教會對於典藏史料的措施與心態。另外一個重要的地方，就是希望學者能夠同時闡發教會史料中所反映出來當時臺灣社會與政治的情況，讓研究者也可以藉教會史料來佐證近代臺灣歷史的發展。

　　此次會議獲得各方良好的反應。首先是學術界踴躍的參與及提供論文，他們的著作可以分成兩類。在史料貯藏與分析上，耶魯大學神學院圖書館特藏部主任Martha Smalley（司馬倫）女士，特別撰文介紹耶魯大學神學院中有關臺灣的典藏。耶魯大學神學院是收藏基督新教史料最豐富的地方，而過去學界殊少注意到該檔案館中之臺灣教會的史料，故司馬倫女士的文章讓臺灣學界認識到他們的收藏。同樣的，香港浸會大學圖書館助理館長黃淑薇女士也特別前來發表專文，介紹浸會大學如何建立基督教史料的特藏部，成為今天亞洲基督教的史料中心之一。張妙娟教授則對臺灣基督長老教會的「臺灣教會史料館」（臺灣基督教會創設最早、館藏最豐富的檔案館）加以研究，一方面討論其館藏史料的保存與管理，另一方面也擇要介紹其重要史料的內容，有助於學者對此檔案館的了解。王成勉與王政文的文章則分別對於教會相關史料的保存、管理及研究方向的創新提出討論與建議。

　　第二類的論文是集中在對於特殊史料的意義與分析。學者們介紹許多非常有特色的史料，並呈現其中豐富的史料價值，如古偉瀛教授探討天主教的主要史料《教友生活周刊》之研究、李宜涯教授對於中原大學董事長張靜愚日記的探討、黃子寧對於楊雲萍所藏文書之長老教會白話字文獻的研究、鄭睦群對於臺灣基督長老教會地方教會議事錄的研究、倫敦大學亞非學院的資深教授狄德滿（Rolf Gerhard Tiedemann）介紹英國長老教會檔案中對於臺灣政治與文化的描述、班達（Jonathan Benda）教授討論了Oberlin College檔案館中有關東海大學的史料、日本學者高井ヘラー由紀由紀則提供日本教會刊物中對於臺灣的報導。無論是美國、英國與日本都有各式各樣與臺灣關係密切的教會史料，而這些資料不僅對於教會史極為重要，更含括到對臺灣社會的許多層面的報導。可以說每一項特殊史料的介紹，都引起與會者高度的興趣與討論。

　　這次會議也引起教會界高度的注意與參與。我們原本是邀請單國璽樞機主教前來做主題演講。他也很高興的答應了，可是到會議前三週，他的肺癌被發現轉移，必須再做化療。他在化療後親自打電話給我表示無法前來，聽到他平靜而又真摯的口氣，實在是非常感謝與感動。就在這個緊急的時候，承蒙古偉瀛教授幫忙，代為邀請到狄剛總主教來擔任主題演講人，非常謝謝他的精彩演講。教會界的積極參與還特別在會議安排的「圓桌論壇」中表現出來。許多教會機構都派員參加這次的會議，我們也邀請一些教會機構介紹他們的史料典藏。如臺灣神學院的鄭仰恩教授願意來主持這論壇，做專題介紹的有：臺灣浸會神學院查時傑教授，輔仁大學天主教史料研究中心陳方中主任，臺灣神學院史料中心盧啟明研究助理，臺灣基督教青年會協會尹遴秘書，臺灣信義會陳志宏監督，以及中華福音神學院圖書館莊秀禎館長。從他們的參與和介紹史料，可以感受到教會界開始關注史料，也遠比以前更加開放。

這次研討會後我們仍然進行學術把關，將會議參與者的文章送交國內外的資深學者進行外審。部分文章因為未能完全符合會議的主旨，或是需要過於重大的修正，我們只有割愛。各篇文章的作者後來也都參考了外審意見做了修改。所以現在刊出的論文，都是經過嚴格的外審與論文的修正，相信會得到學術界的認可，也有助於日後臺灣史與教會史的研究。

最後，會議的舉辦與此專書的出版有諸多要感謝的地方。首先是會議籌備小組、出席會議的學者以及教會界的熱情參與，對我們來說是最大的鼓勵。其次，國科會、中央大學研發處、中央大學文學院、臺灣基督教史學會的經費贊助，讓我們在主辦會議上得以免除經費上的困擾。另外，中央大學歷史研究所在會務、出版上的協助，使得各項工作進行順利。而中央大學出版中心慧眼將書稿納入出版計畫，以及遠流出版公司曾淑正主編的細心編務，才使得這本書能以今日的面貌呈現。這本論文集的出版，相信對於日後教會史、臺灣研究、宗教研究都有開創性的貢獻，這也是我們向所有幫助者最好的致謝方式。

王成勉
誌於中央大學歷史研究所
2013年10月24日

【一・綜合史料分析】

十九世紀臺灣基督徒研究與史料探討

王政文

東海大學歷史學系助理教授

摘要

　　本文的主要目的是探討十九世紀臺灣基督徒的相關研究與史料。首先，說明十九世紀臺灣基督徒研究的重要性，指出臺灣基督教史的論述應跳脫傳統以教會及傳教士為主軸的框架，逐步建立以信徒為主體的研究及歷史論述。其次，回顧以往有關十九世紀臺灣基督徒的研究成果，分析相關討論議題及研究所使用的資料，說明過去研究的侷限以及待開發的史料與議題。文中將現存十九世紀臺灣基督徒的相關史料，歸納為：一、教會檔案；二、書報雜誌；三、傳教士著作與回憶錄；四、基督徒著作；五、官方檔案等五類資料，分別加以說明。最後，舉出「洗禮簿」與「信徒名冊」等待開發資料，在十九世紀臺灣基督徒研究上的運用空間。

關鍵詞：十九世紀臺灣、基督徒、史料、洗禮簿、信徒名冊

一、前言

本文的主要目的是探討十九世紀臺灣基督徒的相關研究與資料。首先，檢視以往臺灣基督教史研究中以教會及傳教士為主軸的書寫脈絡，說明被忽略的十九世紀臺灣基督徒研究的重要性，並指出臺灣基督教史的論述架構應跳脫傳統「福音史觀」的框架，研究的對象也應從傳教士轉移至信徒，開拓研究視野，逐漸發展以信徒為主體的觀察及歷史論述。在解釋上也應跳脫現代化理論下重視教會醫療、教育及社會貢獻的論述模式，並反省以往研究理論的缺陷及新研究方向的可能性。其次，觀察以往有關十九世紀臺灣基督徒的討論及研究成果，分析過去相關討論議題及研究所使用的資料，由此說明過去研究的侷限以及待開發的史料與議題。

本文的重點亦在介紹及說明現存十九世紀臺灣基督徒的相關史料，歸納並分析：一、教會檔案；二、書報雜誌；三、傳教士著作與回憶錄；四、基督徒著作；五、官方檔案等五類資料。說明各類史料中有關信徒的資料性質，了解這些史料的立場及其背後所呈現的社會意涵。

最後，介紹待開發的資料；舉出「洗禮簿」與「信徒名冊」在信徒研究上有待開發的空間，及如何將這些資料運用在十九世紀臺灣基督徒的研究上。另外，像是信徒的著作、當事人的記錄、後人對前人的回憶、族譜、訃文、照片……等資料，都有待開發和利用。透過現存史料的爬梳，及待開發資料的挖掘，再配合田野調查、口述訪問，逐步建立紮實的十九世紀臺灣基督徒研究。

二、議題的重要性

基督教的歷史研究大多重視傳教士的傳教過程，教會的擴張與宣教的方式成為教會史的研究重點。臺灣基督教史的研究多數是從宗派發展、福音傳播等視野來探討基督教的發展與變遷。有關臺灣基督教史人物的論述，大部分亦都偏向於來臺的傳教士，對於本地信徒的研究則相對缺少。臺灣基督教史的主體應是本地信徒與教會，然而著名的傳教士卻成為論述的主軸，成為歷史書寫的主角，是強勢的、是主動的，信徒卻反而成為配角，改宗者（convert）被忽略，被弱智化、被動化。[1] 相對於歷史書寫下傳教士的積極作為，本地信徒成為被動的接受者。就宗教角度而言，傳福音是教會的首要任務，信徒的改宗（conversion）和信仰歷程應成為討論重點，但在臺灣基督教史的書寫中，教會對社會、教育、醫療的貢獻卻成為討論重心。

受到新文化史及後現代思潮的影響，史學最大的轉向是探討的主題由政治制度史轉為社會文化史，重視的對象由權力者轉向社會底層。近來從「東方主義」的研究延伸出「主體」與「客體」相互認識的議題，以往直線式宣教史的研究受到挑戰，研究者開始重新思考傳教者與接受者之間的關係。而殖民論述與從屬群體（subalterns）的研究指出被忽略的異質部分，期望找回失語者的文化，說明被壓迫的種族、階級、性別並非如同所書寫的，這引起基督教史研究對接受者的關注。同時，新文化的研究理論也強調，文化差異是一種動態的概念，反應交往過程中的互變過程，引發對霸權文化與土著文化關係的討論，教會史研究也應重新思索基督教文化與當地文化的關係。回顧早期以「現代化理論」、「帝國主義侵略」、「互動交流」解釋基督教的作品，已經遭受「後學」的挑戰。後現代主義揚棄一元解釋及西方中心，後殖民主義使研究重點移向原本遭忽視的「它者」及底層的聲音，而對東方主義的反省，更讓我們注意論述者的說話位置。

新的研究趨勢與方法理論，迄今尚未反映在臺灣基督教史的研究上。近年來中外學界有關基督教在華史的研究，不論在研究對象與問題意識上，都積極與新的理論及方法對話。[2] 臺灣基督教史的研究架

---

1 James T. Richardson, "Studies of Conversion: Secularization or Re-enchantment?," in Phillip E. Hammond, ed., *The Sacred in a Secular Age: Toward Revision in the Scientific Study of Religion* (Berkeley: University of California Press, 1985), pp. 104-121.

2 參見Nicolas Standaert著，劉賢譯，〈文化相遇的方法論：以十七世紀中歐文化相遇為例〉，收入吳梓

構勢亦有必要突破傳統研究者的宣教式研究，跳脫傳統「福音史觀」的框架，而以傳教士為主軸的論述也應轉為以信徒為主體的觀察。在解釋上應跳脫現代化理論下重視教會醫療、教育及社會貢獻的論述模式，而方法上也不應侷限於傳統式的實證史學。

　　戰後學界對於基督教史的研究是由近代史領域中衍生出來，研究重點在了解東西文化的交流與衝突，研究的架構多放在現代化理論或外交史領域中進行。現代化理論認為人類社會必須由傳統轉型向現代，而西化是現代化，傳教士將西方文明帶至東方。因而這類的研究肯定傳教士在交流中的角色，強調基督教在社會、教育、醫療等方面的貢獻，說明教會對臺灣社會現代化的啟蒙。[3] 而教案研究或外交史領域的基督教研究，目的不在了解基督教史，旨在探求涉外事件的處理，大多在討論政治架構下的中西交流模式，或說明西力東漸下社會交流衝突的原因。[4] 因而關心的主題是中外關係或仇外因素，而不是基督教。

　　另外，觀察相關基督教史研究的論述觀點，研究者經常出現兩種盲點：其一是過度誇耀基督教的偉大，而呈現出美化傳教過程的歷史面貌。其二是過於批評挾著西方武力侵略傳入的基督教，進而只注重到其外來與反教的一面。這兩種論述方式都是在描述基督教發展過程中經常見到的現象。研究者當注意到，在西方興起背景下東來的基督教，其本身的宗教性及其與東方文化的交涉過程，並要反省本身的觀

明、吳小新主編，《基督教與中國社會文化：第一屆國際年青學者研討會論文集》（香港：香港中文大學崇基學院宗教與中國社會研究中心，2003），頁31-80。相關討論見陳慧宏，〈「文化相遇的方法論」——評析中歐文化交流研究的新視野〉，《臺大歷史學報》，第40期（2007年12月），頁239-278。

3 董芳苑，〈論長老教會與臺灣的現代化〉，收入張炎憲編，《臺灣近百年史論文集》（臺北：吳三連史料基金會，1996），頁183-211；周宗賢，〈清末基督教宣教師對臺灣醫療的貢獻〉，《臺灣文獻》，第35卷3期（1984年09月），頁1-10。

4 呂實強《中國官紳反教的原因》一書是代表作品。他指出儒家傳統的「華夷之辨」、「人禽之辨」及「循理精神」，傳教事業的侵略性質，以及中國社會習俗與官紳現實利益等，均構成反教的主要原因。呂實強，《中國官紳反教的原因（1860-1874）》（臺北：中央研究院近代史研究所，1955）。其他教案研究如：林文慧，《清季福建教案之研究》（臺北：臺灣商務印書館，1989）；蔡蔚群，《教案：清季臺灣的傳教與外交》（臺北：博揚文化事業有限公司，2000）。

察角度立場，才能為基督教史做一正確的註解。[5] 以往基督教史主要集中在宣教史、教派史或是教案史，宣教史與教派史過度重視傳道人或差會的事業，教案史則是強調中外關係及東西文化的衝突。臺灣基督教史的研究多集中在討論基督教教育、醫療、社會福利機構以及傳教士等主題上，大體上仍以考證源流、探討組織發展傳布及社會貢獻為主。因而從目前研究可以發現，我們需要跳脫舊的研究框架，反省現代化理論及東西交流架構的基督教史研究範式，將基督教研究帶入一個以信徒為主體的新基督教史研究領域。

十九世紀的臺灣基督教徒是「第一代」（初代）的基督教徒，他們的信仰並非繼承家人的信仰，也與社會中的傳統信仰有極大差異。換言之，「第一代」教徒是家庭中第一代改宗為基督徒的，他們改變與家人及周遭人的宗教信仰，這個過程多數經歷「革命」或「衝突」。因此十九世紀的臺灣基督教徒在信仰歷程中面臨極大的挑戰，他們在改宗的過程中也要比其他世代的人來得掙扎。臺灣基督教史的論述中，經常討論傳教士初到臺灣傳教的「艱辛」過程，但卻鮮少討論第一代信徒在信仰上的「艱辛」遭遇。重視十九世紀臺灣「第一代」信徒的研究，除了讓我們認識以往被忽略的底層外，也思考信徒改宗的過程，亦有助於我們了解異文化的交會在社會中的掙扎與體現過程。

筆者認為，臺灣基督教史的研究，除了重視傳教士及教會的貢獻、發展及重大事件外，應逐漸修正以往以教派或傳教士為主軸的臺灣基督教史，而改以信徒為主體，擴充臺灣基督教史的研究面向。朝向觀察信徒的改宗歷程與社會處境，而不單是傳教士的社會貢獻；重視信徒的生命抉擇，而不只是教會的宣教方式或內部組織。亦期望研究方式能跳脫傳統教會史論述下，重視傳教士傳教的研究範式，而將焦點放在異文化跨界下的臺灣社會脈絡中來思考，這樣的目的在使研

---

5 Nicolas Standaert，〈廬山真面目──我們能不能了解別的文化？〉，《二十一世紀》，第16期（1993年4月），頁115-118。

究者重新思考傳教者與被傳教者之間的互動關係，凸顯信徒的主體性與歷史意義，呈現臺灣基督徒的生命史。

三、相關研究

回顧最早的臺灣基督教史研究著作，多數是傳教士整理差會或教區的官方報告。[6] 其後相關的臺灣基督教史著作仍是以長老會出版的教會史、年譜、各地教會簡史及紀念刊物為主，[7] 同時培養出一批重視教會歷史的傳道人。[8] 這些著作多數總結教會檔案史料，以傳教發展及教會組織為主軸，且具宗教關懷。

近年來關於臺灣基督教史的研究漸趨活躍，然在史料與研究成果上仍不成比例，目前許多教會都存有大量的檔案、報刊等資料，然而學界與教會卻都忽略這方面的研究與史料保存。[9] 就目前臺灣基督教史的研究成果而言，仍以博碩士論文為研究的主力。研究的主題以原

---

6 例如：William Campbell (甘為霖), *Formosa under the Dutch: Described from Contemporary Records, with Explanatory Notes and a Bibliography of the Island* (London: Kegan Paul, 1903); *An Account of Missionary Success in the Island of Formosa* (London: Kegan Paul and Trubner, 1989); Jas Johnston (莊士頓), *China and Formosa: The Story of The Mission of The Presbyterian Church of England* (New York: Fleming H. Revell, 1897; Taipei: Ch'eng-wen Reprinted, 1972); Edward Band (萬榮華), *Working His Purpose Out: The History of the English Presbyterian Mission, 1847-1947* (London: Publishing Office of the Presbyterian Church of England, 1947).

7 參見賴永祥編，〈基督教臺灣宣教史文獻〉，收入臺灣基督長老教會總會歷史委員會，《臺灣基督長老教會百年史》（臺南：臺灣基督長老教會，1965），頁495-529。

8 例如：陳清義，《北部臺灣基督長老教會的歷史》（臺北：北部臺灣基督長老教會傳道局，1923）；郭和烈編著，《北部臺灣基督長老教會簡史》（臺北：北部臺灣基督長老教會大會事務所，1952）；楊士養，《南臺教會史》（臺南：臺灣教會公報社，1953）；《信仰偉人列傳》（臺南：人光出版社，1995）；徐謙信編著，《北部臺灣基督長老教會年譜》（臺北：北部臺灣基督長老教會大會歷史部，1955）；《臺灣北部教會暨神學院簡史》（臺北：臺灣神學院出版部，1972）；黃武東、徐謙信編，《臺灣基督長老教會歷史年譜》（臺南：人光出版社，1959）；《臺灣基督長老教會歷史年譜——第二部‧日據時代編》（臺南：臺灣教會公報社，1962）；鄭連明、鄭連德、吳清鎰、徐謙信編著，《臺灣基督長老教會北部教會九十週年簡史》（臺北：慶祝設教九十週年歷史組，1962）；黃六點主編，《臺灣基督長老教會北部教會大觀——北部設教百週年紀念刊》（臺北：臺灣教會公報社，1972）；黃茂卿，《臺灣基督長老教會太平境馬雅各紀念教會九十年史（1865-1955）》（臺南：臺灣基督長老教會太平境馬雅各紀念教會，1988）；《臺灣基督長老教會迪階‧觀音山教會早期五十年史（1877-1927）：英國長老教會東部宣教》（花蓮：觀音山教會，1991）。

9 王成勉，〈臺灣基督教史料之研究〉，收入林治平主編，《臺灣基督教史——史料與研究回顧論文集》（臺北：宇宙光傳播中心，1998），頁237-272。

住民議題、長老教會史、政教關係等為重心，在研究方法上則以文獻及訪談為主。就研究的宗派而言，目前除長老教會外，其他宗派在史料出版與研究上仍相當缺乏，主要原因在於：長老教會為臺灣基督教中最大的宗派，人數及會堂數最多，且歷史最悠久、史料保存最為豐富，加上長老會有臺灣、臺南、玉山三所神學院與神學研究中心，故擁有豐富的研究基礎。[10]

　　有關十九世紀臺灣基督徒的研究相當缺乏，關於信徒改宗及社會處境與身分認同的議題在基督教史中也很少出現，有趣的是這個議題卻經常出現在「平埔」研究中。學者在探討平埔族社會變遷時，一定會發現到十九世紀平埔族「集體改宗」信仰基督教的現象。如果某一個原住民改宗基督教是單一現象，學者恐會加以忽略，但從北部的噶瑪蘭到中部的巴宰族、南部的西拉雅與馬卡道都出現了平埔族集體改宗的現象，這個十九世紀平埔族的集體改宗現象便無法忽視。張隆志在討論巴宰族時指出，基督教傳入巴宰族與康熙後期漢通事張達京進入岸裡社的方式類似，均為憑藉醫療治病途徑獲得社眾的信任，並且引進新的文化經驗，如何深入比較漢文化與基督教信仰對於巴宰族群發展的影響，應是理解巴宰族群乃至平埔變遷的重要關鍵。[11] 陳秋坤在討論岸裡社番產外流和土著貧困化時，從自保及抗衡的角度說明岸裡社人為何在漢人優勢的社會經濟勢力下，選擇改宗基督教。[12] 洪麗完在研究岸裡社時指出，岸裡社因基督教醫療傳道而引起集體改宗運動，不僅改變聚落景觀，更影響社民生命禮俗的改變，同時也認為應

---

10 關於長老教會的研究回顧，已有吳學明、康鈺瑩、張妙娟等人為長老會的研究作一系統之回顧。參見吳學明，〈日治時期臺灣基督長老教會研究的回顧與展望〉，收入林治平主編，《臺灣基督教史——史料與研究回顧論文集》，頁213-236；康鈺瑩，〈臺灣基督長老教會博碩士論文研究趨勢之回顧與展望〉，《思與言》，第37卷2期（1999年6月），頁155-172；張妙娟，〈臺灣基督長老教會史研究之回顧與展望——以近二十年來學位論文為中心〉，《史耘》，第6期（2000年9月），頁133-150。

11 張隆志，《族群關係與鄉村臺灣——一個清代臺灣平埔族群史的重建與理解》（臺北：國立臺灣大學出版委員會，1991），頁163-165。

12 陳秋坤，《清代臺灣土著地權——官僚、漢佃與岸裡社人的土地變遷，1700-1895》（臺北：中央研究院近代史研究所，1994），頁224-232。

進一步探究改宗的真正原因。[13] 似乎平埔族研究者都注意到十九世紀末平埔族改宗的社會變遷，但對於何以造成及其影響卻未深入追問，留下亟待努力的課題。歷史學家已關注到基督教與平埔族之間的關係，多數研究也指出基督教的傳入造成平埔社群的社會變遷，然而為何平埔族會出現集體改宗現象？這種現象無法單以傳教士的個人作為或基督教的醫療傳道、社會福利事業來解釋，改宗的過程與影響仍有待進一步深入探討。

回顧此一議題，洪秀桂認為經濟生產方式的改變是巴宰人改信漢人宗教的原因，原本打獵捕魚改為農耕，因此夢占、鳥占、禁忌、巫術隨之消失，且改信漢人土地公，而後改宗基督教乃因牧師熟悉醫術，最高神祇也可與耶穌相比擬。[14] 邵式伯（John R. Shepherd）認為《天津條約》後傳教士地位提高，享有相當權力。平埔族為漢文化之邊緣，無法和漢人競爭，因而改宗基督教，藉此走向財富地位之途徑，進而指出平埔族人的改宗是為了尋求對抗漢人的意識型態。[15] 陳偉智認為噶瑪蘭人改宗不是馬偕（George L. Mackay）個人的努力與魅力，而是當時的族群情境，在遭遇強大的漢化陰影與族群身分認同危機等社會性因素下，促使噶瑪蘭人集體改宗。[16] 陳志榮指出噶瑪蘭人藉教會支持得以繼續維持「加留餘埔」政策，日治後傳教士無法繼續行醫，而保護政策也取消，因而教會喪失吸引力。[17] 吳學明注意到第一代信徒「靠番仔勢」入教的現象。[18] 簡炯仁在討論天主教與萬

13 洪麗完，《臺灣中部平埔族——沙轆社與岸裡大社之研究》（臺北：稻香出版社，1997），頁414-415。

14 洪秀桂，〈南投巴宰海人的宗教信仰〉，《國立臺灣大學文史哲學報》，第22期（1973年6月），頁445-509。

15 John R. Shepherd, "From Barbarians to Sinners: Collective Conversion Among Plains Aborigines in Qing Taiwan, 1859-1895," in Daniel H. Bays, ed., *Christianity in China: From the Eighteenth Century to the Present* (Stanford: Stanford University Press, 1996), pp. 120-137.

16 陳偉智，〈族群、宗教與歷史——馬偕牧師的宜蘭傳教與噶瑪蘭人的族群論述〉，《宜蘭文獻》，第33期（1998年5月），頁43-72。

17 陳志榮，〈噶瑪蘭人的宗教變遷〉，收入潘英海、詹素娟主編，《平埔族研究論文集》（臺北：中央研究院臺灣史研究所籌備處，1995），頁77-98。

18 吳學明，〈臺灣基督長老教會入臺初期的一個文化面相——「靠番仔勢」〉，《鄉土文化研究所學報》，第1期（1999年12月），頁101-130。

金、赤山的平埔族關係時，指出天主教透過「教會—墾佃」的土地關係，促使傳教與當地平埔族的生計形成一種相輔相成的關係。[19] 詹素娟指出馬偕入宜蘭傳教時正是噶瑪蘭社會變化最快速的時期，蘭陽平原生態環境改變，噶瑪蘭人在缺乏土地，無從維持舊經濟活動的前提下，生活日益艱辛。而噶瑪蘭人傳統宗教與漢人民間信仰、祖先祭祀混淆，語言也逐漸福佬化，噶瑪蘭人開始離開原居地、尋找新天地。進而指出因為在基督教世界裡人人平等，馬偕與處於社會下層的噶瑪蘭人一同吃、喝，一起生活，一起分享宗教情感。馬偕的成功在於他觸摸到十九世紀末噶瑪蘭社會的脈絡，藉由宗教的關懷與安慰，取得噶瑪蘭人的認同與肯定。[20] 葉春榮反駁邵式伯認為平埔族是藉著基督教來對抗漢人的說法，認為平埔族改宗基督教是個動態的過程，就外在因素來講，是基督宗教挾著強大的資本主義勢力，派遣傳教士到全球各地，散發救濟品以吸引信徒；就平埔內在的因素來說，因為西方傳教士的醫療服務，送舊衣服、麵粉給信徒，實際上改善信徒的生活，也就是出於實際的理由，因此吸引許多平埔人改宗基督教。[21]

　　從十九世紀基督教在世界各地的宣教事工中，我們發現一個有趣的現象，即基督教在世界各地原住民部落的宣教都比同時期在較具文明規模的社會來得成功。在十九世紀的非洲與1860年後的中國，這個現象都相當明顯，[22] 同樣的情形也出現在臺灣。相關研究指出基督教在原住民等邊陲社會具有吸引力，乃是因為邊陲社會可藉由代表西方勢力的基督教而獲得政治庇護、醫療服務，並引基督教勢力來對抗本地主流社會的文化霸權。早期的教會史家賴德烈（Kenneth S. Latou-

---

19 簡炯仁，〈天主教道明會與赤山、萬金的平埔族〉，《臺灣文獻》，第50卷1期（1999年3月），頁103-128。

20 詹素娟，〈馬偕宣教與噶瑪蘭族群空間〉，收入許功明主編，《馬偕博士收藏臺灣原住民文物——沉寂百年的海外遺珍》（臺北：順益臺灣原住民博物館，2001），頁26-33。

21 葉春榮，〈宗教改信與融合：太祖與神明的交換〉，收入葉春榮編，《建構西拉雅：研討會論文集》（新營：臺南縣政府，2006），頁199-225。

22 Andrew F. Walls, *The Cross-Cultural Process in Christian History: Studies in the Transmission and Appropriation of Faith* (Maryknoll, New York: Orbis Books, 2002), pp. 85-173.

rette）就指出少數民族集體改宗的行為是為了獲得基督教勢力來對抗敵對（adversary）族群的文化霸權。[23]

再觀察十九世紀臺灣漢人信徒的研究，陳梅卿分析加拿大及英國長老教會中漢人信徒改宗基督教的過程，認為漢人入教的動機大同小異，主要是基於：一、現實生活中條件之惡劣，希冀宗教之庇護，又對原有神祇失望，因而改宗基督教；二、由於醫療獲得好感；三、家庭因素；四、友情或因接觸而引起好感。陳梅卿指出其中無人因求救贖、永生等基督教理想入信動機而入信，同時也注意到信徒間通婚，基督徒家族的出現及第二、三代基督徒社會地位的提升。[24] 查時傑透過族譜資料描述臺南高長家族及屏東吳葛家族的發展，說明來自底層的基督徒透過教會組織及教育來提升社會地位。[25] 邵式伯認為基督教無法在漢人社會中發展的主要原因並不是文化差距（cultural distance），而是漢人在改宗基督教時必須付出相當大的社會成本。[26] 吳學明運用《臺灣教會公報》分析信徒改宗的原因，認為主要有：一、遭遇現世種種困頓者；二、醫療受照顧感念者；三、為靠洋勢入教者；四、反悔自己的過錯，怕受到處罰者；五、為心靈救贖而入教等類型。[27] 謝國斌認為在十九世紀末的臺灣，漢人改信基督教不但無助於在主流社會的晉升，反而可能會被社會冠以「漢奸」等惡名而被貶抑，原先處於邊陲弱勢地位的人，被摒除在財富與名利等社會價值及主流社會結構之外，[28] 因此改宗其他宗教並不會有太大的社會成本。

---

23 Kenneth S. Latourette, *A History of Christian Missions in China* (New York: Macmillan, 1929), p. 310.

24 陳梅卿，〈清末加拿大長老教會的漢族信徒〉，《臺灣風物》，第41卷2期（1991年6月），頁33-55；陳梅卿，〈清末臺灣英國長老教會的漢族信徒〉，《東方宗教研究》，新3期（1993年10月），頁201-225。

25 查時傑，〈光復初期臺灣基督長老教會的一個家族——以臺南高長家族之發展為例〉，《國立臺灣大學歷史學系學報》，第18期（1994年12月），頁157-178；查時傑，〈記臺灣基督長老教會的一個大家族——屏東吳葛家族之發展〉，收入周宗賢主編，《臺灣史國際學術研討會：社會、經濟與拓墾論文集》（臺北：國史館，1995），頁109-123。

26 Shepherd, "From Barbarians to Sinners," pp. 120-137.

27 吳學明，〈臺灣基督長老教會的傳教與三自運動——以南部教會為中心〉（臺北：國立臺灣師範大學歷史研究所博士論文，2001），頁68-80。

28 謝國斌，〈基督教在原住民聚落之發展與影響——以南臺灣西拉雅平埔族聚落為例〉，《成大宗教與文

相關十九世紀臺灣基督徒的研究，除了由平埔研究及改宗研究著手的討論外，張妙娟亦以《臺灣教會公報》為研究基礎，發展出基督徒教育、[29] 本地傳道師等相關研究，[30] 並延伸討論至日治時期的主日學教育。[31] 近年來碩博士論文則有王政文從信徒的日常生活、身分認同、社會處境等方面，來探討十九世紀的臺灣第一代基督教徒。[32] 黃子寧透過從萬金天主堂的領洗簿等資料，探討天主教在萬金的發展及平埔信徒與漢人、客家人的族群關係。[33] 另外，延伸至日治時期有關基督徒的討論，則有王昭文探討基督徒知識份子與社會運動的關係，[34] 盧啟明討論日治末期基督徒「傳道報國」的身分認同問題。[35]

　　綜觀上述對於十九世紀臺灣基督徒的研究，可知以信徒為主體且全面性的研究，仍有待開發，特別是信徒在面對價值衝突、身分認同以及基督徒生活調適等議題上。是故，若能將各類資料加以整理，再綜合前人的研究成果，縫合、彌補其中的不足之處，改變觀察基督教史的傳統視野、結合新方法與新理論，或許可以對十九世紀臺灣基督徒有新的詮釋，進而提出新的臺灣基督教史研究架構與方向。

化學報》，第6期（2006年6月），頁93-120。

29 張妙娟，《開啟心眼——《臺灣府城教會報》與長老教會的基督徒教育》（臺南：人光出版社，2005）。

30 張妙娟，〈出凡入聖——清季臺灣南部長老會的傳道師養成教育〉，《臺灣文獻》，第55卷2期（2004年6月），頁151-174。

31 張妙娟，〈日治前期南部長老教會的主日學教育〉，《興大歷史學報》，第22期（2010年2月），頁79-103。

32 王政文，〈天路歷程：臺灣第一代基督徒研究（1865-1895）〉（臺北：國立臺灣師範大學歷史學系博士論文，2009）。

33 黃子寧，《天主教在屏東萬金的生根發展（1861-1962）》（臺北：國立臺灣大學出版委員會，2006）。

34 王昭文，〈日治時期臺灣基督徒知識份子與社會運動（1920-1930年代）〉（臺南：國立成功大學歷史系博士論文，2009）。

35 盧啟明，〈日治末期臺灣基督徒「傳道報國」認同之研究（1937-1945）〉（臺北：國立臺灣師範大學歷史學系碩士論文，2011）。

四、相關資料探討

　　十九世紀的臺灣基督教徒多數是無聲的,是社會的邊緣;他們多半都是當時社會的下層階級。[36] 信徒的知識水準不高,經濟能力也不強。[37] 因此,只有少數信徒能留下文字著作。我們除了從少數信徒留下的著作做分析外,建構十九世紀的臺灣基督徒史,將面臨的兩大問題:一是方法,一是史料。從現存的史料來觀察,研究必須要透過傳教士著作、教會檔案及第二、三代基督徒的回憶資料來進行,然而有更多的新史料等待開發,例如教會的信徒名冊、洗禮簿、家譜、家族資料、戶口資料、地方教會誌、訃文,研究中並配合口述訪問與田野調查,便能逐步建立十九世紀的臺灣基督徒史。下面從現有史料及待開發之史料來作介紹分析。

　　(一)教會檔案:(1)收藏於倫敦大學亞非學院(School of Oriental and African Studies, University of London)的《英格蘭長老教會海外宣教檔》(*The Presbyterian Church of England Foreign Missions Archives, 1847-1950*),收入會議記錄、傳教士書信、著作,教會傳教單張、手冊等。[38] (2)收藏於加拿大長老教會檔案事務所的《加拿大長老教會檔案》(*The Presbyterian Church in Canada Archives*),臺灣神學院藏有其中有關臺灣部分的相關微捲。[39] (3)甘為霖(William Campbell)編的《臺南教士會議事錄》(*Handbook of the English Presbyterian Mission in South Formosa*)留下許多十九世紀臺灣信徒的相關記錄,記載有關信徒發生的事件及事件處理的經過等資料。[40]

---

36 臺灣基督長老教會總會歷史委員會編,《臺灣基督長老教會百年史》,頁13、22。

37 Edward Band著,詹正義譯,《巴克禮博士與臺灣》(臺北:長青文化事業公司,1976),頁34-37。

38 *The Presbyterian Church of England Foreign Missions Archives, 1847-1950*.《英格蘭長老教會海外宣教檔》(PCE-FMA)(中壢:中原大學宗教研究所藏)。參見魏外揚,〈英國長老會海外宣教檔案中臺灣部分之評介〉,收入林治平主編,《臺灣基督教史——史料與研究回顧國際學術研討會論文集》,頁153-170。

39 Kim M. Arnold, "Hand in Hand: An Analysis of the Archival Documentation Pertaining to Taiwan as Held by the Presbyterian Church in Canada Archives and Records Office. 1875-1998",收入林治平主編,《臺灣基督教史——史料與研究回顧國際學術研討會論文集》,頁171-193。

40 William Campbell, *Handbook of the English Presbyterian Mission in South Formosa* (Hastings: F. J. Parsons, LTD.

（二）書報雜誌：1885年由巴克禮（Thomas Barclay）創辦的《臺灣府城教會報》。1892年更名為《臺南府教會報》，1893年更名為《臺南府城教會報》，1906年更名為《臺南教會報》，乃至1932年的《臺灣教會公報》，是研究臺灣基督教史不可或缺的資料。[41] 其中保存當時傳教士及教徒對臺灣的記載、時事批評、回憶、教會訊息、信徒學習的教義、靈修及信仰生活等資料。許多信徒在學習白話字後，在教會報上發表文章，成為最好的研究材料。教會報中更留下許多後代信徒對十九世紀臺灣信徒的回憶，包括家人、親友或教會同工對前代信徒的記錄。另外，《教務雜誌》（Chinese Recorder）、[42]《中國叢報》（The Chinese Repository）、[43]《使信月刊》（The English Presbyterian Messenger）[44] 中，也有許多來臺傳教士留下對信徒的一手報導及觀察。天主教方面也有郭德剛（Pablo Fernandez）整理道明會（Dominican）傳教士的報告與書信，其中有對信徒信仰及遭遇的描述。[45]

（三）傳教士著作與回憶錄：十九世紀傳教士與外國人來臺遊記、日記、考察報告等相當豐富。舉凡馬偕、甘為霖、巴克禮、李麻（Hugh Ritchie）、梅監務（Campbell N. Moody）等傳教士都留下大量日記、書信、回憶乃至研究作品。[46] 並可輔以當時西方人士對臺灣

1910; Reprinted 臺南：教會公報社，2004).

41 參見翁佳音，〈室藏《臺灣府城教會報》介紹〉，《臺灣史田野研究通訊》，第17期（1990年12月），頁47-49；吳學明，〈《臺灣府城教會報》及其史料價值〉，收入吳學明，《臺灣基督長老教會研究》（臺北：宇宙光，2006），頁187-210。張妙娟，《開啟心眼——《臺灣府城教會報》與長老教會的基督徒教育》。

42 參見李金強，〈從《教務雜誌（Chinese Recorder）》看清季臺灣基督教的發展〉，收入李金強，《聖道東來：近代中國基督教史之研究》（臺北：宇宙光，2006），頁87-99。

43 張秀蓉編，A Chronology of 19th Century Writings on Formosa（臺北：曹永和文教基金會，2008）。

44 《使信全覽》（臺南：臺灣教會公報社，2006）。臺灣教會公報社於2006年重新翻印英國長老教會自1850年至1947年的《使信月刊》（The Messenger，刊名在不同年代有不同名稱），全套75集，定名為《使信全覽》。

45 Pablo Fernandez, One Hundred Years of Dominican Apostolate in Formosa (1859-1958) (Philippines: University of Sto. Tomas, 1959; Taipei: SMC Publishing Inc. Reprinted, 1994); Pablo Fernandez著，黃德寬譯，《天主教在臺開教記——道明會士的百年耕耘》（臺北：光啟出版社，1991）。

46 參見魏外揚，〈來臺基督教宣教士傳記之研究〉，收入林治平主編，《從險學到顯學：2001年海峽兩岸三地教會史研究現況研討會論文集》（臺北：宇宙光出版社，2002），頁587-603。

的描述記錄、著作，或來臺遊記、日記。[47] 這些傳教士們的著作與回憶錄中，保存許多關於信徒的記錄，雖然沒有系統，且分散不集中，但仍可透過爬梳比對逐一整理。

四、基督徒著作：十九世紀的臺灣教徒多數是來自底層，他們起初多數不識字、無法書寫，也因此難以留下太多的文獻記載，故這方面的資料較少、分散而不集中。《臺灣府城教會報》中保有部分信徒和本地傳道師的記錄和短篇作品，例如：劉茂清對基督徒辦理喪事的看法，[48] 胡肇基對縛腳的論述……等。[49] 報中也載有教會或後代基督徒對早期基督徒所寫的傳記、回憶資料。[50] 另外，比較具有代表性的如李春生的《主津新集》、《主津後集》、《民教冤獄解》、《民教冤獄解續編補遺》、《耶穌聖教讖諆備考》、《天演論書後》、《東西哲衡》、《宗教五德備考》、《哲衡續編》、《聖經闡要講義》等。[51] 其次有後人對前人的回憶資料，例如：李嘉嵩《100年來》、[52] 細川瀏《小鱗回顧錄》、[53] 高俊明回憶錄、[54] 陳五福回憶錄、[55] 偕萬來自述，[56] 還有相關散見於報章雜誌的記載與回憶。而賴永祥的《教會史話》[57] 及「賴永祥長老史料庫」中，[58] 收錄相當豐富的信徒略歷、家族簡譜、訪談記錄、後人回憶、訃文等資料。另外，也可運用

---

47 參見費德廉（Douglas Fix）、羅效德編譯，《看見十九世紀臺灣——十四位西方旅行者的福爾摩沙故事》（臺北：如果出版社，2006）。費德廉網站中收集相當豐富有關十九世紀來臺外國人所留下的記錄，參見http://academic.reed.edu/formosa/。

48 劉茂清，〈論喪事〉，《臺灣府城教會報》，第57-62張，1890年2月至6月。

49 胡肇基，〈縛腳論〉，《臺灣府城教會報》，第111卷，1894年6月，頁63-64。

50 有關《臺灣府城教會報》的主筆與撰稿人討論，請參見張妙娟，《開啟心眼——《臺灣府城教會報》與長老教會的基督徒教育》，頁101-104。

51 李明輝、黃俊傑、黎漢基編，《李春生著作集》，第一至五冊（臺北：南天書局，2004）。

52 李嘉嵩，《100年來》（臺南：人光出版社，1979）。

53 細川瀏，《小鱗回顧錄》（臺南州嘉義郡：加土印刷所，1927）。

54 高俊明、高李麗珍口述，胡慧玲撰文，《十字架之路——高俊明牧師回憶路》（臺北：望春風文化事業公司，2001）。

55 張文義整理記錄，《回首來時路——陳五福醫師回憶錄》（臺北：吳三連臺灣史料基金會，1996）。

56 偕萬來口述，楊功明訪問，李忠賢記錄，〈偕萬來先生自述〉，《宜蘭文獻》，第6期（1993年11月），頁27-38。

57 賴永祥，《教會史話》，第一至五輯（臺南：人光出版社，1990-2000）。

58 賴永祥長老史料庫http://www.laijohn.com/Index.htm。

基督徒家族族譜，如：《臺南高長家族族譜》、[59]《一五〇年來吳葛親族》、[60]《潘睦派下潘氏族譜》。[61]

　　五、官方檔案記載：主要有《教務教案檔》、[62]《籌辦夷務始末》、[63]《總理各國事務衙門檔案》、[64]《法軍侵臺檔》[65] 等，而光緒年間清政府多次下令清查淡水廳及新竹縣境的教堂，因而在《淡新檔案》中留下許多文獻及教堂地圖、教堂建築繪圖，成為珍貴記錄。[66] 另外，由中國第一歷史檔案館與福建師範大學歷史系合編的《清末教案》，收集的資料包括第一歷史檔案館所保存的清政府檔案、英國會議文件、美國對外關係文件史料、法國外交文件及《使信月刊》中關於教案的史料。[67] 教案的主角除了是傳教士外，有許多案件是發生在教徒身上，這些案件中記載許多關於基督徒的資料。

　　從現存的基督教史料來源，可以發現大體分為四類：第一類是傳教士及教會所留下來的報告、檔案、刊物及文宣品等。第二類是基督徒所留下來的著作。第三類是反教人士所留下來的反教言論及書籍。第四類是官方的教務教案及外交或地方檔案。教會史料多屬傳教性質，有其撰寫動機與限制，而傳教士對臺灣的描述關係到異文化差

---

59 高昭義編著，《臺南高長家族族譜》（臺南：編者家族自印，1996）。

60 汪乃文、吳振乾編，《一五〇年來吳葛親族》（屏東：吳氏家族自印，1990）。

61 潘稀祺，《潘睦派下潘氏族譜》（臺中：潘啟南派下家族，1996）。

62 中央研究院近代史研究所編，《教務教案檔》，第二至五輯（臺北：中央研究院近代史研究所，1974-1977）。

63 臺灣銀行經濟研究室編，《籌辦夷務始末選輯》，臺灣文獻叢刊第203種（三冊）（臺北：臺灣銀行，1964）；臺灣銀行經濟研究室編，《籌辦夷務始末選輯補編》，臺灣文獻叢刊第236種（臺北：臺灣銀行，1967）；寶鋆等修，《籌辦夷務始末（同治朝）》，收入沈雲龍主編，《近代中國史料叢刊》，第62輯（臺北：文海出版社，1971）。

64 《總理各國事務衙門檔案》（臺北：中央研究院近代史研究所檔案館藏）；呂實強，〈總理衙門檔案中有關臺灣之史料〉，《臺灣人文》，創刊號（1977年10月），頁51-58。

65 臺灣銀行經濟研究室編，《法軍侵臺檔》，第一至四冊（臺灣文獻叢刊第192種，臺北：臺灣銀行，1964）。

66 《淡新檔案》（臺北：國立臺灣大學圖書館藏）；淡新檔案校註出版編輯委員會編，《淡新檔案（二）》，第一編 行政（臺北：國立臺灣大學，1995）；戴炎輝、陳棋炎、曾瓊珍，〈有關臺灣基督教兩件資料〉，《臺灣文化》，第6卷2期（1950年5月），頁61-72。

67 中國第一歷史檔案館、福建師範大學歷史系合編，《清末教案》中國近代史史料叢刊，第一冊：中文檔案（1842-1871）（北京：中華書局，1996）。中國第一歷史檔案館、福建師範大學歷史系合編，《清末教案》中國近代史史料叢刊，第六冊：英國議會文件選譯（北京：中華書局，2006）。

距。是故，我們應從不同角度解讀史料，提出新的歷史解釋，有意識的運用文本和詮釋理論，打破史料真實與虛構的界線，察覺實際間的落差，進而反省論述者的說話位置，重視被忽視的「它者」及底層聲音，跳脫舊有的解釋框架。[68] 由此，新的觀察角度使得史料可以重新開發，舊史料也有新意義。

五、待開發史料

這裡筆者用幾件史料做為例子，來說明十九世紀臺灣基督徒史研究的可能性與未來發展。「洗禮簿」與「信徒名冊」是最需要開發的一項史料，關於「信徒名冊」的史料發掘與利用，目前仍有極大發展空間。

以北部教會為例，北部教會保存有相對完整的十九世紀信徒名冊，這份名冊的原稿目前收藏在淡水「滬尾偕醫館」展示中心。該名冊現名「北臺灣信徒名冊」，共計載有：滬尾、五股、八里坌、和尚洲、水返腳、新港社、大龍峒、基隆、大溪新店、新莊、崙仔頂、紅毛港、竹塹城、桃仔園、中港街、艋舺街、打馬煙、番社頭、波羅辛仔遠、奇立板、掃笏社、新社、打挪美、埤頭、斗門頭、奇母蘭、武暖社、奇立丹、大竹圍、加禮宛、流流仔、大里簡、亞里史、蘇澳街、奇武荖、南方澳、真珠里簡、頂雙溪、辛仔罕、三結仔街、羅東、礁溪、銃櫃城、龜山、垢籠、枋橋、三角湧、北關口、頭城、後山岐萊加禮宛等50所教會的信徒受洗資料。

「信徒名冊」在時間上從1873年1月9日馬偕在淡水舉行第一次受洗儀式，記載至1890年。信徒名冊中主要記載信徒名單、受洗日期、年紀、性別，部分信徒並記錄有簡略事蹟、擔任職務、死亡時間。名冊中除上述教會信徒資料外，另有臺北教會本地牧師名冊，和淡水縣

---

68 古偉瀛，〈中華天主教史研究方法的淺見〉，收入古偉瀛編，《東西交流史的新局：以基督宗教為中心》（臺北：國立臺灣大學出版中心，2005），頁27-48。

教會長老名目（載有：大稻埕、八里坌、水返腳、崙仔頂、新店街、五股坑、和尚洲、基隆頭、桃仔園的長老資料）、宜蘭縣教會長老名目（載有：達仔美、番頭社、奇立板、加禮宛、流流仔、波羅辛、南風奧、奇武荖、真珠里簡、埤頭社、掃笏社、辛仔罕、武暖社、大竹圍、奇武蘭、奇立丹、斗門頭、打馬煙、亞里史的長老資料）、淡水縣執事名目（載有：五股坑、新店街、和尚洲、崙仔頂、新莊街、八里坌、三角湧、艋舺街、水返腳、新社的執事資料）、宜蘭縣執事名目（載有：達仔美、番頭社、奇立板、加禮宛、流流仔、波羅辛、南風澳、奇武荖、真珠里簡、埤頭社、掃笏社、辛仔罕、武暖社、大竹圍、奇武蘭、奇立丹、斗門頭、打馬煙、銃櫃城、亞里史的執事資料）……等有關信徒資料。

透過「施洗簿」或「信徒名冊」可以建立起許多十九世紀教徒的初步輪廓，例如各地信徒人數、年齡、受洗年齡等量化資料，也可從「信徒名冊」中了解信徒改宗後其家庭成員改宗的情況、在教會的服事狀況……等。再透過檔案、傳教士記錄、後代回憶資料，逐步比對爬梳信徒之間的家庭、人際網路，如此將可挖掘出相當豐富的信徒及其或家族的信仰生命歷程。事實上，除了北部教會外，南部教會亦有豐富的信徒資料，位於長榮中學的「臺灣基督長老教會歷史資料館」館藏32冊的《教會成人名冊》和35冊的《教會小兒名冊》。[69] 另外，天主教亦保有豐富的領洗簿資料。[70] 訪查許多地方教會也都會有「施洗簿」或「教徒名冊」等相關資料留存，而這些資料是建立「十九世紀臺灣基督教徒史」的最重要史料，卻也是最有待積極開發和使用的史料。現在的教會也經常會有「會友聯絡冊」、「小組名單」之類的通訊資料，但這些隨手可得的資料，卻經常不被重視。

另外，信徒留下的資料也有很大開發的空間。例如，郭添、郭朝成（父、子）的後代子女將郭朝成的毛筆著作原稿整理成《傳道行

---

69 《教會成人名冊》、《教會小兒名冊》，臺南：臺灣基督長老教會歷史資料館藏。

70 例如：〈萬金堂區領洗簿整理記錄（1862-1900）〉，收入黃子寧，《天主教在屏東萬金的生根發展（1861-1962）》，頁339-383。

程》上冊、下冊兩大冊，共1,200頁。[71]《傳道行程》以傳記及報導體裁記載當時的所見所聞及第一代信徒的信仰歷程，從內容中可以發現許多信徒間的人際關係、信仰過程，這些資料都是建構臺灣基督徒史的重要資料。

我們可以發現，「明末清初的天主教徒」在學術界是相當熱門的研究議題，而這個議題也有非常精彩且豐富的研究成果。黃一農在探討明末清初中西文明的第三類接觸中，以兩頭蛇形容夾在中西兩大傳統之間的第一代天主教徒，說明第一代天主教徒由於長期在儒家傳統和生活禮俗中，其處境及心理掙扎衝擊遠較後人強烈。[72] 相反的十九世紀的教徒，不論是在中國的教徒或臺灣的教徒，都幾乎缺乏討論，而且沒有成為一個專門議題，很重要一個原因便是資料上的不完整。所以我們可以發現到，若是能妥善利用「信徒名冊」，配合家族資料、相關回憶記載，並透過傳教士及官方文書中記錄，十九世紀的臺灣基督教徒史，便可以逐漸浮現出輪廓，進而成為一個重要的研究議題；若是再加上田野調查和口述訪問、新史料的挖掘，的確有機會建立一部十九世紀臺灣基督徒的生命史。

六、結語

有關十九世紀臺灣基督教徒的資料相當零散、不完整，但透過不斷努力的蒐集與拼湊，希望以往沒有被重視的教徒史，能逐漸浮現輪廓。藉由舊史料的整理與新史料的發現，並配合進行田野調查與口述訪問，相信臺灣基督教史的論述，不僅是只有以傳教或傳教士為主軸的書寫脈絡，也能發展出以「教徒」為主軸的臺灣基督教史或臺灣基督徒生命史。

---

71 郭朝成，《傳道行程》，上、下冊（郭朝成子女自印，2006）。郭朝成在《臺灣教會公報》中亦經常以筆名「安貧生」發表文章。

72 黃一農，《兩頭蛇：明末清初的第一代天主教徒》（新竹：國立清華大學出版社，2005），頁vii、463-482。

在「臺灣基督徒」的研究中，除了歷史學的討論外，更應該藉助社會學、人類學、宗教學與心理學的研究方法。「真的社會學是歷史」，[73] 歷史與社會學的互動有助於對「過去」與「現在」的探討，可以豐富歷史解釋的面向，更可以經由社會學和社會科學理論，來深化歷史解釋的看法。這「不是把理論應用到歷史，而是利用歷史深化理論。」[74] 不同的學科對基督教有不同的注意焦點及研究方法，期望「臺灣基督教史」的研究亦能藉助不同學門的研究方法及社會科學理論來加強探究，採取「方法學上的多元主義」來進行，[75] 以增加研究的深度與廣度。

探討臺灣基督徒時我們無法切割其所處的社會脈絡，更無法忽視信徒改宗的處境與自我認同衝突。西方學界隨著1960年代新興宗教興起而出現的「改宗」研究與理論，將有助於教徒研究的探討。各種改宗理論從宗教到社會、心理層面的探討，從教義吸引力或注意生命轉折時的宗教追尋，到強調社會網絡（social network）與理性選擇（rational choice）的研究，[76] 都可與臺灣的教徒研究進行對話，進而發展出臺灣基督徒史研究的理論基礎。換言之，「十九世紀臺灣基督徒」的研究，除了歷史分析外，更希望建立一個解釋體系，除了重新建構一個以基督徒為主軸的歷史架構外，更希望尋求理論層次的對話與建立。

---

73 Robert N. Bellah, "Durkheim and History," in Robert A. Nisbet, *Emile Durkheim with Selected Essays* (Englewood Cliffs, New Jersey: Prentice-Hall, Inc., 1965), p. 154.

74 Arthur L. Stinchcombe, "What Theory in History Should Be and Do," *Theoretical Methods in Social History* (New York: Academic Press, 1978), p. 1.

75 蔡彥仁，〈晚近歐美宗教研究方法學評介〉，《東方宗教研究》，新1期（1990年10月），頁264-288。

76 John Lofland, *Doomsday Cult: A Study of Conversion, Proselytisation, and Maintenance of Faith* (New York: Irvington Publishers 1981); Ullman Chana, *The Transformed Self: The Psychology of Religious Conversion* (New York: Plenum Press, 1989); Lewis R. Rambo, *Understanding Religious Conversion* (New Haven: Yale University Press, 1993); Lawrence A. Young, ed., *Rational Choice Theory and Religion: Summary and Assessment* (New York: Routledge, 1997); Rodney Stark and Roger Fink, *Acts of Faith: Explaining the Human Side of Religion* (Berkeley: University of California Press, 2000).

臺灣教會史料分布與典藏之研究

王成勉

國立中央大學歷史研究所教授

摘要

　　過去幾十年對於臺灣教會史的研究，已經有相當的數量，但是研究者往往是各就其便，從手邊可以掌握到的資料入手，而缺乏對教會史料與相關的官方檔案有整體的了解。以致在學術界的作品不多，也未能產生令各方滿意又有廣泛影響力的作品。

　　本文試圖整體的討論臺灣的教會史料，從官方機構、學術機構與教會機構三個角度來分析各自史料的收藏情況與特色。本文不止是綜覽式的分類介紹各式史料，而是希圖更進一步探討各種史料的典藏與特色。同時提出相應的改進教會史料收藏與發展的方向，供學術界、教會界與圖書館界參考。

關鍵詞：臺灣、教會史料、分布、典藏

一、前言

　　過去幾十年對於臺灣教會史的研究，雖說不上成果豐碩，可是相關的著作也屢屢出現在會議、期刊、學位論文與專書中，在整體數量上也相當可觀。但是研究者往往是各就其便，從手邊可以掌握到的資料入手，缺乏對教會史料整體的了解。同時對相關的官方檔案，也利用的不夠完全。主要的原因多半是對官方史料與教會檔案史料的特質缺少了解，同時也沒有注意到史料中若干的缺失與盲點，以致多年來在學術界少有產生令各方滿意又有廣泛影響力的作品。

　　本文試圖整體的討論有關臺灣教會的史料，就官方機構、學術機構與教會機構三個角度來分析各自史料的收藏情況與特色。本文並非是概覽式的分類介紹各式史料，而是希圖能呈現此三類教會相關史料的典藏與特色。由於這三類機構在收藏教會與教會相關史料的動機與目的不同，性質上自有差異。但是若是研究者能夠加以交互運用，則在史料的內容與觀點上可以產生互補與對照的功能。這種現象正可以反映教會在臺灣發展的不同面相，以及教會與社會的互動關係，值得教會界與學術界加以注意，俾能發展出更深入與更全面的探討。

二、官方檔案

　　教會與教會機構是融入在全國各個地方與社會的各個層面，所以政府許多部門都有教會相關的資料。但是過去因為沒有檔案法的制度，所以外界既不知有那些資料留存，更無由得知相關部會是如何研擬與處置教會和教會機構的案件。由於教會方面涉入的層面太廣，難以將各個部門的資料詳細介紹。如內政部有民政司「宗教輔導科」在管理宗教事務，每隔幾年就會要各教會總會呈交該教會的發展資料，然後編輯成《宗教簡介》一書。[1] 教育部對於「宗教教育」與「教會

---

1 過去已經出版的記錄如下：馬琰如等編輯，《宗教簡介》（臺北：內政部民政司，1991）；黃崇烈等編

學校」有非常多的文件與檔案，最早期的已移交國史館，後期的移交檔案管理局[2]。行政院大陸委員會則有兩岸宗教交流的研究報告，衛生署的資料有教會醫院的相關記載。至於地方政府對於地方上所有宗教的教產、組織與負責人都有登錄，散見地方上各種機構中。故無論是中央或地方政府都有相關的記錄。

（一）中央部會資料

中央部會所保存的教會相關史料差異很大。現舉「外交部」與「警政署」為例，來顯示相關資料的重要性與特殊性。除了極少數的本土教會外，臺灣大多數的教會是外國差會所創建的，所以與外國教會來往，或是傳教士入臺都會經過外交部，同時外人在華與教會機構所引起的社會事件，也會被外交部設檔記載。

學術界與教會界長期以來對於警政單位中所保存教會相關檔案一直不夠了解。由於過去臺灣的政教關係發展得並非平順，所以警政情治系統如何看待若干教會、又到底有那些留存相關的資料，值得加以探索。國史館依臺灣省警務處檔案所編纂出版的《臺灣省警務檔案彙編——民俗宗教篇》，對此點透露出重要的訊息。[3] 現以「耶和華見證人教會」為例，[4] 來看當時政府情治部門的監控情況。由於「耶和華見證人教會」的立場是反對教友服兵役，所以遭到情治單位的猜忌，認為違反國家的制度，因此透過各個系統加以監控。

輯，《宗教簡介》（臺北：內政部民政司，1993）；黃慶生等編輯，《宗教簡介》（臺北：內政部民政司，2000）；黃慶生等編輯，《宗教簡介》（臺北：內政部民政司，2003）；黃慶生等編輯，《宗教簡介》（臺北：內政部民政司，2005）。

2 該局至2001年才成立。

3 何鳳嬌編，《臺灣省警務檔案彙編——民俗宗教篇》（臺北：國史館，1996）。

4 「耶和華見證人」（Jehovah's Witnesses）起源於1870年美國賓州匹茲堡的一個聖經研究班，發起人為查爾斯·泰茲·羅素（Charles Taze Russell）。該團體是以逐戶向人做見證，並分發聖經書刊為特色。「耶和華見證人」在臺的事工是從日據時期開始，也是由日人傳入臺灣。於1927年時，「耶和華見證人」派遣一位在美國出生的日人，到日本展開傳布福音的工作。由於「耶和華見證人」素以主張和平，政治中立著稱，過去在勸阻信徒服兵役的事情上，未能得到政府的理解，故有信徒因為良心因素拒服兵役而被判刑的事件。請參見王成勉，〈基督教〉，《嘉義市志》卷十《宗教禮俗志》（嘉義：嘉義市政府，2005年8月），頁188-189。

首先是「臺灣警備總司令部」依據「國家安全局」的文件，認為該教會有不法的活動，然後發文給「內政部」，要求對該教會的刊物《守望臺》、《儆醒》的內容「逐期嚴格審查」，若有不妥或禁止發行，或予以剪頁發行。該文件中亦反對《王國月刊》中附送羅馬字母拼音資料，要加以查扣。第二、對於關鍵的傳教士反戰爭的言論，則要「加強布線密偵」。第三、請「臺灣省警務處」繼續收集該教會負責人名單，建卡列管，並協調「外交部」嚴格管制外籍教士入境。這份文件並知會「高雄縣警察局」與「臺北市警察局」。[5]

　　從上述的文件中，可以看出有好多個情治單位與政府部門都涉入監管教會的行動，包括高雄縣警察局、臺灣警備總司令部、臺灣省警務處、國家安全局、內政部、外交部、臺北市警察局等。他們透過檢查出版品，建立領導人名冊，管制傳教士出入境，以及「有關單位循『偵防』途徑加強布線密偵」，對此教會監控。雖然其他相關單位的文件未能在此檔案集中配合展現，但此文件已顯示端倪。政府各單位對於「不法活動教會」的態度與措施，在《臺灣省警務檔案彙編——民俗宗教篇》一書中，被情治系統監控的基督教機構還有「新約教會」、「日本基督教循理會」、「摩門教——基督教末世聖徒會」。[6]

　　過去有非常多的傳教士來華宣教，出入境都要透過外交部，而教會人士的出國也需要透過外交部，所以在外交部的檔案中也有不少的教會史料。現在根據外交部檔資處的北美司檔案目錄來了解當初他們所保存的教會史料。在1949年以前的資料，有一些傳教士的社會案件成為專檔，如「和州美以美會被竊」（1929）、「美教士聞聲在海州被害」（1931）、「美教士柏立美在安定被劫」（1933）、「福州烏石山青年會被搶案」（1934）。根據外交部的記錄，在1949年以前的檔案，是轉交給國史館來典藏。在1949年以後的檔案則轉存於中央研

---

5 參觀何鳳嬌編，《臺灣省警務檔案彙編——民俗宗教篇》，頁550-551。
6 參見何鳳嬌編，《臺灣省警務檔案彙編——民俗宗教篇》，頁523-549, 563-579。

究院近代史研究所。這些則是有關臺灣的檔案，包括「基督教長老會牧師謝榮良等出國（戴正毅、林宗生等）」（1975）、「臺北基督教兒童合唱團訪美」（1976）、「宗教團體活動」（1977）、「雷震遠神父」（1979）、「美地方教會建林口萬人聚會堂」（1987）、「新約教徒示威索賠」（1987）、「山地教會」（1985）。從外交部相關檔案的名稱來看，除了教會人物與團體出入境的資料外，似乎包括了宗教外交與外籍傳教士在華的專檔。如果進一步的分析，或許可以看出政府與外交部門對於宗教人士的運用、管制與態度。如果對應歐洲司的檔案目錄或許可以看到外交部對於天主教國家（特別是教廷）的宗教外交。[7]

（二）地方政府資料

在地方縣市也有一些官方的記載，透露出教會的相關資料，如筆者過去曾經參加過《嘉義市志》的寫作，負責《嘉義市志》中「基督教會」的撰寫。[8] 由於職務上的需要，所以可以參閱嘉義市政府中有關教會的登記清冊。過去每隔一段時間，嘉義市政府就會要地方上的各個教堂申報相關的資料，這些資料透露出當地一些教會的資訊，可以作為研究的佐證。嘉義地區雖然不能算是臺灣重要的縣市，但是在基督教發展史上有特別的地位。其是「真耶穌教會」與「貴格會」在臺灣發展的源頭。現從「真耶穌教會」與「臺灣基督教長老會」這兩個教會的教堂登錄資料來做為檢索的線索。首先是關於「真耶穌教會嘉義教會」的登錄資料。從登記的資料可以看出，該教會在1931年就成立，資料中不但有教會負責人的個人資料，也有教會的人數、興辦事業、各種活動、出版品以及教會的財產。從連續幾次的申報，更可以看出該教會在地方的發展。以「長老教會嘉義東門教會」為例，該

---

7 關於外交部與中華民國駐梵蒂岡大使館的外交史料已經編出，見陳方中、吳俊德主編，《中梵外交關係六十年史料彙編》（臺北：輔仁大學天主教史料研究中心，2002）。
8 王成勉，〈基督教〉，《嘉義市志》卷十《宗教禮俗志》（嘉義：嘉義市政府，2005年8月），頁163-193。

教會成立的更早,首先於1873年創立,後來教堂在1973年改建,申報的資料中也有詳細負責人、聚會活動、財產的資料。這些在地方上的資料很少為學術界注意和使用。

在學術界中,專門為教會檔案、史料加以保存的機構並不多,過去中研院近代史研究所曾經將總理衙門的資料編成《教務教案檔》[9]、《近代中國對西方及列強認識資料彙編》[10],對學術研究有重大的貢獻,也是今天研究教案最主要的依據,但是後來就沒有像這樣大部頭的史料編著。在中研院中另外一個保有相當完整單一教會史料的單位,就是民族學研究所。該所透過關係收集到聖公會的主要檔案——《聖公會臺灣教區歷屆年會會議記錄,1961-》,成為一大特色。所以今天要研究聖公會在臺灣的發展,需要到民族學研究所的圖書館參閱這份資料,惟該所目前尚無相關的研究人員進行聖公會的研究。

三、教會史料

教會與教堂史料,是一件廣為分布而頗令學者難以掌握的資料。更令學術界為難的,是每個教堂到底保存那些史料,是否對外開放,往往沒有通則,而是落入太多的教會個案的決定。而每個個案又會因人事、情況異動而變化,所以是永遠沒有定案的問題。

教會史料可以分為宗派的檔案與各自教堂所保存的資料。現在先以幾個較有特色的宗派檔案館來介紹,一般而言在臺灣收藏最豐富與數量最大的即是「臺灣基督教長老會歷史資料館」,該檔案館不止是有長老會總會的會議記錄,相關教會組織機構的移交清冊,甚至有宣教士的信函、照片與傳教士在百餘年前運來臺之印刷機,所以在文物兩方面都有很好的收集,而此檔案館過去比較受到學界的注意和使

---

9 陸寶千、張貴永、呂實強編,《教務教案檔》(臺北:中央研究院近史所,1974-1981)。

10 中央研究院近代史研究所編,《近代中國對西方及列強認識資料彙編》(臺北:中央研究院近代史研究所,1972)。

用。[11] 至於在臺北的臺灣神學院，也設有「史料中心」，對於教會的歷史文物也有相當可觀的收藏，包括早期的神學用書，傳教的譯經，宣教的小冊，和早期牧者與神學院老師對於教會發展與臺灣風土的短篇研究成果。[12]

過去外界比較不熟悉的宗派，其實也有很好的收藏，一直到了近年才開始對外界和學界開放。例如「真耶穌教會」在臺灣是很有歷史的教會，早期日據時代就在南部有很大的發展。就信徒數字方面來說，曾經是臺灣第二大的宗派。但是該教會長期以來很少與學界和其他教會界來往，所以對於該教會資料保存情況、宣教策略、人事更迭與教堂的分布和歷史，都少為外界所知。一直到近年才有研究真耶穌教會領導人與教會發展的學術論文發表，也才讓外界知道「真耶穌教會」有很好的史料收藏，[13] 同時「真耶穌教會神學院」有專人教授這方面的歷史，以及相關資料的保管。

另外一間過去較少與教會界來往的團體就是「教會聚會所」（或稱「召會」）。雖然學界對於聚會所的領導人物有一些研究，[14] 但是

---

11 有關該檔案館史料的研究，請參閱本書張妙娟的論文〈「臺灣基督長老教會歷史資料館」館藏史料之研究〉。

12 有關「臺灣神學院史料中心」之介紹與收藏，請參見該中心網站：http://www.taitheo.org.tw/ front/bin/cg-list.phtml?Category=171。

13 有關真耶穌教會的碩士論文，在2008年明顯的增多，很可能是教會有了較開放的政策，同時教會檔案也較易取得。從國家圖書館可搜尋到的碩士論文有：曾敏菁，〈阿美族長老教會與真耶穌教會之比較研究——以成功地區為例〉，國立政治大學民族學系碩士論文，1999；張藝鴻，〈utux、gaya與真耶穌教會：可樂部落太魯閣人的「宗教生活」〉，國立臺灣大學人類學研究所碩士論文，2000；黃恩霖，〈改宗、世俗化與復振：一個都市真耶穌教會的研究〉，國立清華大學人類學研究所碩士論文，2001；李桓崴，〈真耶穌教會與大林鎮郭家之宗教及社會參與〉，國立臺南大學臺灣文化研究所碩士論文，2008；施和樂，〈臺灣真耶穌教會的教會活動與會堂分布之關係〉，逢甲大學土地管理所碩士論文，2008；張心怡，〈臺灣真耶穌教會的發展（1925-2008）〉，中興大學歷史所碩士論文，2008。

14 研究聚會所的碩士論文相當不少，主要是從社會學、宗教學與歷史學的角度來討論，近幾年相關的論文有：李銘倫，〈「地方召會」之研究〉，國立中山大學中國與亞太區域研究所碩士論文，2013；胡聖民，〈青少年參與臺北市召會活動之休閒效益與幸福感〉，台北市立體育學院休閒運動管理學系碩士班碩士論文，2012；許秀敏，〈李常受教會觀之研究——「神的經營思想」之詮釋與實踐〉，中原大學宗教研究所碩士論文，2011；劉秋華，〈李常受的羅馬書釋義及其生機救恩論〉，中原大學宗教研究所碩士論文，2010；汪長欣，〈基督徒在「神聖」與「世俗」之間——以「臺北市召會聚會所」的基督徒為例〉，臺灣大學社會學研究所碩士論文，2009；李佳福，〈倪柝聲與中國「地方教會」運動（1903-1972）〉，國立臺灣師範大學歷史研究所碩士論文，2009；彭淑卿，〈論倪柝聲的末世論教會觀〉，中

外界對於聚會所的內部資料（非出版的神學書刊）、卻是不得而知。一直到最近幾年，才有重大的變化，不但聚會所的人事參與相關的研討會，同時更發表有關聚會所領導人物的研究論文。尤其重要的是成立了「倪柝聲文物與地方教會展覽館」，主動邀請外界人士前往參觀。「聚會所」近年來出人出錢，頻繁與學界合辦會議，如在2011年12月2~3日，在淡水舉辦「2011近現代中國基督教神學思想」學術研討會，2013年8月8~9日在香港舉辦「中國本土化基督教神學發展」國際學術研討會；2013年12月6~7日在木柵舉辦「2013現代中國本土基督教神學之發展」學術研討會，以及在福州舉辦數次相關的會議，且已有會議論文集出版。[15] 可以預見「聚會所」將來會開放更多的研究資料，也會促成研究成果。

在神學院方面，也逐漸的開始設立研究中心與史料中心，例如臺灣神學院成立「基督教思想研究中心」[16]、「史料中心」；臺南神學院「雙連宣教策略研究中心」[17]，及與長榮大學共同創立的「臺灣基督教與文化研究中心」[18]；中華福音神學院成立了「信仰與文化研究中心」[19]。而最積極的發展就是建構了「神學圖書資訊網」，將中華信義神學院圖書館、中華福音神學院圖書館、玉山神學院圖書館、浸信會神學院圖書館、聖光神學院圖書館、臺南神學院圖書館、臺灣神學院圖書館、中臺神學院圖書館等臺灣八所神學院圖書館的館藏聯合目錄，由信望愛網站提供技術支援，書目總量約45萬冊，為全臺灣最

原大學宗教研究所碩士論文，2009；林枝葉，〈從新興宗教的觀點論述基督教地方召會——以高雄縣林園地方召會為例〉，高雄師範大學臺灣文化及語言研究所碩士論文，2008。在「臺灣教會史料國際學術研討會」（2011年12月2-3日，國立中央大學文學院國際會議廳）中，亦有蔡蕙光發表的文章〈教會聚會所典藏資料分析：以聚會所在臺灣的初期福音開展為中心（1949-1962）〉。

15 這些會議主要為中港台學者參與，會議名稱不同，但是聚會所的人士經常撰寫論文，以「倪柝聲」、「地方教會（即聚會所）」為主，會議論文質量參差不齊。目前已出版的會議論文集為：林四皓、周復初編著，《不死就不生：2011近現代中國基督教神學思想學術研討會論文集》（台北：橄欖出版有限公司，2012）。

16 請參見該研究中心網站：http://www.taitheo.org.tw/front/bin/cglist.phtml?Category=20。

17 請參見雙連宣教策略研究中心網站：http://www.ttcs.org.tw/。

18 請參見臺灣基督教與文化研究中心網站：http://sites.cjcu.edu.tw/fccrc/page_c01001.html。

19 請參見信仰與文化研究中心網站：http://www.ces.org.tw/web/reserch_01.html。

大的神學圖書資源網站，可以說是了解臺灣這些神學院收藏最好的地方。[20]

筆者曾經在二十年前向國科會申請了一項三年計畫調查全臺灣教會的史料貯存。這個計畫有兩個目的，第一個是了解到教會界到底保存多少史料與那些史料，第二個是教會對於史料保存的歷史意識為何，他們能否從歷史的察覺中認知自我，與外在環境，進而尋求自我的定位，與確定未來的方向。該項計畫自1992年11月開始執行，到1996年才告一段落。[21] 從這項調查所顯示的一些成果，透露了許多有趣的訊息。關於史料的統計、分析的部分，已經在過去的學術會議中發表。[22] 現在則進一步的探討一些教會對於史料保存的情況以及處理的心態。所謂教會史料，當時分為六項：（1）教會會議記錄；（2）個人手札、信件、照片；（3）專論、紀念集；（4）教會期刊，週、月報；（5）論文、研究報告；（6）稀有書籍、特殊收藏[23]。這項調查所得到的結果是一則以喜、一則以憂。喜的是有許多教會史料在進行調查時仍然存在，憂的是教會界在開放與保存上仍然有很多問題。

現在舉幾間教會的史料作為討論的例證。第一間教會為新北市的「八里長老教會」。該教會創立於1874年，而保存的資料也從1874年開始，包括教會內小會、地方教會、長執會、年度會員大會等會議記錄。但是這些資料都不對外開放，至於傳道人聯誼會、會員大會手冊、照片等則是對學術界與教會學者開放，另外《小羊月刊》、《臺灣教會公報》、《週報》、《基督教論壇報》等出版品也是對學術界

---

20 詳請參閱「神學圖書資訊網」之網站：http://ttlib.fhl.net。

21 該項國科會三年計畫是「臺灣地區基督教史料調查研究計畫（I）（II）（III）」，進行時間分別為1992年11月至1993年10月，1994年8月至1995年7月，1995年8月至1996年7月。此項計畫在執行上有所耽延，主要是筆者此期間工作轉換，申請此計畫時在淡江大學，開始執行時則剛轉至中興大學任教，而後在1994年8月轉往中正大學任教，方才完成此項計畫。

22 王成勉，〈臺灣基督教史料之研究〉，《臺灣基督教史——史料與研究回顧國際學術研討會論文集》（臺北：宇宙光出版社，1998），頁237-272。

23 這個分類乃是參酌美國調查各機構有關中國教會史料的大型計畫，然後加以修改而來，這些分類是要測量教會是否認知到各種史料的性質，又做何種保藏。至於美國當年的調查計畫，請參見Archie Crouch, *Christianity in China: A Scholars' Guide to Resources in the Libraries and Archives of the United States* (N.Y.: M. E. Sharpe, 1989).

與教會學者開放。雖然這間教會歷史悠久，也保存了教堂重要的會議資料，應該是可以作為研究參考的地方。但是該教會在開放的情況上，卻是封閉的。真正關鍵性和可以了解教會發展的東西，都不對外開放。即使是外間都可以取得的出版品，該教會也只做有限度的開放。這可以反應出在管理史料方面的保守心態。事實上在筆者設計調查問卷時，對開放與不開放之間，有第三項選擇，就是「須經申請許可」。但是這教堂對於所有的資料都沒有去勾選這一項，顯示至少在訪問當時，受訪人認為這些真正關係到教會決策與發展的歷史材料，沒有任何對外開放的可能。同時，在進行史料調查時，也發現當時受訪的人士對於資料的了解與保管也有不清楚的地方，例如其將《基督教論壇報》也列為1874年開始出版[24]，而將《臺灣教會公報》的起始年份列為1874年也是明顯的錯誤。[25]

　　同樣的情況也出現在其他很有歷史的教會。如在中部的「溪湖長老教會」，成立於1898年，保存的資料也是從1898年開始，包括「小會會議記錄」、「牧長會議記錄」、「各種團契會議記錄」，可是這些重要又有歷史的會議記錄都不對外開放。而對於學術界與教會學者開放的資料，為《七十週年紀念冊》、《八十週年紀念冊》、《九十週年紀念冊》、《週報》等。所以都可以看出他們也是無意將主要史料提供出來。北臺灣最早的「淡水長老教會」雖然在史料開放上是保守的，但是對於歷史文物則是成立小型的史料館，將馬偕家族的物品予以陳列，包括生活用品、醫藥器材、銅板、幻燈片、標本箱、《三字經》、餐碟、偕媽蓮日文聖經、偕醫館建材等，應是北臺灣唯一有史料館的教會，這與南臺灣的太平境馬雅各紀念教會史料館遙遙呼應[26]，為深具歷史意識，又願意展示歷史文物的教會。這一方面固然

24　《基督教論壇報》是一份在臺灣發行的基督教報紙，創立於1965年10月30日，最早是採週刊發行，後來曾經為三日刊、二日刊。

25　《臺灣教會公報》（創辦初期的名稱為《臺灣府城教會報》），是1885年7月12日開始在臺灣發行，詳請參閱：張妙娟，《開啟心眼──《臺灣府城教會報》與長老教會的基督徒教育》（臺南：人光出版，新樓書房發行代理，2005）。

26　關於太平境馬雅各紀念教會史料館之介紹，請參梁唯真，〈見尋本溯源──太平境馬雅各紀念教會史料

是長老教會在臺發展歷史悠久，另一方面則是長老教會比較注重歷史文物的保存。

四、挑戰與展望

臺灣的神學院與主要宗派機構至少都有幾十年的歷史，已經到了必須要思考與處理史料的時候。一方面是開始有堆積如山的史料，從教堂到分會、宗派的各種會議、各種出版品，很難有足夠的空間貯藏，更難定出一個保存的標準。同時，在經費、空間與管理（開放）制度都有壓力的情況下，侷限了積極處理史料、應用史料的思考，成為今天教會史研究和教會史料保管的重大挑戰。

如果未來要有一個健康的教會史料發展，至少有三項事工（ministry）或觀念值得積極推動和注意。[27] 這三項事工不是單一的人物、職位或機構可以單獨處理的，而是需要整個神學界與教會界的自覺與動員，同時是要經過一場長期的努力，未來才能看到豐碩的結果。

（一）專業化的人員與參考工具的建立及整合

過去教會界對於圖書與檔案不夠重視，最好的例子就是負責圖書、史料的人士多非是專業人員。好像這種工作是任何基督徒就可以來擔任，多為兼差性質，而他們的工作只定位在保藏與管理而已。只要收藏品與圖書不短少、有地方放，他們就完成了任務。

但是真正理想的史料、圖書人員，一定要有現代圖書管理的觀念。只有專業人員，才能夠和同業、讀者與研究人員有良好的互動，

與歷史撰述之分析研究），發表於「臺灣教會史料國際學術研討會」（2011年12月2-3日，國立中央大學文學院國際會議廳）。

27 「事工」（ministry）有狹義與廣義的兩種定義，一為教會特定的服事，另一為廣義為教會與民眾提供的服事。見 "Ministry," in Sinclair B. Ferguson, David F. Wright and J. I. Packer, *New Dictionary of Theology* (Downers Grove, IL: Inter-Varsity Press, 1988), pp. 430-433.

更能將現代的科技應用在管理方面。在教會史料的保存，國外教會的檔案館有很好的先例。例如，許多神學院圖書館可以用分工的方式共同來保存教會的出版品。臺灣並不大，並不需要每個神學院圖書館都要有全套的圖書、期刊和各項出版品。如何建立有特色而且分工良好的合作系統，在收藏與使用上互相支援，應是神學院圖書館界首先要思考的。

進一步來說，神學圖書館合作時，是否能夠跨越宗派的藩籬，是另一項關鍵。雖然在收藏與使用方面，各圖書館優先考量到自己宗派的立場，這是難免之事，可是應該可以在收藏方面予以突破。臺灣神學院的圖書館有了一些新措施，筆者稱之為「寧靜革命」。記得約在二十年前，筆者在臺灣神學院圖書館使用資料時，該館在本地教會出版品的收藏上，幾乎是只有長老教會的出版書冊。但是筆者在2011年上半年再度前往參訪時，有好幾排書架是臺灣各地教會的週年紀念集，其中很多是非長老教會系統的教堂週年紀念冊。從歷史研究者的眼光來說，自然會希望能身處於一個具有深度與廣度的圖書館，能夠進行大架構與比較歷史的研究。也就是說，讀者可以參考到更大的背景，了解到基督教在臺灣的發展，而不是只看單一的宗派。同時，歷史研究必須進入比較歷史的境界，才能看出單一歷史的特色。如果臺灣神學院圖書館的做法不是一個獨特的個案，則這個趨勢是很有意義也是值得鼓勵的。

（二）「圖書館事工」（Library Ministry）

臺灣教會史多年沒有順利開展的原因，就教會內部而言，有很大的因素是因為神學院未著重「教會史」的課程，以致培養出來的教會領袖與教會負責人沒有足夠的「歷史觀」與「歷史訓練」。但是另外一項重要的原因，是教會界未留下與開放足夠的教會歷史材料，致使歷史研究者沒有可以著力的空間，無法寫下真實、感人又與切身相關的作品來豐富教學與訓練學生。

要能打破這個惡性循環，必須從提倡「圖書館事工」（Library

Ministry）來做起。就是負責史料、圖書的檔案館員或圖書館館員必須了解，自己所負責的工作，不再只是資料管理，而是能夠自覺到手邊的東西，是上帝在臺灣帶領的物證，其中包含了多少宣教上的血淚與流汗，這些資料應該也必須被使用和廣傳。

隨著電腦與網路的利用，神學院的圖書館與檔案館也增加了這些研究的利器。而這些網路資源不只是便利了自己的學生或是自己宗派的成員，也讓外界可以一窺這些機構收藏的豐富，以及相關研究活動的訊息。但是這些發展似乎只做到連線的使用。也就是說，很多資料並未數位化，同時在開放上也做的不夠積極。神學院圖書館好像從未與學術界研究教會史的人有過座談。如果神學院圖書館的館員連最多使用教會資料、最多在寫作教會史的人需要什麼都不清楚，那如何讓這方面的館藏發生作用。

其實要了解神學院和教會界的史料，特別是其中的珍藏與重點，有一個捷徑可循，就是參考神學院學生的碩、博士論文。現在有越來越多神學院學生撰寫教會歷史的論文。（例如臺灣神學院、中華福音神學院、衛理神學研究院等都有不少關於歷史研究的學位論文。）從這類論文的增加，亦透露出神學院學生的興趣與相關老師的要求。而神學院的學生，比較能夠獲得宗派與教會的信任，因而在訪談人物與教會史料的收集及使用上，往往會突破一些教會的限制，得到內部的觀點與資料。因此分析神學院的碩士論文，特別是這些論文最後的書目及參考文獻，是了解教會史料的良好方法。但是因為目前神學院學生論文未加入國家圖書館的「臺灣博碩士論文知識加值系統」，可以被上線與搜尋的非常少，所以神學院學生的論文普遍的未被學界所注意和使用。這是學術界與神學院圖書館均應努力的地方。

有了「圖書館事工」的認識以後，教會界與神學院圖書館及檔案館的工作人員就能夠站在積極的立場，主動的去收集史料，提供史料，甚至進一步的編纂史料，並可以和相關單位合作，將其收藏做成資料庫。[28] 這裡可以利用耶魯大學與普林斯頓大學兩校的神學院圖書館做為例子。普林斯頓大學當年是第一個編輯中國教會史料的機構，讓許多份民國時期的教會期刊成為縮微膠片。而耶魯大學現在做的更廣，把該圖書館藏的重要期刊亦製成為縮微膠片。

而教會界與神學院圖書館的館員，在配合教會史的收藏與研究上，他們更需要熟悉通史（特別是教會通史），和歷史學者座談，了解研究的趨勢和需求，這樣才能提供協助，讓教會史料能做最大的發揮，也同時讓教會的歷史研究能夠更加進步。耶魯大學特藏部就顯示出這個良性的循環。首先是有很好的庫藏，收有很多重要機構、傳教士的檔案和文件，然後吸引到很好的學者與研究人士前來利用，產生出許許多多重要的教會史研究，而這樣的名聲與貯藏特色吸引了更多的教會和機構願將他們的資料捐給耶魯大學。[29] 今天耶魯大學特藏部為西方首屈一指的教會史料典藏單位，主要是在圖書館事工上建立了這個良性循環。而長期在耶魯大學特藏部擔任館長的司馬倫（Martha Lund Smalley）女士，就是建立今天豐富館藏與特殊地位的主要推手之一。[30]

（三）「堂史」運動

過去教會界把教會史寫作不是看的太嚴肅就是看的太簡單，這兩種心態也都影響到教會歷史的撰寫。第一種心態，就是把教會史當成很嚴肅又很艱難的事情，認為總會人士或是資深的牧者才能執筆，而且是不容任何其他人士插手或置喙。這種情況下教會史或堂會史往往

---

28 例如司馬倫（Martha Lund Smalley）女士就把耶魯大學神學院特藏室中傳教士有關南京大屠殺的史料編成專冊，成為此方面的重要出版史料。Martha Lund Smalley, ed., *American missionary eyewitnesses to the Nanking Massacre, 1937-1938* (New Haven, Conn.: Yale Divinity School Library, 1997).

29 傳教士捐給耶魯大學神學院圖書館的資料可參考：Martha Lund Smalley, *Missionary Papers at the Yale Divinity School Library* (New Haven, Conn.: Yale Divinity School Library, 1994)。許多新捐的傳教士檔案，可查該神學院圖書館的特藏部的網頁。

30 關於耶魯大學神學院圖書館的歷史與史料，請參閱本書司馬倫（Martha Lund Smalley）女士的文章"Documenting the Church in Taiwan: the Perspective from Yale University"。

一拖再拖，幾十年過後還是找不到適合的人來寫作，最後是歷史無存與史料散亂難尋。

而太簡單的看待教會史的人，則是認為只要把教會資料整理一下，依年代列出一些活動就是歷史。所以教會界可以產生大批的紀念集，從人物到建堂紀念集都有。但是其中的問題大同小異。主筆者多未受過歷史的訓練，敘事很多沒有經過考證，不但在時間與敘述誤謬，而且往往資料不足。例如其中所附的照片常沒有附上照片中每位的人名與拍攝時間。編輯的人沒有想到，再經過幾十年，讀者都不認識照片中人，這樣所附的照片就變成猜謎，失去意義。但是這種情況經常可以在教會出版品中見到。

更嚴重的事，就是教會人士常常用報喜不報憂的心態來編輯教會的歷史。絕大部分教會歷史出版品都是極其隱諱或是一筆帶過的方式來處理教會的人事問題與紛爭。這種不敢面對歷史的心態，寫出來的歷史失真。只能算是一種感恩見證集，反而缺少真實與感動的力量。聖經中並沒有避諱一些人物的跌倒或錯誤，更一再敘述重建聖殿的困難與問題，所以要寫出真實的歷史，才符合聖經的歷史寫作。

因此教會界亟需進行撰寫「堂史」的運動。讓教會的各個教堂與機構的主其事者有歷史的概念，反思上帝的心意與帶領，不但留下資料，同時把發展的歷史事實寫作下來。[31] 在寫作歷史的同時，應該尋求歷史專業人士的合作，把教會的歷史變成「信史」，做為「見證」。為了配合這個歷史的寫作，應該有系統的把資料留存，或加以數位化的處理，從週報、各種會議記錄、各種活動介紹與報告、差傳資料，以迄單張、通信等等都可以分類留存。

「堂史」是與信徒最直接、最有感觸的歷史。也是所有教堂的參與者共有的經驗。這是教堂的牧師、長老、執事與信徒都能發揮的工作。經過教會成員自己的經歷與寫史、大家的分享及參與，能共同感

---

31 臺灣神學院的鄭仰恩教授頗為注意教會歷史教育，曾出版：鄭仰恩主編，《臺灣基督長老教會歷史教育手冊》（臺北：使徒出版，臺灣基督長老教會歷史委員會發行，2010）。

受到上帝的工作，也往往能因此重新找出起初的感動，進而整理出將來發展的路線。從教會歷史的觀點，有了堂史可以把各個教會在地方發展中連起來，成為一個面，看出教會與社會的整體互動。而有了堅實的堂史，更能協助整個宗派史，甚至臺灣教會史的寫作。

　　與國外的教會史料比較起來，臺灣教會最欠缺的史料是日記與通信。似乎臺灣教會界過於注重個人的隱私，沒有把日記或書信、文件交付檔案館保存的習慣。但是缺少了這類東西，在歷史寫作上也缺少了更真切的寫作材料。對於這個缺憾，可以補足的地方就是展開「口述歷史」的工作，由教會、總會或神學院圖書館進行「口述歷史」的訪問。利用文字與音訊等設備，能很有效的將受訪人的資料保存下來。這項工作必須是由受過這方面訓練的人員來進行。「口述歷史」並非僅是採訪，或是讓受訪者暢所欲言，而是有主題、有驗證，又能讓關鍵事項很好的呈現。[32]

五、結語

　　臺灣教會史料的保存與研究正處於一個重要的關口。在檢討這些史料時，同時會呈現樂觀與不樂觀的兩個面向。比較不樂觀的地方，是過去由於政教關係敏感、教會經濟困乏、學界關注不足的外在原因，以及教會人士對於教會歷史不夠注重的內在原因，造成史料與相關文物的流失與棄置。另外一個欠缺，是教會界過去沒有及時進行個人史料的「徵集」，特別是「口述歷史」的缺乏。這些內在與外在的問題，致使臺灣教會歷史的著述與研究一直無法順利的開始。

　　但是在研究臺灣教會史料時，也發現幾道光明的曙光。就是教會相關史料其實是無所不在。從政府的中央部會到地方政府的調查資料，無不顯示教會的發展和內容。這些資料和教會的資料可以相互佐

---

32 坊間已有不少介紹「口述歷史」的書可以參考，如唐諾・里齊（Donald A. Ritchie）著，王芝芝譯，《大家來做口述歷史》（臺北：遠流，1997）。

證，產生的作品將會是更周延、更可以看出教會與社會的互動性。同時教會界（甚至單獨教堂）還是有許多史料留存，神學院也開始推動教會史相關的研究，相關的圖書館與史料館也成立與開放，使得臺灣教會史的研究將來有很大開展的空間。

近年來在中國教會史方面，有多本深受學術界注意的著作出版。[33] 也許大家面臨的問題是，為什麼幾十年來我們看不到一本令人滿意的臺灣教會史？[34] 這個問題是歷史學界與教會界都要反省的問題。教會史的寫作是一項長期又極為辛苦的工作，一方面需要有良好歷史訓練的人士投入這個冷門的領域，另一方面又需要教會界願意開放史料、予以配合，而這兩方面都是我們應該積極努力的地方。

---

33 如以基督教在華的通史而言，就有 Nicolas Standaert, ed., *Handbook of Christianity in China, Vol. 1* (Leiden; Brill, 2001); R.G. Tiedemann, *Handbook of Christianity in China, Vol. II* (Leiden: Brill, 2010). Daniel H. Bays, *A New History of Christianity in China* (Malden, MA: Wiley-Blackwell, 2011).

34 現有的幾本臺灣基督教會通史為：Hollington K. Tong, *Christianity in Taiwan: a history* (Taipei, Printed by China Post, 1961)，惟此書的中文譯本並不理想：董顯光，《基督教在臺灣的發展》（香港：董顯光，1962）；李政隆，《臺灣基督教史》（臺北：天恩，2001）；林金水主編，《臺灣基督教史》（北京：九州出版社，2003）。

中國基督教史料蒐集的機遇與合作

黃淑薇

香港浸會大學圖書館特藏及文獻組主任

摘要

本文主要是介紹香港浸會大學圖書館基督教在華發展史文獻部，在蒐集基督教在華史料所得的經驗，及如何掌握發展機遇，與其他圖書館和教會合作。

香港浸會大學圖書館基督教在華發展史文獻部成立於1996 年，其目的是為學者在亞洲地區，提供一個專門研究基督教在華發展歷史的中心。

鑑於過去十多年，有關基督教的研究、學術會議文章及出版物與日俱增，同時香港浸會大學也增加了許多與基督教有關的課程和研究項目，因此，對基督教史料的需求也日益增加，藉這樣的機遇，文獻部就向圖書館要求增加更多資源，並得到批准。我們在蒐集資料時，也不斷有新的嘗試，與其他圖書館合作，購買他們部分館藏拍成的縮微膠卷。本部並於2010年得到耶魯大學神學院圖書館全數資助，與香港五間教會及基督教機構合作，將其刊物數位化及製成縮微膠卷。因此，耶魯大學神學院圖書館及本館，都收藏全套數位影像和縮微膠卷，大量增加了基督教在華發展的研究資料。

關鍵詞：基督教史料、華人基督教、館藏發展、香港浸會大學圖書館、數位化、耶魯大學神學院圖書館

一、前言

香港浸會大學圖書館的基督教在華發展史文獻部（下稱文獻部）成立於1996年10月1日，目的是要在亞洲地區為學者提供一個專門研究基督教在華歷史的中心。基於此，本部專注蒐集一切與中國基督教徒、傳教士、教會歷史有關的史料，不論任何基督教教會，任何國別的記錄，一手或二手的資料，本部皆兼收並蓄，包括信件、手稿、專論、期刊、縮微膠卷等。目前，現存檔案及書刊超過4,988種，共6,594冊，縮微資料近28,400件。

自2000年，文獻部的發展方向重新定位，由創辦初年側重蒐集早期傳教士及歐美差會檔案，改向以福建、華南地區，近代華人教牧及教會為主。此外，由於文獻部地處香港，且本校由浸信會創辦，故對香港教會及浸信會史料的蒐集亦加以重視[1]。

二、文獻部的源起

文獻部的成立源於當年任職於香港浸會大學（下稱浸大）歷史系的史百川教授（Prof. Barton Starr）的推動。1980年代中，史百川教授研究倫敦會傳教士馬禮遜（Robert Morrison, 1782-1834）的生平及事業時，獲得校內外的撥款，他因此購置大量有關馬禮遜的縮微資料[2]。但在尋找資料的同時，他進一步發現從事中國基督教史研究的學者，往往未能在中國本土上找到所需的史料，反而要遠渡至歐美國家尋找相關資料。1995年，他與浸大宗教及哲學系費樂仁教授（Prof. Lauren Pfister）撰寫建議[3]，後更邀請歷史系的李金強教授及剛

---

1 李金強，〈感謝的話〉，《基督教在華發展史文獻部十週年紀念特刊（1996-2006）》（香港：香港浸會大學近代史研究中心，2006），頁52。

2 同前註。

3 Starr, J. Barton, "In Celebration of the 10th Anniversary of the Opening of the Archive on the History of Christianity in China," in *Special Issue for the Celebration of the 10th Anniversary of the Archive on the History of Christianity in China (1996-2006)*(Hong Kong: Modern History Research Centre, 2006), p. 17.

回母校任教的黃文江先生連署，向校方提出成立文獻部，專責蒐集基督教在華史料，讓學者在香港就能夠獲取重要研究史料，免卻遠赴重洋之苦。校方接納該建議後，於1996年10月1日在大學圖書館設立文獻部，並組成文獻部委員會，管理文獻部的建設與運作[4]。

文獻部發展至今已屆十七年，雖然在館藏、讀者服務及數碼化計劃等各方面仍未能與其他歷史悠久的研究機構及圖書館相比，但在大中華地區以至於亞洲區內，已為人認識是專門研究基督教在華發展史的中心。現在，無論在館藏、設備及讀者服務各方面都比初成立時，更加豐富及多元化。

三、文獻部的發展過程

文獻部在蒐集中國基督教及教會史料的工作，大致可分為三個階段。在不同的階段，我們因應不同的內在因素及條件、客觀環境及難得的機遇，定下不同的館藏發展策略，以增加館藏及讀者服務。

（一）建設時期（1996年10月～1999年6月）

文獻部成立之初，直接隸屬於浸大圖書館的讀者服務部。但由於當時圖書館經費有限，未能投放大量資源在文獻部的發展上，故此，文獻部無論在人力、資金及設備上都比較貧乏。本部在最初的兩年，幸好得到一位在美國退休的圖書館員Marie McKay女士義務幫忙，負責文獻部的管理行政、館藏發展，及提供讀者服務。Marie McKay女士於1998年8月離任之後，前香港浸信會神學院圖書館員Vivian Holder女士接任，至1999年12月。

在這成立初期，由於資金緊絀，文獻部未能大量購買藏書，Marie McKay女士便將浸大圖書館部分有關在華基督教史及中國教會

---

4 李金強，〈感謝的話〉，《基督教在華發展史文獻部十週年紀念特刊（1996-2006）》（香港：香港浸會大學近代史研究中心，2006），頁52。

發展史的書籍，撥歸文獻部所有，供讀者使用。然而，在蒐集基督教及教會史料的工作上，進展仍然緩慢。本部的停刊出版物及檔案，主要來自私人捐贈。

1996年10月，居港數十年，曾於香港中文大學任教的施其樂牧師（Rev. Carl T. Smith）將他在數十年內蒐集的中國基督教資料中，揀選部分送給文獻部。施其樂牧師醉心研究中國大陸、香港及澳門的基督教及教會歷史，其收藏的研究資料種類繁多，數量驚人。他也把部分資料送交香港政府歷史檔案館。他捐給文獻部的史料，包括300多件有關香港、澳門、中國大陸基督教史的書籍和檔案文件，如*Papers of Clergy and Ministers' Group Meeting*。同年，浸信會出版社捐出美南浸信會西差會傳教士Lila Watson在1927~1949年於臺灣及香港傳教工作的原始資料。

1997年3月經施其樂牧師引薦，Betty Wai博士捐出Lady Ride Collection，其中包括於1859年5月5日 Gallowtree Gate Church寫給理雅各博士（Dr. James Legge）的一封信。這封信寫在一張32×46.5公分的羊皮紙上，內容是有關理雅各博士來港傳教，返英休息時，收到教會發出的感謝信。教會更送上一袋金，希望幫助理雅各博士在港傳教。理雅各博士的哥哥，正是該會的牧師。另外還有位於馬禮遜牧師墓西端的中文字拓本，長闊為25.3×8公分。

同年，更獲得美南浸信會國外傳道部港澳差會（Hong Kong-Macao Baptist Mission of the Southern Baptist Convention Foreign Mission Board）的檔案資料。此外，浸大圖書館獲中國神學研究院圖書館准許，將其晚清時期的基督教有關古籍52種掃描，複製成光碟，存藏於文獻部供讀者使用。

1998年2月，Swiss East-Asia Mission捐出一冊於1819年出版，由馬禮遜編寫的《漢英字典》的第二部分第一冊（*Dictionary of the Chinese Language* in Three Parts. Part II, vol. 1）給文獻部。

為了要解決資金短缺這個大難題，Marie McKay女士及史百川教授便嘗試向海內、外機構申請撥款。Marie McKay女士於1997年的短短兩個月內便聯絡了44間機構，為文獻部籌募經費。因著在史百川教授及費樂仁教授的努力下，文獻部在1998年獲得美國Henry Luce Foundation捐贈12萬美元供本部發展之用。該筆捐款分三年發放，主要是用於員工培訓及購買設備，例如電腦、影印機、古籍掃描機及縮微資料閱讀機等。1998年4月，文獻部獲本校「教學發展基金」撥款，購買設備及縮微資料。因此，本部的設備便得以改善。由於Henry Luce Foundation指定不可以動用捐款於購買書籍，所以，我們的藏書並未能因此而大量增加。但因為縮微資料並非書籍，所以我們便可以運用部分撥款購買縮微資料。事實上，自1998年起數年間，文獻部採購的縮微資料中，有超過一半是因Henry Luce Foundation撥款而購買的，其中有歐美國家的基督教差會檔案，範圍包括十八至二十世紀美洲及歐洲基督教差會及傳教士在中國的生平及事工，例如 *Wesleyan Methodist Missionary Society (London) Archives*、*Church Missionary Society Archives*及*Archives on the Council for World Mission, 1775-1940*。其他的縮微資料則是有關基督教及中國教會的書刊，例如*Nineteenth Century Books on China*、*China Christian Year Book*，*China's Millions*、*West China Missionary News*、*American Theological Library Association Serials*。如果沒有以上兩筆撥款，我們絕對無法大量採購這些每卷售價為100美元或100英鎊以上的縮微資料。

總而言之，文獻部在首三年的起步階段期間，得以成功蒐集館藏，主要是依賴圖書館館藏的轉移、熱心人士的捐贈、歷史系和宗教及哲學系教授撰寫撥款申請書，以及Henry Luce Foundation的巨額資助。另一方面，Marie McKay和Vivian Holder兩位女士在制定讀者服務和政策、購置部門設備等工作已是十分繁重，所以她們未能花太多時間去蒐集館藏資料；加上她們對中文的認識有限，所以在蒐集中文資料，尤其是原始資料上，倍感困難。

（二）打穩根基時期（1999 年 7 月～2005 年中）

第二階段是文獻部進入鞏固基礎，邁步向前的時期。這時，浸大圖書館管理層認識到文獻部需要一位能掌握中、英文，了解香港及內地情況，具備檔案管理專業知識的主管來管理，才能有長遠發展。於是，圖書館方面便向亞洲基督教高等教育聯合董事會（United Board for Christian Higher Education in Asia）申請撥款，連同Henry Luce Foundation的部分捐款，於1999年1月保送筆者到美國伊利諾州惠敦市（Wheaton）進修六個月。筆者在惠敦學院（Wheaton College）的葛培理中心檔案館（Billy Graham Centre Archives）內受訓，同時在芝加哥市郊的Dominican University 修讀檔案管理一科及訪問美國多間檔案館和大學圖書館。該培訓計劃完成後，筆者於1999年6月底返港。

這時，圖書館也開始推行架構改組。1999年7月2日開始，基督教在華發展史文獻部便與當代中國研究部及大學文獻部正式合併，成為特藏及文獻組（下稱特藏組），而筆者便成為該新部門主管至今。此外，館方亦將圖書館四樓的部分地方重新裝修，建成特藏組的辦公室及讀者閱讀室，而全職員工就增至四人。

1998年中，梁王以煥女士接任為香港浸會大學圖書館館長。梁館長上任前曾在美國的大學圖書館工作超過二十年，經驗豐富，見識廣博，她為我們帶來很多新思維及創新的圖書館發展理念。首先，她鼓勵我們學習及利用日新月異的圖書館及資訊科技於工作及服務上。她認為浸大圖書館應發展具有特色的館藏，而不是與其他有悠久歷史、資源豐厚的大學圖書館在館藏數量上爭一日之長短，即所謂貴精不貴多。環顧香港其他院校圖書館，她發現沒有一間擁有較具規模的中國基督教館藏。所以，梁館長便計劃加快發展特藏組，而圖書館管理層這個決定，正是對本部的發展及蒐集中國基督教及教會文獻的工作有莫大幫助。

在2000年2月圖書館邀請美國惠敦學院葛培理中心檔案館的Paul Ericksen先生來港擔任文獻部發展顧問，為文獻部日後的發展提供寶貴的意見，並在留港期間參與了一連串介紹本部工作及教會檔案的活動，包括：

1.「檔案與教會歷史」活動——由浸大圖書館及浸大歷史系合

辦，當中包括兩場有關口述歷史和中國內地會的講座。

2. 基督教檔案整理工作坊——文獻部獲得香港華人基督教聯會資助，Ericksen先生和筆者特別為155位圖書館及教會人士分享檔案整理的方法。

3. 特藏組更在圖書館內及互聯網上舉辦了相關展覽，直至該年3月初。

在2004年，圖書館得到政府撥款進行擴展工程，特藏組便因此得以擴展空間，新增的面積達到一倍以上。

在這階段的初期，文獻部採購中國基督教及教會的書刊和縮微資料，仍是由Henry Luce Foundation的撥款和圖書館特別經費支付，而文獻部仍未能爭取到固定的館藏發展經費，因此，館藏數量無法迅速增長。

在制定文獻部長遠的發展政策時，筆者深信如果缺乏足夠的人力及資源，發展必會受到侷限，遑論要實現大量增加館藏的宏願。而讀者需求與資料供應又有著莫大的關係，假如讀者對文獻部的館藏及服務需求增加，文獻部在圖書館的重要性或會直接提升，因而可以向管理層要求增撥資源，使本部可以取得固定的資金去採購藏品。因此，在1999至2004年期間，我們加強宣傳文獻部的工作，並且好好把握幾個難得的機遇，去爭取迅速發展的機會。

· 學術界對中國基督教史的重視

近二十年，有關中國基督教史的研究發展蓬勃。從表1所示，筆者以「中國」、「臺灣」、「香港」、「教會」、「基督教」及「傳教士」等關鍵詞在三個中、英文的論文數據庫搜尋，可見自1990年起，論文數量已倍增。學術界對中國基督教史研究的重視，令中國基督教及教會史料的需求大增，同時亦鞭策文獻部積極爭取資源，嘗試開拓新途徑去蒐集中國基督教發展史的資料。

表 1：中國基督教史學術論文數量

提供中國基督教史學術論文的數據庫	1990-1999	2000-2009	2010-2011
1) EBSCOhost （英文論文數據庫）			
Church* AND (China or Taiwan or Hong Kong)	1695	2386	295
Christianity AND (China or Taiwan or Hong Kong)	817	1405	217
missionar* AND (China or Taiwan or Hong Kong)	889	1113	179
2) 中國期刊全文數據庫 China Journal Net			
香港或者中國或者臺灣 並且教會	383	965	204
香港或者中國或者臺灣 並且基督教	1188	3082	656
香港或者中國或者臺灣 並且傳教士	752	2115	549
3) 臺灣期刊論文索引系統 Index to Taiwan Periodical Literature			
（KW= 教會）[AND]（KW= 香港 OR 中國 OR 臺灣）	45	87	13
（KW= 基督教）[AND]（KW= 香港 OR 中國 OR 臺灣）	37	68	8
（KW= 傳教士）[AND]（KW= 香港 OR 中國 OR 臺灣）	8	11	2

　　踏入2000年後，學者在研究基督教史的領域內，漸漸重視中國基督教的歷史，探討及推動研究中國基督教或基督宗教的學術團體及機構紛紛成立。在香港浸會大學內，便有「近代史研究中心」、「林思齊東西學術交流研究所」和「中華基督宗教研究中心」。校外則有「中國基督教史研究學會」、「建道神學院基督教與中國文化研究中心」及「香港中文大學崇基學院宗教與中國社會研究中心」。而國內外學者從事中國基督教歷史或相關的研究項目亦為數不少。本校教師當中，以歷史系的李金強教授、黃文江教授、朱益宜教授和宗教及哲學系費樂仁教授為例，他們均從事近代中國天主教及基督教的研究。此外，在本科生的課程設計上，本校宗哲系及歷史系也增加了多個有關基督教的課程，例如中國基督宗教（Chinese Christianity）、香港宗教儀式及實踐（Religious Rituals & Practices in Hong Kong）、基督宗教與文明（Introduction to Christianity and Civilizations）、基督教與中國文化（Christianity and Chinese Culture）、中國天主教史（History of the Catholic Church in China）、十九世紀香港歷史（History of Hong Kong to 1900）及口述歷史（Oral History and Its Local Applications）等。歷史系的教授亦積極鼓勵研究生及本科生開展中國基督教史有關的研究。因此，本校師生對中國基督教史的資料需求便有增無減。

與此同時，中、港、臺三地舉辦有關基督宗教的研討會或交流會亦為數不少，在本港舉辦了七屆的「近代中國基督教史研討會」便是其中一個成功的例子，很多與會的學者，當他們路經香港或專程來港參加會議時，都會到文獻部參觀或尋找資料，所以，來訪的校外人士亦有所增加。總體而言，從表2及表3，可見文獻部的讀者總人次及藏品使用量都有穩定增長。

・讀者增加，爭取經費

有見及此，文獻部圖書館委員會便要求圖書館管理層增設文獻部館藏發展經費，由2004至2005學年度開始，文獻部便每年獲得5萬港元的經費去採購館藏資料。隨後在2007年及2010年，文獻部的館藏經費分別增加至10萬及11萬港元，以採購書刊、善本書、縮微資料及檔案，當中包括來華傳教士的著作和手稿，以至早年傳教士編撰的英漢字典等，例如1866至1868年出版，William Lobscheid編撰的*English and Chinese Dictionary : with the Punti and Mandarin Pronunciation*。

・另闢途徑，蒐集史料

由於很多研究中國基督教史的學者及學生，藉著中國教會、西方差會及宣教士在華工作的史料去探討近代中國在教育、社會、福利、醫療、政治及經濟、文化及翻譯等各方面的發展，所以文獻部要蒐集的史料亦要非常廣泛。除了從書商採購新舊書刊之外，我們要進一步去蒐集善本及未經出版發行的一手資料。

・與中國大陸圖書館合作

我們深信中國大陸的圖書館，尤以在清末民初時興辦的基督教大

表2：基督教在華發展史文獻部使用量統計（1996-2011）

年份	藏品使用量	讀者人次				時數（小時）
		學生	教職員	校外人士	總數	
10/1996-6/1997	-	-	-	-	306	-
7/1997-7/1998	-	-	-	-	864	-
8/1998-6/1999	-	-	-	-	-	-
7/1999-6/2000	1767	-	-	-	408	-
7/2000-6/2001	1411	186	26	98	310	-
7/2001-6/2002	2909	201	43	70	314	-
7/2002-6/2003	1740	146	49	102	297	-
7/2003-6/2004	1406	156	50	84	290	675.51
7/2004-6/2005	2258	227	58	103	388	1140.53
7/2005-6/2006	3237	172	82	169	423	1189.11
7/2006-6/2007	4900	229	111	270	610	1796.59
7/2007-6/2008	5227	149	104	300	553	1495.08
7/2008-6/2009	4219	162	78	294	534	1606.55
7/2009-6/2010	3606	237	84	312	633	1864.91
7/2010-6/2011	4017	224	78	316	618	2730.57
7/2011-10/2011	789	21	23	140	184	823.03

學內，一定仍然保存為數不少有關基督教在華發展史的書籍。1999年，筆者藉著到上海參加圖書館研討會之便，到上海華東師範大學（前聖約翰大學）圖書館了解他們的館藏及查詢合作的可能性。最終我們揀選了55種中文圖書，請他們將有關基督教在華發展和基督教教義的中文書籍，以及聖經譯本等，拍成縮微膠卷，供浸大圖書館讀者使用。

雖然，這個增添館藏資料的方法無疑是較為費時及昂貴，但不失為一個蒐集中文善本書的好方法。故此，在2003至2004年，我們先後

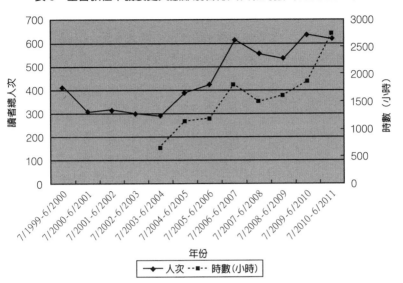

表3：基督教在華發展史文獻部讀者總人次和時數（1999-2011）

與北京師範大學圖書館及上海圖書館進行相同的合作計劃，增加了99種書。這些書刊都事先經過我們查閱核實，確保香港其他院校圖書館沒有收藏，我們才會請中國大陸圖書館複製成縮微膠卷。

· 加強宣傳

　　文獻部獲批的發展經費有限，在蒐集一手資料及絕版書刊上，我們仍需依賴熱心人士的捐贈。鑑於文獻部只有寥寥數年的發展，認識我們工作的人恐怕不算多。因此，我們便開展一連串的宣傳活動；我們除了在香港的兩份基督教週刊上撰文介紹文獻部的工作及在圖書館內舉辦展覽外，我們也藉著歷史系在校內舉辦有關中國基督教史的會議及研討會期間，展覽相關的館藏資料及介紹我們的服務。藉此吸引更多海內外學者及研究人員使用文獻部的資料，捐贈書刊和一手資料給我們。

　　自2001年起，聯合國教育、科學及文化組織（UNESCO）將文獻部列為香港其中一間民間宗教檔案館。2002年，文獻部網頁改版，我們增添了《近代中國基督教史研究集刊》的論文撮要、教會成立檔案部的實用手冊、文獻部館藏資料列表及文獻部數碼化計劃的連結。另外，2005年至今，特藏組同時被列入Thomson Gale出版社的*Directory of Special Libraries and Information Centers*名冊內。相信這兩條網上訊息都有利於文獻部的宣傳工作。

‧ 善用科技，介紹館藏，推廣服務，爭取讀者，吸引捐贈

我們宣傳的工作之一是介紹文獻部藏品及工作。1980年代起，資訊科技及數碼技術發展迅速，互聯網的使用亦日益普及；這一切都有助圖書館建立高質量的文獻資訊系統、大型的數據庫系統及網絡信息系統。如果我們能利用數碼技術的方便及互聯網無遠弗屆的優勢分階段為有研究及教學價值的資料建立索引及全文數據庫，提供開放性的研究及教學資料，供公眾及研究人員在互聯網上免費使用，達致資源共享共建的目標，支持中國基督教歷史教學人員及研究學者的工作，我們相信一定可以獲取更多人認同文獻部的工作，也可以令讀者人數增加。

2003年初，文獻部搜集有關基督教在華發展的畢業論文資料，編製目錄，上載文獻部網頁內。收錄的論文為中、港、臺三地神學院及大學博、碩士生的論文。同年10月，文獻部將美國葛培理中心檔案館於1997年捐贈的225張玻璃幻燈片及玻璃負片掃描及編目，推出"China Through the Eyes of CIM Missionaries" <http://www.hkbu.edu.hk/library/electronic/libdbs/lantern.html> 數據庫，該批原屬於中國內地會（China Inland Missionary）的圖像，記錄了1900至1930年代的中國地貌、人物剪影、建築、經濟及社會狀況。在2004年6月，推出「當代中國基督教發展剪報數據庫」 <http://www.hkbu.edu.hk/library/electronic/libdbs/cccc.html>，該數據庫載有1,660篇剪報的索引。此批剪報搜羅自1950至1976年於九個國家或地區出版的中、英文報章及期刊，共約123種。主要報導中國政府的宗教政策和基督教在中國發展

的情況。全數由「友聯研究所」搜集得來。當中不乏一些值得研究的題目，包括「三自愛國運動」、教會和神學院的發展，有關天主教徒和基督教徒的審訊。同年8月，文獻部把本校教授挑選出來的本科生論文全文載入圖書館的 "HKBU Honours Project Database" 數據庫 <http://libproject.hkbu.edu.hk/was40/advancesearch?channelid=27228>。這些論文內容都是有關中國基督教發展史，此後，文獻部把更多本科生論文加入此數據庫。這些數據庫都是上載到互聯網上供公眾人士免費查閱，於2010年7月至2011年9月，「當代中國基督教發展剪報數據庫」和 "China Through the Eyes of CIM Missionaries" 分別錄得467,926及25,129次的點擊率。

總而言之，文獻部這幾年的宣傳活動，主要是將網頁改版，並將文獻部的館藏資料加以利用，建設資料庫及索引，上載互聯網供公眾人士免費閱覽及使用。除自發性舉辦館藏展覽外，我們亦懇請本校教授向校外學者及研究人員推介文獻部所藏資料及其利用價值。而筆者更不時與歷史系和宗教及哲學系的教授合作，在他們上課時介紹本部的藏品，如何利用文獻部的資料於學習及功課上。

這些宣傳項目令到認識文獻部的學者人數與日俱增，讀者人數亦有所上升，經轉介或主動捐贈的私人藏書及檔案亦有所增加，包括本校前任校長謝志偉博士、副校長陳彥民博士家屬及退休英文系Gillian Bickley教授合共捐贈超過300箱的一手檔案及書籍。臺灣王爾敏教授、香港浸信教會、香港華人基督教聯會教會歷史資料室及其他教牧捐出為數約730本的書刊及教會刊物。別具收藏價值的珍品則有長洲浸信會及前浸會大學圖書館高級副館長吳業立先生分別送贈1880年清朝的教會土地契約一份及1894年出版的《新約全書》；該《新約全書》跟當年獻給慈禧太后的《新約全書》屬同一版本。由此可見，捐獻其實是文獻部蒐集珍貴的檔案資料、善本書刊及未經出版的教會刊物的主要途徑。

（三）加速發展階段（2005 年中至今）

在這個階段，文獻部進入加速發展步伐、爭取資助、尋找合作夥伴以增強館藏的重要時期。

文獻部除了使用本部的採購經費增添書刊及縮微資料外，私人捐贈仍是蒐集基督教在華及教會史料的重要來源之一。2005至2006年，我們便收到超過1,500冊書刊，當中不乏已停刊或從未正式發行的教會資料。文獻部相信讓更多人知道本部的服務及作業，我們蒐集資料的工作會更為方便。因此，文獻部再接再厲，舉辦更多多元化的活動，希望讓更多人認識我們的工作。

2006年10月，我們藉著文獻部成立十週年的機會，與本校歷史系及香港基督教協進會執行幹事陳劍光博士合辦一連串的慶祝活動，其中包括四個展覽、一個座談會及出版《基督教在華發展史文獻部十週年紀念特刊（1996-2006）》一書，介紹文獻部過去十年的工作及發展。於2007年4月，與世界華人福音事工聯絡中心及臺灣基督教宇宙光全人關懷機構在本校合辦一個大型的公開展覽。該「自西徂東——馬禮遜牧師入華宣教二百年歷史圖片展」共展出183幅珍貴罕見的歷史圖片，紀念首位赴華基督教傳教士馬禮遜牧師入華宣教二百年。

此外，文獻部嘗試利用先進的資訊科技去介紹文獻部的藏品。在2005年9月及2008年12月，我們分別完成了「杜葉錫恩數字化資料」和「基督教古籍數據庫」。「杜葉錫恩數字化資料」數據庫<http://www.hkbu.edu.hk/ library/electronic/libdbs/elsie.html> 是一個索引及全文圖像的數據庫。杜葉錫恩博士於1947至1955年間，在中國內地及香港宣教，1956年她辭任傳教士一職，投身香港的教育及社會運動。該數據庫收集了杜葉錫恩博士，1970至1999年發表的223篇演講稿及自資出版的9本書刊。另一個名為「基督教古籍數據庫」則是2008年由文獻部及香港浸會大學校牧葉敬德博士合作建立的全文數據庫。其收錄的36冊於清末民初出版的中文古籍，主要是聖經註釋，其次為有關基督宗教的著作。文獻部將葉敬德博士的36冊古籍掃描後，再將全文電子檔案上載互聯網供公眾人士免費查閱。雖然文獻部並沒有獲取這批古籍的擁有權，但藉著數碼化及互聯網技術，將該批沒有版權的古籍納入為文獻部的藏品之內，同時方便公眾人士在網上查閱，可謂一舉數得。

對於採購海外文獻的工作，文獻部也不敢有所鬆懈。2006年，我們向英國牛津大學Bodleian Library提出合作建議，請他們把98種在十九世紀出版的基督教古籍拍成縮微膠卷供文獻部讀者使用，該批從「Bodleian Library China Protestant Missionary Tracts Collection」藏書挑選出來的古籍，全部都是西教士翻譯的中文書，部分內容是採用中國地方方言翻譯而成的，當中包括有寧波、杭州、廣東、上海、廈門、蘇州等地的方言。在蒐集一手檔案資料一事上，我們於2007年向美國耶魯大學神學院圖書館查詢複製該館收藏的「Archives of the United Board for Christian Higher Education, 1882-1974」縮微資料，該批原屬於亞洲基督教高等教育聯合董事會（United Board for Christian Higher Education in Asia）的檔案資料主要記錄了1882至1974年間在中、臺兩地基督教大學的發展歷史，當中包含書信、會議文件及大學刊物等，是研究在華基督教會辦學的重要資料。這批縮微膠卷原是非賣品，但文獻部本著為讀者提供原始檔案資料的宗旨，冒昧向該館提出請求。經該館與亞洲基督教高等教育聯合董事會商討後，我們終於成功購得該批縮微資料。

除書刊及檔案外，文獻部也蒐集博、碩士論文。在2006年，圖書館購買ProQuest學位論文全文檢索系統時，我們便挑選了250篇有關基督教在華發展史的博士及碩士論文全文供讀者使用。

四、「香港教會刊物數碼化計劃」

時至今日，許多香港教會對捐贈其檔案及出版物仍抱觀望態度，不願割愛。另一方面，教會在保存及維護這些資料時每因缺乏資源而感到吃力。有感於此，文獻部便推行另類蒐集計劃，利用資訊科技的優勢及爭取校外基金的資助，與教會共同合作，推出「香港教會刊物數碼化計劃」。

　　該計劃源起於2005年3月，當時筆者應邀到新加坡出席美國耶魯大學神學院圖書館（下稱耶魯大學）發起的 "Documentation of Christianity in Asia" 諮詢交流會。參與機構還有新加坡三一神學院（Trinity Theological College）和泰國Payap University的神學院（McGilvary Divinity School）及大學檔案館（Payap University Archives）。會上，各代表熱烈討論蒐集亞洲區基督教資料的迫切性及如何更有效推動有關工作。與會者一致認為蒐集亞洲區基督教資料的工作確實未如理想，遂計劃結成聯盟，向亞洲基督教高等教育聯合董事會申請撥款，資助一個先導計劃去完善亞洲區基督教資料蒐集的工作。各成員同意在互聯網上建立連結，方便公眾查找亞洲地區內基督教有關資料；調查及蒐集區內教會及基督教資料的所在地；在所屬地區舉辦一個諮詢會，邀請區內神學院、大專院校及相關機構商討共同蒐集有關資料的可行性；舉辦工作坊，教導如何成立教會檔案館等。雖然我們的申請最終被拒絕，聯盟成員仍決定推行該先導計劃。後於2006年組成 "Documentation of Christianity in Asia Consortium"（DCIA）「亞洲基督教文獻蒐集計劃」< http://www.library.yale.edu/div/DCIA/>。在2008年更邀請到在馬來西亞的沙巴神學院（Sabah Theological Seminary）（Kota Kinabatu）、馬來西亞神學院（Malaysia Theological Seminary）（Seremban）及衛理神學院（Methodist Theological School）（Sibu）加入。

　　之後，文獻部隨即在香港展開工作，2006年開始蒐集香港教會及大學圖書館所藏有關中國基督教及教會的檔案及書刊，將資料輸入 "DCIA Guide" 資料庫內，並於2013年完成「香港基督教文獻數據庫」<http://library.hkbu.edu.hk/electronic/libdbs/dcic.html>供公眾人士在網上查閱。

　　2008年1月，文獻部在本校舉辦諮詢會，邀請21位來自中、港、臺及澳門的22位教會領袖及學者，探討各地有關在華基督教史料的收藏狀況及挑戰，繼而討論蒐集及保存文獻的可行方案。

其後，文獻部邀請香港聖公會、基督教香港信義會、中華基督教會香港區會、香港浸信會聯會及香港基督教協進會作更深入的詳細討論。以上五間香港主流基督教會及教會機構，發展悠久，甚具代表性。筆者遂建議這些教會及教會機構將其出版的月刊和週刊借給我們數碼化，完成後，我們會將全部刊物歸還，同時亦會將刊物的圖像檔案送給他們。文獻部負責所有行政、書刊數碼化及籌募經費的工作，五間教會及教會機構則只需要集齊所有刊物交給我們處理。文獻部與五間教會及教會機構經過一輪商討後，便準備所需資料，於同年3月向「世界傳道會／那打素基金」申請撥款。雖然申請被拒，但文獻部得到五個合作夥伴的鼓勵，再接再厲，向美國耶魯大學查詢 "Kenneth Scott Latourette Initiative for the Documentation of World Christianity" 計劃的詳情後，便著手準備申請書。經過一年多時間的商討及修改申請書，文獻部在2010年3月正式向耶魯大學提交撥款申請，最終我們的申請獲得接納，同年7月，文獻部便展開此項為期八個月的「香港教會刊物數碼化計劃」（Preservation of Denominational Periodicals in Hong Kong）。

（一）計劃內容及權責

該計劃其實比我們最初向「世界傳道會／那打素基金」提交的計劃更為完善，對各方更為有利。責任分配上，文獻部全權負責所有行政、數碼化工作及所需的器材及技術；耶魯大學需要向文獻部撥款9,238美元及將刊物的數碼TIFF圖像轉化成縮微膠卷；香港聖公會、基督教香港信義會、中華基督教會香港區會、香港浸信會聯會和香港基督教協進會則負責收集其出版的整套月刊及週刊，送交文獻部處理。

在工作安排方面，文獻部請以上五間教會及教會機構將他們的月刊及週刊分批送交我們，然後我們將刊物放置於一個冷凍櫃內達72小時，使櫃內溫度快速下降，將溫度保持在攝氏零下34度，以達到除蟲及去霉菌的作用。書刊經過這清潔程序後，文獻部的職員會逐本檢查，核實年份及期數，如有缺頁或缺期，便囑咐有關教會機構增補。文獻部之後利用新購的善本書掃描機把合共4,387期教會刊物數碼化（見表4），將圖像檔案存在外置硬盤內。文獻部使用的Zeutschel OS-1200C型號的善本書掃描機是德國製造，在掃描書籍時，不會發出破壞紙張的紫外光，並且可以將檔案以多種檔案格式儲存，檔案格式包括未壓縮的TIFF、PDF、JPEG及Thumbnail等。各教會機構也需自備一個外置硬盤儲存上述圖像檔案。另一方面，文獻部必須將全部數碼圖像檔案儲存在三個外置硬盤內，分批運送到耶魯大學，讓他們將全部TIFF圖像檔案轉化為縮微膠卷。

該計劃完成後，所有五間教會及教會機構可以免費得到其刊物的數碼圖像檔案及35mm的縮微膠卷各一份；文獻部及耶魯大學可以保存全套刊物的數碼圖像及縮微膠卷，供圖書館讀者使用。耶魯大學會將縮微膠卷的母帶放在一間符合國際儲存縮微資料標準的儲存庫內作永久保存。經相關教會機構同意後，耶魯大學可將縮微膠卷複製賣給其他圖書館或檔案館。當五間教會及教會機構日後有充足的資源，他們可以將其刊物的數碼圖像上載到互聯網上供公眾人士免費查閱。在此，文獻部沒有任何複製或售賣該批刊物圖像檔案或縮微膠卷的權利。

（二）互惠互利

文獻部這個「香港教會刊物數碼化計劃」，不單蒐集、保存及維護香港教會資料，同時也讓資訊流通，成為提供珍貴研究史料的新渠道。

對這五間教會及教會機構而言，他們不但可以藉這計劃徵集其出版的月刊及週刊，日後，無論任何人要查閱該批刊物，都可以直接到文獻部或該教會及教會機構使用電腦閱讀刊物的電子全文版本，而不需要使用刊物的印刷本。此外，由於文獻部已將所有刊物除蟲去霉及清潔，五間教會及教會機構便可以將該批刊物妥善保存，避免因為人手翻閱而導致不必要的破損。如果教會及教會機構把數碼圖像全文上載互聯網，就可以使公眾人士更方便，去查閱教會資料及了解教會的

表 4：「香港教會刊物數碼化計劃」刊物細目

1. 香港基督教協進會

i.《信息》（*Message*），1976年5月～2009年12月（共295期，月刊）

ii. *News and Views*，1978年12月～2009年秋（共115期，季刊）

2. 中華基督教會香港區會

i.《會訊月刊》，1957年6月～1994年5月（共444期）

ii.《匯聲》，1994年6月～2009年12月（共184期）

3. 基督教香港信義會

i. 《信義通訊》，1951年5月～1960年3月（共82期，不定期出版）

ii.《佳音》（*Good Tidings*），1960年4月～1972年3月（共144期，月刊）

iii.《信義會刊》，1971年12月～1972年12月（共4期，不定期出版）

iv.《信義會報》，1974年1月～1975年11月（共20期，不定期出版）

v. 《信義報》，1966年1～12月，1976年2～12月，1980年8月～1984年6月，1985年6月～
2009年12月（共170期，不定期出版）

4. 香港聖公會

中文刊物：

i. 《港粵教聲》（*Kong Yuet Diocesan Echo*），1946年11月～1948年12月（共24期）

ii. 《港澳教聲》（*Diocesan Echo*），1953年3月～1982年11月（共351期，月刊）

iii.《教聲》（*Echo*），1982年11月～2009年12月（共1414期，週刊）

英文刊物：

iv. *Outpost*, 1920年～1975年10月（共173期，不定期出版）

v. *Diocesan Echo*, 1967年6月～1968年11月；1981年6月～1998年10月（共172期，1968
年12月～1981年5月期間停刊）

vi. *Echo*, 1998年11月～2009年12月（共111期）

5. 香港浸信會聯會

i. 《香港浸會月刊》，1935年1月～1938年4月（共39期，月刊）

ii. 《香港浸信會聯會月刊》，1938年5月～1940年1月；1946年6月～1975年12月（共
367期，月刊）

iii.《晨星季刊》，1940年1月～1940年12月（共4期）

iv. 《浸聯月刊》，1977年1月～1994年12月（共133期，月刊）

v. 《浸聯通訊》，1990年9月～1996年12月（共27期，月刊）

vi. 《浸聯會刊》（*Baptist Today*），1995年4月～2004年12月（共52期，月刊）

vii.《浸情》（*Baptist Link*），2005年2月～2010年8月（共34期，月刊）

事工及發展。

　　由這計劃可以看到文獻部在蒐集教會及基督教在華史料的工作時，利用善本書掃描機的高端科技，因著耶魯大學的撥款，將珍貴的教會資料數碼化；讓公眾人士可以在文獻部和耶魯大學查閱該批刊物的數碼圖像及縮微膠卷作研究之用。這樣的做法，就不會侵犯教會機構的刊物擁有權，更重要的是，該批刊物得到妥善的保存的同時，也可以讓學者及研究人員能夠有機會查閱這批珍貴史料。

五、總結及展望

　　蒐集中國教會及基督教史料的工作是艱辛的。文獻部所蒐集的這些史料，有許多都不是經出版社公開發行而獲得，而相關教會機構往往也不願將舊史料捐贈。因此，文獻部除了在市場採購外，仍需要做更多的宣傳工作，利用先進的資訊科技將館藏資料數碼化，建立資料庫，讓讀者服務完善，同時也要讓更多人認識文獻部的工作及藏品，從而吸引熱心人士捐贈。

　　另一方面，我們需要掌握機遇，找尋合作夥伴及校外撥款，善用科技將刊物數碼化，推行對各方有利的計劃。由於「香港教會刊物數碼化計劃」的蒐集史料模式得到理想成效，耶魯大學遂與浸大圖書館於2012年2月達成長期合作的協議，進一步推廣保存華人基督教文獻的數碼化計劃。耶魯大學會每年從 "Kenneth Scott Latourette Initiative for the Documentation of World Christianity" 基金撥款資助文獻部，而文獻部會主動邀請更多國內外的華人基督教教會及機構商討參與該計劃，目的是將華人基督教有關的書刊、年報、機構及個人檔案、原始及出版刊物等數碼化，以保存教徒生活及信念、教會活動及華人基督教史料。在現階段，香港一間基督教出版社及一所中國基督教文化研究中心已經同意將他們收藏的教會及基督教資料數碼化及轉成縮微膠卷。筆者相信，日後必定會有更多基督教教會及機構參與其中。在教會及機構得以保存華人基督教文獻的同時，耶魯大學及文獻部亦可以蒐集更多史料供讀者使用。總括而言，在蒐集教會及基督教在華史料上，文獻部只有一個方法，就是嘗試，繼續嘗試。

後記：2012至2013年期間，參與浸大與耶魯大學圖書館合作的「保存華人基督教文獻數碼化計劃」的教會及機構共有五間，分別為香港基督教協進會、基督教文藝出版社、漢語基督教文化研究所、聖光神學院和基督教台灣信義會。

【二・教會檔案典藏與研究】

「臺灣基督長老教會歷史資料館」館藏史料之研究*

張妙娟

高雄應用科技大學通識教育中心退休副教授

摘要

　　臺灣基督長老教會發展迄今已有一百四十七年的歷史，其存留之教會史料與文物不僅見證教會發展之軌跡，亦是研究臺灣近代社會變遷的重要佐證。目前有關臺灣基督長老教會的史料與文物之收藏以位於臺南市私立長榮中學的「臺灣教會史料館」創設最早，館藏數量亦最豐富。2008年12月臺灣基督長老教會宣教基金會與國家圖書館簽訂「臺灣基督長老教會史料圖書文物數位化計畫」，更使這批古老史料的保存邁向一大里程碑。本文首先探討「臺灣教會史料館」的設置緣起和發展，繼而說明目前館藏史料的保存與管理現況僅止於初步的整理和保管，主要因為保存空間和專業設備不足，又缺少專業管理人才，至今仍缺少一份完整詳盡的館藏清冊，館藏史料也未編碼上架。近年已有史料重刊和館藏數位化的努力，大幅提升閱讀查詢和研究的功能，但建立一座專業化的教會檔案館仍是根本之道。本文最後亦擇要介紹其重要史料的內容，期能對有志於臺灣基督長老教會歷史的研究者提供些許參考。

關鍵詞：臺灣長老教會、教會史料、教會歷史、臺灣基督長老教會歷史資料館

＊撰寫本文期間特別感謝前臺南市長榮中學蘇進安校長、校牧室鄭加泰牧師、朱忠宏牧師、張明容老師、臺灣長老教會歷史委員會委員阮宗興先生、以及國家圖書館黃文德先生接受訪談，並多方協助查證資料，謹致謝忱。

一、前言

　　基督新教傳入臺灣可上溯至十七世紀荷據時期，自1865年英國長老教會（The Presbyterian Church of England）傳教士來臺灣積極拓展醫療、教育的佈道策略之後，教會更見茁壯。本土化的臺灣基督長老教會立足於臺灣迄今已有一百四十七年的歷史，歷經清朝、日本殖民、中華民國等政權更迭，所存留的教會史料與文物跨越百餘年，不僅見證臺灣長老教會發展之軌跡，亦是研究臺灣近代社會變遷不可或缺的佐證。目前有關臺灣基督長老教會的史料與文物之收藏大致分散在臺灣長老教會歷史資料館（本文以後簡稱為「臺灣教會史料館」）、總會研發中心、臺灣神學院史料中心、真理大學、淡江中學、彰化基督教醫院、馬偕紀念醫院，以及臺南新樓基督教醫院等處。這其中又以位於臺南市私立長榮中學的「臺灣教會史料館」創設最早（雛型可上溯至1950年南部大會歷史資料室），館藏數量亦最豐富。

　　2008年12月臺灣基督長老教會宣教基金會與國家圖書館簽訂「臺灣基督長老教會史料圖書文物數位化計畫」，此一為期三年的數位典藏工作堪稱是這批古老史料保存工作的一大里程碑。數位化典藏不但有益史料之保存，更有助於未來研究者之檢索運用，關於臺灣長老教會的研究成果將日漸豐碩應是指日可待。本文擬先探討「臺灣教會史料館」的設置緣起和發展，繼而說明目前館藏史料的保存與管理現況，最後擇要介紹其重要史料的內容，期能對有志於臺灣基督長老教會歷史的研究者提供一些參考。

二、「臺灣教會史料館」的設立與發展

　　「臺灣教會史料館」的創設可溯源自1950年黃武東牧師所設立的「南部大會歷史資料室」，以後隨著黃牧師職務的調動和臺灣基督長老教會組織的重整，「南部大會歷史資料室」的文物曾經搬遷到臺北總會保存（1957-1975），1976年又遷回臺南神學院，1987年再遷至臺南私立長榮中學，以下就館藏品存放地點之遷移分為四階段加以說明。

（一）南部大會歷史資料室（1950-1956）

1950年黃武東牧師就任臺灣基督長老教會南部大會的第一任總幹事，5月收回戰亂時期被佔住的新樓醫院房舍，作為南部大會事務所辦公場地[1]，當時所發現的英國傳教士文物包括馬雅各醫師（Dr. James Laidlaw Maxwell, 1836-1921）的書桌、臺灣第一部教學用的幻燈機、各教會信徒的受洗記錄（共64冊）以及南部中會、大會的議事錄等。黃武東遂在其事務所設立了「南部大會歷史資料室」，收藏這批文物以及他早期所收集的聖餐餐具、梅監務牧師（Rev. Campbell N. Moody）街頭佈道用的喇叭及其他文件[2]。這是第一批的史料館藏品。

（二）臺北總會歷史資料室（1957-1975）

1951年3月臺灣基督長老教會總會正式成立，黃武東被推舉為首任議長，設總會事務所於每屆議長辦公處[3]，但直到1957年2月第四屆總會召開，通過設置總會事務所於臺北市[4]，並選舉黃牧師為第一任總幹事。依照「總會強化案」的規定，撤銷南部大會，並將所有之事業機關和財物移交給總會，原屬於「南部大會歷史資料室」的相關文物因而搬遷到臺北總會事務所（當時總會事務所是租用加拿大母會位於臺北市中山北路二段的傳教師宿舍）[5]。1965年為慶祝長老教會宣教一百週年紀念大典的相關活動中，總會亦設立「歷史資料展覽

1 黃武東，《黃武東回憶錄》（臺北：前衛出版社，1988），頁198。
2 賴永祥，〈獻辭：歷史資料館的育成──敬悼黃武東牧師〉，《教會史話》第三輯（臺南：人光出版社，1995），頁241。
3 黃武東，《黃武東回憶錄》，頁204。
4 同前註，頁251。
5 同前註，頁253。

組」，由徐謙信牧師擔任組長，籌備「紀念歷史文物展覽會」，於同年6月16~22日假臺南神學院的巴克禮紀念館展出，分為一般文物、醫療傳道、神學教育、普通教育、教會教育、山地傳道、文字傳道、視聽傳道、以及迫害史等單元[6]，可說是第一次正式向社會大眾公開展示這批珍貴史料和文物。1966年當黃武東牧師卸任總幹事後，這批文物也隨著遷移保存在臺北長春路的總會事務所內。

（三）臺南神學院「臺灣教會史料館」（1976-1987）

1976年高俊明牧師接任總會的總幹事，總會成立「臺灣教會歷史資料館管理小組」，文物從臺北總會事務所再遷往臺南神學院，並於校內最古老的建築物巴克禮樓正式設立「臺灣基督長老教會歷史資料館」，由林信堅牧師擔任館長。同年4月20日為慶祝臺南神學院創校一百週年，再度舉辦一次文物展覽。

此後林信堅牧師在《臺灣教會公報》上撰文呼籲和徵集長老教會相關的史料文物，陸續獲得各界慷慨的捐贈，包括木刻對聯、匾額、木版、銅版、《臺灣府城教會報》、舊聖詩、舊音樂課本、服飾、珍貴書刊、相片等，1980年也得到偕叡理牧師（Rev. George Leslie Mackay）孫女贈送的偕牧師遺物，收藏更豐富。[7]可惜的是，從臺北搬遷到臺南的過程中不但有些文物遺失，連文物移交清冊也闕如。

（四）臺南長榮中學（1987迄今）

1987年得臺南長榮中學蘇進安校長之助，文物移至長榮中學校史館。1988年第三十五屆臺灣基督長老教會總會通過設立「教會歷史委員會」[8]，並決議邀黃武東牧師自美國回臺灣協助整理。經過長榮中

---

6 臺灣基督長老教會總會歷史委員會編，《臺灣基督長老教會百年史》（臺北：臺灣基督長老教會，1965），頁361-362。

7 賴永祥，〈獻辭：歷史資料館的育成——敬悼黃武東牧師〉，《教會史話》第三輯，頁242。

8 總會歷史委員會是為推行教會歷史文獻資料之整理、編輯與發行等相關事工而設置的，委員九人均為義務職，目前暫設於臺南長榮中學的「臺灣基督長老教會歷史資料館」是由該委員會負責。參見賴永祥，〈聚珍堂史料發刊總序〉，未編頁碼。

時間	大事記要
1950	黃武東牧師就任臺灣長老教會南部大會首任總幹事，在新樓醫院設立「南部大會歷史資料室」。
1951	黃武東牧師就任首屆總會議長，同年10月至1953年間赴英國進修，並蒐集臺灣教會史料，所得甚豐：如母會機關報 *The Presbyterian Messenger*、馬雅各醫生的親筆函、蕃仔契、保護鳳山禮拜堂的日本政府告示、新樓地契、臺南神學院地契、甘為霖牧師的著作共 5 冊。
1957	黃武東牧師就任總會總幹事，南部大會歷史資料室文物遷往臺北市中山北路總會事務所。
1965	為慶祝長老教會設立一百週年，在臺南神學院、臺北雙連教會舉辦「紀念歷史文物展覽會」。
1966	黃武東牧師辭卸總幹事，文物隨總會事務所的遷移存放於臺北市長春路。
1976	文物再遷往臺南神學院，於巴克禮樓設立「臺灣基督長老教會歷史資料館」，林信堅牧師任館長。
1987	得長榮中學蘇進安校長協助，文物移至長榮中學史館保存。
1990	長榮中學第二實習大樓落成，五樓成為校史館及「臺灣教會史料館」現址。

資料來源：賴永祥，《教會史話》第三輯，頁 241-243。

　　　　黃武東，《黃武東回憶錄》，頁 196-199、225-254。

學校史館阮綠茵老師的協助清查，得知收藏品「約有1,500件，包括書籍171冊、議事錄約300冊，手稿6件，文件一堆，銅鉛版66塊，木刻55件，圖10張，印章102顆，照片多數，玻璃版幻燈片61張，匾額16件，器物46件，傢俱5件，建材8件，衣服14件，塑像1件，雕像1件，土像6件，樂器及附屬品4件，木船1艘，雜誌有 *The Messenger*、《臺灣教會公報》、《瀛光》……等；已登錄入檔者共155件（打字印出藏品簡目1頁，登錄清單7頁）。」[9] 1990年9月21日長榮中學校慶，第二實習大樓落成，校史館開幕，同時展出教會史料，五樓成為長榮中學校史館及「臺灣教會史料館」現址[10]。

三、館藏史料的保存與管理現況

有關「臺灣教會史料館」珍藏的史料與文物之保存概況，筆者擬以其典藏是否提供利用分為收藏期和開放期兩階段來說明。第一階段收藏期是指1950~1976文物收藏在南部大會和總會事務所期間，只有在1965年的宣教百週年紀念活動中展出一週（參見頁81-82），其餘時間不曾對外開放利用。第二階段的開放期是指1976年迄今，設有專責單位管理，也對外開放借閱和展覽。

（一）收藏期（1950-1976）

此一時期這批館藏品先後存放在臺南新樓醫院和臺北的總會事務所（中山北路與長春路），前長榮中學蘇進安校長回憶他擔任長老教會總會歷史委員會委員時，曾經在臺北長春路事務所看過這批史料文物裝箱堆置在二樓和三樓之間的夾層空間，如同「放在倉庫一般」[11]。

1976年文物由總會事務所南遷到臺南神學院，當時雖有專屬空間，但總會與神學院均未編列史料館的人事、維護費之預算。在長期經費不足之下，加上巴克禮樓建築日久老舊失修，遭逢漏雨浸溼，文物資料多有毀損。在林信堅牧師出國期間，曾有幾次竊賊闖入而遺失文物，如偕叡理牧師娘的衣服、蕃仔契、聖餐具等珍藏品均下落不明[12]。由此也顯示巴克禮樓年久失修，並非妥善的館藏處所。因此，這段期間這批史料的保存狀況其實只是整批資料集中存放，沒有特別

---

9 賴永祥，〈黃武東晚年的心願〉，《教會史話》第四輯，頁19。
10 賴永祥，〈獻辭：歷史資料館的育成──敬悼黃武東牧師〉，《教會史話》第三輯，頁243。
11 蘇進安校長口述，張妙娟電話訪談，2011年10月26日於鳳山。
12 賴永祥，〈黃武東晚年的心願〉，《教會史話》第四輯，頁20。

受到重視並加以整理或對外開放運用。

　　1987年，長榮中學蘇進安校長擔任總會歷史委員會委員之後，前往臺南神學院視察史料保存狀況時，卻發現當時的巴克禮樓（今已拆除，僅留建築基座）屋頂漏水，一部分史料已受潮毀損，而且門鎖也遭破壞，史料多有遭竊遺失，因此他自告奮勇提供長榮中學的校史館作為史料存放地點[13]。經過總會同意之後，在一次颱風來臨前夕，由「長榮中學百年史編輯室」的同仁（張牧、阮綠茵、葉瑞鈺）和兩位工友趕緊搶救搬遷。所有的文物運到長榮中學校史館（舊址），並利用館內的一半空間先展出部分史料。浸溼的典籍和不堪展出的文物，經曝曬、除塵另存放在特別教室內。後來，黃武東牧師由美國回來多次到學校指導，直到1990年再搬遷至新建實習大樓的五樓[14]。

　　在此二十六年的收藏期間，這批史料可說是專屬於長老教會內部的檔案，只有1965年為推動臺灣基督長老教會宣教百週年紀念大典而編輯出版《臺灣基督長老教會百年史》、辦理「紀念歷史文物展覽會」時對外開放，長老教會內部有關的撰寫者和籌劃人員應該是少數曾經查詢和運用過這批史料的人員了。

（二）開放期（1976年迄今）

　　1976年4月20日「臺灣教會史料館」於臺南神學院的巴克禮樓正式開館，為了讓各界了解教會歷史發展之腳蹤，林信堅牧師自同年2月15日起連續在《臺灣教會公報》撰文介紹這批重要的蒐集品，連載的主題名為〈臺灣教會史料館蒐集品簡介〉，直到1978年2月5日總計撰寫了36篇[15]。這些介紹文章可說是這批館藏資訊首度對外公開，雖然不是實物的公開展覽，但透過文字詳細說明和附加圖示仍可看出這

---

13 蘇進安校長口述，張妙娟電話訪談，2011年10月26日於鳳山。

14 蘇進安校長口述，張妙娟電話訪談，2011年10月26日於鳳山。張明容口述，張妙娟訪問，2011年10月21日於臺南。阮宗興口述，張妙娟訪問，2011年10月24日於臺南。

15 林信堅，〈臺灣教會史料館蒐集品之一——馬雅各醫生致巴克禮博士親筆信函〉，《臺灣教會公報》，第1250期，民國65年2月15日，第四版。

批館藏品生動地記錄教會發展的軌跡及其珍貴性。

由於這些館藏品的介紹資訊，加上1987年史料搬遷到長榮中學之後經過整理公開陳列展示，吸引不少外界人士的注意，尤其1990年新的展示空間布置完成後，經常有中外學者前往查閱史料文獻，有關臺灣基督長老教會的歷史研究成果日益增多，更有許多教會人士或學校團體前往參觀。「臺灣教會史料館」搬遷到長榮中學之後，可說是這批館藏史料蒐集保存狀況和運用情況最好的時期。

目前的保存空間分為展覽室和閱讀室兩大部分，館藏內容豐富而珍貴。展覽室內有訂製精美的玻璃櫥櫃，陳列了許多教會歷史文物（如臺灣最古老的印刷機、幻燈機和玻璃幻燈片、臺灣和澎湖地圖木刻原版、臺灣教會公報插圖用的銅版畫原刻版、巴克禮牧師的睡袍等），還有重要文獻和書籍原件（如《臺灣府城教會報》、馬雅各醫生的親筆信、梅監務牧師的手稿筆記和傳記等）。閱讀室的空間面積比較小，擺設開架式的書櫃存放史料書籍，可惜有些珍貴的文獻如《使信月刊》（The Messenger）只有簡單的以公文袋裝存。就一所保存發展歷史逾百年的教會史料館而言，目前的史料保存狀況實有許多待改善之處。

首先是保存空間和專業設備不足：由於閱讀室的空間面積較小，目前放置在閱讀室的史料仍有許多是分袋擺放或裝在紙箱裡未上架陳列，閱讀者每次使用皆需逐袋檢索再取出閱覽，不但耗時不便，也使這批古老的史料在多次翻閱後增加破損的風險，對文物的保存是一大危機。此外，展覽室和閱讀室只有兩座防潮櫃，其他史料和文物並非在恆溫、防潮、防酸、防塵的環境中被保存，當有外賓申請參觀或閱覽時才開放冷氣，以南臺灣如此長期高溫炎熱的氣候其實是相當不利文物之保存。

第二是缺少專業管理人才：檔案管理是一門專業，自1976年史料搬遷至臺南神學院，由林信堅牧師擔任史料館館長起這批史料才算是有專人管理，在長榮中學保存時是由蘇進安校長指派秘書室張明容老師兼管，負責接待外界參觀與借閱，但兩者皆非專業或專職的檔案管理人員，因此在檔案的保存或管理上無法有專業性的改進實在是無可厚非。或許由於「臺灣教會史料館」隸屬於總會的歷史委員會，長榮中學只是保存展示的單位，權責單位的歷史委員會若能向總會爭取在經費預算上多加挹注、並在史料館的管理規劃上多加指導，相信會更有成效。

第三是「臺灣教會史料館」至今仍缺少一份完整詳盡的館藏清冊：筆者目前搜尋到的館藏清冊（文獻部分）共有四份[16]，分別是（1）1976年5月27日由黃武東牧師移交給臺南神學院的「臺灣基督長老教會總會財產清冊」、（2）1993年吳文雄牧師編製的「臺灣教會史料館藏書目錄」、（3）2002年張妙娟編製的「臺灣教會史料館館藏目錄」、（4）2003年日本京都大學駒込武教授的「長榮中學校史館所藏資料仮目錄──教會關係資料之部（簡略版）」。筆者試將此四份目錄內容整理比較如表2。

檢視上述目錄可以發現，四份目錄不僅登記的史料數量不一，分類類目和註記的資料也有不同。除黃武東的清冊沒有分類之外，吳文雄、張妙娟、駒込武三位的分類類目不同，吳文雄編製的目錄總數量689筆最多，駒込武的目錄只編入與教會歷史有關的資料，所以數量只有265筆，此外張妙娟和駒込武的目錄也註明較多的出版資料和史料狀況。筆者推測，會出現不同的目錄原因可能是編製者未發現或無法取得過去已有的目錄，另外則是對以前編製的目錄感到不夠完整，所以自己重編。不論如何，為裨益日後的使用者方便檢索，實有必要重新清點館藏品（包括展示的文物），並將此四份目錄重新彙整和校訂成為一份比較詳細完整的書目。

第四是館藏史料未編碼上架：目前館藏史料已有初步分類擺放在

---

16 阮綠茵採訪整理，〈訪黃武東牧師暢談教會史料館重要史料蒐集由來〉，《母校長中》，第79期，1990年3月，頁52。若是根據上文，1965年百年紀念展覽後將資料按照號碼做成清冊收藏於總會事務所資料室，但是屬於北部教會的一部分資料則由徐謙信牧師退還提供者。1987年，蘇校長重擔任歷史委員會委員，撥出校史館一半空間和舊工藝教室收藏展示，整理出一份清冊送交總會，並影印一份留長中。1990年黃武東牧師又曾經整理一份，但目前筆者未找到這些目錄，僅能以手邊所有的四份目錄做分析。

表2：「臺灣教會史料館」館藏史料清冊比較表

時間	編者	分類	總數量（單位：筆）	史料描述	出版資料
1976	黃武東	無	245	無	無
1993	吳文雄	1. 議事錄（總會、大會、中會、地方教會） 2. 南部教會姓名簿 3. 設教週年紀念刊 4. 宣教師記錄 5. 臺南神學院 6. 總會出版物 7. 臺灣教會公報 8. 期刊雜誌 9. 國內出版物 10. 國外出版物 11. 教師考試論文 12. 雜項待整理資料	689	無	有註明出版年份
2002	張妙娟	1. 聖詩 2. 文件檔案 3. 白話字書籍（教理書、議事錄） 4. 英文書籍 5. 日文書籍 6. 中文書籍 7. 報紙 8. 雜誌 9. 長榮中學校史資料	613	有註明刊行語文、手稿、原件、影印本、破損情況等資料	有註明作者、編者、出版時間、出版社、總頁數

| 2003 | 駒込武 | 1. 聖經
2. 聖詩
3. 白話字教理書
4. 漢文教理書
5. 教會史
6. 會議記錄（1945以前）
7. 會議記錄（1945以後）
8. 教會名冊（成人、小兒）
9. 教會公報
10. 瀛光
11. 英文資料（1945以前）
12. 英文資料（1945以後）
13. 教會紀念週年誌
14. 文件 | 265 | 有註明史料存放的書架位置 | 有註明作者、編者、出版時間、出版社 |

書架上，陳列於展示櫃的也都有簡略文字說明卡，但卻沒有固定的編碼和陳列位置，因而若是使用者閱覽之後未照原有位置歸還，後來的使用者就很難再找到。以筆者為例，即使曾經逐一清查過這批史料，編過目錄，如今重回史料館也無法確切找到所需要的史料文獻，耗時費力，無庸置言。由此可見史料沒有分類、編碼、定位，不論對於管理人員或使用者都會造成莫大困擾，妨礙史料之運用，而使用者不斷的翻閱這些古文獻，更加速史料之破損，實是更大的危機。

綜上所述，「臺灣教會史料館」在館藏品的保存和管理上都亟待突破，事實上，多年來長老教會歷史委員會也不斷努力在尋找建立一棟專業檔案館來妥善保存史料的可能性，可惜至今尚未能定案[17]。

除此之外，歷史委員會成員之一的阮宗興先生則致力於重刊珍貴

---

17 阮宗興口述，張妙娟電話訪問，2011年11月10日於鳳山。

史料，一則推廣介紹讓更多人認識長老教會歷史珍貴的信仰遺產，二則讓使用者更便於閱讀，也保護史料不致受損。近年來歷史委員會與臺灣教會公報社合作重刊出版的史料共有三套：第一套是2003到2007年陸續刊印的《聚珍堂史料叢書》10冊，第二套是2004年出版的《臺灣教會公報全覽：臺灣第一份報紙》77冊，第三套是2006年出版的《使信月刊全覽》（*The Messenger*, 1850-1947）75冊，並有數位圖檔DVD光碟發行。這些重刊的史料都是有關長老教會歷史研究最基礎的素材[18]，如今能重刊流傳，對於史料的保存和運用均有極大貢獻。

　　檔案的數位化是現今檔案保存的趨勢，2008年底，為妥善保存和應用這些典藏文獻，國家圖書館與臺灣基督長老教會宣教基金會簽訂「文獻資料數位化合作計畫協議書」，著手進行史料數位化工作，以提供學術研究和民眾利用。這項為期三年的計畫是「臺灣教會史料館」保存工作的一大里程碑，分為書冊、文件、手稿、書信、照片、以及文物六大類，同時進行文獻圖書和歷史文物的數位化，不過並非全面清查，只有擇要挑選一部分典藏品做處理。目前第一階段的數位計畫暫告一段落，國家圖書館網站中的「臺灣記憶系統」網頁上已建置有「臺灣基督長老教會文獻（測試版）」連結，提供503筆書籍資料的檢索[19]。初期開放的這批史料都已有全文內容數位化處理，主要包括羅馬字（白話字）版教理書、教科書、大會、中會議事錄等，但美中不足的是缺少有關文獻圖書的介紹和說明文字，又因檢索系統仍在測試階段，現在只能看到書目，一般閱覽者並沒有權限使用內容查詢。

四、重要館藏史料的介紹與運用

　　臺灣基督長老教會不論是就時間縱軸來看（設立迄今長達一百

---

18 有關這些重刊史料之內容將於本文第四節介紹。

19 參考國家圖書館網站：http://memory.ncl.edu.tw/。

四十七年），或就空間地理的擴展來看（從沿海平地、離島到高山原住民）、或教會組織的發展（從教會、醫院、學校、到社會服務機構等）都擁有許多面向的研究路徑和課題，「臺灣教會史料館」收藏的是自1865年設教以來的圖書史料與文物，其種類、數量繁多，可提供教會歷史研究的素材真是不勝枚舉。由於史料繁雜，筆者不可能逐一閱覽所有史料，加上教會史料的分類至今學術界仍未有定論[20]，以下僅能就館藏文獻的特色分別介紹幾項重要的基礎史料。

（一）雜誌報刊

1. 《使信月刊》（*The Messenger and Missionary Record of the Presbyterian Church of England*）

這是英國長老教會總會在倫敦發行的月刊型雜誌，其中的〈海外傳教〉（Foreign Missions）專欄刊載其轄屬之海外傳教事業動態，早期來臺灣的傳教士寫給總會的報告和書信大多收錄於此，可說是研究臺灣長老教會歷史最原始的史料。這本月刊的名稱曾多次變更，1845~1867年稱為 *The English Presbyterian Church*，1868~1878稱為 *Messenger and Missionary Record of the Presbyterian Church in England*，1881~1884年改為 *Outlook*，1884~1885年及1891~1906年稱為 *Presbyterian*，1885~1891年稱 *Presbyterian Messenger*，1906~1907年稱 *Monthly Messenger of the Presbyterian Church in England*，而自1908年以後就改名為 *The Presbyterian Messenger*。[21]

「臺灣教會史料館」所收藏的是黃武東牧師從英國攜回的原件，自1864年1月號到1947年12月號，其中1882年、1885年、1886年的全

---

20 參見王成勉，〈臺灣基督教史料之研究〉，《臺灣基督教史研討會論文集》（臺北：宇宙光出版社，1998），頁259-265。Archie R. Crouch 在其 *Christianity in China：A Scholar's Guide to Resources in the Libraries and Archives of the United States* 一書中將教會史料分為十三類，王成勉在其「臺灣地區基督教史料調查研究計畫」中則區分為會議記錄／教會報告，個人手札、來往信件、照片等，專論小冊子／紀念集／建堂紀念集，教會機構期刊／教會週報，博碩士論文／學術性研究報告，稀有書籍等六類。本文介紹的臺灣教會史料館的館藏品皆屬較早期的文獻，因而沒有採用上述的史料分類法。

21 賴永祥，〈英國長老教會的宣道〉，《教會史話》第一輯，頁248。

缺，總共計71個年份[22]。2006年臺灣教會公報社翻印重刊的《使信月刊全覽》則將1850~1863年、1882年及1885~1886年的內容都補齊了，資料更為完整詳盡。

這套雜誌記錄了英國長老教會近百年來在臺灣、中國、印度半島、歐洲地中海等地區的宣教史料，包括傳教士報告、各項宣教會議記錄、讀者來函、信仰見證、捐獻財務、甚至是兒童與青少年教育的教材、故事、插圖與照片。這套豐富完整而珍貴的史料，不僅是研究英國長老教會海外傳教事業的基礎史料，也是研究臺灣長老教會和母會互動關係、早期英國傳教士對臺灣社會的民情風俗觀點與傳教策略的最好材料。

2. 《臺灣教會公報》

這是臺灣歷史上第一份定期出刊、且迄今發行最久的報紙，亦為臺灣長老教會的機關報。1885年由英國長老教會傳教士巴克禮牧師在臺南創辦，稱為《臺灣府城教會報》（1885.7~1891.12），目的在鼓吹信徒學習白話字、傳遞教會消息，並提供聖經義理之解讀與靈修文章，以勉勵信徒更深刻認識基督教義，實踐信仰生活[23]。最初為幫助多數不識漢字的信徒閱讀而採用廈門音羅馬字刊印，日後隨著臺灣政權更迭而在日治時期加入日文版，中華民國時期加入中文版副刊以配合推行國語運動，1969年3月由於國民黨政府的禁令而停用羅馬字，12月以後全部使用中文刊印，羅馬字版的教會報從此走入歷史。

自晚清創辦以來迄今一百二十七年，共經歷四次更名，為因應清末和日治時期地方行政組織的調整，1893年改稱《臺南府城教會報》、1906年改名《臺南教會報》，1913年5月第二次「臺灣大會」決議南北長老教會合稱「臺灣基督長老教會」後遂改稱《臺灣教會報》，1932年3月又合併南北中會的《教會新報》、《福音報》和

---

22 賴永祥，〈資料館藏使信月刊〉，《教會史話》第四輯，頁12。「臺灣教會史料館」收藏有1864-1947年份《使信月刊》，臺灣神學院史料中心則保存有1850-1944年份的《使信月刊》。
23 巴克禮，〈巴牧師的信〉，《臺灣教會報》，第500卷，1926年7月，頁1。

《芥菜子報》改稱為《臺灣教會公報》[24]。該報雖經幾次更改報紙名稱，惟創刊宗旨未曾稍改，始終堅持宗教教育的理想性。在報紙內容方面可謂包羅萬象，包括各地教會消息、聖經教義闡釋、長老教會所屬之教育、醫療事業動態、國內外社會時事以及生活新知等[25]，為晚清以來的基督徒提供一項新的教育途徑。

2004年臺灣教會公報社重印《臺灣教會公報全覽：臺灣第一份報紙（1885-2002）》，共有77冊，每冊約600頁，這套鉅著內容記錄了一百一十七年間三次政權輪替下的臺灣社會與長老教會內部的變遷，實在是難能可貴的民間觀點史料。總之，《臺灣府城教會報》開創了羅馬字報紙之先聲，保存自清季以來廈門音閩南方言之原貌，為研究臺灣社會的語言和文化保存了珍貴素材。該報記錄了許多近代臺灣社會變遷的歷史文獻，而且是一份迥異於官方的庶民記錄，堪稱是臺灣基督長老教會最具代表性的本土文化資產，也是一部橫跨臺灣百年歷史的百科全書[26]，值得臺灣教會歷史和臺灣史的研究者深入挖寶。

（二）會議記錄

1. 《臺南教士會議事錄》（*The Handbook of the England Presbyterian Mission in South Formosa*）

1877年英國長老教會傳教士成立「臺南教士會」（Tainan Mission Council）作為在臺灣傳教事業決策之最高會議，該年1月10日起召開第一次會議，每週三聚集一次，直到1910年1月第788次會議為止[27]，每次討論事項決議皆有詳實記錄，是英國長老教會在南臺灣傳教極為

---

24 有關《臺灣府城教會報》的發展沿革，如刊印文字之變化、名稱之更迭詳見張妙娟，《開啟心眼——《臺灣府城教會報》與長老教會的基督徒教育》第三章（臺南：人光出版社，2005），頁91-104。

25 有關《臺灣府城教會報》的內容見張妙娟，《開啟心眼——《臺灣府城教會報》與長老教會的基督徒教育》第三章，頁105-141。

26 阮宗興，〈導讀：介紹一部橫跨臺灣百年歷史的百科全書——《臺灣教會公報》全覽（1885-2002）〉，《臺灣教會公報》全覽（1885-2002）》，Vol. 1，1885-1890，頁9-12。

27 William Campbell, *Handbook of the English Presbyterian Mission in South Formosa* (Hastings: F.J. Parsons, LTD.1910), p. xi.

重要的史料之一。本書由甘為霖牧師（Rev. William Campbell）負責編撰，並撰寫一篇導論，概述在臺傳教事業之成果，包括「議事錄要點（Council Minutes，有307頁）……其前有序（Preface）、目次、緒言（Introduction，有32頁），而後有極詳細的「索引」（Index，有97頁）。編者曾努力將議事錄所出現的每一個人，每一個地方，每一個題目，用字母順（Alphabetically），兼用年代順（Chronologically）表列，加上有相關互見（Cross-references），誠周到。」[28] 其記錄之詳實由此可見。1910年本書出版時，甘為霖並在扉頁聲明：「這本有版權的書為非賣品，僅印行一百本，供私人傳閱。」[29] 查閱此書，「幾乎從1877至1910年間，所有與教會相關的人、事、地都有記錄可查，光是所涉及的中外人名，就高達551個之多。」[30]

目前「臺灣教會史料館」所藏雖為影印本，仍彌足珍貴。2004年臺灣教會公報社重印的《臺南教士會議事錄》，還有臺灣長老教會歷史委員會的委員阮宗興先生加以校注，索引部分則另外印製單行本，讓使用者得以免除前後翻閱對照之困擾，並方便日後增補重印[31]。此外，由於《臺南教士會議事錄》是以英文撰寫，許多本地信徒之姓名、臺灣地名、以及教會名稱皆為羅馬拼音，現在讀者往往難以辨識，阮宗興先生特別在重刊本的書後附錄一張自己查證整理的「漢羅姓氏對照表」，幫助讀者對教會人士姓名有更清楚的辨證，如此周詳的校注不僅嘉惠讀者，亦增加了這本史料的參考價值。

2. 《南部大會議事錄（一）》（1896-1913）、《南部大會議事錄（二）》（1914-1927）

南部大會是指1896年2月24日由臺南各教會的傳道師、代議長老和英國宣教士一起參與討論教會事務的會議，當時稱為「臺南長老大

---

28 賴永祥，〈臺南教士會議事錄〉，《教會史話》第四輯，頁230。
29 甘為霖著，《臺南教士會議事錄》，聚珍堂史料6，阮宗興校注（臺南：臺灣教會公報社重印，2004），頁32。
30 阮宗興，〈導讀：介紹一本特殊的教會史料——兼談校注甘為霖的《臺南教士會議事錄》的一些問題〉，《臺南教士會議事錄》，頁16。
31 同前註，頁27。

會」，1912年南北聯合成立「臺灣大會」之後改稱「臺南中會」[32]。這是臺灣本地信徒和英國傳教士一起分擔教會事務決策的開始，對臺灣教會邁向自治的意義重大。在每次會議當中所討論的皆是攸關臺灣教會發展的重大議題，例如制定各種教會規章、按立本地牧師、傳道師薪水的籌措、分設堂會等，另外還有例行業務報告（如澎湖宣道會、佈教慈善會等）、教會治理和信徒問題的討論等。南部大會的會議記錄可說是教會制度變革與地方教會發展的第一手記錄[33]。

　　現在館藏的《南部大會議事錄》的原件是毛筆正楷書寫，極為工整，沒有頁碼，除了議程、決議事項的記錄之外，其附錄文件也極具參考價值，如教會人物小傳（包括許廷芳長老、潘明珠牧師、宋以利沙伯牧師娘、甘為霖牧師、宋忠堅牧師等小傳）、章程規條（臺南小學六年章程、勸懲婚姻規條、聘牧師書式等）。2003年重印的《南部大會議事錄》共兩冊，皆為未曾刊印過的漢文手稿本，也是臺灣歷史上首見的議事錄。編輯者加上了目錄和頁碼，尤其在目錄上附註本地牧師封牧、人物小傳和附件名稱是一大進步，更方便讀者檢索查閱。不過需要注意的是，議事錄通常只摘要記錄提案和決議，有關討論過程中的細節尚須同時比對、參閱《臺灣教會公報》、《臺南教士會議事錄》或其他史料方足夠完整[34]。

3. 各項會議議事錄

　　臺灣長老教會是採用長老制做為治理教會的體制，設有小會、中會、大會和總會四層級，每一層級各有職掌權責[35]，定期開會的議事錄都是了解臺灣長老教會發展歷史的重要史料。「臺灣教會史料館」除了珍藏上述《臺南教士會議事錄》、《南部大會議事錄》之外，還蒐集各層級會議的議事錄，雖然不盡完整，仍相當具有參考價值。

---

32 臺灣基督長老教會歷史委員會編，《臺灣基督長老教會百年史》，頁105。

33 黃德銘，〈導讀〉，《南部大會議事錄（一）1896-1913》（臺南：臺灣教會公報社，2003），未編頁碼。

34 同前註。

35 臺灣基督長老教會總會編輯小組，《認識臺灣基督長老教會》（臺南：人光出版社，1986），頁68-73。

1993年吳文雄牧師整理的館藏目錄所羅列的各層級會議議事錄細分為大會議事錄、南部大會議事錄、北部大會議事錄、臺南中會議事錄、臺北中會議事錄、東部中會議事錄、七星中會議事錄、臺北中會議事錄、新竹中會議事錄、臺中中會議事錄、嘉義中會議事錄、臺北中會議事錄、高雄中會議事錄、壽山中會議事錄、屏東中會議事錄、太魯閣中會議事錄、排灣中會議事錄，以及地方教會議事錄等共18項，達250筆。其中還包括一些教會機構重組時財物的移交清冊，如長榮女中、長榮中學、彰化基督教醫院、南部女宣道局、南部傳道局、山地宣道會、澎湖宣道會等。這些文件檔案都是研究臺灣長老教會制度沿革和各地教會發展時非常值得重視的記錄。

（三）羅馬字教理書

　　自1865年起英國長老教會的傳教士即以廈門音的羅馬字（又稱白話字）作為向臺灣住民傳教的媒介，1885年又進而創辦以羅馬字刊行的《臺灣府城教會報》作為教導信仰、傳遞教會消息，以及基督徒吸收新知的文字媒介。晚清以來長老教會的基督徒在日常生活中無處不應用白話字，舉凡聖經、報紙到教會學校上課的教材皆以白話字刊行，能夠流利讀、寫白話字成為可以受洗、被教會接納、進入教會學校就讀的要件之一，更是本地傳道人考試必有的測驗。清代傳統教育只有少數富家子弟能入學、且以科舉考試為目標，清季臺灣長老教會的白話字教育則是屬於全民教育，不分男女老幼，沒有年齡限制，甚至連一向被社會放棄的盲人也在甘為霖牧師的努力下於1890年在臺南創設「訓瞽堂」，並同樣使用白話字學會點字系統[36]，百餘年來白話字的使用遂成為臺灣長老教會發展歷史中的重要特徵。

　　羅馬字的書籍文獻也是「臺灣教會史料館」館藏的一大特色，根據2003年張妙娟整理的館藏目錄，白話字的教理書就有162筆，除了前面提到的各層級會議議事錄，還包括：

36　William Campbell, *An Account of Missionary Success in the Island of Formosa, Vol.II,* pp. 651-667.

（1）兒童主日學教材：如《幼葉》、《普世主日學學課兒童課本》、《簡易白話字教本》、《主日學教材》等。這些教材有助於了解長老教會內部兒童信仰教育的內涵，有些教科書甚至是世界各國的主日學教育的教材。

（2）信徒靈修書籍：如《耶穌的生活和教示》、《天路歷程的大意》、《闢邪歸正》、《理家要略》、《天路指明》、《真道問答》、《每日靈糧》、《三字經新撰白話字註解》等。大體而言，這些靈修書籍都是由當時歐美傳教士在中國佈道與教育信徒時所用的書籍翻譯成羅馬字刊行，對於基督教教育與中國文化的衝擊是很好的分析材料。

（3）教育理論：如《主日學中心的問題》、《基督教教育實際指導》、《基督教教育》、《適應兒童心理學—日曜學教授法》等。這些著作大都是為了培育教會主日學的師資、或促進本地信徒對信仰教育的反思而寫成，也是研究長老教會基督徒教育必備的參考資料。

（4）教會歷史：如《北部臺灣基督長老教會的歷史》、《北部臺灣基督長老教會簡史》、《教會成人名冊》、《教會小兒名冊》等。其中特別值得一提的是《教會成人名冊》32冊和《教會小兒名冊》35冊，這批原件保留了臺灣各地教會（遠至琉球、臺東觀音山、馬公、大嶼、瓦硐）的信徒動態資料，名冊內記錄了在教會受洗信徒的姓名、性別、年齡、父母姓名、受洗日期、施洗牧師姓名等資料，無論是對個人家族、家譜或地方教會歷史的研究都是很重要的線索。

（四）傳教士的著作

傳教士是臺灣傳教事業的前鋒，他們在母國所受的訓練和長期對宣教地區文化的觀察是決定宣教策略的依據，由於需要定期向母會報告，他們存留的書信或記錄都是研究臺灣教會發展的第一手資訊。「臺灣教會史料館」收藏不少英國長老教會傳教士的著作，以下試舉數例介紹：

1. 甘為霖牧師（1841-1921）

他在臺灣服務的時間長達四十五年二個月（1871-1917），除了傳教工作之外，著述甚勤，留下許多有關臺灣研究的重要歷史作品。《法波蘭語信仰個條書》（*The Articles of Christian instruction in Favorlang-formosan*, 1896）、《荷蘭統治下的臺灣》（*Formosa under the Dutch*, 1903）是他蒐集、選譯荷蘭統治臺灣時期的宣教文獻和傳教策略的研究成果，「資料非常的豐富，幾乎可以算是無法閱讀荷蘭文獻的學者要研究十七世紀臺灣歷史的一部百科全書。」[37] 賴永祥長老也肯定他「確實開拓了荷蘭臺灣宣教史研究的路徑。」[38] 《臺灣佈教之成功》（*An Account of missionary Success in the Island of Formosa*, 1889）與《福爾摩莎素描》（*Sketches from Formosa*, 1915）是他在臺灣傳教所記載的見聞實錄，有助於了解外國傳教士眼中的臺灣印象。另外還有羅馬字相關的著作，如《聖詩歌》（1900）、《治理教會》（1905）、《廈門音新字典》（*A Dictionary of the Amoy Vernacular spoken throughout the prefectures of Chin-chiu, Chiang-chiu and Formosa*, 1913）。

2. 巴克禮牧師（Rev. Thomas Barclay）

巴克禮牧師在臺灣服務六十年，重要貢獻包括創辦臺南神學院、《臺灣府城教會報》、翻譯新舊約羅馬字聖經等，他的著作最多保留在《臺灣教會公報》的撰稿中，經常苦口婆心呼籲信徒遵守教義、本地傳道師要慇勤學道、宣導教會的決策等。近來聚珍堂史料叢書所重刊的《巴克禮作品集》（*Formosa For Christ*）是他為英國長老教會的外國宣道及青年福祉委員會所寫的一本小書，目前原書已絕版。

3. 連瑪玉（Marjorie Landsborough）

連瑪玉是蘭大衛（David Landsborough）醫師的夫人，曾經撰寫

---

37 有關甘為霖的著作介紹，詳見賴永祥，《教會史話》第一輯，頁107-114, 187-194。林昌華，〈甘為霖牧師（William Campbell）：一位十七世紀臺灣教會史的研究者〉，《臺灣風物》54卷1期，2004年3月，頁167-182。阮宗興，〈甘為霖及其書信集〉，2006.11.30，賴永祥長老史料庫網站，http://laijohn.com/index.htm。

38 賴永祥，《教會史話》第一輯，頁112。

三本介紹臺灣社會民風見聞和信徒見證的書：《美麗的福爾摩沙》（*In Beautiful Formosa*, 1922），《福爾摩沙的故事》（*Stories from Formosa*, 1924）及《福爾摩沙的故事續集》（*More Stories From Formosa*, 1932）。這些故事是為英國教會的主日學學生而撰寫，目的是介紹臺灣的傳教工作，激勵教會繼續關心海外宣教、鼓勵青年投入傳教行列，可說是主日學的課外讀物[39]。目前臺灣教會公報社重新出版的是《福爾摩沙的故事》和《福爾摩沙的故事續集》二書合編，並附有導讀和各篇故事的詳細解說，由於連瑪玉以傳教士的角度來描述臺灣社會民風和女性信徒的生命史，也可作為了解日治時期臺灣的社會文化和當代女性的生活素材。

4. 余饒理（George Ede）

余饒理曾擔任長老教中學校長，館藏的作品有《三字經新纂白話註解》、《聖道問答》、《萬國記錄》。其中《三字經新纂白話註解》是長老教中學學生必考的書，「每字附註白話讀音和字義，每句有臺語譯文及完整的白話字註解，尤其對歷史有詳細說明。相信在中國境內用漢文或方言都還沒有人出版過如此好的書籍，對學生教師有用，對初習漢文的外國宣教師，亦不失為一本有用的工具。」[40]《聖道問答》、《萬國記錄》都是從漢字版本翻譯成羅馬字的教材，以利教會信徒和中學學生學習，余饒理對於教學的關注和親編教材的用心由此可見。

5. 梅監務（Rev. Campbell N. Moody）

梅監務牧師是1895到1924年在彰化地區和蘭大衛醫師一起合作醫療佈道的「一位露天佈道家、歷史神學家、聖樂家、屬靈的聖徒」。他的英國同工稱他為「英國乞丐」，他的臺灣同工稱他為「臺灣的保

---

39 王昭文，〈導讀：蘭醫生媽講臺灣故事──《福爾摩沙的故事》解說〉，《福爾摩沙的故事》，聚珍堂史料1，2004年，頁15-19。

40 *The Monthly Messenger*, April, 1895, p. 84；轉引自賴永祥，〈余饒理三字經註解〉，《教會史話》第四輯，頁31。

羅」[41]。他的著述也很豐富，如《異教徒之心》（*The Heathen Heart,* 1907）、《福爾摩沙的聖徒》（*The Saints of Formosa,* 1912）、《佈道論》（羅馬字版，1914）、《早期改教者的心思》（*The Mind of the Early Converts,* 1920）、《古早的教會》（羅馬字，1922）、《國王的客人》（*The King's Guests,* 1932）等。最近聚珍堂史料叢書出版的是梅監務以前比較不受注意的羅馬字著作結集而成《梅監務作品集》，包括《羅馬書一到八章》，白話字原名為《羅馬信一到八章：新翻譯的白文及註解、解釋、講》、《佈道論》、《古早的教會》、《談論道理》。另外值得一提的是，現存「臺灣教會史料館」還有梅監務牧師的第二任妻子洪伯祺（Peggy Arthur Moody）撰寫的《宣教學者梅監務》（*Campbell Moody, Missionary and Scholar*）一書的打字複寫本，這次也一併在聚珍堂史料叢書出版，對梅監務牧師個人的研究、臺灣中部地區教會和信徒生活的描述都提供了很好的參考。

五、結語──期待一座專業管理的教會檔案館之建立

史料是歷史研究的基礎，「史料之不具或不確，則無復史之可言。」[42] 沒有史料，就無歷史，教會歷史自然也不例外。古老史料得來不易，可遇不可求，雖珍貴，但也脆弱容易毀損或遺失，梁啟超就曾提醒：「思想行事留痕者本已不多，所留之痕，又未必皆有史料的價值，有價值而留痕者，其喪失之也又極易。因必有證據，然後史料之資格備，證據一失，則史料即隨之湮沉。」[43]

因此史料的保存妥善與否攸關著歷史證據的存留、日後歷史研究的成果和歷史的重建與詮釋，其重要性不言可喻。1992~1997年王成勉教授曾進行為期四年的「臺灣地區基督教史料調查研究計畫」，實

---

41 鄭仰恩，〈英國乞丐？臺灣保羅？──梅監霧牧師小傳〉，《臺灣教會人物檔案（一）》（臺南：人光出版社，2001），頁56。
42 梁啟超，《中國歷史研究法》（臺北：里仁書局，民國83年），頁83。
43 同前註。

地訪查1,048家教會或教會機構對於教會史料的保存和管理情況，發現超過一半以上教會沒有設立教會圖書館和檔案室，可見許多教會不太重視自己的史料，也沒盡到妥善保管的責任。因此提升各教會對自己內部檔案和信徒資料的重視、並保存檔案的歷史意識的努力實在刻不容緩[44]。臺灣長老教會是目前臺灣歷史最久遠的宗派，「臺灣教會史料館」的館藏誠然十分豐富而有價值，不只文獻藏書多，還有琳瑯滿目的教會文物，除了見證百年來臺灣基督教的文化與教會發展，也是臺灣社會的重要文化資產，值得更多的關注與珍惜。否則隨著時間流逝，未加妥善保存的古老史料仍難免損壞或遺失，不免徒留遺憾。

現代資訊科技的進步使得檔案管理日益專業精進，完整的檔案管理包含了檔案的蒐集（如徵集、點收、鑑定等）、整理（如分類、編目、立案、描述等）、保管（如維護、數位化等）和應用（如提供檢索、調閱、研究、推廣、教育等），而檔案管理的最終目的是為促進檔案的開放和運用，充分發揮檔案的功能與社會共享，並提升其文化價值[45]。目前「臺灣教會史料館」的史料管理其實僅止於初步的整理和保管，近年來雖然有史料重刊和館藏數位化的努力，大大增加閱讀查詢和研究的方便性，較之以往研究者需親自前往臺南逐櫃尋找，翻閱破損原件的情形已大有改善。然而就長遠目標而言，建立一座專業化的教會檔案館來整理、保存和應用這些珍貴史料才是根本之道。所謂專業化的教會檔案館不只是建築空間（典藏庫房、文物修護室、展示廳等）和硬體設備（恆溫、恆濕、防治蟲害、火災感測等監控系統設備），還需要培養檔案管理的專業人才，配合完善的管理制度（統一規劃和集中管理等[46]）。如此長遠浩大工程，不是一朝一夕可達到，但行遠必自邇，若能體會珍貴史料的毀壞流失危機迫在眉睫，開放史料的運用可以充分彰顯史料的價值，裨益教會歷史的重建，則一點一滴的努力都將有成功之日，是所至盼。

---

44 王成勉，〈臺灣基督教史料之研究〉，《臺灣基督教史研討會論文集》，頁239-265。
45 凌寶華，〈檔案應用與使用者研究〉，《檔案季刊》，第5卷4期，2006年，頁117-130。
46 邢祖援，〈檔案管理的基本精神和展望〉，《研考雙月刊》，第15卷3期，1991年6月，頁9。

Documenting the Church in Taiwan: the Perspective from Yale University

Martha Lund Smalley

Yale Divinity School Library

Abstract

This paper will describe collections at the Yale University Divinity School Library that document missionary activity and the development of the Church in Taiwan. A survey of relevant archival sources, periodicals, reports, pamphlets, and books will be presented to describe the types of documentation collected and the methods for acquiring them. The presentation will include an overview of the archival program at the Divinity School Library, describing the acquisition, processing, description, preservation, and dissemination of primary source materials. In addition to describing Yale holdings, we will also review methods for utilizing national databases and Internet resources to identify and access materials related to the subject.

Keywords : archives, primary sources, bibliographic information, Yale

This essay provides background information about the collections of the Yale Divinity School Library, discusses available types of documentation related to Christianity in Taiwan, and explains methods for discovering relevant resources.

The Day Missions Collection of the Yale Divinity School Library contains materials related to the missionary movement and world Christianity. The Yale Divinity School Library is Yale University's primary research collection for the study of Christianity. It contains more than 500,000 volumes of books and periodicals, plus more than 4,500 linear feet of original format archival and manuscript material. In addition, the library regularly acquires microform or digital collections that document the missionary movement and world Christianity, which are historically a strong emphasis of the Library's collection. (See Photo 1)

The Day Missions collection was formed by George Edward Day, a professor of Hebrew at Yale who had an avid interest in foreign missions. After his retirement, Day dedicated himself to building a collection of books related to missions, which he gave to Yale, forming the Day Missions library in 1892. Day and his wife, Olivia Hotchkiss Day, also left an important bequest to insure the maintenance and growth of the Day Missions Library.

Another important player in the development of the Day Missions Collection was Kenneth Scott Latourette (1884-1968), who served as D. Willis James Professor of Missions and World Christianity at Yale Divinity School for many years. (See Photo 2) Latourette established an endowment fund specifically focused on acquisition of materials related to the missionary movement and world Christianity for the Yale Divinity Library. A portion of this bequest is now used for the Latourette Initiative, a proactive program to preserve and provide access to the documentation of world Christianity. The Latourette Initiative provides funding for the digitization and creation of preservation microfilm of published and archival resources documenting the history of Christian missions and the life of the churches in countries where missionaries served.

The Yale Divinity School Library's collections related to China are particularly strong because of the China Records Project. This Project was initiated in 1968 by National Council of Churches of Christ in the U.S.A. to insure the preservation of the personal records of former missionaries to China. Yale Divinity Library was chosen as a central repository for Project and received records of more than 300 former China missionaries during the initial five year grant. These collections have served as a magnet, attracting many additional collections in the following years. (See Photo 3)

Various types of materials related to Christianity in Taiwan are available at the Yale Divinity Library. These types would include books, pamphlets, reports, periodicals, personal papers, organizational archives, oral histories, dissertations, databases, and websites. It is one of the great strengths of the Yale Divinity School Library that it brings together in one place all of these different types of material, whether in original format or in microform (microfilm and microfiche.) The generous bequests of the Days and Latourette have allowed the Library to actively acquire a wide variety of materials.

The most important tool for discovering Yale's holdings is Orbis, the open access online library catalog that serves all of the more than twenty libraries at Yale University (http://orbis.library.yale.edu.) Orbis contains records for books, pamphlets, reports, periodicals, and archival collections. It is possible to use the "Advanced Search" option in Orbis to restrict your search to only the Divinity Library. Since nearly all books at the Divinity Library relate to Christianity, this is a handy way to limit a search to materials related to the church and missions without having to use a lot of keywords to define that limit. So, for example, a keyword search for "Taiwan or Formosa," restricted to the Divinity Library at Yale, results in 337 hits, all of which would relate in some way to missions or Christianity in Taiwan. Of course there would be other documentation in the Divinity Library that relates to Christianity in Taiwan for which the keywords "Taiwan" or "Formosa" do not appear in the Orbis record – particularly items such as periodicals and reports.

An alternate keyword search, for "Taiwan Christianity", without restricting to Divinity Library, results in 278 hits. This brings up the point that many Chinese language materials at Yale are cataloged by the East Asia Collection, rather than the Divinity Library, so searches that are not restricted to the Divinity Library may also reveal fruitful results.

Pamphlets with distinct titles and authors are cataloged in Orbis as well as more substantial books. We use a simplified form of cataloging for pamphlets and an unclassified sequential call number system. These conventions allow us to process and make available more material than would be possible if we applied the same cataloging rules to all items. It is also worth noting that the Yale Divinity Library collects materials in all languages, not just English.

Also appearing in Orbis are title records for periodicals and reports, which may contain important information about Christianity in Taiwan even though the keywords "Taiwan" or "Formosa" are not in the Orbis record. For periodicals and reports, it is important to identify relevant organizations and search for their publications directly. For example, in the 1938 *Directory of World Missions*, we discover that mission agencies working in Formosa at that time included three British societies and four Japanese societies, in addition to the Oriental Missionary Society, the Presbyterian Church in Canada, and the Seventh Day Adventists from North America. Examination of additional reference works such as missionary atlases and the *Mission Handbook* may reveal additional agencies working in Taiwan in other eras. Knowing the names of these agencies allows us to search directly for their periodicals. The periodical of the Oriental Missionary Society, for example, the *Missionary*

Standard, will undoubtedly contain valuable information about mission work in Taiwan, since it was one of the fields of work for that society.

Other examples of periodicals available at Yale Divinity library (in Orbis) include:

- Collectanea Theologica Universitatis Fujen
- New China Review
- Occasional Bulletin : Taiwan Church News
- Ricci Bulletin = Taibei Li Shi Xue She Nian Gan
- Shen Xue Yu Jiao Hui
- Sino-Christian Studies : an international journal of Bible, theology & philosophy = Han yu jidu jiao xue shu lun ping / Chung Yuan Christian University
- Tai-oan Kau-hoe Kong-po
- Taiwan Journal of Theology
- Theologies and Cultures
- Ying Guang

An additional source of periodicals is the Yale Divinity Library's collection of documentation received from the United States Catholic China Bureau, our Record Group No. 194. Periodicals in this collection include:

- Amor Newsletter Published in Taiwan by Asia-Pacific Meeting for Religious Women, Asian Service Center
- China Church News Published in Taiwan by the Jesuit China Service
- Inside China Mainland Published in Taipei, Taiwan by Institute of Current China Studies
- Taiwan Church News (Uniform Title: Occasional bulletin [Presbyterian Church in Taiwan]); Published in Tainan, Taiwan by Taiwan Church News;
- Taiwan Communique (Washington D.C. edition) Published in

Washington, DC by International Committee for Human Rights in Taiwan

There are also archival holdings at the Yale Divinity Library, including personal papers, organizational archives, and oral histories. It is possible to search for these types of materials in Orbis, Yale's online catalog, by restricting a search by "Type" to "Archives or Manuscripts." A search for "Taiwan or Formosa" limited by "Archives or Manuscripts" and the Divinity Library results in 27 hits, including original format personal papers and organizational archives, microform collections of organizational archives, and archivally-organized publications of organizations.

An example of a personal papers collection is the Donald MacInnis Papers, our Record Group No. 204. (See Photo 4) The Orbis record for this collection links to a finding aid, which provides more detailed information about MacInnis and the contents of the collection. These finding aids appear, and can be searched for directly, in the Yale Finding Aids Database (http://findingaids.library.yale.edu). The finding aids, which follow accepted North American standards, contain two basic parts. The first part is the "front matter", which includes administrative information about the collection, biographical information about the person or agency involved, and an introduction that describes the papers. The second part is a folder listing of the collection contents, i.e., a listing of the folder labels. The collection contents are typically divided into "series" and "sub-series," which are logical groupings of the material that are established by the archivist to make the collection more accessible to the researcher.

In the biographical chronology of the MacInnis Papers, for example, we see that MacInnis served as a Methodist missionary in Taiwan from 1953 to 1966. The contents listing shows us that there is one folder of correspondence from this time period, contained in Box 28, Folder 260. This is not a large amount of material but it includes both "circular" letters and personal letters written by MacInnis during this time period that can shed important light on his work and the state of the church in Taiwan. (See Photo 5)

Another example of a personal papers collection is the papers of Lillian R. Dickson, who served with the Canadian Presbyterian Mission and "The Mustard Seed" mission in Taiwan from 1927 to 1975. In this case, a relatively small collection of personal papers has been included in our China Records Project Miscellaneous Personal Papers Collection, a gathering together of small collections into one finding aid. Biographical information and contents listings are provided in a more compact way for these smaller collections. Despite being only two boxes, the Dickson papers include an interesting variety of materials, including reports, writings, circular letters, personal correspondence, brochures, and photographs. (See Photo 6)

An example of an organizational archives held at Yale would be the archives of the United Board for Christian Higher Education in Asia, a support agency for institutions of higher education in Asia. In our Record Group No. 11A (first addendum), for example, there are records related to three institutions in Taiwan: Soochow University, Tainan Theological College, and Tunghai University. Once again, a finding aid provides a folder-by-folder description of the material contained in the collection. Since the United Board is an ongoing organization, Yale receives archives from it on an ongoing basis. The second addendum (Record Group No. 11B), for example, contains additional files related to Tunghai University. (See Photo 7)

As mentioned earlier, the Yale Divinity School Library actively acquires microfilm or microfiche collections of archives of mission agencies. An important collection related to mission work in Taiwan is the archives of the Presbyterian Church of England. This collection contains 2,841 fiche made from the originals located at the School of Oriental and African Studies in London. The collection documents the work of the Presbyterian Church of

England Foreign Missions Committee and the Women's Missionary Association in China, Taiwan, Singapore, Malaysia and India. Included are correspondence, minutes and reports from the years 1847-1950. Special subjects include opium trade, coolie trade, treaties and life in the Treaty Ports, Japanese colonialism in Taiwan, Chinese Nationalism in the 1920s and the Sino-Japanese War. The guides to these microfilm and microfiche collections tend to be much less detailed than the finding aids we create for our original format collections, but there is a very substantial amount of documentation available.

Also included in a library catalog search for archival materials at Yale are a set of materials that we call "Historical records." These are actually primarily published materials – constitutions, leaflets, brochures, reports, etc. – from organizations. We have chosen to organize them in an archival manner rather than cataloging each individual item. This strategy is partially to save time in cataloging, but we also believe that it is more useful to have these types of non-monographic material gathered together as a group.

Oral histories are the final type of archival material that I will mention. At Yale we typically describe any collections of oral histories with finding aids. An example would be American Lutheran Church Women in Mission Oral History Project. Some archives repositories, such as the Billy Graham Center Archives in Wheaton, Illinois, create separate records for individual oral history interviews.

Another important type of document for the study of Christianity in Taiwan is dissertations. There are two sources of information about dissertations that I will note. Most important is the "Dissertations and Theses" database that can be licensed from the vendor ProQuest. This database provides abstracts and full text for most of the dissertations that it indexes. Though it does not provide full text, another important resource is a database hosted by the Yale Divinity School Library called "Researching

World Christianity: Doctoral Dissertations on Mission since 1900" (http://resources.library.yale.edu/dissertations/). This database incorporates compilations of missions-related dissertations published in issues of the *International Bulletin of Missionary Research*, and has been expanded in its scope to include English-language doctoral dissertations without regard to country of origin, dissertations dealing with Christianity outside the West, dissertations presented since 1900, and all doctoral level dissertations and theses including the D. Min. and D. Miss. The database contained information 6,087 dissertations as of August 2009.

Databases and online resources that the Yale Divinity School Library provides access to through its website provide additional resources for the study of Christianity in Taiwan. Many of these online resources are freely available on the web. The Yale Divinity Library's "Missions and World Christianity" subject guide (http://guides.library.yale.edu/missions_resources) attempts to provide a consolidated point of access to them. This guide includes links to sites such as Elder John Lai's website on the history of Christianity in Taiwan (http://www.laijohn.com/). Also of particular note is the Chinese Christian Texts Database (http://www2.arts.kuleuven.be/info/eng/OE_sinologie/CCT/), a research database of primary and secondary sources concerning the cultural contacts between China and Europe in the seventeenth and eighteenth centuries. Our guide also provides links to online full text of the *Chinese Recorder*, an important primary source periodical, some issues of which can be keyword searched online.

Another important resource is the Ricci Roundtable database hosted at the University of San Francisco. The Ricci Roundtable incorporates information from the important reference work *Christianity in China: a scholars' guide to resources in the libraries and archives of the United States*. A search of the "Archives" category of the Ricci Roundtable reveals numerous repositories that hold archival material related to Christianity in Taiwan. The

"Institutions" category contains important information about agencies and institutions at work in Taiwan. The great advantage of the Ricci Roundtable is that it is available for free. At Yale, we have access to other licensed databases that provide information about where archival holdings exist, such as ArchiveGrid. A search in ArchiveGrid for "Taiwan missionaries", for example, provides links to 76 different collections held throughout North America.

We have touched on numerous types of documentation that provide relevant information about the topic of the church in Taiwan. It is important for researchers to seek out as many different types of documentation as possible because these different types of records reveal various angles of the story. Diaries and personal letters written to family members, for example, are likely to contain more introspective and unguarded reflection. Communications with a mission board, and "circular letters", may offer more thorough, but also more "politically correct" reporting. Periodicals, brochures, and reports prepared for distribution to the general public and financial supporters of the mission board or church are designed to garner support. Newspapers and reports that go beyond the control of the mission board or church offer an outside perspective. Secondary literature offering historical analysis is obviously of interest to researchers as well as primary sources. Although Yale does not have large holdings in these areas for Taiwan, I would note that there is increasing interest in maps and photographs as historical documents. (See Photo 8)

As we have opportunity the Yale Divinity School Library is digitizing from its holdings and making materials available on the Internet. Our "Online Resources" site (http://www.library.yale.edu/div/onlineresources. html) provides consolidated access to these materials, as well as to training materials related to archival processing and description.

Photo 1: Day Missions Reading Room, Yale Divinity School Library

Photo 2: Kenneth Scott Latourette

Photo 3: China Records Project (http://www.library.yale. edu/div/spc/chinarec.htm)

Donald MacInnis Papers Record Group No. 204	Overview	
ble of Contents	**REPOSITORY:**	Yale University Divinity School Library 409 Prospect Street New Haven, CT 06511 Email: divinity.library@yale.edu Phone: (203) 432-5301
Title Page Overview Collection Contents ⊞ Series I. Research files , 1899-2002 ⊞ Series II. Writings, 1945-1995 ⊞ Series III. Personal Papers, 1948-2004 ⊞ Series IV. Collected Material, 1928-2004 ⊞ Series V. Audio-visual Material, 1908-1999	**CALL NUMBER:**	Record Group No. 204
	CREATOR:	MacInnis, Donald E.
	TITLE:	Donald MacInnis Papers
	DATES:	1899-2005
	PHYSICAL DESCRIPTION:	Total archival boxes 41 plus 2 oversize; total linear
Navigation options: *Expand Menu* / *Collapse Menu*	**LANGUAGE(S):**	In English.
	SUMMARY:	The bulk of this collection consists of research files missions in China. Correspondence, writings, colle book *China Chronicles from a Lost Time: The Min* missions in Fujian province. The collection also inc documentation of MacInnis, who was a missionary the National Council of Churches of Christ in the U Research Program

Photo 4: Finding aid for Donald MacInnis Papers (http://hdl.handle.net/10079/fa/ divinity.204

LETTER FROM FORMOSA

226 West Lane
Model Village
Taichung, Taiwan
September 20, 1955

Dear friends:

We have waited too long to write our second letter. Please forgive us. In this letter we will try to bring you a general picture of our life and work in Taiwan today.

TRUCKS, GUNS, & RICE FIELDS

I stood at a corner of our main cross-town street recently, heading for the home of a church member, when a convoy of military trucks began rumbling past. This was a heavy artillery unit equipped with the latest super-size American trucks, each as big as a two-story house. Chinese driver and crew perched high above us in the cab, while each truck towed a mammoth 105mm howitzer, the final trucks in the long convoy pulling supply and ammunition trailers. I roughly guessed the cost of each truck and gun at US$40,000, 25 units worth over a million dollars.

I looked around me then at the neighborhood where we lived. At one end of the street stood the Buddhist temple, gilded, well-kept. Opposite the temple was a row of "overcome difficulty" homes, mainlander refugees in squatters' bamboo huts where we have a weekly literacy class for the women. Next to them was a flour mill, a sprawling primary school crammed with clamorous youngsters, a soy sauce factory, the government rice control office, a men's barbershop with women barbers, a row of farmers' market stalls, two rice shops, a brothel, a World Health Organization (WHO) maternal & child health clinic, a pool hall, another brothel, a laundry, a basket shop on wheels, a bamboo and tinware shop,

Photo 5: Example of "circular" letter written by Donald MacInnis while serving in Taiwan

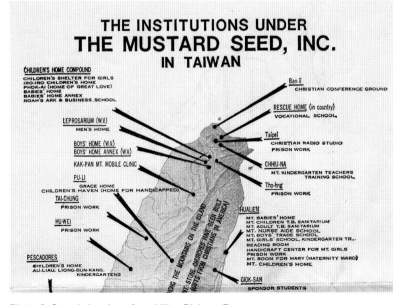

Photo 6: Sample brochure from Lillian Dickson Papers

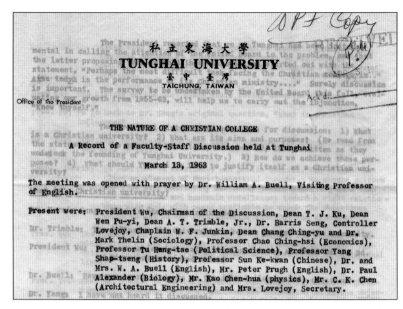

Photo 7: Sample document from records related to Tunghai University in the archives of the United Board for Christian Higher Education in Asia

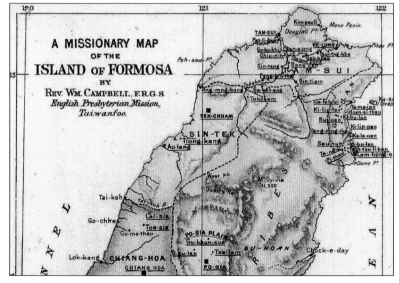

Photo 8: Missionary map contributed by the Yale Divinity Library to the ATLA Cooperative Digital Resources Initiative (http://www.atla.com/digitalresources/)

"Ye Are Witnesses": Tunghai University and Taiwan through the Archives of the Oberlin Shansi Memorial Association, 1955-1979

Jonathan Benda

Department of English, Northeastern University

Abstract

Between 1955 and 1979, the Oberlin Shansi Memorial Association (OSMA) sent selected Oberlin College graduates to Taiwan to teach English at Tunghai University and engage in intercultural exchange. While Taiwan and Tunghai University are only briefly mentioned in the "administrative history" notes in the OSMA Finding Guide, the records of OSMA (RG 15), which are located in the Oberlin College Archives (OCA), include a substantial record of the activities of the Oberlin graduates (called "representatives," or "reps") while in Taiwan and upon their return to Oberlin. The records also enable us to trace the secularization of the OSMA and its changing policies toward Tunghai University through a study of the Association's detailed letters, reports, and meeting minutes.

The records of OSMA in the OCA are also significant for the study of church history in Taiwan. The interactions – and sometimes conflicts – between the young Oberlin reps and the more conservative Western Christian community at Tunghai throw into relief how the missionary work at Tunghai was made difficult not only by cultural differences between Westerners and Chinese, but also by the complications brought about by generational differences and different definitions of Christianity among the Westerners themselves.

The records of OSMA also provide for a focus on the different venues in which OSMA administrators, reps, and other OSMA-associated parties talked and wrote about not only Association's activities, but also the political and social concerns about Taiwan during the early Cold War and Vietnam eras. The archives' detailed collections on the one hand give a clear sense of an organization very much concerned with its own identity and legacy, and on the other hand demonstrate the interaction among global events during the early Cold War and Vietnam eras, the identities and political stances of Oberlin College students and alumni, and the relations between a nominally Christian OSMA and Tunghai University. Finally, the records allow scholars to trace the OSMA's changing policies toward Taiwan and Tunghai as relations improved between the United States and the People's Republic of China.

Keywords: Oberlin Shansi Memorial Association (OSMA), Tunghai university, Shansi, Taiwan, Christian community

Introduction

Between 1955 and 1979, an English teaching and intercultural scholarly exchange program joined Tunghai University with the Oberlin Shansi Memorial Association (OSMA, or "Shansi") of Oberlin College in Ohio. Tunghai, which was a newly established school in 1955, was the beneficiary of the fact that the OSMA had four years earlier been forced out of China after the Communist takeover of the mainland. After a deliberative process that took several years, the OSMA decided to establish an exchange program with Tunghai in which selected Oberlin College graduates would be sent there every year to teach English and engage in intercultural exchange activities. The records of this program's activities are contained in the records of the OSMA, located in the Oberlin College Archives. While Taiwan and Tunghai University are only briefly mentioned in the "administrative history" notes in the OSMA Finding Guide, the records of OSMA (RG 15) include a substantial record of the activities of the Oberlin graduates (called "representatives," or "reps") while in Taiwan and upon their return to Oberlin.

This paper will introduce the records and discuss what this archive can offer scholars of Christianity in Taiwan. The records of OSMA in the OCA are significant for the study of church history in Taiwan. The interactions – and sometimes conflicts – between the young Oberlin reps and the more conservative Western Christian community at Tunghai throw into relief how the missionary work at Tunghai was made difficult not only by cultural differences between Westerners and Chinese, but also by the complications brought about by generational differences and different definitions of Christianity among the Westerners themselves.

The records of OSMA also provide for a focus on the different venues in which OSMA administrators, reps, and other OSMA-associated parties talked and wrote about not only Association's activities, but also the political and social concerns about Taiwan during the early Cold War and Vietnam eras. The archives' detailed collections on the one hand give a clear sense of an organization very much concerned with its own identity and legacy, and on the other hand demonstrate the interaction among global events during the early Cold War and Vietnam eras, the identities and political stances of Oberlin College students and alumni, and the relations between a nominally Christian OSMA and Tunghai University. Finally, the records allow scholars to trace the OSMA's changing policies toward Taiwan and Tunghai as relations improved between the United States and the People's Republic of China.[1]

The OSMA in China, 1908-1951

Before introducing what the OSMA archive has to offer scholars of Taiwan church history, I will briefly introduce the OSMA. The Oberlin Shansi Memorial Association was founded in 1908 in remembrance of Oberlin-associated missionaries who had been killed in Shanxi Province during the Boxer Uprising of 1900. The connection of Oberlin with China is usually traced back to the early 1880s, when "a group of Oberlin men received a great inspiration... under the instruction of Dr. Judson Smith, then Professor of Church History in the Oberlin Theological Seminary."[2] Students and faculty at Oberlin, a Congregationalist college, were passionate about the spread of Christianity in the Western United States and in other parts of the world that the Gospel had not yet reached. Smith's inspired students volunteered to go to China under the auspices of the American Board of

---

1 Portions of this paper have been adapted from my Ph.D. dissertation, "The Future of Asia: The Oberlin Shansi Memorial Association, Tunghai University, and the Rhetorics of Intercultural Exchange, 1955-1979" (Syracuse University, 2011).

2 *The Shansi Memorial Association: A Strategic Missionary Opportunity* (Oberlin, OH: The Tribune Press, 1908), p. 3.

Commissioners for Foreign Missions (ABCFM, also a Congregationalist organization).[3] During 1882, a "band" of seven Oberlin-connected missionaries and their wives arrived in Taiyuan, Shanxi Province, roughly 300 miles southwest of Beijing.[4] A year later they settled in the nearby city of Taigu.

Ellsworth Carlson describes the mission of the Oberlin band as consisting mainly of "making converts to the Christian faith."[5] In addition to this major task, Oberlin band members also attempted to establish schools. Carlson notes that before 1900, "Western learning" – but not the English language – began to be taught in the schools. He describes the curriculum as "a kind of compromise between what was taught in Chinese schools and what the missionaries were most anxious to teach" – Christianity.[6] The Chinese were suspicious of the foreign missionaries, so the attempts at both proselytizing and teaching were only moderately successful. However, it is important to note the increasing emphasis being placed on education, despite the reluctance of many in the ABCFM to "dilut[e] the religious nature of the missionary endeavor in China in the instruction of secular subjects."[7] Part of the reason behind this increasing emphasis was probably due to the increasing progressivism of Oberlin College. John Barnard traces the "weakening hold of evangelicalism" at Oberlin and the greater concern with social issues during the 1880s.[8]

---

3 Ellsworth C. Carlson, *Oberlin in Asia: The First Hundred Years, 1882-1982* (Oberlin, OH: Oberlin Shansi Memorial Association, 1982). Carlson was an OSMA rep to Shanxi from 1939-43 and later a professor of history at Oberlin (and closely connected with the Shansi program throughout his life).

4 At the time, "Shanxi" (山西) was romanized as "Shansi." Hereafter, "Shanxi" will be used to refer to the province in China, and "Shansi" will be used to refer to the Oberlin Shansi Memorial Association and its related projects.

5 Carlson, *Oberlin in Asia*, p. 10.

6 Ibid., p. 13.

7 Wen-Hsin Yeh, *The Alienated Academy: Culture and Politics in Republican China, 1919-1937* (Cambridge, MA: Harvard University Asia Center, 1990), p. 61.

8 John Barnard, *From Evangelicalism to Progressivism at Oberlin College, 1866-1917* (Columbus, OH: Ohio State University Press, 1969), p. 59 passim.

The work of the Oberlin band was interrupted abruptly in 1900 with the deaths of 18 Oberlin missionaries and their children in Shanxi. The Oberlin missionaries were killed, along with Chinese converts, by participants in the Boxer Uprising. The Boxer Rebellion became symbolic for the Oberlin College community, with a dual focus on memorializing those Oberlin people who had been "martyred" in Shanxi and on continuing the mission of Oberlin in Shanxi. Memorialization of the martyrs took the form of a Memorial Arch that was built on Tappan Square on the campus of Oberlin. The Arch was dedicated in 1903.[9]

The second part of the process of remembering the Oberlin martyrs was initiated with the founding of the Oberlin Shansi Memorial Association in 1908.[10] One year earlier, a school named Ming Hsien (銘賢 "Remember the Worthy")[11] had been established in Taigu, Shanxi Province, jointly by Oberlin and H. H. K'ung (Kong Xiangxi), who was from "a wealthy banking family" in China.[12] The Ming Hsien school offered a Western-style education to boys (a separate school for girls was also established by K'ung).

As Mary Tarpley Campfield writes, when the traditional examination system in China was abolished in 1905, "modern education and western education were synonymous, and the missionaries practically cornered the market on this newly prized commodity."[13] Xiaoye You notes that mission

---

9 Bronze plaques on the Arch read, "MASSACRED" and list the names of the Oberlin-associated American missionaries and children killed. The phrases "NEITHER COUNT I MY LIFE DEAR UNTO MYSELF" and "THE BLOOD OF MARTYRS THE SEED OF THE CHURCH" are carved into its sides, and "YE ARE WITNESSES" and "THE LORD REIGNETH" are carved above the walkway that passes through the Arch.

10 Carlson, *Oberlin in Asia*, p. 19.

11 Ibid., p. 20. Modern discussions of the school, like Carlson's, often use a different Romanization system, spelling its name "Ming Xian." I will adopt the spelling that was used at the time, except for when quoting from modern sources.

12 Ibid., p. 19. K'ung later became the husband of Song Ailing, sister of Song Meiling, Chiang Kai-shek's wife, and of Song Qingling, Sun Yat-sen's wife. This marriage eventually put K'ung in the position of financier to the Chinese Nationalist Party (Kuomintang, or KMT) under Chiang.

13 Mary Tarpley Campfield, "Oberlin-in-China, 1881-1951" (Unpublished doctoral dissertation, University of Virginia, 1974), p. 108.

colleges, which began to be established in China in the late nineteenth century, "required that students demonstrate satisfactory English ability before entering college."[14] This kind of expectation, combined with the strong influence of mission schools on Chinese higher education after 1905, positioned missionary-run secondary schools like Ming Hsien as important participants in the English-teaching market in China. Missionaries with the ABCFM, most having studied at Oberlin College or Seminary, began teaching at Ming Hsien from the beginning, and the school became famous for its English program; as Campfield observes, it "rather quickly acquired the reputation of being the best preparatory school in the province, largely because its excellent English instruction so well prepared its graduates for heavy English requirements of China's modern universities."[15]

Between 1907 and 1917 the number of students at Ming Hsien rose from seven to more than 80.[16] The success of the English program at Ming Hsien resulted in a need for more teachers. In 1918, the OSMA began to send selected Oberlin graduates to Ming Hsien to teach English. However, like many Western-run educational and missionary activities in China, Ming Hsien was shut down in 1951 as a result of the Communist takeover of the country.

The OSMA Archives

The OSMA Archives constitute Record Group 15 and take up approximately 132.35 linear feet.[17] According to the statement of Scope and

---

14 Xiaoye You, *Writing in the Devil's Tongue: A History of English Composition in China* (Carbondale, IL: Southern Illinois University Press, 2010), p. 33.

15 Campfield, "Oberlin-in-China", p. 133.

16 Ibid.

17 Oberlin College Archives. "Oberlin Shansi Memorial Association Records, 1881-2012," http://www.oberlinlibstaff. com/archon/index.php?p=collections/controlcard&id=5 (accessed October 14, 2013). A digital collection of some

Content, "Records of the Oberlin Shansi Memorial Association were acquired in fourteen lots between 1967 and 1991," and more files have been transferred to the Archives since then.[18]

Files are divided into the following subgroups:[19]

Subgroup I. Oberlin China Band

Subgroup II. Administrative Records

Subgroup III. Program Areas

Subgroup IV. Representatives

Subgroup V. Publications and Publicity

Subgroup VI. Architectural Plans and Maps

Subgroup VII. Audio-Visual

Records related to Shansi's work in Taiwan are found throughout Subgroups II through VII. It is notable, however, that the first subgroup of the OSMA archives consists of documents written as part of the work of the Oberlin China Band. Since the OSMA was established in memory of those missionaries, by including the Oberlin China Band's records, the OSMA archive embodies and enacts Shansi's collective identity by telling a particular story of the organization's origins. As rhetorician Barbara Biesecker has asserted, the archive "always already is the provisionally settled scene of our collective invention, of our collective invention of us and of it."[20] The presence of the Oberlin China Band records in the OSMA archives, then, is

---

Shansi materials entitled "Shansi: Oberlin and Asia" has been set up and can be found at http://www.oberlin.edu/library/digital/shansi/index.html. However, the scope of the digital collection is limited to materials that date from between 1880 and 1950, and the introduction to the site contains no mention of Tunghai University or Taiwan (or, to be fair, of any other programs besides the ones at Shanxi).

18 Oberlin College Archives. "Administrative Information," "Oberlin Shansi Memorial Association Records, 1881-2012," http://www.oberlinlibstaff.com/archon/index.php?p=collections/controlcard&id=5 (accessed October 14, 2013).

19 Ibid.

20 Barbara A. Biesecker, "Of Historicity, Rhetoric: The Archive as Scene of Invention," *Rhetoric & Public Affairs* 9, no. 1 (2006): 124.

itself an act of invention that (provisionally) establishes the Oberlin China Band as the cradle of the OSMA. As shown above, the origins of the OSMA were clearly rooted in the deaths of the Oberlin China Band members. Their "martyrdom" loomed large in the early administrative rhetoric of the OSMA, although the Oberlin community (particularly the student body) became more and more uncomfortable with the Christian missionary roots of Oberlin's association with Asia.

The OSMA archives are extraordinarily extensive, spanning the hundred-year history of the Association and including detailed records of both the major and mundane activities of the organization. Why such extensive records were turned over to the Oberlin Archives is not entirely clear, but the "Scope and Contents"; also, information that accompanies the list of the Oberlin Archives' holdings of OSMA records suggests how users of the records might read them. The writer (archivist Roland Baumann?) notes that the post-1950 records "trace the secularization of OSMA and document the transformation of its programs."[21] As we will see, the secularization of Shansi was a slow and conflicted process (in fact, the word "process" itself might be too neat a way of describing what happened), as was the way in which Shansi's programs were transformed. The scope and content statement invites users of the archives to find the story of Shansi's secularization and transformation in the records – a story that is actually a somewhat convoluted narrative.

The statement goes on to note that "[a]dministrative correspondence [in the archives] offers a look at the role of cultural exchange in both higher education and international relations (and <u>vice versa</u>)."[22] The records also demonstrate the importance of writing in the operations of the OSMA. In the days before the Internet or even the ability to make inexpensive

---

21 Oberlin College Archives. "Scope and Contents," "Oberlin Shansi Memorial Association Records, 1881-2012," http://www.oberlinlibstaff.com/archon/index.php?p=collections/controlcard&id=5 (accessed October 14, 2013).

22 Ibid.

international telephone calls, the Association had to maintain its networks via a variety of written genres. These included detailed meeting minutes that recorded not just votes taken on motions but also summaries of Trustee discussions; at times, the minutes even took the form of a conversation among the present committee members.[23]

There are several possibilities for why the minutes would be so detailed. More detail in minutes could more effectively coordinate the work of the Trustees and the Executive Committee by invoking a common "official" memory of previous discussion. Since the Executive Committee (made up of a select group of Trustees) was responsible for decision making when the Trustees were not meeting, and since the two committees shared equally in the authority over Shansi's administration, it would be important for the two parties to have clear memories of what each other was doing.

A related reason is suggested by the advice of a consultant to non-profit organizations. Leslie T. White writes that non-profits have legal obligations that board members must ensure are met in order to minimize the risk of a legal claim. She continues, "An effective method to minimize the chance of such a claim and to aid in its defense is to maintain detailed records of the board's activities. Thorough documentation of the Board's actions also provides a system for monitoring the members' fulfillment of their legal duties. The minutes of the board's meetings are a good place to start."[24] This

---

23 Admittedly, it's hard to determine how much was left out of the minutes. When one looks at the amount of detail, however, one is left with the impression that the secretary has given a fairly "complete picture" of what took place. The "illusion" of completeness (and objectivity) is occasionally challenged, however. One place where we do see an alternative interpretation of the events of a meeting is in a report Wynn Fairfield submitted to the Trustees in December of 1955; in the first part of this report, his memory of the November 14, 1954 annual Trustees' meeting is different from that of that meeting's minutes: he recalls a disagreement which is not mentioned in the minutes. (See Wynn C. Fairfield, "A Study of Opportunities for the Future Program of The Oberlin-in-China Memorial Association," Dec. 1, 1955. Minutes of Executive Committee and Board of Trustees, 1956, RG 15, Subgroup II, series 2, Box 3, OCA.)

24 Leslie T. White, "Directors & Officers–the Importance of Board Minutes," Croydon Consulting website, http://croydonconsult.com/minutes.htm (accessed July 12, 2008).

consultant's comments are reminders of how the work of the Association – and that work's textualization – is linked to a variety of groups, some of which did not participate directly in Shansi's work. In view of White's advice, the minutes might be said to mediate Shansi's legal relationships to its contributors, to the schools (and countries) where Shansi reps were sent, to the reps themselves and their families, and to the State of Ohio where the Association was registered as a not-for-profit corporation.

In addition to meeting minutes, the OSMA archives include correspondence among the organization's various constituencies. Such correspondence includes reports written by Trustees or other parties who were commissioned to investigate opportunities for Shansi or evaluate the progress of Shansi's projects in Asia. These reports sometimes took the form of letters written to the chair of the Board of Trustees or, alternatively, took the form of formal reports, including executive summaries, subheadings, and appendices.

Many of the reports are notable for the individuality of the authorial voice. Reports speak on behalf of a variety of people – both those who were spoken to in the process of composition and those who were simply spoken for – but the reports also often show the attitudes and points of view of their authors. In that sense, the authors make arguments in the reports, rather than simply "reporting" in the sense of providing objective information about the topic. On at least one occasion, the 'directions for use' that accompany the reports signal the fact that the writer recognizes the perspectival nature of the information provided. Wynn C. Fairfield, for instance, admits in his 1955 report to the Trustees that he is including personal judgments in the section covering "The Problem of Geographical Location," but argues that these views are "reported with complete humility and no illusions as to their authoritative character." He continues, "One of the tasks of the Trustees in considering this report will be to examine these judgments critically and to determine whether they are sufficiently sound to serve as a factor in selecting the project or projects to be undertaken."[25]

Other types of reports include those written by administrators in the Association, such as Margaret Leonard (the Executive Secretary for many years) and Carl Jacobson (the Executive Director beginning in the mid-1970s). These reports, which were addressed to the Trustees, usually focused on the activities of the previous year and raised issues or problems to be discussed at the annual Trustees meeting. In addition, returned reps also wrote reports to the Trustees, either upon their return to the United States or upon the conclusion of their third year as a "returned rep" at Oberlin.

The texts that arguably received the widest exposure among both Oberlin students and other Shansi constituencies were the "rep letters." These were letters written by Shansi representatives in order to share their experiences with the Oberlin community. Rep letters took many forms, including stories of trips taken, retellings of local legends, language lessons, descriptions of geography, descriptions of classroom teaching experiences, book reports, and even poetry. The rep letters (and the occasional rep-written articles that were published in the Oberlin College newspaper, the *Oberlin Review,* and in the *OSMA Newsletter*) were important in the construction of the public face of the rep program.

Private correspondence, as can be imagined, covered a wide variety of topics, from disagreements going on between constituencies involved in the Shansi-Tunghai project, to complaints about culture shock, to requests for compensation for medical treatments. The writer of the Scope and Contents statement notes that such "correspondence ... paints a detailed picture of the impact of cultural exchange on the individual."[26] Thus, to some extent, it is possible that letters detailing such minor things as requests for compensation

---

25 Wynn C. Fairfield, "A Study."
26 Oberlin College Archives. "Scope and Contents," "Oberlin Shansi Memorial Association Records, 1881-2012."

for dental bills can give us some insight into the reps and their relationships to Shansi and to Taiwan, and more generally, perhaps, some understanding about the material conditions that were part of intercultural exchange. However, one challenge that I experienced working with the writings of the Oberlin reps was that I was asked to contact former reps to get their permission to cite their writing in my work. This requirement made me hesitant about approaching the former reps with too many requests to quote from their writing – particularly their personal letters to Oberlin. I elected not to make a great deal of use of these documents, only citing them when it seemed to me to be absolutely necessary and when I could get specific consent from the writers. This requirement is something that other scholars will need to consider when using the OSMA archives.[27]

Early Conflict Between Reps and Missionaries at Tunghai

Despite that limitation, the OSMA Archives can contribute to the study of Christianity in Taiwan by providing insight into the different understandings of Christianity that characterized the foreign missionaries at Tunghai, the Chinese Christians there, the Oberlin reps, and the OSMA Trustees. An example of how these different versions of Christianity came into contact can be found in a letter written by Shansi Trustee Ellsworth Carlson that raised some problems concerning the relationship between foreign missionaries at Tunghai and some of the Oberlin reps. During his 1957 trip to Asia under the auspices of the OSMA, Carlson wrote six letters to the Trustees regarding his visit to Tunghai. His April 22, 1957 letter to the

---

27 Despite that requirement, work in the Oberlin College Archives is encouraged by the staff, and researchers can apply for financial support through the Archives' Frederick B. Artz Summer Research Grants Program. Information about the Frederick B. Artz Summer Research Grants Program can be found at http://www.oberlin.edu/archive/artz/index.html.

Shansi Trustees about the religious situation at Tunghai focuses entirely on the religious situation at Tunghai and its relation to the reps. Carlson begins by tracing his understanding of the recent history of Protestantism in Taiwan. Noting that after the end of World War II, Taiwan was "the target of a major Protestant missionary attack," Carlson describes the conservatism of the missionary community at Tunghai. According to Carlson, Tunghai Chaplain William Junkin was "convinced that the main purpose of Tunghai is to win Christian decisions, and that anything else that the university accomplishes can be justified only to the extent that it contributes to winning Christian decisions." Carlson quotes Junkin as describing the Shansi reps as "mighty fine young people" who displayed good morals. Since Junkin didn't consider reps to be Christians, he was therefore afraid their presence would suggest to the Chinese students that it was possible to be a good person without being a fundamentalist Christian. Junkin was not alone – as Carlson writes, "When I arrived here four weeks ago, the more conservative members of the missionary community were waiting for me, and within a few days I had heard four accounts of the problem that the reps present to the Christian program of the university, with a climax coming in a session that both [Carlson's wife] Bobbie and I had with Rev. and Mrs. Junkin."[28]

Despite the missionaries' view of the reps as being "hostile" to the Christian program at Tunghai, Carlson depicts the reps as "more troubled and

---

28 Ellsworth Carlson, To Florence M. Fitch, 28 March 1957. (2 1/3-page letter.) Reports to the Trustees, 1956-58, #11, RG 15, Subgroup II, Series 7, Box 3, OCA. Interestingly, Carlson seems to have a change of heart after writing the first letter. In a brief letter written on April 22 (about a month after his first letter), he says that his emphasis on "the need to get someone [as a senior rep] 'fairly soon'" was a product of his "distress at the whole religious situation, and some uncertainty" about how to handle that situation. "Now that I'm rather confident that we should go ahead pretty much as at present so far as our attitude toward the reps' participation in religious activities are [sic] concerned, I'm not as concerned about having an older person around to handle that problem as I was." Ellsworth Carlson, To Florence M. Fitch, 22 April 1957. (1-page letter.) Reports to the Trustees, 1956-58, #11, RG 15, Subgroup II, Series 7, Box 3, OCA.

uncertain than anything else."[29] He expresses the view that the previous chaplain, who was more of an intellectual than Junkin, could have given "some sympathetic help to the reps in thinking through their religious problems," but feels Junkin could not do it. In this context, Carlson emphasizes the need for a senior Shansi rep to come from Oberlin, in order "to help cushion the impact of a youthful and not overly pious group of reps on a rather conservative missionary community."[30]

It should be noted that the religious issue was more of a problem in Tunghai's early years than later on, when Tunghai moved away from an American model of a small Christian college. However, it clearly caused some consternation to both the fundamentalists at Tunghai and to Carlson, who didn't write about the religious problem until he was away from Tunghai (in fact, he wrote from Manila) because, as he wrote, "I felt the need to make sure that emotional reactions were not having too much influence on my thinking and the need to put some perspective around the picture that I had been drawing."[31]

Another example of the conflict between more conservative missionaries and Oberlin is a 1960 letter from Tunghai President Wu Teh-yao to Ellsworth Carlson concerning the possible hiring of a former Shansi rep to be a "senior rep" that would be more steadily involved in the work of Tunghai and would provide the younger reps with guidance regarding their own intercultural exchange work. A sticking point about hiring this particular person was that his wife was a Unitarian. As Wu's letter to Carlson explains:

It is rather difficult to bridge the wide gap between the Unitarian view

---

29 Ellsworth Carlson, To Florence M. Fitch, 22 April 1957. (6-page letter.) Reports to the Trustees, 1956-58, #11, RG 15, Subgroup II, Series 7, Box 3, OCA.

30 Ibid.

31 Ibid.

and our Christian college understanding. We believe every person has a right to his own religious beliefs, but for leaders, such as the senior representative from Oberlin, we are concerned. Tunghai University, as you know, is under the auspices of union Christian work and we are aware of the necessity to share in several interpretations, but at the same time feel the great importance of maintaining a strong university, at all times keeping our purpose Christ-centric.[32]

The clarity of this message is complicated, however, by the presence of a handwritten note at the bottom of the typed letter. That note informs the reader that the above paragraph "is the reflection of the opinion of some of the Western faculty and staff members. <u>Chinese Christians do not make the distinction.</u>"[33] This handwritten note suggests that President Wu was not expressing his own beliefs about Unitarianism's incompatibility with the Christianity practiced at Tunghai. This did not go unnoticed by the Shansi Trustees. Indeed, in the minutes of an April 18, 1960 meeting of the OSMA executive committee, it is noted that the "hand-written P.S.... makes it pretty clear that the framing of the letter was done by Miss [Elsie] Priest rather than President Wu."[34]

These examples demonstrate how different views of Christianity between not only Chinese and Western Christians, but even within the Western Christian community (if it even could be called a community), complicated

---

32 Wu Teh-yao, To Ellsworth Carlson, 31 March 1960. Tunghai U. 1960-62, RG 15, Subgroup III, Series 3, Box 2, OCA.

33 Ibid.

34 O.S.M.A. Executive Committee Meeting, 18 April 1960. Executive Meeting Minutes, 1955-60, RG 15, Subgroup II, Series 1, Box 3, OCA. Elsie Priest, who served as Tunghai's Controller from 1955-1960, had also served at Ginling College and the University of Nanking. See William P. Fenn, *Ever New Horizons: The Story of the United Board for Christian Higher Education in Asia, 1922-1975* (New York: United Board for Christian Higher Education in Asia, 1980), p. 78, 98.

attempts to characterize Tunghai as a Christian college. Such attempts required the negotiation of a variety of traditions, including Christianity as it had developed in Taiwan, the Christianity of Chinese from the mainland, the fundamentalism of the Western missionary community at Tunghai, and the more social Christianity of Oberlin. While the OSMA archives provide little about the Taiwanese and Chinese traditions, they do provide insight into the latter two varieties.

Secularization of the OSMA

An understanding of the changing relationship of the OSMA to its Christian roots is also important to seeing how the Association operated in Taiwan. The records of the OSMA indicate that, contemporaneous with the "religious problem" at Tunghai, there was some movement by Oberlin students involved in Shansi to redefine the organization's mission so as to reduce its emphasis on Christianity. In the early years of the Shansi-Tunghai relationship, Shansi's Christian identity is strongly present in the discussions of the Trustees. The minutes of the Trustee meetings indicate that up until the mid-1960s, most meetings were opened with a prayer. Moreover, during the deliberative process that led to the decision to form a relationship with Tunghai University, the potential for fulfilling the Christian mission of the OSMA had been frequently referred to as an important consideration when making a decision. For instance, a committee report that was discussed at the 1954 Trustees Annual meeting lists as one of the committee's eight presuppositions that "we should seek to serve in a Christian school or college where the work done would be readily identified as an Oberlin-in-China project."[35] Later, an important report prepared in 1955 by OSMA Trustee

---

35 Committee on Future Policy (undated). Min. of Exec. Comm. and Board of Trustees, 1954, RG 15, Subgroup II,

Wynn Fairfield frequently references Shansi's Christian mission, and includes in a chart entitled "An Analytical Scoring of Proposals for Future Program on Certain Points" the criterion of "Christian Significance."[36]

Oberlin students at the time appeared less enthusiastic about Shansi's Christian mission. In June of 1952, the graduating senior members of the OSMA's Student Committee wrote a report to the Board of Trustees suggesting that many Oberlin students themselves disapproved of the missionary identity: "the trustees are probably aware that labeling our work as a 'Christian' project and, especially, working through a mission board, creates a negative reaction among a vocal group on campus who, at the same time, are certainly in favor of seeking international goodwill."[37] The Student Committee felt that many Oberlin students objected to the idea of financially supporting a Christian organization that was supposed to represent all of Oberlin. Subsequently, the Trustees and the Student Committee formed an ad-hoc joint committee to discuss the relationship of Shansi to Christianity. That committee was, however, unable to come up with a unified statement of what they felt that relationship should be and chose to present a multivocal report reflecting the committee members' fundamental differences.[38] An OSMA Trustee on that ad-hoc committee cited the Association's Charter and Regulations, which "state the purpose of the Association to be 'to teach and practice the principles of Christianity and in the furtherance of this purpose to carry on a system of schools.'" He went on to argue,

---

Series 2, Box 2, OCA.

36 Fairfield, "A Study of Opportunities," 43. Fairfield's report, which runs to almost 60 pages and covers future possibilities in seven countries in Asia, was commissioned by the Board of Trustees after the 1954 annual meeting and presented to the Board for discussion at the 1955 annual meeting.

37 "Report from the Graduating Members of the Student China Committee to the Trustees," (June 1952), Student Com. Min, 1945-68, RG 15, Subgroup II, Series 5, Box 4, OCA. The "mission board" referenced was the ABCFM.

38 Summary of the opinions of "the joint committee of trustees and Student Committee members which was set up to interpret the purpose of the Association and the relationship of the representatives to it." Undated. Student Com. Min, 1945-68, RG 15, Subgp II, Series 5, Box 4, OCA.

These purposes are good and as worthy today as when first conceived. The Association has accepted large sums of money, both permanent funds and funds for current use, from donors to aid in the carrying out of these purposes. Even though there were a desire on the part of the Association to alter its fundamental purpose it could not do so without forfeiting the right to hold and use these funds. Therefore, it would appear that the subject of the fundamental purpose and aim of the Association is not open for debate.[39]

This argument attempts to shut down debate by raising the specter of potential insolvency. It seems to have succeeded to some extent because among the Trustees, the issue of Shansi's Christian identity doesn't appear to come up in earnest again until 1972.

While Oberlin College became more secular and Oberlin reps began to represent that secularization, the Association remained, on paper at least, committed to principles of "Christian education." In 1972, however, an evaluation of Shansi's programs was carried out by Lawrence Buell (a former Princeton-in-Asia fellow at Tunghai and a Shansi Trustee); this evaluation formed the basis for a series of resolutions made by the Shansi Trustees at their 1972 annual meeting. He argues that references to Christianity in the Association's charter suggest a commitment to a particular religious "orthodoxy which relatively few people connected with Shansi over the past two decades have actually felt." In addition, he says, "the concept of Christian education carries an implication of moral superiority" which implied that Shansi's goal involved the uplifting of others rather than a "striving for a truly mutual 'respect and understanding,' as the charter elsewhere puts it."[40] While

---

39 Ibid.
40 Ibid., p. 3.

Buell recognizes the desire of some to retain the term "Christian education" in order to maintain a connection with Shansi's heritage, he concludes that the term can only result in a lot of people continuing to misunderstand Shansi's goals and identity.

As Buell expected, there was some hesitation about approving this recommendation. As the minutes of the 1972 OSMA Trustee meeting report, "There was expression of concern at dropping the phrase unless some other could be substituted which would indicate the motivation of those who founded the enterprise or would bridge our history in some way." One Trustee suggested "that in dropping the word 'Christian' the idea of service might be lost...."[41] This argument for keeping the phrase "Christian education" seems to rest on two basic assumptions: one, that the idea of service was important to Shansi's identity, and two, that the idea of service depended on a Christian orientation – that an idea (or ideal) of service was not possible without a Christian identity. Despite these concerns, however, Buell's recommendation was eventually accepted by the Trustees.

"Rep Letters" about Changing Taiwan

The OMSA records include a rich amount of material for scholars who are interested in how Taiwan's changing society appeared to Americans. Rep letters written back to the Oberlin community, rep-written articles published in the *Oberlin Review*, texts of speeches given to Oberlin students and faculty by returned reps, and final reports written by returned reps for review by the Shansi trustees are all full of fascinating observations, reactions, and analyses of the reps' experiences in Taiwan. Some of the rep letters have been collected

---

41 O.S.M.A. 1972 Annual Meeting, November 10-11, 1972. Minutes of Executive Committee, Board of Trustees. 1972, RG 15, Subgroup II, Series 1, Box 4, OCA.

in an anthology entitled *Something to Write Home About: An Anthology of Shansi Rep Letters 1955-1988*. However, one of the criteria for inclusion in this anthology was "long-term interest",[42] which means that while some of the letters in the anthology can provide readers with a sense of particular moments in Taiwan's postwar history, scholars who want more than a taste of the young Americans' views of changing Taiwan need to go to the archives.

Rep letters from Taiwan, of which there are approximately 140 in the archives, covered a wide variety of topics of interest to students of Taiwan history. To name a few: teaching and cultural differences between the US and Taiwan pertaining to education (not surprising, considering the reps were in Taiwan to teach), Taiwan's economy (including a letter from the 1950s about a visit to a sugar factory and a letter from the early 1960s about a department store in Kaohsiung), and problems of youth and gender relations (including a letter about budding feminism among female Tunghai students[43]). There are also two letters by different reps about President Chiang Kai-shek (one about seeing his train go by during a trip to the mountains and another about his funeral).

Early records regarding the presence of Shansi in Taiwan also include discussion of an experimental rep program at the Presbyterian Chang Jung Boys' School in Tainan. Two reps were sent there for a year to teach English. These reps then spent the second year of their two-year term at Tunghai. In their rep letters (written from Taiwan) and final reports to the Trustees (written upon their return to Oberlin), they demonstrated a great deal of sympathy for the students and teachers of Chang Jung, sympathy that probably grew out of the reps' progressive political leanings and their view of

---

42 "Introduction," *Something to Write Home About: An Anthology of Shansi Rep Letters 1951-1988* (Oberlin, OH: Oberlin Shansi Memorial Association, 2000), p. viii.

43 For more discussion of this letter, see my article, "Difficult Writing: Representation and Responsibility in Narratives of Cross-Cultural Encounters," *Intercultural Communication Studies*, 19, no. 3 (2010): 135-148.

the Taiwanese as being oppressed by the Mainlanders. The archives are useful for illustrating for scholars the ways in which young American college graduates would witness Taiwan less than a decade after the 2-28 Incident.

The economic and industrial development of Taiwan is one trend that is visible through the eyes of the Shansi reps. While letters about Taiwan's agriculture and about village life don't completely disappear in the 1970s, the industrialization of Taiwan can be seen in texts like Richard Smith's April 1970 letter (published in *Something to Write Home About*), which notes need for a hypothetical farmer to sell his land to industrial developers in order to be able to send his son to college.[44] Another letter, which discusses family planning, also hints at some of the results of Taiwan's urbanization. Some letters suggest the increasing presence of Western popular music and television programs in Taiwan.

Reading through these letters, one is struck by both the strong observational skills and the strong voices of many of their writers. At the same time, however, it is important to remember that these texts are representations of Taiwan by young Americans who were themselves struggling with their multiple roles as recent college graduates, college English teachers, representatives of the United States to the people of Taiwan, observers of Taiwan, and intermediaries between the people of two institutions: Tunghai University and Oberlin College.[45] As I have written elsewhere, these multiple roles – and the expectations that were part of these roles – could make the task of writing about Taiwan particularly challenging for the reps. Added to this pressure was the feeling some reps had that their writing should have an

---

44 Richard Smith, "Notes on the Land," in *Something to Write Home About*, p. 168.

45 For more on the effects of reps' multiple roles on their writing, see my paper, "'Other Moments' / Moments with Others: Acts of Cultural Translation by an Oberlin Rep in Taiwan, 1958-1959." *Globalization and Cultural Identity/ Translation International Conference*. Proc. of conference, 19 to 20 December 2008, Fo Guang University, Taiwan (Jiaoxi Taiwan: Fo Guang University, 2008), pp. 367-381.

"academic" quality and that anything they wrote – no matter how tentatively expressed – might be taken as established (and unchanging) reality.[46] As the introduction to *Something to Write Home About* suggests, "While [the letters] occasionally offer a novel insight into Asia, their primary charm is that they are reflections of bring young Americans going through the challenges of living and working in an Asian setting, discovering what it is like – at least temporarily – to call the other side of the world, 'home.'"[47]

The OSMA and US-Taiwan-China Relations

The changes in Taiwan that the reps were observing were also noticed by the Shansi Trustees and administration. In the end, the effects of those trends appear to have been part of the reason that Shansi eventually left Tunghai and Taiwan. At the time the decision was made to break off relations with Tunghai, Shansi cast around for other locations in Taiwan to establish a connection. What the organization found, however, was an island where it was hard to find a place to serve. In an article in the Nov., 1978 *OSMA Newsletter*, Shansi Program Planner Carl Jacobson wrote,

> After looking at a number of other institutions I realized... that the reasons for leaving Tunghai are not peculiar to Tunghai; that, in other words, the forces which have changed Tunghai from a small college with an atmosphere conducive to liberal thinking apply throughout Taiwan and are a part of the economic and political reality of the island. Tunghai, like all of the institutions in Taiwan, is being squeezed in a double bind. First, a small student body cannot support

---

46 Jonathan Benda, "Difficult Writing," p. 138.

47 "Introduction," *Something to Write Home About*, p. viii.

a college. Second, times are such that no value is assigned to a liberal arts program. Professional training with an eye to qualifying students for specific careers rules the day and is the hallmark of the successful private schools. Political pressures from the government to curtail critical thinking are felt, even in the classroom at Tunghai. Alexa Hand, now a newly returned rep from Tunghai, had to confront this very issue head-on last year in a newspaper discussion class.[48]

Jacobson's comments suggest that the effects of development in Taiwan, combined with political repression, made forming an association with any universities in Taiwan undesirable. At the same time, however, the records of the OSMA raise other factors that led the organization to its decision to leave. By the end of the 1970s, the OSMA had decided to phase out relations with Tunghai University and had begun to reopen contact with the PRC in hopes of establishing a presence there as China opened up to the West. These actions took place in the contexts of the political changes in the US (and at Oberlin) and Asia brought on by the Vietnam war. By 1979, when the last Shansi rep left Tunghai University, relations between the United States and East Asia were shaken by profound changes brought on by U.S. involvement in the Vietnam war.

However, when the OSMA decided to end its connection to Tunghai, Executive Secretary Margaret Leonard phrased the decision in a letter to Tunghai Foreign Language and Literature Department chairman Ivor Shepherd as the result of the changes at Tunghai: she wrote, "Tunghai isn't what it used to be: a smallish residential university. With the huge increase in students and with over thirty westerners in the English department the reps

---

48 Carl Jacobson, "What on Earth is Shansi Doing?" *Oberlin Shansi Memorial Association Newsletter* 53 (November 1978): 3. Oberlin Shansi Memorial Association Newsletter, 1970- , RG 15, Subgroup V, Series 1, Box 1.

have no Shansi or Oberlin [identity] and they have to go off campus to find student friends, etc. In general, reps aren't having as satisfying experience as reps used to have."[49] The issue of Shansi identity raised by Leonard echoes throughout the meeting minutes and other records related to Shansi's decision to leave.

In spite of the Trustees' decision to eliminate references to Christianity in the OSMA Charter and to emphasize reciprocity between cultures over service to Asia, the OSMA records during the 1970s – in particular the minutes of the Trustees and the Executive Committee – demonstrate a continued concern for Shansi's identity as a Christian service organization. Meeting minutes often portray Trustees who are concerned with Shansi's "identity" at Tunghai. As Tunghai (and the English Department where the Shansi reps taught) grew in size, some in the OSMA felt Shansi was playing less of a major role at Tunghai than it used to. There was a sense that Tunghai didn't "need" Shansi as much as it had in the past.[50] Shansi identity had been considered an important factor in the decision to establish relations with Tunghai in 1955 and it appears again in the last years of that relationship. Shansi identity at Tunghai was clearly tied to the emphasis on Shansi as a benefactor: in arguing for the need for Shansi to have identity at Tunghai, one OSMA Trustee argued that it was "natural for us [Shansi] to want identity." Other Trustees are reported as giving reasons why Shansi should want identity: "Mr. Holbrook commented that Shansi is giving Tunghai more than reps. It has given buildings, pianos, faculty research grants. What other organization does that? Princeton merely places people in jobs in Asia."[51]

---

49 Margaret H. Leonard, to Mr. Ivor Shepherd, 15 Dec. 1977. Tunghai University, 1977-80, RG 15, Subgroup III, Series 3, Box 2, OCA.

50 In his response to an earlier version of this paper, Professor Ku Hung-ting of Tunghai University argued that Taiwan's economic development and the increasing sense of Tunghai's identity as a Chinese university also contributed to the feeling that Tunghai didn't need Shansi's help as much as it used to.

51 O.S.M.A. Executive Committee Meeting, March 26, 1974. Minutes, 1974, RG 15, Subgroup II, Series 1, Box 4,

Shansi's "identity" at Tunghai, then, seems to have been seen by Trustees mainly in terms of recognition for its contributions to the school. This view of the relationship of Shansi to Tunghai seems to have been shared by some at Tunghai: in responding to a 1975 questionnaire distributed among Tunghai administration, faculty, and students, the president of Tunghai expressed appreciation for what Shansi had done for the school. Moreover, a professor named Y. P. Mei (Mei Yi-pao) wrote the following in his response to the questionnaire, in regards to the "Promotion of the Oberlin-Shansi ideal":

> I was flabbergasted when I found out how little people at Tunghai knew or cared about Oberlin and Oberlin-Shansi. A young colleague of mine in the humanities program is a Tunghai graduate of 5-6 years' vintage. When I spoke to him briefly about Oberlin-Shansi and Oberlin, he was much excited and enthused, partly because he had never heard about either except in name. He did not know even what "Ming-Hsien" Hall, the hall OSM built for Tunghai, meant and I had to tell him that it meant "Remember Martyrs" and who some of the martyrs were.[52]

Mei's argument about Shansi's identity at Tunghai is clearly rooted in the past, referencing the "Martyrs" in the name of the Ming Hsien T'ang in a way that would probably make Wynn Fairfield, who suggested the name for the building, quite proud. When Fairfield suggested "Ming Hsien T'ang" for the building, he argued that it would cause people to think about martyrs and

---

OCA.

52 Y. P. Mei, to Halsey Beemer, July 11, 1975. Tunghai – Eval. of Shansi, 1975, RG 15, Subgp III, Series 3, Box 2, OCA. In his response to an earlier version of this paper, Professor Ku Hung-ting also noted that when he was a student at Tunghai, he and his classmates did not know anything about Oberlin Shansi or what the name "Ming Hsien" referred to.

might lead to people at Tunghai asking about Shansi's missionary past.[53] Like Fairfield, Mei connects Oberlin and Oberlin-Shansi to Tunghai by invoking Shansi's past in China and frames Shansi's identity in terms of Christian service and martyrdom.

Mei goes on to argue that "more need[s] to be done about 'selling' Oberlin-Shansi and its history and ideals. Since the Tunghai administration is so inert, the 'Reps' are the natural ones to take up the burden. The spirit of the OSM Assoc behind its projects and activities, is somet[h]ing beautiful to hear. To do his whole job, the 'Rep' should impart and impress some of that spirit on the Tunghai student body. It is good education."[54] However, it would probably have made the reps quite uncomfortable if they had been asked to be spokespeople for the "old" Shansi spirit. The moment for having reps talk about Shansi and Oberlin to Tunghai students or for having assemblies about Shansi was long past. For one thing, the other instructors at Tunghai wouldn't have been happy to listen to the reps 'brag' about Shansi. For another, the reps themselves wouldn't have been comfortable with such an assignment. Reps would be unlikely proselytizers of such outdated notions of Shansi's mission as embodied in the "Shansi spirit."

At the same time that some Trustees were criticizing Tunghai University in terms that suggested their emphasis was on service, however, Shansi was trying to downplay that very ideal in favor of a focus on reciprocity. Lawrence Buell's 1972 evaluation of Shansi itself grew out of changes that were taking place at Oberlin, affecting both the Shansi program in general and the Shansi reps in particular. Part of the impetus for a reevaluation of Shansi came out of the kind of discourse regarding Shansi that was published in articles in the student newspaper, the *Oberlin Review*. As Cynthia Elek, the writer of one

---

53 See "Recommendations of the Executive Committee With Respect to the Future Work of the Association." Minutes of Executive Committee and Board of Trustees, 1956, RG 15, Subgroup II, Series 2, Box 3, OCA.

54 Y. P. Mei, to Halsey L. Beemer, Jr.

1971 article about Shansi, asked, should the Shansi program "become more of an Asian-expert training ground with service only on the side, or should it maintain its practice of sending English teachers in the older tradition?"[55]

Even more pointed than Elek's question were the comments in a letter by J. Clayton Miller, a former rep to China from 1930-1932, that responded to Elek's article.[56] After criticizing the "cultural imperialism" of the program in its past and present form and advocating a more research- (or learning-) oriented rep program, he writes about Taiwan: "If the reports as to the police-state character of the Generalissimo's [President Chiang Kai-shek's] government are correct, the question then may be raised as to whether Oberlin wishes to be identified further with that government or not. This decision of course carries with it perforce how Oberlin wishes to be related to the indigenous Formosans."[57]

Miller's perspective raised the question of how and whether the OSMA should relate to the martial law government in Taiwan, even as the United States government was deliberating the same question. This was no coincidence; Elek's article quoted Taiwan reps Rick and Elizabeth Smith as arguing that the reps were "'playing out American foreign policy in a very small role.'" Some at Oberlin were quite vocal that Shansi should not relate to the government of Taiwan at all. For instance, a 1967 article in the *Review* on the Oberlin Student Senate's decision to allocate funds to Shansi mentioned a student at the Senate meeting who "questioned Shansi support of Tunghai University in [Taiwan]. 'I suggest that the Senate not send money to this university,' he said. 'I certainly don't want to support the education of people

---

55 Cynthia Elek, "Fuller Trip Highlights Need for Shansi Change," *Oberlin Review*, January 15, 1971.

56 J. Clayton Miller, "Miller Mulls Shansi; Imperialists All?" [Letter to the editor.] *Oberlin Review*, February 5, 1971. "Clipbook V", RG 15, Subgroup V, Series 2, Box 4, OCA.

57 By "indigenous Formosans" Miller is probably not referring specifically to the Aborigines in Taiwan.

who are going to support Chiang's plans to invade mainland China.'"[58] The Student Senate's Financial Committee decided in the end to allocate $900 to Shansi, but this quoted student was not the only person expressing such a negative opinion of Chiang's government. In fact, at the 1970 Trustee meeting it was suggested that members of the Shansi Student Committee "talk with [Oberlin] student leaders, like Senate members, Review staff, and students who are hostile to Chiang."[59] And, of course, there was J. Clayton Miller's letter, which expressed a distinct hostility to the Chiang government.

J. Clayton Miller's letter also answers Elek's article by arguing for changing the rep program into a more study-oriented one, a point which is significant because it follows the trend of pairing anti-imperialist arguments with the image of Asia as a site for research or learning. This trend is also visible in the minutes of the 1970 annual Trustee meeting, where Shansi Student Committee co-chairman (and future Shansi rep to Taiwan) Tim Liang reported on "some student criticism of our working in Taiwan and to the changing needs and desires of American students. They would be more interested in study fellowships and teaching in other fields than English."[60] Critiques of imperialistic tendencies or of Shansi's involvement with the oppressive government in Taiwan and arguments for study fellowships typically went together in discussions about the future of Shansi. While they would appear to be two different issues, one dealing with what is arguably a matter of ethics and the other dealing with a matter of student motivation or

---

58 Keith Ervin, "Senate Allots Funds, Delays Two Decisions." *Oberlin Review* Mar. 21, 1967. "Clipbooks V", RG 15, Subgroup V, Series 2, Box 4, OCA.
Traditionally the reps had been paid through allocations from the Oberlin Student Activity Fee; however, for several reasons, over time the allocation was reduced until it was eliminated entirely. Carlson refers to a "gradual phasing out of support from the student activity fee [which] made it necessary for the Association to pick up full responsibility for financing the rep program...." (Carlson, *Oberlin in Asia*, p. 51.)

59 O.S.M.A. 1970 Annual Meeting, November 7, 1970. Minutes of Executive Committee, Board of Trustees. 1970, RG 15, Subgroup II, Series 1, Box 4, OCA.

60 Ibid.

interest, there was some attempt to make both matters issues of Shansi's proper responsibilities, both to Asia and to Oberlin.

Reps themselves had strong views about what the rep program should or should not be. In 1971, Rick and Elizabeth Smith criticized the Taiwan program for being "'antiquated' in its missionary overtones."[61] In a report presented to the Executive Committee in 1976, Shansi Program Planner Carl Jacobson noted that "among potential reps and in the criticism of returned reps notable is an uneasiness about the idea of 'service' and all of its paternalistic overtones. This clings to us despite the fact that the two brochures we use now and the statement which prefaces the 1972 resolutions all address the issue."[62]

Criticisms of Shansi's role in Taiwan and at Tunghai were contemporaneous with the changing stance of the US toward Taiwan and China. In the early 1970s, the future of the Shansi-Tunghai connection was linked to the possibility of a relationship with China. The "Resolutions Adopted by the Board of Trustees of the Oberlin Shansi Memorial Association" from November 1972 (and the Buell report and the Trustee meeting discussion on which the resolutions were based) cite an agreement among Trustees for Shansi to stay at Tunghai "at least for the present, but keeping its eye for the future on possible opportunities on the mainland. (This does not of course mean that Shansi should terminate it[s] Taiwan affiliation precipitously if an opportunity on the mainland arises; any future changes in the China program should be made very carefully and responsibly.)"[63] While the Trustees hasten to add that the Tunghai connection wouldn't be cut off "precipitously," the agreement does appear to signal that the OSMA's

---

61 The Smiths are quoted in Elek's article. Elek, "Fuller Trip Highlights Need for Shansi Change."

62 Report from Carl Jacobson, Shansi Program Planner, October 1976, Minutes of Executive Committee, Board of Trustees. 1976, RG 15, Subgroup II, Series 1, Box 5, OCA.

63 "Resolutions Adopted by the Board of Trustees of the Oberlin Shansi Memorial Association."

association with Taiwan and its potential relationship with China are mutually exclusive.

It is notable that this option was being discussed around the time that U.S. President Nixon had gone to China (February 1972), so such possible opportunities for exchange with China were being raised in the expectation that China would soon be "opening up" to the U.S. The idea of future opportunities in China and their impact on relations with Taiwan should be understood in light of Nixon's visit to China and of the Shanghai Communiqué of February 28, 1972.[64] In that document, the U.S., while distancing itself from an outright declaration of agreement with the PRC regarding Taiwan's belonging to (the People's Republic of) China, basically commits itself in the long run to removing its military forces from Taiwan in order to facilitate a peaceful resolution of the "Taiwan question." Shansi, "playing out American foreign policy in a very small role," was also moved to consider how its relationship to Taiwan would influence its possible connections to China – or rather, how its possible connections to China would influence its relationship to Taiwan.

As the possibility for normalization of relations with the PRC became more and more real, the desire to work out academic connections with China also led to a heating up of activity among academic exchange organizations such as the Committee on Scholarly Communication with the People's Republic of China. In the case of Oberlin, Shansi's association with Tunghai again needed to be considered in light of this academic "ping pong diplomacy." A motion made in a report from a subcommittee regarding relations with China (date-stamped Nov. 8, 1976, Office of the Provost) suggests the kind of thinking going into the process:

---

64 "Joint Communiqué of the United States of America and the People's Republic of China," February 28, 1972. Taiwan Documents Project, http://www.taiwandocuments.org/ communique01.htm (accessed October 15, 2009).

Motion #5 – For the time being the Association assumes that consideration of the possibility of an exchange with the PRC does not affect our present program at Tunghai University in Taiwan.

Comment: The simple fact is that we do not know how a possible exchange with the PRC would affect, or be affected by, the Tunghai connection. It would seem to follow that until we find out there is not much point to jumping to a conclusion. There would appear to be two or more conceivable outcomes to the Taiwan "problem." (1) As [part] of an agreement to normalize relations with the PRC, the U.S. might simply write off Taiwan, by agreeing that it is part of China and by terminating separate relations with it. At least in the long run our relationship with Tunghai would then be terminated by action of governments, whether Shansi chose to do so or not. Conceivably in the short-run, prior to the time when the PRC established effective [control] over Taiwan, some interim relationship with Tunghai might be maintained, but this would not appear to be likely. (2) As part of an agreement to normalize relations the U.S. and the PRC might negotiate some special arrangements with respect to Taiwan. On occasion the Chinese have spoken approvingly of the "Japanese model," referring to the fact that the Japanese broke diplomatic, military, and treaty relations with Taiwan but continued economic and cultural relations. The "Japanese model" seems to assume some measure of Taiwanese "autonomy" or separation from the Chinese mainstream. Under a Japanese model we might possibly have an exchange with the PRC and maintain a Tunghai connection. But even with such a model, we might find that we couldn't both have our cake and eat it. But we come back to the main point that is that we don't know what the options will be, and until we find out we should hang on at Taiwan. (p. 3)[65]

While the motion concludes that the program at Tunghai is not affected by the possible relationship with China, the key phrase in the motion is the "For the time being" that begins the motion. As with the earlier Recommendation, time plays an important role in the statement of commitment to Taiwan. "For the time being" immediately signals a recognition that at some point in the future the relationship with Tunghai will probably be affected by a future exchange with China. The "Comment" section ends with the image of "hang[ing] on at Taiwan" as Shansi waits for a clearer idea about what China will do. ("Hang on" is significant, too, for the image it presents of a temporary connection that might be cut at any time.) This clearly puts the PRC in an agentive position in this process. As with its relationship with the United States, Taiwan's relationship with Oberlin Shansi is controlled by the decisions that China makes.

In the end, whether it was due to a loss of Shansi "identity" at Tunghai or to the possibility of rekindling relations with China, the OSMA Trustees voted in November 1977 to phase out relations with Tunghai. The Shansi-Tunghai relationship operated at many levels. At one level, it was a microcosm of U.S. Cold-War-to-Vietnam-era foreign policy. But on another level, it was more than that, and to try to map the decisions of the Shansi Trustees directly onto the foreign policy decisions of the U.S. government is an oversimplification of the complex organizational decisions of the OSMA. The decision, as I have tried to explain here, needs also to be understood in the contexts of the secularization of Oberlin's and Shansi's missions; the professionalization of Oberlin's interest in Asia; and the post-Vietnam rhetoric

---

65 "Report of the sub-committee of the Executive Committee established (pursuant to a motion passed at the September 17, 1976 meeting of the Executive Committee) to explore the possibilities for and issues related to the establishment of an exchange with the People's Republic of China." 1976, RG 15, Subgroup II, Series 2, Box 5, OCA.

of reciprocity that influenced Shansi's relationship with Asia, complicating the service motive of the past.

Conclusion

The archives of the OSMA are unique in their presentation of the work of an organization that transitioned from a focus on Christian mission work in Asia to one of a secular educational relationship with its Asian counterparts. Of particular interest to scholars of Taiwan church history is how Shansi's work with Tunghai complicates the image of Western missions work in Taiwan by introducing an organization that itself was in flux even as it operated with a changing institution (Tunghai) in a changing country (Taiwan). Tunghai and Shansi both became more secular institutions as a result of different pressures that they experienced in martial law Taiwan and in the increasingly secular atmosphere of Oberlin College. The OSMA archives are valuable for the amount of detail they provide the researcher about the operations of Shansi, both at its home base in Oberlin College and on the campus of its partner for over two decades, Tunghai University.

Researchers willing to seek out and gain the permission of former Oberlin reps will also find valuable resources in the reps' letters to the Oberlin campus, their more personal letters to people at Oberlin, and in their final reports to the Shansi Trustees. These records have many stories to tell about how young Americans confronted the challenges of living in and trying to understand another culture. The reps' insights into their experiences of Taiwan, like much of the Shansi collection's records about OSMA work in Taiwan, are largely unexplored and deserve attention.

【三・教會出版資料論析】

The Japanese Narrative on Taiwan Church History during the Japanese Colonial Period as Revealed by Japanese Church Periodicals

Yuki Takai-Heller

Research Fellow, Meijigakuin University

Abstract

The primary interest of the articles about Taiwan that appeared in the various news periodicals of Japanese church denominations during the Japanese colonial era was Japanese churches and their activities in Taiwan, rather than the Taiwanese people or Taiwanese Christians. However, through these articles one can also observe some interesting cross-cultural aspects about Taiwanese churches and Taiwanese Christians, especially where there were connections between Japanese and Taiwanese Christians. Based on a list of Taiwan-related articles that appeared in eight major church news periodicals published in Japan between 1895 and 1942, this paper aims to analyze the general tendencies of those articles according to the different periods, and to explore how such a Japanese Christian narrative might contribute to the present historiography of Christianity in Taiwan.

Keywords: Japanese church periodicals, Taiwan church history, *Fukuin Shinpo*, narrative, historiography

Introduction

The history of Japanese churches in Taiwan during Japanese colonial rule had not been thoroughly investigated until I wrote about it in Takai-Heller (2003).[1] That the Japanese churches in Taiwan were the churches of the colonizers made the topic rather sensitive; and partly because of this, the existence of the individual Japanese churches in Taiwan, which once existed but now are no more, had been left out of the Japanese and Taiwanese historiographies of churches. The histories of these churches were about to fade away with the passing away of those who were once members of these churches.[2]

In addition to the above, the lack of historical material was a significant factor why these Japanese churches did not attract attention and were being forgotten. As I searched for primary sources, I did come across important printed materials such as *Taiwan Kirisuto Kyoho* 台湾基督教会報, weekly periodicals issued by the *Taihoku Nihon Kirisuto Kyokai* 台北日本基督教会, and *Taiwan Seinen* 台湾青年, monthly periodicals issued by the Taiwan YMCA run by Japanese Christians.[3] While these periodicals did provide detailed information about the activities of Japanese Christians in Taihoku, many issues were missing from both periodicals.[4] Other materials, such as church minutes or lists of church members, remained only sporadically

---

1 Yuki Takai-Heller, *Nihon Tochi-ka Taiwan ni Okeru Nihonjin Protestant Kyokai-shi Kenkyuu* 日本統治下台湾における プロテスタント教会史研究(1895-1945) Vol. I: Main Text & Vol. II: Supplementary Materials, unpublished PhD dissertation, International Christian University (2003).

2 Surprisingly, there were only two published histories of individual Japanese churches; *Taihoku Nihon Kirisuto Kyokai Shoshi, Kenchiku Koji Hokokusho, Kaido Kenchiku Hokokusho* 台北日本基督教会小史・建築工事報告書・会堂建築費報告書 (1916); and *Taihoku Nhion Kumiai Kirisuto Kyokai 20 Nenshi* 台北組合基督教会二十年史 (1932).

3 *Taihoku Nihon Kirisuto Kyokai* was established in November 1896, the Taiwan YMCA in 1898. Note that *Taiwan Seinen* issued by the Taiwan YMCA had no connection with *The Tai oan chheng lian* 台湾青年issued in Japan by Shinminkai 新民會.

4 See Appendix A. for the list of extant issues of news periodicals issued by Japanese churches or Christian movements in Taiwan during the colonial period.

available, either kept by Taiwanese churches that were once Japanese churches, or by individuals.

In order to fill in this hole and reconstruct histories of the thirty or more Japanese churches from scratch, a kind of base material that would cover the entire colonial period, as well as all denominations of Japanese churches that existed in Taiwan, was going to be necessary. That was when I turned my attention to the news periodicals of Japanese church denominations, which were being published weekly, bi-weekly, or monthly in Japan proper. These periodicals are now almost all on microfilm,[5] and the indexes and titles of the periodicals published by the mainline churches (Presbyterian, Congregational, Anglican, and Methodist) have been compiled and published in ten volumes.[6] These church news periodicals carried reports and essays written by Japanese Christians who lived in or travelled to Taiwan, and proved to be the most consistent source of information for reconstructing the history of Japanese churches in Taiwan. Lists of Taiwan-related articles, reports, or notes (hereafter "articles")[7] that appeared in these news periodicals are included in the second volume of my dissertation, which is downloadable.[8] Although these Taiwan-related articles were primarily about the progress of Japanese church work in Taiwan, quite a few articles actually dealt with, or referred to Christianity in Taiwan in general, as well as the relationship between Japanese and Taiwanese Christians. The purpose of this paper is to analyze the tendencies of these articles that appeared in the news periodicals of Japanese church denominations according to the different

---

5 *Kindai Nihon Kirisutokyo Shinbun Shusei* 近代日本キリスト教新聞集成, 1875-1945, Nihon Tosho Center. The periodicals issued by the Japan Salvation Army is not included here.

6 *Kirisutokyo Shinbun Kiji Soran* キリスト教新聞記事総覧, vols. 1-10 (Nihon Tosho Center, 1996).

7 Note that the lengths of these articles, reports, and notes vary between a few lines to a few pages.

8 https://box.yahoo.co.jp/guest/viewer?sid=box-l-qp3okhm6hoqeqxryxe4pywifmu1001&uniqid=92ce7d99-9e89-48d6-a5ce-588430ab1db1&viewtype=detail (volume II); https://box.yahoo.co.jp/guest/ viewer?sid=box-l-qp3okhm-6hoqeqxryxe4pywifmu-1001&uniqid=ecf3bad6-66cc-4637-982d-993dca3b6ce4&viewtype=detail (volume I).

periods, and to present my view on how to utilize effectively those articles for the study of the history of Christianity in Taiwan.

Characteristics of Japanese church periodicals

When Western Protestant missionaries first entered Japan in the late 1850s, they engaged in educational work, as the propagation of Christian faith was still forbidden. Japan at the time was striving to join the West by adapting herself furiously to Western civilization, while barricading against the advance of Christianity among her peoples. Varying responses to Christian faith among the elites in the early Meiji era suggest Japan's dilemma between the desire for a state religion that would serve as a "spiritual backbone" to accompany the newly adopted modern civilization and resistance against the foreign takeover of the Japanese mind and spirit through Christian influence. Creation of Tenno-sei 天皇制 (the Japanese Emperor system), as a "pseudo-religion" that was Japanese in spirit but had the appearance of modern civilization, was the Japanese answer to this dilemma. Tenno-sei also worked as a spiritual device that would convince people to accept the tremendous changes that was being caused by the emergent "conversion" to Western civilization.[9]

Whereas Japan as a whole effectively avoided Christianity by creating a "pseudo-religion", some of the ex-Samurai (warrior) elites accepted Christian faith through the educational work of the above-mentioned missionaries. For these first generation Christians, Christianity was primarily a religion of "civilization." Being as nationalistic and progressive as those who rejected Christianity, they believed that Christianity would lead their country to the

---

9 Komagome Takeshi, "'Bunmei' no Chitsujo to Misshon: Ingurando Choro Kyokai to 19 seiki no Buriten, Chugoku, Nihon" 「文明」の秩序とミッション：イングランド長老教会と19世紀のブリテン・中国・日本, *Nenpo Kindai Nihon Kenkyu* 19 (Yamakawa Shuppan, 1997), pp. 1-43.

true state of civilization. Naturally, they shared such beliefs as Japan having a "civilizing mission" toward Taiwan and the rest of Asia, which they perceived as still "barbarous."

Shrouded in the above background, it was in 1875 in Osaka, that the first Christian weekly newspaper in Japan was published. By the 1890s all major church denominations in Japan were publishing their own periodicals.[10] Most of these periodicals, reflecting the mentality of Japanese Christians at the time, were highly nationalistic and progressive. They aimed chiefly at exchanging views among Japanese Christians, enlightening Japanese culture, and propagating the Christian faith. Sharing reports on evangelical progress was also an important task.[11] However, by the 1910s, they were basically circulated only among members of their respective churches, functioning primarily as "in-church" newspapers.[12]

Fukuin Shinpo 福音新報, which was started by Uemura Masahisa 植村正久 of *Nihon Kirisuto Kyokai* 日本基督教会, carried the largest volume of articles related to Taiwan.[13] This was owing to the fact that *Nihon Kirisuto Kyokai* shared the same Reformed and Presbyterian tradition as the missions and churches in Taiwan that were dominated by the Presbyterians at the time, which is likely to have strengthened *Nihon Kirisuto Kyokai's* sense of mission for Taiwan. *Nihon Kirisuto Kyokai* eventually became the largest Japanese church denomination in Taiwan, having established churches and evangelical stations in all major cities in the colonial Taiwan. *Nihon Kirisuto Kyokai* often received help from Taiwanese churches and Christians, as well as Western

---

10 See Appendix B for the list of titles of the news periodicals and the approximate numbers of Taiwan-related articles.

11 "Fukuin shuho no hakkan ni tuski ichigen su 福音週報の発刊につき一言す." *Fukushin Shuho* 1 (Mar. 14, 1890), cited in Yosuke Nirei, "Toward a Modern Belief," *Japanese Journal of Religious Studies* 160, 2007. "Kirisutokyo Sekai 基督教世界," *Nihon Kirisutokyo Rekishi Daijiten* (Kyobunkwan, 1988).

12 "Christian Literature in the East: I. Japan." *International Review of Missions* (1913), pp. 690-701.

13 As shown in Appendix B, there were actually a larger number of articles carried in Anglican periodicals, but far longer articles were carried in *Fukuin Shinpo*.

missionaries, in the process of starting out their churches in Taiwan. *Nihon Kirisuto Kyokai* in Taiwan also explored the possibilities of establishing a formal alliance with the Taiwanese Presbyterian Church – a sentiment never shared by the Taiwanese side. "Union" between the Japanese and Taiwanese churches was only realized, in an unfortunate way, when all churches in Taiwan were forced to join *Nihon Kirisuto-kyo Taiwan Kyodan* 日本基督教台湾教団 in 1944 under the leadership of the Japanese church leaders in Taiwan who tried to "protect" Taiwanese churches from being crushed by the Japanese military government.[14]

The second largest Japanese church denomination in Taiwan was *Nippon Seikwokai* 日本聖公会, the Anglican Church in Japan.[15] Their weekly paper, *Kirisuto-kyo Shuho* 基督教週報 (later *Kyokai Hyoron* 教会評論) carried the largest numbers of articles relating to Taiwan among all the periodicals issued by Churches in Japan. Their monthly papers *Nichiyo Soshi* 日曜叢誌 and *Tokyo Kyoho* 東京教報 also carried a significant numbers of Taiwan-related articles. As Japanese Anglicans had struggled with Western missionaries' dominating the allocation of mission fields within Japan proper, they had high hopes for Taiwan, which they considered to be the first "mission field" of the *Nippon Seikwokai*, where they would undertake evangelical work independent from Western missionaries. However, their work met with many difficulties in Taiwan, partly because they received no support from the Western missionaries nor the local Christians or churches. The Presbyterian

---

14 Yuki Takai-Heller, "Nihon Tochi-ka Taiwan ni okeru Protestant Kyokai no 'Godo' Mondai: 1930 nendai oyobi 1940 nendai wo chuushin ni日本統治下台湾における台日プロテスタント教会の「合同」問題――一九三〇年代および一九四〇年代を中心に一," *The Journal of History of Christianity* (The Society of Historical Studies of Christianity, Japan, 2005), pp. 59, 109-141.

15 Of special note is women's contribution to Anglican work in Taiwan. *Nippon Seikokwai Fujin Dendoh Hojokai* 日本聖公会婦人伝道補助会 raised funds for work in Taiwan, Korea, and Manchuria, and sent out female missionaries. Their annual report, available for read in the Province Office of Nippon Seikwokai日本聖公会管区事務所 in Tokyo, is an excellent source for the history of Japanese Anglican work in Taiwan.

missionaries, highly skeptical of the Anglican "invasion" into work among the Taiwanese, distanced themselves from the Japanese Anglicans. With no local Christian support or enough financial resource from their home church, they had no choice but to limit their work solely to the Japanese. Naturally, their reports contained little reference to Taiwanese churches or Christians, in contrast to the reports carried in *Fukuin Shinpo*.

Nihon Kumiai Kirisuto Kyokai 日本組合基督教会 established their first church in Taiwan in 1912. This remained their only church in Taiwan except a small gathering of Taiwanese Christians that was established as a church in connection with the *Kumiai* Church in 1937. The reports from the *Kumiai* churches in Taiwan were carried mainly in *Kirisuto-kyo Sekai* 基督教世界 (later, *Kirisuto-kyo Shinbun* 基督教新聞). One of the characteristics of the Japanese Christians in *Kumiai* churches in Taiwan was their strong sentiment for the Taiwanese people, especially young people. Meetings of Taiwanese students were held regularly at *Kumiai* church in Taihoku. Many were active in the YMCA, where often both Japanese and Taiwanese students were involved. Ministers and leaders of the *Kumiai* churches often possessed friendly relationships with Taiwanese Christians and Western missionaries on personal levels, though not on an organizational level.

Nihon Mesojisuto Kyokai 日本メソヂスト教会, the Methodists, were the last among the mainline churches in Japan to start work in Taiwan. When they established churches in Taihoku in 1932 and Tainan in 1934, they were highly conscious of establishing *naitai yuwa* 内台融和 churches where Japanese and Taiwanese Christians would merge and cooperate. Their reports were carried in *Gokyo* 護教（later, *Kyokai Jiho* 教界時報, *Nihon Mesojisuto Shinbun* 日本メソヂスト新聞, or *Nihon Kirisuto-kyo Shinbun* 日本基督教新聞）．

In contrast to these four mainline churches which made little impact among the Taiwanese, the work of *Nihon Holiness Kyokai* 日本ホーリネス

教会, the Japanese Holiness Church, advanced rapidly in Taiwan both among the Japanese and Taiwanese in the 1920s and 1930s, often "poaching" Christians from existing churches. Reports about the evangelical work of Japanese Holiness churches in Taiwan were carried in *Hono no Shita* 焔の舌 (later, *Kiyome no Tomo* 聖潔の友 or きよめの友, then *Reiko* 霊光). These periodicals are the most essential historical source for the history of the Taiwanese Holiness Church, as all church documents and records were confiscated in 1942 together with church property when the Japanese government forced all Holiness churches to dissolve.

Nihon Kyuseigun 日本救世軍 (the Japan Salvation Army) issued a bi-weekly paper titled *Toki no Koye* ときの声 (later, *Nihon Kyuseigun Shinbun* 日本救世軍新聞, *Asa no Hikari* 朝の光).[16] Their work in Taiwan was launched shortly after the Japanese Holiness Church. Though the Japan Salvation Army also made some impact among the Taiwanese through their social work as well as their cooperation with the colonial government such as promoting the use of Japanese language among the Taiwanese, it was not the equivalent of the Holiness church.

Japanese narrative of Taiwan and Christianity in Taiwan – Analysis of the articles that appeared in *Fukuin Shinpo*

As was typical in Japan at the time, news periodicals of Japanese church denominations at the end of the 19th century exhibited a general inclination toward progress, enlightenment, and modern Western civilization, coupled with a strong sense of nationalism and self-identity that wavered between a sense of inferiority toward the West and superiority toward the East.

---

16 *Toki no Koe* is not on microfilm, but all back numbers are kept compiled in Yamamuro Gunpei Kinen Kyuseigun Shiryokan 山室軍平記念歴史資料館 in Tokyo.

Naturally, the narrative on Taiwan found in these Japanese church periodicals reflected these tendencies, but the articles reveal that the Christian nature of the periodicals made the narrative slightly different from that of secular Japan. For instance, there seemed to be an acute awareness that the Japanese in Taiwan were the first to have to be civilized as they were shamelessly acting like "barbarians". On the other hand, in the eyes of the Japanese authors, the Taiwanese churches seemed to be having more "success" than the Japanese churches, which might have made the Japanese feel that Taiwan was in one sense a more "Christianized," if not a more "civilized," region than Japan. The narrative changed over time, reflecting the changes in the times and in the relationship between the Japanese and Taiwanese Christians.

Below is an analysis of *Fukuin Shinpo*, the articles of which most clearly reveal the state of contact between (mainline) Japanese churches and the Presbyterian churches in Taiwan.

The Beginning (1895-1910)

Following Taiwan's cession to Japan in 1895, Japan subjugated Taiwan by military force. Subsequently, a large number of Japanese emigrated to Taiwan. Surprisingly, there were quite a large number of Japanese Christians, both among the soldiers who participated in the military subjugation and among the civilians who emigrated. Filled with a sense of "civilizing mission," Japanese Christians sought contact with Western missionaries and local churches, and wrote about the encounters in reports sent to their churches back home in Japan. Reports by the three Christian *jugun imonshi* 従軍慰問師 (Japanese pastors dispatched from churches in Japan proper to visit and minister to Japanese soldiers) who were in Taiwan, are of particular interest, as they travelled all over Taiwan and the Penghu Islands, describing in detail what they saw and experienced.

The Christian *imonshi* in Taiwan were in one sense inspectors for the future Japanese church work in Taiwan. Hosokawa Kiyoshi 細川瀏, one of the *imonshi* and a Presbyterian minister, communicated with Taiwanese Christians and Western missionaries as a representative from the Presbyterian Church in Japan, thus making connections for Japanese Christians throughout Taiwan. Reports by *imonshi*, soldiers, and civilians alike, were carried in the news periodicals of their respective church denominations and provided Christians in Japan with knowledge of Taiwan and Christianity in Taiwan.

The common frame of understanding in the minds of the Japanese at the time, regardless of whether they were Christian or non-Christian, was that Taiwan was a "barbarous" region that needed to be civilized through Japanese colonial rule. This mentality did not easily change even after Japanese Christians visited Taiwan and encountered Christians in Taiwan. Nevertheless, their descriptions of Taiwan and Christianity in Taiwan remained relatively objective. Obviously, Japanese Christians were curious to know what churches in Taiwan were like. Japanese Christians would visit local churches wherever they went and report what they observed; often they were deeply impressed. They also tried to grasp the overall situation of Protestant Christianity in Taiwan. These reports, some short and some lengthy, provide significant information about the state of Christianity in Taiwan at the end of the 19th Century. There were about 25 articles between 1895 and 1897 that were written about Christianity in Taiwan, in *Fukuin Shinpo* alone.

Relationship building between Japanese Christians and Taiwanese Christians/ churches/ evangelists, as well as Western missionaries, started out amiable and reciprocal. Many articles were about encounters between Japanese and Taiwanese Christians. While still engaged in combat with the Taiwanese guerrillas, Japanese Christian soldiers occasionally had opportunities to befriend Taiwanese Christians, gathering together in churches for worship and fellowship. Civilians, on the other hand, gained opportunities for fellowship with Christians in Taiwan as they simply sought places of worship. They would typically attend Taiwanese churches for Sunday worship services, and, as the number of Japanese Christians increased gradually, Taiwanese churches would offer the use of their buildings on Sunday afternoons, which would also be attended by Taiwanese church members. Thus was the pattern most Japanese Presbyterian churches followed at the beginning, until the early 1900s.

The kind of reciprocal relationship described above did not last once Japanese churches were firmly established. In the case of Taihoku, Japanese Christians maintained a close relationship with missionaries and Taiwanese Christians until they achieved financial independence and launched the erection of the new building. The completion of the building in 1900 owed much to Li Shunsei 李春生 (Li Chhung-seng), who donated a 300 *tsubo* land and 2,000 yen. Ironically, once the Japanese Christians ceased to need any support from the Taiwanese Christians, their intention to ally or unite with the Taiwanese church became evident, in such a way the Taiwanese side resisted, being aware of the possibility that the Japanese would control the new "united" church.[17] It was in this way that joint worship services between the *Taihoku Nihon Kirisuto Kyokai* 台北日本基督教会 and *Bangkah* Church 艋舺教會 ceased to take place after 1898, the same year Taiwan-related articles disappeared from *Fukuin Shinpo*.[18] Throughout the 1900s and 1910s, almost no reports on Taiwanese churches or Western missionaries appeared in *Fukuin Shinpo* except 1901, the year George MacKay died. This lack of mention reflects the widening gap between Japanese and Taiwanese Christians.

To conclude, the general subjects of Taiwan-related articles that appeared

---

17 Letter from Thurlow Fraser to R. P. Mackay, Mar. 16, 1904, Presbyterian Church in Canada Box 3, File 31, United Church of Canada Archives.

18 See Takai-Heller 2003, Vol. I, Chapter 2.

in *Fukuin Shinpo* during this inception period, can be listed as follows:

a) Christianity in Taiwan in general, often coupled with discussion about the role of Japanese churches in the Christianization and civilizing of Taiwan;

b) Conditions of individual local Taiwanese churches where Japanese Christians traveled or were assigned;

c) Western missionaries;

d) Stories of Japanese-Taiwanese Christian encounters;

e) Sufferings of Taiwanese churches and Christians during the Japanese military subjugation, including calls for financial support for churches that suffered;

f) Launching work of Japanese churches and news about Japanese Christians and ministers, often with reference to Taiwanese support in the early part of the inception period, but little or no reference to the Taiwanese after approximately 1900, and

g) Messages sent from Taiwanese churches to churches in Japan at the onset of the Japanese rule.

1910s and 1920s

By the 1910s, it became evident to all concerned that forming an alliance between Japanese and Taiwanese Christians would be difficult, with one being the ruler and the other being the ruled.[19] References to Taiwanese churches and Christians in *Fukuin Shinpo* also remained almost nonexistent throughout the 1910s and the 1920s. The exception was the years 1915-1916, when a group of Taiwanese and Japanese Christians in Taihoku, together with Kenneth Dowie, a Canadian missionary, tried to reorganize the Taiwan YMCA, which had been virtually a Japanese organization, into a joint

---

19 Thurlow Fraser, "Recent Work in Formosa," *Presbyterian Record* (July 1904), p. 301.

organization of Taiwanese, Japanese, and Western Christians. During this time, a few articles with reference to Taiwanese churches and the YMCA movement appeared. This trans-church venture initially seemed to work out better than the "union" plan that *Nihon Kirisuto Kyokai* had envisioned, but even this joint YMCA plan only revealed more starkly the gap between the Japanese and the Taiwanese and by 1920 it fell apart.[20]

A breakthrough for the Japanese Presbyterian church in making a connection with Taiwanese Christians and impacting the Taiwanese youth came from a different direction. A new generation of Taiwanese Christians, who had studied in Japan proper and thus possessed more affinity for the Japanese than the older generation, was emerging. A majority of church-related Taiwanese youth received their higher education or theological training in Christian schools and seminaries in Japan, such as *Doshisha* 同志社, *Meijigakuin* 明治学院, *Aoyamagakuin* 青山学院, *Tokyo Shingakusha* 東京神学社, and so on. Other Taiwanese church youths who studied in government schools in Japan or secular private schools would attend Japanese churches. Through their immersion in Japanese Christian cultures, these educated youths and seminary graduates were able to understand and communicate better with Japanese Christians once back in Taiwan. Those whose names appeared in *Fukuin Shinpo* in the 1910s and 1920s typically had some personal connection with Uemura Masahisa. They included Li Chugi 李仲義 (Li Tiong-gi), Chin Seigi 陳清義 (Tan Chheng-gi), Shu Tenrai 周天来 (Chiu Thian-lai), Ryu Shinho 劉振芳 (Lau Chin-hong), and Rin Mosei 林茂生 (Lim Bo-seng). Unlike most of these individuals whose

---

20 Yuki Takai-Heller, "Nihon Tochi-ka Taiwan no Kirisuto Kyokai ni okeru Ibunka Koryu: Taiwan YMCA no Jirei wo Chuushin ni 日本統治下台湾のキリスト教界における異文化交流：台湾YMCAの事例を中心に," *Cultural Encounters in Asia* (Tokyo: Meiji Shoin, 2004), pp. 210-233; "Shokuminchi Tochi-Kozo ni okeru Kirisuto-kyo to Sono Ekkyo-sei ni Kansuru Ichi-Kosatsu – 1910 nendai no Taiwan YMCA to K. W. Dowie wo Chuushin ni 植民地統治構造におけるキリスト教とその越境性に関する一考察：1910年代の台湾YMCAとK. W. ダウイを中心に," *Doshisha American Studies Journal* 45 (2009), pp. 39-65.

names appeared only in the news of churches and members, Shu actually contributed articles, which were of purely religious nature, completely unrelated to Taiwan (1730: 1928.10.18, 1739: 1928.12.20). On the other hand, Ryu's name appeared in connection to the report about the *Tokyo Taiwan Kirisuto-kyo Seinen-kai*東京台湾基督教青年会, which is significant as this particular history has not been made clear.

Another point of breakthrough came through Sai Baika 蔡培火 (Chhoa Poe-hoe), one of the key members of the early Taiwanese political movement in Tokyo, who became a Christian in 1920 in Japan through Uemura Masahisa's strong influence.[21] Through Uemura's personal connection to Sai, a politician and a member of *Nihon Kirisuto Kyokai*, Tagawa Daikichiro 田川 大吉郎, became deeply sympathetic with the politically oppressed state of the Taiwanese, and together with Uemura openly professed support for the Taiwan Parliament Petition Movement 臺灣議会設置運動. Thus, a series of articles appeared in *Fukuin Shinpo* in the 1920s, expressing support for these emerging political movements in Taiwan. Uemura also hoped that Sai would assist the work of *Nihon Kirisuto Kyokai* in Taiwan in his spare time, but this was never realized.[22] In the 1920s, Sai contributed two articles in *Fukuin Shinpo*, "Taiwan Dendoh wo Kaishi Seyo 台湾伝道を開始せよ (A call to launch evangelical work among the Taiwanese)" (1367: 1921.09.08) which was addressed to the Japanese churches in Taiwan, and "Nangoku yori 南国 より (From a southern country)" (1767: 1929.02.21), written in Chinese, which was addressed to the Taiwanese in Japan.

In short, *Nihon Kirisuto Kyokai*'s connection with Taiwanese Christians during this period was almost completely limited to those who studied in

---

21 *Fukuin Shinpo* 2162 (1937.08.05). Yuan Xinyi 顏欣怡, *Qingnian Cai Peihuo de Shenfen Celue – Riben Dazheng Sichao de Taiwan Yishi* 青年蔡培火的身分策略——日本大正思潮下的台灣意識, Master's thesis submitted to National SunYat-Sen University (2007), pp. 7-10.

22 *Fukuin Shinpo* 2164 (1937.08.19).

Japan. Subjects of Taiwan-related articles that appeared in *Fukuin Shinpo* during this period can be summarized as below:

h) Reports about Japanese churches – over 95% of all Taiwan-related articles in the 1910s and 1920s;

i) Short news about individual Taiwanese Christians who studied in Japan and had close connections with *Nihon Kirisuto Kyokai* in Japan proper, especially with Uemura Masahisa;

j) Articles written by Taiwanese Christians;

k) Reports written by Japanese ministers about their itinerant work in Taiwan, in which reference was made to Taiwanese Christians who had close relationships with Japanese Christians; and

l) Reports about the Taiwanese Presbyterian Church, written by Chin Seigi, who studied in *Tokyo Shingakusha*, the Presbyterian seminary in Tokyo.

The 15-year war period (1930s-1945)

The number of articles relating to Taiwan increased again in the 1930s, reflecting the atmosphere of the island under the pressure of the military government to promote "*naitai yuwa* 內台融和 [merging of the Taiwanese and the Japanese]." In spite of the fact that the ultimate purpose of this slogan was to mobilize the Taiwanese people to contribute to the war effort in the same way as the Japanese, not the granting of equal rights and opportunities, it still created an air among Christians, though mostly Japanese Christians, that the time was ripe for the "union" or *yuwa* between Taiwanese and Japanese Christians. This optimistic air was in stark contrast to the grim reality that was dawning on Taiwanese churches and missionaries, who were receiving increasing pressures from the colonial government and the Japanese colonists to "Japanize" if they wished to survive. This was most evident in mission schools where shrine worship and use of the Japanese language were forced. On seeing Taiwanese churches and missionary work in crisis, Japanese churches in Taiwan understood that their role was to act as the protector of the Taiwanese Church, taking it over from the Western missionaries. The Taiwanese Church, on the other hand, approached the head office of the *Nihon Kirisuto Kyokai* or *Nihon Kirisuto-kyo Renmei* 日本基督教連盟 in Japan proper for "alliance" or "cooperation" for the sake of survival. These two directions seemed to fit, but the intention of the Japanese Church leaders to safeguard the Taiwanese church through Japanese ministers in Taiwan and the Taiwanese intention to gain help directly from Church leaders in Japan proper never seemed to meet. Even Taiwanese Christians' cooperation with a series of *naitai yuwa* ventures had the air of a reluctant compromise for the sake of survival.

Around the year 1932, when the North Presbyterian Church celebrated the 60th anniversary of the launch of mission work by the Canadian Presbyterian Mission, *Fukuin Shinpo* carried a few articles about late George MacKay, *Bangkah Church*, and the related celebration (1841, 1907, 1957, 1976). From around the year 1934, when a shrine worship scandal shook the Presbyterian Middle School in Tainan, Taiwan-related articles started to increase in *Fukuin Shinpo* again, showing *Nihon Kirisuto Kyokai's* growing concern for and interest in Taiwanese churches and their recognition that a closer relationship would be necessary.

The year 1935 marked the beginning of a new stage in the relationship between Japanese and Taiwanese Christians. An informal gathering of Taiwanese and Japanese Christians was organized in February under the leadership of Kami Yojiro and Chin Keishu 陳渓圳 (Tan Khe-chun), pastors of *Taihoku Nihon Kirisuto Kyokai* and *Sianglian* Church 双蓮教会 respectively.[23] In April 1935, when a large earthquake hit Taiwan, the tie between the Japanese and Taiwanese churches seemed to strengthen. Kami

---

23 *Taiwan Seinen* 臺灣青年 68 (Mar. 1935).

Yojiro travelled through a wide area of Taiwan, visiting many Taiwanese churches that suffered partial or complete destruction of their buildings, and handing them relief donations collected from Japanese Christians (2054, 2055, 2056). Eight months later, in November, a large-scale convention took place in *Taihoku Kokaido* 台北公会堂, the public hall, during the exposition commemorating the 40th anniversary of the Japanese colonial rule in Taiwan.[24] Over a hundred Christians, both Taiwanese and Japanese, were on the preparation committee, and the participants neared 2,000 people. From around this time, *Fukuin Shinpo* started to carry reports about Taiwanese churches along with Japanese churches (2050, 2063, 2072). Thus, in 1935 there were over 20 articles written about Taiwanese churches and mission work in Taiwan. In 1936 and 1937, there was ongoing interest in promoting *naitai yuwa* among Christians. Of particular importance were Saba Wataru's 佐波亘 reports of his trip to Taiwan (2091-2095). However, after 1938, the number of Taiwan church-related articles dropped down close to zero, with only some very short articles.

Below is a list of the subjects of Taiwan-related articles that appeared in *Fukuin Shinpo* between 1930 and 1943. The overall characteristic of the tone during this time was a conviction in the benefit of the *naitai yuwa* between the Taiwanese and Japanese Christians.

m) Reports about Japanese churches as well as Taiwanese churches, with reference to the possibility of the merging of the two groups, including Saba Wataru's reports.;

n) Celebrations of the 60th anniversary of the launch of Christian work in northern Taiwan, the 70th anniversary of launch of Christian work in southern Taiwan, and the 60th anniversary of Thomas Barclay's work in Taiwan, including revival meetings conducted by the Rev.

---

24 For the Christian Convention of 1935, see Takai-Heller 2004.

Song Shanjie 宋尚節, which were articles that were mostly written by Takeda Kohei 武田公平, professor of Tainan Theological Seminary;

o) Reports about the small-group fellowship between Taiwanese and Japanese Christians, and the big-scale convention on the island, both of which promoted naitai yuwa between the two groups;

p) Taiwanese Presbyterian Middle School and other mission schools, and the issues confronting them such as shrine worship, use of the Japanese language, appointment of Japanese headmasters, and so on;

q) Short news about individual Christians most of whom studied in Japan, including Shoki Coe 黃彰輝 (Ng Chiong-hui), Shi Kunho 施鯤鵬 (Si Khun-pheng), and Ro Bunhuku 盧文福 (Lou Bun-hok); and

r) Warnings about the True Jesus Church, written by Chin Seigi.

The efficacy of using news periodicals of churches in Japan for the study of the history of Christianity in Taiwan

As discussed above, the characteristics of Taiwan-related articles that appeared in *Fukuin Shinpo* during the 50-year Japanese colonial rule changed dramatically over time. The articles in the first three or so years showed the Japanese Christians' genuine interest in Taiwan as the object of Christianization and modernization. Taiwanese Christians as well as missionaries were perceived as partners for this civilizing venture. From 1899 to 1930, the content of the articles became almost completely limited to the work of Japanese churches in Taiwan. The exceptions were those articles expressing support for the Taiwanese political movement that appeared from time to time in the 1920s, as well as references to those Taiwanese Christians who studied in Japan and had personal connections to Uemura. However, the general disinterest in Taiwanese churches and Taiwanese Christians stayed the same. From 1930 onwards, under the pressure of militarism, Japanese Christians in Taiwan once again tried to promote a close alliance with the Taiwanese Christians. This mood dominated the articles that appeared through the 1930s.

The overall trend of the articles that appeared in *Fukuin Shinpo* mostly paralleled those news periodicals of other Japanese church denominations. The Holiness periodicals were an exception, as their work was geared by and toward both the Japanese and the Taiwanese from the start.

Having analyzed the general tendencies and characteristics of the Japanese Christian narrative of Taiwanese churches and Christians, it is noted that these articles possess historical value for the study of the history of Christianity in Taiwan, in the following three ways.

Firstly, the articles from 1895 to 1897 contain valuable observations of churches and Christians in Taiwan as seen through Japanese eyes. The same can be said about the articles from the 1930s that contain reports about Taiwanese churches. Secondly, the articles manifest the state of Japanese-Taiwanese Christian encounters and relationship building, which is an important part of the reality of Taiwanese churches and Christians in Taiwan during the Japanese colonial era that deserves more attention. The articles also provide information about individual Taiwanese Christians who had close connections with Japanese Christians. Thirdly, those articles that are primarily about Japanese churches and Japanese Christians in Taiwan are not completely cut off from the history of Christianity in Taiwan. While the history of Christianity in Taiwan primarily centers around the Taiwanese people who are the main actors of Taiwan today, it is a fact that in colonial Taiwan the Japanese on the island also understood themselves as belonging to Taiwan. In that sense, more heed should be given to the history of Japanese churches in Taiwan in the historiography of Christianity in Taiwan, regardless of any personal sentiments toward the history of Japanese colonialism.

Appendix A

Extant issues of news periodicals issued by churches and YMCAs in Taiwan during the Japanese colonial period, in Japanese

	Title	Issued by:	Years of issue	Extant issues	Held by
1	*Taiwan Kirisuto Kyoho* 臺灣基督教報	Taihoku Nihon Kirisuto Kyokai 臺北日本基督教會	1906-1944	Nos. 129-169 (1917.3~1922.10)	An individual in Taipei. The author got permission to make a photocopy in March 1999.
				Nos. 317-418 (1935.8~1944.9)	Taiwan University Library
2	*Taiwan Seikwokai Kaiho* 臺灣聖公會會報	Taihoku Seikwokai 臺北聖公會	Unknown	Nos. 187 (1939.2~3), 203-4 (1940.7~1940.8)	An individual in Tokyo
3	*Taihoku Kyodan* 臺北教壇	Taihoku Nihon Kumiai Kirisuto Kyokai 臺北日本組合教會	Unknown	Nos. 258-262(1939.1~5), 280(1940.11)	Doshisha University Library

4	*Taiwan Seinen The YMCA of Taiwan* 臺灣青年	Taiwan YMCA 臺灣 YMCA	Unknown-1944	Nos. 56-188 (1934.3~1945.3)	Originally held by an individual in Nagoya; donated to Doshisha University Library by author in 2000.
				No. 53 (「臺灣之青年」1929.3.31), Nos. 55 -189 (1930.09.20~1945.4-5)	The National Council of YMCAs in Japan 日本YMCA聯盟, Tokyo
5	*Taiwan Kirisutokyo Seinenkai Renmeiho* 臺灣基督教青年會聯盟報	臺灣基督教青年會聯盟	1933?-unknown	Nos. 2-4 (1933.7~1934.1)	Originally held by an individual in Yokohama. The author got permission to make a photocopy in 1999, and donated a duplicate to Taiwan Theological Seminary in 2013.
6	*Taiwan Kirisuto Kyokai Ho* 臺灣基督教會報	The Presbyterian Church in Taiwan (issued in the north) 北部臺灣基督長老教會	1942.12-1944.7	1-10, 12-14 (1942.12~1944.7)	Tainan Theological Seminary Library

Appendix B

Approximate number of Taiwan-related articles/ reports/ notes in news periodicals of Japanese Church Denominations that possessed churches in Taiwan

	Titles (the underlined title is the typical denotation of the periodical)	Issued by	Frequency of issues	Number of Taiwan-related articles
1.	*Fukuin Shuho* 福音週報 ⇒*Fukuin Shinpo* 福音新報	Nihon Kirisuto Kyokai 日本基督教会 (Presbyterian)	weekly	745
2.	*Kirisutokyo Shuho* 基督教週報 ⇒*Kyokai Hyoron* 教会評論	Nippon Seikwokai 日本聖公会系 (Anglican)	weekly	775
3.	*Nichiyo Soshi* 日曜叢誌	Nippon Seikwokai 日本聖公会 (Anglican)	monthly	79
4.	*Tokyo Kyoho* 東京教報	Nippon Seikwokai 日本聖公会 (Anglican)	monthly	43
5.	*Kirisutokyo Sekai* 基督教世界 ⇒*Kirisutokyo Shinbun* 基督教新聞	Nihon Kumiai Kirisuto Kyokai 日本組合基督教会 (Congregational)	weekly	369
6.	*Gokyo* 護教⇒*Kyokai Jiho* 教界時報⇒*Nihon Methodist Shinbun* 日本メソヂスト新聞⇒*Nihon Kirisutokyo Shinbun* 日本基督教新聞	Nihon Methodist Kyokai 日本メソヂスト教会 (Methodist)	weekly	128
7.	*Hono no Shita* 焔の舌⇒*Kyome no Tomo* きよめの友⇒*Kiyome no Tomo* 聖潔の友⇒*Reiko* 霊光	Nihon Holiness Kyokai 日本ホーリネス教会 (Holiness)	weekly	216
8.	*Toki no Koye* ときのこゑ⇒ときの声⇒*Asa no Hikari* 朝の光	Nihon Kyuseigun 日本救世軍 (Salvation Army)	bi-weekly	135

臺灣天主教重要史料：
《教友生活周刊》初創期之研究[*]

古偉瀛

國立臺灣大學歷史學系教授

摘要

　　由於臺灣天主教會七個教區未有專設的檔案室，史學家若想要研究當代臺灣天主教史，往往苦於史料缺乏。在許多堂區陸續慶祝成立一百週年之際，雖然有紀念特刊的發行，但其中史料並不豐富，而且準確性不夠。唯一較容易入手，資訊和史料也較豐富的是臺北總教區創刊於1953年的天主教《教友生活周刊》，連續發行了五十五年，於2008年8月10日發行最後一期後改組成《天主教周報》，發行至今，因此這份報刊是重要史料來源。

　　本文主要討論此一刊物從創立到1970年代對臺灣天主教史研究的重要性。作為一個教區的周刊，服務全臺，創立的經過、特別是早期從危機到逐漸穩定，其經營管理上的情況、此刊物所代表的價值觀，以及由於環境和編者立場，所產生的特色與限制。

關鍵詞：臺灣天主教、教區、教友生活周刊、主教、羅馬教廷

＊作者特別感謝兩位匿名審查者的建議及指正，已按所提意見，加以修訂。

一、前言

要研究臺灣的天主教會歷史，當然最有用的是檔案，但今日臺灣教區並無檔案室的設置，近六十年來的臺灣天主教史料，目前最有用的應該是從1953年開始發行的天主教《教友生活周刊》，這份由臺北總主教區出版的周刊是為全臺灣的教區及教友服務的，而且一直出版到2008年才轉型成《天主教周報》，仍然是此地天主教歷史資料很重要的來源。由於發行較早又較少，全臺只有少數機構收藏，而且並不完整，最完整的據我所知只有臺北總教區，但仍有零星的殘缺，承該報目前負責人慨允借閱，在此特別致謝。

由於此周刊包含有教會史的各個層面的消息，例如國際教會的要聞，或教廷的重要事情，還是臺灣與教會有關的各種情況，因此可以相當程度的反應臺灣天主教的發展與變遷。本文就以此刊為基礎，將來龍去脈，特別是從初創時期到逐漸穩定的前幾年的發展，以及其特色和重要性加以整理，以供參考，並就教於方家。

二、該刊的創立與發展

臺灣天主教史在1950年後有了重大變化，因為中共建政，大批西方傳教士及國籍神職轉來臺灣，臺灣監牧區也一分為二，原來的道明會轉到南部發展，北部則由國籍修會主徒會負責，這當然是由於當時教廷的傳信部秘書長是主徒會會祖剛恒毅樞機（Celso Costantini）[1]，而且中國教會已於1946年建立聖統制，逐漸朝向地方教會的建立，所以主徒會的郭若石被任命為臺北監牧區監牧，一年後擢升為臺北總主教。在此一新時代的開始，主徒會致力於中華文化的學習和傳播，相當重視知識份子的傳教。承襲自利瑪竇以來的文字傳教法，

---

1 剛樞機在1953年1月策封樞機後才辭去傳信部秘書長職，見主徒會編印，《剛恒毅樞機主教使華七十週年論文集》（臺北：主徒會，1992），頁151。

仍舊是在地域遼闊的中華大地最有用的福傳方式，來臺前的大陸天主教會早已有了中文教會報紙，對日抗戰前最有名的要算是上海的《聖教雜誌》，戰後又有一些復刊的教會報章，我們看一下牛若望的報導：

> 民國四十一年十一月，結束了我在新嘉坡的工作，便搭船準備回臺灣，……到臺的日期，模糊記得是 [民國四十二年] 四月十二日。到臺後先拜訪了教區首長郭若石總主教，……，我向郭總主教說：「那麼，我想恢復重慶時代的『教友生活』，專門為教友閱讀的一個小刊物。」郭總主教予以贊成，且很慷慨大方地當時就拿出一千元美金，向我說：「你拿去作為開辦費，以後需要，另想辦法。」於是「教友生活」就決定了在臺北出版。郭總主教同時對我說：過不久從歐洲回來的一位中國神父，是一位飽學之士，對於國學有特別研究，等他回來後，你們倆合作合辦這個刊物吧。這位神父就是成世光，現在的臺南教區成主教。果然不久成神父回來了，我同他談了「教友生活」的計畫，他也同意，於是在那年的七月一日「教友生活」的創刊號面世了。它的體積很小，只十六開小張，前面一二三頁都是理論的文字，第四頁是一些教會新聞的報導。出版後一般反應還好，份數日增，不到半年，便已超過萬份。[2]

成世光主教對同一件事也有如下的親身報導：

> 民國四十二年，我與溫中祥神父結伴，由比利時回來，五月十八日在基隆港登岸。承蒙郭總主教厚待，被安置在主教公署。以後溫神父負責堂區傳教，我則被派與牛若望蒙席發行教友生

2 牛若望，〈教友生活的創刊與經營〉，《教友生活周刊・慶祝教友生活周刊創刊廿週年紀念特刊》，1008期，1973/06/28，1版。

活周刊。

教友生活的發行宗旨,是為每主日供給教友及慕道者一些教會知識,和教會動態。版面不大,只有十六開面四頁。第一頁是一篇道理,通常由牛蒙席執筆,偶而牛蒙席也要我塗鴉,變換一下口味。第二頁是介紹本週的一兩位聖人或聖女,作為教友們的生活楷模,這一部分歸我負責。第三頁報導國內教會的動態;第四頁報導國際教會的動態。[3]

當然由於消息的多寡會影響版面的微調,每週四印出,以便郵政服務能在星期日送到教堂或訂戶的手中,於是刊物上發刊的日期都寫成星期日,配合教會的瞻禮單,這種做法一直沿用至今日,只是提早一天,通常週三出版,週末前可以寄到。

我們從當年的發刊辭「啟」見到創刊的主旨:

我們在人力物力貧乏的條件下,辦這一個小刊物,其旨趣就是在服務;因為條件差,服務不周,勢所難免,這個小刊物,一定很難滿足大家的願望;不過要期望它服務周到一些,就必需各位神長和教友們,給我們兩種幫忙:一是精神的,一是物質的。

精神的幫忙,就是給我們指導:這個小刊物有什麼缺點,各位對它有什麼期望,我們誠懇地企望著各位的教誨,各位以為它是孺子可教,我們也一定如同孺子一般,接受各位的訓導:可不要使它在字紙簍中長眠,或者供零售商的驅使。

物質的幫忙,不是要各位給我們金錢的補助,也不是給我們多拉幾個訂戶,現在我們是義務服務,經費是由郭總主教籌墊;因此所謂物質的幫忙,就是希望各位神長教友,供給我們豐富

3 成世光,〈教友生活的創刊與發行〉,《教友生活周刊·慶祝教友生活周刊創刊廿週年紀念特刊》),1008期,1973/06/28,1版。

的材料：理論的文字，報導的消息；各位都是生活經驗豐富，寫出來的東西，必定生動動人；各位所管理，所居留的區域，教會的動態，教務的進行，必定都有記錄的價值；給我們寫來，非常歡迎，隨時披錄，如此可以互相觀摩切磋，促進教務的進展。

謹候教，是為啓。

社址：臺北市和平東路一段一八八巷一號

電話：二六九七六[4]

聲明顯然是針對各堂區的本堂神父及教會領導們而發，此外，周刊也表達了作為「教友感情聯繫的橋樑」的期待。[5] 發行一年後，主編牛若望及成世光等人集資在永和買了一間小屋作為社址，離開臺北市和平東路的主教辦公室。[6]

發行到兩週年時，主編有如下的報導：

本報創刊兩週年

本報的服務，一方面提供教友們知的材料，一方面也貢獻教友們行的方法。希望教友們知的愈多，行的愈廣，然後是知無不行，行必有果，養成知行合一的教友生活，走上神修的最高境界：融洽於天主。

本報創刊時，初只兩千份，第一年終了，增至五千份。現在是第二年的結尾，已由五千份增至九千二百份；而各地要求增多份數及新訂的函件，還在繼續著來。預計兩三月後，可出版到一萬份。其中十分之九供應本省的教友，其餘應華僑教友的要求，分寄到南美、北美、香港、印尼、馬來、北非和歐洲等

---

4 《教友生活周刊》，1: 1，1953/07/05。

5 〈答鞏純如先生〉，《教友生活周刊》，2: 2，1954/06/27。

6 他們當時多少都有一些自己爭取到的存款，見成世光，〈鹽齋拾遺〉，《成世光全集》004（臺南：聞道，2010，1987年初版），頁06。

地。[7]

該文並要求各地神長共同努力，編出一本介紹教義的書籍。值得注意的是兩年的時間內，訂閱的份數已將近一萬，可以說相當受到歡迎。在第四年終了時，此刊又標明了〈「教友生活」的宗旨〉：

第一、每週供給教友研究道理的材料，和實踐教友生活的方法。
第二、報導聖教會各地的動態，使教友明瞭國內外聖教會的大勢。

並表示「歡迎‧希望」：

本報歡迎教友直接訂閱，每份全年定費新臺幣十元，外加郵費五元（定十份以上者郵費免）。希望每個教友家庭有教友生活一份，希望每位教友在主日天能夠看到教友生活。它會隨著時間的前進，逐漸告訴你要緊知道的道理，和應當遵守的教規。遇有問題時，請隨時寄來，本報將盡力為你解答。[8]

啟事中表明要求訂費，這與從前贈閱不同，顯然有了經濟上的需要，這是因為總主教郭若石資助半年後，改由教廷駐華使館支持，但不到兩年，黎培理突然宣布停止資助，使得此刊差一點宣布停刊，在報上發表聲明。[9]（詳見下節）

如前節所述，一開始主其事者是牛若望與成世光，三年後，1956年牛被調去越南，由成主持，一年後，成又接任臺中的衛道中學校

---

7 〈本報創刊二週年〉，《教友生活周刊》，2: 50，1955/06/12

8 〈教友生活的宗旨〉，《教友生活周刊》，4: 50，1957/06/05。

9 聲明強調財政困難，若不得即時支援，將於數月後停刊，見〈本報緊急啟事〉，《教友生活周刊》，3: 4，1955/07/24。

長，1957年起，由耀漢會的趙雅博主持[10]，他們為了撐下去，「起初是由我們每個參加社務的人，每月捐出十五元美金，更好是說，我們工作人員，每個都是枵腹從公，各人找自己的生活。後來這種情形逐漸改善，由於各位本堂神父與教友們的支持，教友生活的成本可以回收，……在這期間，由於成主教的建議，將永和鎮教友生活社址，廉價出售，牛若望副主教慷慨將售出後應得之金錢全部拿出，作為支持教友生活之發行，教友生活就在這種情形下，繼續的生長下去。」[11]

發行至第五年時，有一次重要聲明，將此刊宗旨重新整理並直接徵求訂戶，不再由各地的本堂神父收發及代繳報費，其聲明如下：

（一）

《教友生活》，偏重在道理方面，新聞報導僅佔四分之一的篇幅。這可能使它顯得嚴肅，枯燥一點。而且它的性質是雜誌的，不是日報的，所以排版法也缺少新奇變化。

這個問題，我們一開始就研究過，考慮過。採取雜誌性質而不採取日報性質的原故，是因為：本報第一著重的是道理介紹，其次才是報導聖教會各地的動態。在這樣的目標下，雜誌的形式似乎比日報的形式，更合於本報的身分。

……宗旨是如此，但實際作起來，也不能盡如理想。第一我們抱歉的，是有些道理未能寫得深入淺出。天主的道理本身已夠深奧，再加上本報同人的才拙，表現的就更晦澀。第二、我們也抱歉有些道理篇幅寫得過長，減少了讀者快讀的興味。

……

（三）

以前的時候，本報沒有直接訂閱的辦法，教友們是向本堂神父

---

10 成世光，〈教友生活的創刊與發行〉，《教友生活周刊・慶祝教友生活周刊創刊廿週年紀念特刊》，1008期，1973/06/28，1版。

11 趙雅博，〈教友生活的成長〉，《教友生活周刊・慶祝教友生活周刊創刊廿週年紀念特刊》，1008期，1973/06/28，1版。

處取閱。如今我們多犧牲出一份時間，專門為直接訂閱的教友服務，設法使每個教友家庭或每位教友，主日天都能看到《教友生活》。[12]

　　這份刊物每年訂費10元，郵費5元，民國46年後正式成為臺北總教區刊物，但主要的面向是臺灣的天主教會。牛若望蒙席民國46年12月中旬離臺赴越，「教友生活」業務就奉託耀漢會趙雅博神父負責。一度曾把社址遷移到該會景美附近新建的會院。趙神父接替後，於是改善擴大版面，先改為四開一張，最後改為對開一張，內容也加以充實。自田耕莘樞機出長臺北總教區後，更加重視此一刊物，將此刊改為樞機主教公署公報，亦即「教區公報」，並召開「擴版編訪」會議。[13] 趙神父的回憶：

　　　等到臺北教區由田樞機出長以後，成主教受命輔理主教，高公使接任教廷公使，本人與高公使曾暢談數次，並將教友生活的擴充計畫，詳細報告給高公使，他非常同情，他說：如果田樞機答應，在每年教廷撥給教區的津貼上，可以多撥兩千美元，作為支持並擴大教友生活周刊的經費。由於田主教認為不太相宜，事情未能成功，但教廷在那年還是撥出了一千元的津貼，而臺北總教區也每年慨撥五百美元。
　　　當教友生活周刊未曾找到支援以前，在成主教與本人的策劃之下，教友生活的版面已經改變了，變成了一種小型報紙型，共有四欄：新聞、教義、家庭、兒童。兒童版並有國音符號，從各處搜集教會小故事，當時頗得一般兒童與家庭主婦的歡迎，發行數字計到八千份。
　　　等到教區有了津貼以後，教友生活由八開擴充到四開，第一版

12〈第五卷的開始〉，《教友生活周刊》，5: 1，1957/06/12，1版。
13《教友生活周刊》，1960/06/26，4版。

國際要聞，並有社論。第二版教義。第三版家庭、兒童。第四版國內要聞。

　　為了刊載各地的教會消息，每個本堂都派任記者。比較值得注意的是此刊國際新聞又快又多，這是因為「國外消息的來源除有航空版的觀察報以外，我每週三次在早晨五點半收聽梵蒂岡電臺由王伯尼蒙席主持的中文教會消息廣播，並作記錄刊出，這樣有很多消息往往比其他的報紙早一、二週」。[14]

　　後來由於趙神父工作太忙，遂由劉鴻蔭神父接替，不久後即擴成為對開版面。後來再由項退結神父短時間來接替，從1968年8月到1969年1月。在此期間，此刊開始接收廣告，以挹注發行費用，[15] 最後由李善修神父主持，[16] 這已是創刊十五年後的事了，也是《教友生活周刊》定型化的開始。

　　李善修神父在海外多年，接任前特地全省走透透查訪各地神職及教友，他掌握的情況以及對本刊的理解如下：[17]

　　一、教友生活周刊的宗旨，顧名思義乃為發揚基督福音，促進教友的神益。……二、教會報刊負有領導教會輿論的責任，凡為教友有關的問題，不論是應倡導的善舉，或是應糾正的缺點，報刊負有首先提出作客觀公正商討的責任，……三、在中國宣揚天主教必須與中國固有倫理道德相配合，……四、激發教友的反共愛國精神。……五、倡導教友傳教工作：按聖保祿

14 趙雅博，〈教友生活的成長〉，《教友生活周刊·慶祝教友生活周刊創刊廿週年紀念特刊》，1008期，1973/06/28，1版。

15 項退結，〈我對教友生活的短期瓜葛〉，《教友生活周刊·慶祝教友生活周刊創刊廿週年紀念特刊》，1008期，1973/06/28，1版。

16 牛若望，〈教友生活的創刊與經營〉，《教友生活周刊·慶祝教友生活周刊創刊廿週年紀念特刊》，1008期，1973/06/28，1版。

17 李善修，〈教友生活周刊的現狀〉，《教友生活周刊·慶祝教友生活周刊創刊廿週年紀念特刊》，1008期，1973/06/28，1版。

宗徒的訓示，每位教友藉聖洗聖事成為基督奧體的肢體，每個肢體應自動發揮其效能，促進自己及全體的利益。這是每位教友生活中最重要的一環，為此二梵大公會議在教友傳教法令中特別強調這一點。……六、注意教友家庭面臨的現代困難，如人工節育及墮胎問題等，……七、關懷天主教青年……協助他們成為虔誠教友、忠貞國民。

三、經營與經費

任何事業都需金錢，《教友生活周刊》開始時的經費開銷幸好有詳細記錄，不但可知當時的收支情形，還可以感受一下當時的物價狀況：

關心本報的教友，或許願意知道它的經濟狀況吧。先說開支一方面。出版兩千份時，每期印刷費是新臺幣三百六十元，郵費除外，出版五千份時，是五百三十元，出版九千二百份時，是八百二十七元。如今每期發出的報，大小包共二百零四件，郵費八十元。

經濟的來源，分兩個時期：最初六個月，是由臺北郭總主教籌墊，到四十二年底，郭總主教的經費終止，遂改由教廷駐華公使黎總主教津貼。期間承蒙教友們捐助一部分。四十三年度捐款總額：合新臺幣四千四百元，四十四年度開始到現在，捐助總額：是三千八百九十元。有人建議，請教友們個別訂閱，但因報型微小，個別訂閱，過於繁瑣，而且本報目的，純是服務，如有一位教友因訂閱繁瑣，而放棄讀教友生活的機會，便已失去了本報的服務精神。我們願意自由中國的教友，凡少有閱讀能力的，每主日都可以得到一份教友生活，藉此增多對天主的認識，加強信德的生活。所以我們自始即要求各位本堂神父的協助，請他們給教友分散教友生活，也請他們在可能的範

圍內，為本報募捐，如每位本堂神父，能一年一次，向所屬的
教友勸捐，為補助本報的費用，那是我們最渴求不過的事。[18]

發行半年後，由教廷駐華公使接手資助，同時仍繼續募款：「本
報啟事：出版屆一年，本由郭總負擔，自聖誕節起，改由黎公使補
助，但希望呼籲讀者每年捐助五元即可自給自足。」[19] 但不久卻有
了變化，牛若望蒙席的回憶：

> 那時教廷公使黎培理也到了臺灣，聽說在臺灣有這麼一個頗受
> 教友們歡迎的刊物，有一天便把我叫去說：「我要這個刊
> 物！」他的意思是：「我要支持這個刊物，算作教廷公使館的
> 工作之一，你不要再拿教區的補助，我給你們經費。」我聽了
> 他的話，便向郭總主教報告了一切。郭總主教聽說有人要拿
> 錢，不必教區再負擔任何費用，他當然同意了。
> 原來這個小刊物，開始時是採贈閱辦法，郭總主教拿了一千元
> 美金，作為印刷和郵電費。過去的半年，已開銷了四百元，剩
> 餘的六百元，郭總主教又要回去了。以後每個月「教友生活」
> 的經費便由教廷使館支領，逐漸發展，發行數字，由一萬份超
> 過兩萬份。但好景不常，大約又過了半年時間，黎公使突然聲
> 明：以後他不再負責教友生活的印刷等費了。「既有今日，何
> 必當初」！[20]

此刊在黎培理撤資後刊登了一則「本報緊急啟事」：

> 本報自開辦迄今，經濟方面是首由郭總主教續由黎公使予以支

---

18 〈本報創刊二週年〉，《教友生活周刊》，2: 50，1955/06/12。
19 〈本報啟事〉，《教友生活周刊》，1: 49，1954/06/06。
20 牛若望，〈教友生活的創刊與經營〉，《教友生活周刊·慶祝教友生活周刊創刊廿週年紀念特刊》，
　　1008期，1973/06/28，1版。

持的；因此以往都是義務贈閱，猥蒙各地神長及讀者不棄，發行數字日增，現在已有萬份。惟近頃黎公使招編者談話，聲稱「教廷補助費未來，教友生活的經費須由各教區主教，各位神長及讀者維持，不得再仰仗公使館的津貼」；上峯既如此措施，本報同人，只有服從。故今後本報的存亡，胥視各位主教，神長，讀者之扶助如何。如至八月中，經費無著，即行停刊。特此奉告，敬希亮察。[21]

一時之間，好像岌岌可危。

　　或許有人會問，教廷為何臨時撤資，這其實是有緣故的。其中一個重要原因是此刊物重視教會地方化，由強調中華文化及知識傳教的神職主編，刊登的文章像是最重國籍神職及中華教會的雷鳴遠神父的紀念文章等，這恐怕不是黎公使所樂見的。由雷鳴遠神父一手創辦的國籍修會耀漢會會長曹立珊神父有一段回憶，他認為《教友生活周刊》「它重整『中國教會國籍化』的大旗，負起再倡導『教會國風化』的中興使命，像前進軍。（民國）四十四年為了『雷鳴遠神父傳』的出版，筆者曾被臺灣當時教會最高當局召去受申斥，該書初稿也被沒收。當時教會在臺最高當局除了禁止雷傳出版外，並指斥『教友生活』周刊是傳播雷神父思想的專刊。而雷神父的思想（他說），並不適合臺灣教會。」[22]

　　很顯然這是黎公使不再支持此刊的原因；另一原因可能是此時教會支持中華民國政府的反共政策[23]，或許是教廷希望與政府保持距離而撤資。面對此危機，牛若望「和成神父商量後，就決定『自立更生』，於是變更了贈閱辦法為訂閱辦法。好在那時各位本堂神父和善

---

21 〈本報緊急啟事〉，《教友生活周刊》，3：4，1955/07/24。

22 曹立珊，〈教友生活周刊與教會中國化之倡導〉，《教友生活周刊‧慶祝教友生活周刊創刊廿週年紀念特刊》，1008期，1973/06/28，2版。

23 民國四、五十年代常見週刊有向蔣總統致敬電文及擁護蔣中正總統連任的消息。例如〈為　總統祝壽〉，《教友生活周刊》，524，1963/10/31。

心教友們訂閱者極為踴躍，訂戶在一萬份以上，於是『教友生活』也就穩定住了。」[24]

停刊危機解除，牛、成兩位陸續他去，由趙雅博接任，前文提到，1958年田耕莘樞機返國後接任臺北總教區，對於經費有了更穩定的安排，每年資助500美元。

此刊由八開在1960年6月改為四開，趙後因教職太忙，1962年7月，由成世光邀請，劉鴻蔭擔任主編，1964年2月再由四開改為對開；1967年又進行改版，除了改為四開外，最特別的是有稿費：「來稿一經刊出，略致薄酬，每千字酌酬新臺幣三十元至六十元。其版權即為本刊所有。但神父與修女之大作暫不致酬」。[25]

這種情況很難維持，一年後就取消了，1968年1月4日的「緊急啟事」：

> 一、奉羅總主教指示，自農曆新年後，投寄本報一切稿件不再發稿酬，深望各位作者見諒，並冀仍本以往之熱忱，支持本報。
> ……自本期起本報零售一份為新臺幣六角，較前加一角，全年五十期共三十元。本報啟[26]

而且自1968年2月起（738期），又改回對開一大張。[27]

1968年1月，劉鴻蔭神父說：「為了避免阻礙教友生活的發展，本人只好就此下臺。」還為此事特別發出登報啟事。[28] 此後就由項退

---

24 牛若望，〈教友生活的創刊與經營〉，《教友生活周刊·慶祝教友生活周刊創刊廿週年紀念特刊》，1008期，1973/06/28，1版。

25 〈本刊改版啟事〉，《教友生活周刊》，689，1967/02/23。

26 〈緊急啟事〉，《教友生活周刊》，734，1968/01/04。

27 《教友生活周刊》，738，1968/02/15。

28 《教友生活周刊》，737，1968/01/25刊登下列啟事：「啟事一、本人已辭去教友生活社社長職務，……今後對於教友生活社一切事務概不負責。二、以後各種稿件及接洽業務函件，請勿再寄給本人。三、在過去五年內，猥蒙各位同道協助及支持，特此由衷致謝，恕不另函。劉鴻蔭謹啟一月二十三日。」

結暫代，一年後由李善修負責。

此刊創刊十五年後，一切都上軌道，除了財政，李善修神父說：

> 關於社內經濟，當民國五十八年一月本人接任時，收支就不平
> 衡。接任後第二年，印刷費連續上漲，數字驚人，周刊訂費只
> 漲價一次，無法隨印刷費連續漲價，教區對周刊之津貼亦無法
> 再予增加，周刊之支出赤字遂成了教友生活社之致命傷。在這
> 山窮水盡之時幸有總教區的一些位熱心同道，慷慨解囊，才幫
> 助「教友生活」度過了這個難關。第二年的難關雖已度過，但
> 第三年的支出赤字將如何解決，不能不及早籌劃，幸有印刷界
> 一位教外朋友建議本刊放棄活版法，採用打字照像印刷，他為
> 本人詳加解釋並介紹本刊同仁到一教外周刊社去觀摩。民國六
> 十年十月間，由姚宗鑑神父之協助，本社以特廉價購置中文打
> 字機兩架，由本社打字員打周刊全部稿件，再由社內同仁拼
> 版，然後交印刷廠照像付印。這樣一來，印刷費數字直線下
> 降，對本社經濟確係一大幫助，教友生活周刊至此才喘一口
> 氣。但與收支平衡仍有一段距離……[29]

財務安定，版面也定型化了。周刊一共八版，一版為教會要聞；
二版及三版為國際及國內教會要聞，第二版有代表教會立場的社論，
通常由教會內的學者專家輪流執筆，三版並有中外一週大事；第四版
為國際要聞；五版為一週的聖經及禮儀；六版為社會與家庭；七版為
青年與兒童，當時還有「白露修士」等進口的教會著名漫畫；八版則
為副刊，當時常投稿的有郭晉秀、大海及盧克彰等人。

---

29 李善修，〈教友生活周刊的現狀〉，《教友生活周刊‧慶祝教友生活周刊創刊廿週年紀念特刊》，1008
期，1973/06/28，1版。

四、周刊早期的特色

這樣的一份天主教會辦的周刊，在長達五十六年的出版過程中，有著與其他世俗周刊不同的特色，但也多少限制了其閱讀的對象。茲就其從創刊到1970年教會發展高峰期間的主要特色總結如下：

（一）教廷與國際要聞

1. 有些教會的新規定，只有在此刊物上看得到，此處僅舉一例。例如在彌撒禮儀當中的重要部分「領聖體」，以前規定很嚴，但1957年有了「聖體齋新規定」：「教宗於1953年放寬舊日之聖體齋後，今又予以簡化：（1）領聖體前三小時內，不要吃東西；（2）領聖體前一小時不要喝東西（清水除外）。」[30] 又如教廷對於新型態新工具在禮儀時的禁用規定，例如教廷聖禮部於1956年3月7日發表公告，重申聖座禁令如下：

> 聖堂中行禮節時，不許放送留聲唱片或錄音器，以代替唱經班。
>
> 一九三九年聖禮部已經公布過此項禁令：聖堂中作彌撒或行別的禮節時，不准用聖歌唱片，代替人的唱經。與此相同的，是在堂中放送收錄好的道德或要理問答亦在禁止之列，即使沒有神父講道理，也不許用此方法。
>
> 聖堂中不許放演電影，即使講要理的片子也不許。舉行大禮彌撒時Missa solemnis，在奉獻經Offertorium的中間，不准唱本國文的聖歌。[31]

2. 當時對新教友很有吸引力的救濟物資的分配也在此刊物上登

---

30 〈聖體齋新規定〉，《教友生活週刊》，4：42，1957/04/10。
31 〈聖座重申禁令〉，《教友生活週刊》，4：48，1957/05/22，2版。

載：

美天主教福利會　救濟衣物已分配臺灣得五十萬磅

（益世社紐約通訊）一九五三年感恩節週內，在美國神職發起下，美國教友所捐募之衣物及其他救濟品共計九百五十七萬四千磅，已經分配給十九個國家。該次運動係由美國天主教福利委員會戰時救濟服務處所發起。韓國所得最多，計三百六十萬磅，分配原則，係根據各地確實所需，而無種族宗教之歧視。戰時救濟服務處頃發表分配情形如下：

歐洲方面英國四千磅，奧地利四十萬磅，德國一百萬磅，義大利一百二十萬磅，的利雅斯特二十萬磅，馬爾他五萬磅，希臘二十萬磅，法國五萬磅。

亞洲方面：黎巴嫩七十五萬磅，迦薩二十五萬磅，巴基斯坦與印度各十五萬磅，新嘉坡五萬磅，韓國三百六十萬磅，香港三十萬磅，越南二十萬磅，自由中國及日本各五十萬磅。[32]

（二）國內教會要聞

1. 報導當時重要教會領袖來臺的消息，並同時表達本地教會的期待，例如1959年教廷傳信部署理部長來臺，此刊登了一篇〈歡迎雅靜安樞機〉，提出下列訴求：「（一）在臺應有總修院的建立；（二）輔仁大學的復校；（三）傳教近代化：聖保祿宗徒曾說：『就合一切人，為救一切人』，這兩句話說明傳教應注意時代需要……。」[33]

2. 本地教會的創舉及教會本地化倡導，例如報導教會逐漸地方化的過程，[34] 舉行教區會議，或是成立中國主教團，建立全國傳教協進會以取代大陸時期的公教進行會等等。茲舉1967年5月14日聖神降臨節召開的臺北總主教區的教區會議來說明。刊物上不但大幅報導此會議的舉行，並指出其歷史意義，因為這次會議「是中國聖統制成立以

---

32 〈美天主教福利會　救濟衣物已分配臺灣得五十萬磅〉，《教友生活周刊》，1: 35，1954/02/28。

33 〈歡迎雅靜安樞機〉，《教友生活周刊》，6: 36，1959/2/26。

34 例如趙雅博，〈雷鳴遠王老松會見記略〉，《教友生活周刊》，3: 11，1955/09/11。

來正式教區的第一次教區會議，也是第二屆梵蒂岡大公會議後我國的第一次教區會議，並被視為繼承自1805年四川教區會議以來的一次重要教務會議，因為前此都是宗座代牧主教的會議，而不是DIOCESE的會議」，報導的標題如下：臺北教區會議隆重揭幕！羅總主教任大會主席，討論如何將基督介紹給世界，將信仰的寶庫為所有人開放，通過上　總統致敬電引文[35]。另外，像是耶穌會楊信義成為首位在臺晉鐸神父的消息[36]，這也是耶穌會入臺傳教後的重要大事。

　　3.對重量級教友狀況的報導，例如國內教友擔任要職的情況：政府來臺初期，有不少國會成員也一同來臺，此刊物也報導在國大代表中教友的情形：

> 第一屆國會議員中，就有兩位教友：馬相伯、艾知命。
>
> 民國二十一年……國難會議在洛陽開會，被邀請的也有幾位教友：馬相伯（徐景賢代）、魏丕治、張懷、吳有惠等……行憲國民大會中，教友代表，已在二十人以上，而此次國民大會，據所知道的，已經有四十名。[37]
>
> 國大教友代表共四十人　精神團結以謀教國利益
>
> 于斌（黑龍江海倫縣）；陳特向（廣東：工會）；達鑑三（山西陽城）；郭鴻群（河北安次）；章企民（浙江孝豐：全國婦女）；邱藜光（廣東陸豐）；談明華（青島市）；劉伯含（河北冀縣）；英千里（北平市）；馮著唐（河北河間）；宋曼西（河南西平：婦女團體）；張太僕（安東通化）；宋選銓（貴州郎岱）；何芝園（浙江江山）；張體謙（山西清源）；霍濟光（河北井陘）；楊浚明（廣東：自由職業）；范爭波（河南修武：自由職業）；方聞（山西五臺）；黃倫（廣東）；范振民（東北區：教育會）；沈雲龍（浙江）；周良輔（河北遵

---

35 《教友生活周刊》，701，1967/05/18。

36 《教友生活周刊》，2: 18，1954/10/31首次晉鐸於臺灣。

37 《教友生活周刊》，1: 34，1954/02/17。

化）；宋澎（河南）；張秀亞（黑龍江：婦女團體）；王學義
（山東濟南：農會）；果端華（漱江）；李亞倫（安東）；游
再浮（河北永年）；王懷義（山西平魯）；張明倫（合江
省）；岳朝相（山東省利津縣）；夏蔬園（山東）；李致華
（黑龍江訥河縣）；高仲謙（陝西）；江良伯（安徽立煌）[38]
隨後又發現有兩名，加以補登：徐志道（江蘇海門）；高崇禮
（山西岢嵐）。天主教代表，現共有四十二人。[39]

又如對於留在大陸的教友領袖的報導，例如在上海僅次於陸伯鴻
的第二號教友實業家朱志堯，亦即耶穌會神父朱恩榮的父親，江蘇海
門主教朱開敏的姪子在上海去世的消息。[40]

4. 國內教會領袖的介紹：新的主教，包括樞機主教及總主教的任
命，都發行慶祝特刊，深入報導這些神職的個人歷史，成為頗珍貴的
史料。例如1966年5月羅光升任臺北教區總主教，即發行《羅光升臺
北總主教特刊》[41]，有數文論其一生；7月成世光任臺南主教，也發
行《成世光就職臺南主教特刊》[42]，田耕莘樞機主教1957年去世時，
報導更多，方豪教授就寫了一篇傳記[43]，其中的內容比起他日後撰成
的《中國天主教史人物傳》中的要詳細得多。[44] 1969年4月底于斌升
任樞機主教則早有國內外報紙廣為報導，此刊的訊息並非特別突出。

5. 對於青年知識份子的重視，大專天主教同學會消息的報導：為
了在臺灣傳教能有較廣較深的基礎，主徒會出身的郭總主教相當重視
知識青年的福傳，剛好在臺大任教的方豪神父也特別重視明末清初以
來對傳統文化重視並適應的教會方針，因而在1950年代對於天主教臺

---

38 《教友生活周刊》，1: 34，1954/02/17，4版。

39 《教友生活周刊》，1: 35，1954/02/28，4版。

40 〈朱志堯去世〉，《教友生活周刊》，2: 43，1955/4/24。

41 《教友生活周刊‧羅光升任臺北總主教特刊》，1966/05/12。

42 《教友生活周刊‧成世光就職臺南主教特刊》，1966/07/21。

43 方豪，〈田耕莘樞機傳〉，《教友生活周刊》，711期，1967/07/27。

44 方豪，〈田耕莘〉，《中國天主教史人物傳》（香港公教真理學會，1973），頁341-344。

灣大專同學會的事務看得很重[45]。此刊經常報導全國各大專同學會成立及活動的消息，並以統計數字呈現其生機盎然的樣態。例如1955年的報導：

國立臺灣大學教友新生大增

（本報訊）十月二十三日下午二時，國立臺灣大學天主教同學會借教職員休息室舉行迎新會。經初步調查，該校今年教友新生達七十五人之多，為歷年所未有。計文學院二十七人、法學院十四人、理學院十人、工學院十八人、農學院六人。全校現有教友學生二百四十三人，護校尚未計算在內。

又悉：該校歷年畢業教友同學一三六人，中途離校三十三人，計六年來先後在校教友同學總數凡四一二人。去年暑假至今年開學，一年內領洗同學約六十人。

迎新會中，並選出洪鐵生同學為總幹事，江炳倫、陳世璉二同學為副總幹事。指導司鐸除勗勉新舊同學努力求學、研究教理、熱心事主外，更囑積極參加各本堂之傳教工作。對於連任二年之王敬弘總幹事，辛勤負責，備加稱許，並以英文新舊約一部為贈，以表紀念。

大專天主教學生注意

新生及舊生更改通訊處者，一年內新領洗者，請速函和平東路一段一八八巷一號總主教府轉大專天主教同學會總會登記。[46]

到了1968年4月又報導，臺北教區大專院校教友學生55（1966）學年度有2,456人；56學年度有2,685人。[47] 相關論述的文章也陸續出

---

45 此點可參見方豪，〈臺北教區大專天主教同學會沿革〉，《方豪六十自訂稿補編》（臺北，1969/12），頁2661-2681；又參見氏著，〈感謝，祝福，回憶，前瞻〉（古亭天主堂暨大專天主教同學會會所落成紀念冊），同前書，頁2682。

46 《教友生活周刊》，3: 19，1955/11/06。

47 《教友生活周刊》，1968/04/11。

現：〈公教大專學生傳教事業草議〉（1968年2月29日），〈在俗教友在革新中的教會〉（3月7日），〈自覺！革新！謹獻給我們所關注之天主教大專同學會〉（6月6日），〈天主教大專同學會沒有存在的必要嗎？〉（7月4日），〈寄望於天主教大專同學會〉（10月20日、10月31日）等文章，這些文章「都很清新有力，不流於俗套」。[48]

（三）梵蒂岡大公會議後的禮儀改革

　　天主教在二十世紀後半最重要的大事就是進行了第二屆梵蒂岡大公會議（Vantican II Concil），最主要的精神就是落實了教會地方化的政策，開會時間頗長，而在臺灣如何實踐此會的決議又花了不少時日，這次歷史性會議以及其對臺灣、香港及澳門教會的影響，可以從此刊物中找到相當多的史料。特別由於臺港澳三地臺灣較大，因此港澳都有代表來臺參與，俾能將日後的決定一體附諸實施。例如1963年10月3日，盛大報導了梵蒂岡第二次大公會議的消息，標題為「梵蒂岡大公會重開，教宗親主持並致詞，刷新教會基督聖寵灌溉大地，忠心呼籲分離弟兄誠心合一」，該頁同時並登載前往參與並採訪的孫靜潛神父所撰〈二期大會前夕的新景象〉。[49] 此刊還為此在第519期時開始增加兩頁的篇幅。[50] 有關彌撒禮儀的改革，1964年就有一篇〈大公會議彌撒部分譯稿各方意見〉：「臺港澳聖教禮儀委員會所設編譯委員會由陳雄為、布培信、李少峰、顧保鵠、羅星塔、宋之均、項退結七位神父組成……。」[51] 次年又有一篇報導：「臺港澳主教團於2月9日開會，決定3月7日起，彌撒中之重要經文以中文舉行。」[52] 三地的教會也藉此大公會議常有互動，例如1964年6月10日臺港澳主教團在臺北市教務協進會大廈舉行會議，由高理耀公使主席，出席者有

---

48 項退結，〈我對教友生活的短期瓜葛〉，《教友生活周刊・慶祝教友生活周刊創刊廿週年紀念特刊》，1008期，1973/06/28。
49 《教友生活周刊》，520，1963/10/03。
50 《教友生活周刊》，519，1963/09/26。
51 〈大公會議彌撒部分譯稿各方意見〉，《教友生活周刊》，572期，1964/10/15。
52 《教友生活周刊》，589，1965/02/25。

于斌……及香港白主教之代表徐誠斌神父，澳門主教因故缺席。[53]
1965年8月臺港澳禮儀會舉行三屆會議：1964年7月及1965年4月舉行
過兩次，此次8月17至19日第三次，以郭若石總主教為主委，澳門代
表何志仁神父，香港代表陳伯良副主教，孫靜潛為秘書。[54] 此年又有
宋之鈞，〈彌撒禮儀測驗意見綜合報告（1）（2）（3）〉。[55]

　　1965年12月8日大公會議閉幕，中華民國政府派張群為特使，提
到解除路德絕罰目前無法實施。但與東正教互相撤銷絕罰。[56] 臺港
澳三地主教團禮儀委員會也在1966年底提出試用中文彌撒常用經
文。[57]

（四）臺灣教會史及人物

　　有些不見於其他刊物，但足為臺灣天主教史之重要文獻者，例如
全臺最早之三位本地司鐸之一李天一神父英年早逝，其生平事蹟可能
只見於此刊物。

> 道明，〈故李天一大司鐸事略〉
> 本年六月二十五日因患著喉癌絕症，逝世於虎尾若瑟醫院的前
> 溪口本堂李天一神父，係臺灣省雲林縣人，距生於主曆一九二
> 零年六月廿九日，李神父家庭歷代信主虔誠，……於一九四六
> 年十二月廿九日榮膺鐸職，回歸本省，光復後，接充臺北華
> 山、田中、斗南、民雄等地本堂，……十餘年來經其經手授洗
> 進教者不下數千，一九五六年春，奉派洰止溪口鄉開教，……
> 經二年來的披荊斬棘，埋頭苦幹，破異除迷信，轉移整個地方

---

53 《教友生活周刊》，1965/06/17。
54 《教友生活周刊》，1965/08/26；其實早在1961年2月5日的《教友生活周刊》即有登載由香港訪台的徐
　　誠斌神父奉香港白英奇主教之命商權教會用語統一的問題。
55 宋之鈞，〈彌撒禮儀測驗意見綜合報告（1）（2）（3）〉，《教友生活周刊》，1965/11/18、11/25、
　　12/8。
56 《教友生活周刊》，1965/12/15。
57 《教友生活周刊》，683，1966/12/29。

社會風氣，截至目前受洗教友將逾四百，其傳教成果不可不謂
輝煌，……詎竟積勞過度成疾，一病不起，臨終時仍念念不忘
傳教事業，遺言獻車興建聖堂，……李神父遺體安葬於本教區
砂崙聖墓，神父在世只三十又九歲，……。[58]

　　非神職但福傳有貢獻者之史料太少，天主教研究者往往對此引以
為憾，但此刊中卻留下了不少珍貴報導，至少供後人進一步探研。例
如在臺北主教座堂服務之羅銓弟，以及在南部有名的傳道員潘伏
求[59]，都有報導。

臺北民生路主教座堂服務之羅銓弟老先生，服務教堂多年，日
治後期離堂拉車餬口，光復後返堂服務，每天一早來堂準備各
種用品，近午方歸，數十年如一日。本年八月暈倒堂中，十一
月二十九日去世，享年六十八，人尊稱銓伯，聖名多明我。[60]

　　有些修會在華的簡史或是來臺的緣由，都留下珍貴的記錄，例如
主徒會來臺的沿革以及其所屬長安天主堂建造的經過等[61]；擅於管理
學校的聖母昆仲會（Marist Brothers）也有相關的報導，這些報導都
與其入華的簡史一一呈現，頗具價值：

聖母昆仲會於1891年3月8日應北京杜主教之請六位來華。4月
16日至京成立柵欄石門聖母文學會院、上義師範學校及南堂中
小學。1939年，共有修士208人，其中國籍修士76人。學校22
所。1963年高雄鄭天祥主教邀請來臺辦學，王溪泉、劉福亭在

58 道明，〈故李天一大司鐸事略〉，《教友生活周刊》，6: 7，1958/07/23。
59 《教友生活周刊》，1966/05/19。
60 《教友生活周刊》，1964/11/05。
61 《教友生活周刊》，1965/07/29。

高雄，為明誠中學復校，1965年開始招生。[62]

（五）教會倫理及其他雜文

二十世紀後半，第二次世界大戰後，成為美俄兩大集團對峙之局，沒有大的戰亂發生，科技進步迅速，世俗化（secularization）程度加快加深，承平時代，物質享受的多元化，聲色娛樂的推陳出新以及避孕方法的改變，令人眼花撩亂，目眩神迷，相對而言，天主教會的價值觀顯得保守但立場堅定，教會的態度及主張也可從此刊中見到。比較特別而有趣的是在創刊不久，就有「良風團」的成立，是立志以維護善良風俗，倡導觀賞優質電影為職志的團體，以寫信方式提出建團的聲明：

> 給神父和修女們的書信
>
> 可敬的神父和修女們：
>
> 在過去的半年中，我們注意到有許多不良的影片，曾在臺北和全島的戲院中放映。那些不良的影片，對於觀眾，尤其是年青人，會產生怎樣有害的影響，是無庸贅言的。現在一般人，對於犯罪性，離婚，婚姻生活，自殺等等問題，那種毫不在乎的態度，可說都是由這些不良影片，雜誌和書刊所造成的。
>
> 讓我們察看一下，世界其他各國良風團在這方面所有的成就如何？他們檢查不良的影片和雜誌，而加以積極的指導，並且將影片分級，這樣可以使人們，尤其是做父母的人，能夠預先知道那些影片適合他們的孩子看，而那些影片是有害的，而應禁看的。他們這種工作所發生的效果，太顯著了；因此我們天主教伯達院的聖母會，決定在臺灣也同樣組織一個良風團，來推行這種有意義的工作。
>
> 美國的良風團，在好萊塢和紐約，他們都有常務委員會；這委

---

62 《教友生活周刊》，1965/07/08。

員會，經常事先檢查每部好萊塢出品的，或由外國進口的影片，並且根據傳統的道德標準，將這些影片加以分級；因此我們就把他們所分了級的影片名錄和評語節譯，附上以供參考。良風團在臺灣的工作，如果希望能順利進行，那全要靠大家密切的合作才行。我們應該宣誓，或簽訂公約，絕不去看良風團影片指導上所禁看的片子；同時也絕不到那些常放映不良影片的戲院去看戲；我們應該警告當地戲院的負責人：如果他們要放映那些不良的影片，我們就絕不去看；我們只用這種消極抵抗的辦法，戲院的負責人，才會注意選擇適當的影片來放映。做父母的人，和學校的教師們，更應協力推進良風團的工作；我們相信大多數的父母和教師們，對於這種影片的分級和指導，都會歡迎的；但是在這種工作開始時，還須有賴神父們和修女們，經常把良風團的意義，告訴大家；當然，我們要印行一些宣傳品；但是多數的宣傳工作，還是需要就地展開才行。我們這裡附有一份從本年開始，已經在臺北上映過的影片分類表，以後我們每一個月，就出版一份新的分類表；同時臺北教區的教友生活週報，也都會刊載正在臺北上演的影片的分類表。

現在寄上宣誓書或公約書各一份，以便應用（如果需要更多的話請示知即當寄奉）。這些宣誓書或公約書，應交給當地神父，而由他們保存；我們希望每一個教區和學校，要有常務委員會，經常注意當地戲院即將放映的影片，並且應該將這些影片的分級表，張貼在明顯的地方，好讓大家都能看見，而知所選擇。

目前我們對於影片的分級，只限於美國影片和歐洲影片；至於國產片和日本影片，我們正在設法進行中，希望不久，也能將結果奉告。

我們這種工作，還是初次嘗試，如蒙各位神父和修女，有所指示，衷心感激，歡迎。

最後，我們深信各位都會全力支持我們；這樣，我們良風團，必定能夠阻止，而且擊退那些想用不良影片和雜誌，來滲透到我們年青人身心裡的魔鬼。要知道：如果良風團在每一教區和學校裡，都能成功；那麼，就是全國性的成功。我們希望各方面的人士，不分信仰，都來贊助良風團；同時，我們相信純潔的人們，一定會支持一個良風團的存在。

天主教伯達院聖母會良風團常務委員會謹啓

會址：臺北市羅斯福路四段九巷二號

良風團公約

因父，及子，及聖神之名者。亞孟。

凡不純潔，及宣揚和犯罪的影片，我都譴責之。

凡能強化反對製造不端莊，不道德影片的輿論，我願悉心以赴，並和所有抵制他們的人合作。

對那些危害道德生活的電影，我承認有義務為自己陶成一個見解正確的良心。既然作了良風團的團員，我擔保自己絕不去看那些影片，也許願絕不到任何有計畫引人為惡的娛樂場所去。[63]

這是一個由耶穌會主導的青年善會聖母會所成立的團體，在每個星期刊出其分類的結果，舉一個例子，1954年2月17日的電影情況：

甲上，老少咸宜，甲下，宜於成人，丙，絕對禁看；慾海奇花，極端不道德；資料不全，現尚未能查分等級者：蟬妙艷舞。[64]

---

63 《教友生活周刊》，1: 10，1953/09/06。

64 《教友生活周刊》，1: 34，1954/02/17；1961年1月1日好像又恢復了，參見當日的《教友生活周刊》，382，3版。

《教友生活》也刊載有名人物領洗的消息，1957年2月登出故宮博物院院長中央研究院院士蔣復璁的領洗感懷詩：

> 回生上藥沐春和，了悟人天痼宿痾。
> 目激浮雲移疊嶂，心澄碧水止層波。
> 神宮可衛三仇害，御路當承十字磨。
> 技接葡萄因聖寵，歸榮稱頌感恩多。[65]

　　此外，教會也將當時在歐美教會中對於教義或教誡的實際詮釋及主張，加以譯出，例如天主十誡中的第六誡：勿行邪淫，對於國人而言，覺得很模糊又是危機重重，且不易啟口，在此刊中就有很精細的說明，是一篇譯文：

> 天主十誡中的第六誡，一向被認為是最難的一條。而潔德又有「天神之德」的稱呼，……今日的社會，……而孕育出浪蕩不羈，姦淫邪盜，肉慾橫流的情況，……最壞的是竟有很多教友，和異教徒攜手，共度墮落污穢的生活，避孕，墮胎，亂交，重婚，離婚……傷風敗俗的情事，為這些人，潔德的困難是雙重的。

　　這是1957年的文章，所以有關避孕是傷風敗俗，而且大罪小罪也分得很清楚：

違反潔德的大罪
1. 我曾否故意喜歡心靈上引入於罪的不潔思想和想像。
2. 我曾否故意存念以往所有的不潔經歷，而不想以克服。
3. 我曾否以不潔的言語，引起人不好的思想，或在談論這些事

---

[65] 〈四十一年十月三日領洗感懷〉，《教友生活周刊》，4: 36，1957/02/27。

情時，以略知聽者泰半全同意。

4. 我曾否在別人談論淫言穢語時，不急速走開，期待聽聞罪惡的快樂。

5. 我曾否明知自己會陷於嚴重不潔的誘惑，而仍去翻閱一些黃色的書報。

6. 我曾否涉及低級娛樂的場所，或看極端不道德的電影。

7. 我曾否心懷淫念去撫摸，擁抱，和親吻別人。

8. 我曾否手淫，或其他自瀆的行為。

9. 我曾否和別人共犯淫邪大罪。（同性的？異性的或已有婚姻約束的？）

10. 我曾否和自己的親戚犯過此罪。（因為親等，尚有違反第四誡亂倫的大罪）

11. 我曾否期圖獻身於主的人，共犯此罪。（此最上有相反第一誡的褻聖大罪）

12. 我曾否以動物作為洩慾的工具，機會，或其他嚴重的罪行。

13. 我曾否強制他人，遂己獸慾。

14. 我曾否讚許別人犯不潔之罪，或告訴他們這是無法避免的。

15. 我曾否以不潔的輕浮的動作，誘引別人處於重大的危險。

16. 我曾否婚後實行避孕，或不履行婚姻的義務。

17. 我婚後曾否無正當的理由拒絕，或冷遇對方配偶的一再要求。

18. 我曾否於婚後和第三者犯有此罪。（這還犯有相反第七誡公義的大罪）

19. 我曾否對成長的子女，忽略施予在教會性教育的規範。

20. 我曾否放任自己的子女，單獨而長久的和異性廝混。

21. 我曾否租，賣，分送黃色的書報，或類似此種性質的其他什物。

違反潔德的小罪

1. 我曾否一無正當理由，便任意檢閱能動情，或具危險性的書報。

2. 我曾否放縱自己的眼目，隨意顧盼那些危機的人或物。

3. 我曾否對不潔的思想和願望，遲疑不定的去平復。

4. 我曾否對於不合理的情慾和愛戀，不去加力壓抑。[66]

　　像上述的標準，現在看來實為過嚴，不但令人感到自己罪孽深重，而且也很難實行，但這是1957年時教會有些人士的主張。

五、結語

　　以上就《教友生活周刊》發行的緣起，早期經濟狀況，並對此周刊創刊前期，亦即臺灣天主教發展的高峰期（1970年左右）的特色加以說明，最後略談一下此刊對於臺灣天主教史研究的角色。

　　自發行伊始，常常由於編者收聽教廷梵蒂岡廣播電臺華語新聞及早得知而刊布教廷的最新消息，比起從其他管道得知得早而且準確，難怪香港的對口報紙《公教報》的編輯會好奇而詢問這些消息的來源。除了教廷新聞外，歐洲天主教國家以及拉丁美洲的一些教會新聞也有報導，這是其他在臺的刊物所無的。

　　其次是由此刊物可以看到臺灣教會內的新聞及政策之演變。雖然在高雄發行的天主教《善導周刊》也有類似功能，但畢竟南北仍有差異，臺北的消息較為靈通，流通量較廣，重要訊息較可能在《教友生活周刊》上出現，臺灣教會史上的重要大事都是先登載在此刊物上，例如有關臺灣教區的劃分、主教的任命、主教團的創立與改組、教會本地化的過程及發展、第二屆梵蒂岡大公會議的召開以及其決議的落實、禮儀的改革等都是。

---

66 溫德馨譯，〈論潔德〉，《教友生活周刊》，4: 48，1957/05/22，2版。

最後一點是我們可從此刊物上看到臺灣天主教教友宗教生活的實際狀況及其變遷，這也是任何其他刊物所無法見到的。教友對社會的參與，以及如何將教會的精神與中華文化的內涵相融的實際狀況；也能看到教會對於各種先進的科技發展中對於宗教的可能影響進行討論。當然，也可以看到當時教會的保守與限制。此刊物的弱點在於主要的文章過於嚴肅及枯燥，由於要符合教義，又要遵從教會領袖的指導，在動員戡亂的戒嚴時期，加上教會領袖多來自中國大陸，本質上是反對無神論的，在立論的尺度上就有了底線及固定的立場；另外，在家庭主婦及青年兒童的版面，登載的文章並非名家作品，許多還是習作，水準不高，也影響了讀者群。

除了這些缺憾，在此刊慶祝二十週年時，當時的臺北總主教羅光就對它有一概括式的評介：「同時在臺灣，教會卻因人力財力的集中，由一百年祇形成的一個原始教會，建立了一個新興的教會，奠下了中國教會復興的基礎。教友生活周刊便參加了這個新興教會的建立工作，而且記錄了這種工作的過程，將來為編寫中國教會的歷史，積下了許多資料。教友生活周刊不祇是記錄了臺灣傳教的史料，還反映了臺灣傳教的方策。從社論和專論，以及二版三版的文字裡，讀者可以看出二十年來我們傳教的途徑。」[67]

總之，以上是對於《教友生活周刊》發行後的初期階段對於臺灣天主教史研究的重要性之粗淺看法，由於時間關係，本文發表時並未看完這五十年來的所有資料，目前僅就其初創時期的經過，大略瀏覽前二十年左右的資料所整理出來的觀察而已，較完整的理解及整理，俟諸他日。希望讀者能透過本文對於此刊物的起源、性質及其重要性有一大概的了解。

---

67 羅光，〈教友生活周刊與臺灣教會〉，《教友生活周刊・慶祝教友生活周刊創刊廿週年紀念特刊》，1008期，1973/06/28。

臺大楊雲萍文庫之長老教會白話字文獻研究

黃子寧

國立臺灣大學歷史學系博士候選人

摘要

　　本文主要想介紹，由楊雲萍教授（1906-2000）所藏，2001年起經由家屬捐贈，目前原件收藏於臺灣大學「楊雲萍文庫」中之白話字文獻，該批文獻約有89小冊，皆以教會羅馬字書寫，出版年份從早自1892年的《論聖神的功夫》，到1933年的《舊約選錄》，多數為晚清、日治前期的教會出版品。內容多元，包括歷史部分，如《北部基督教長老教會的歷史》；教會羅馬字的學習教材，如《六百字編羅馬字註解》；聖歌、聖詩本，如《詩篇採集》；聖經故事，如《聖誕故事》；禮拜儀式的形式，如《臺灣基督長老教會的典禮》等。這些出版品一方面代表長老教會的傳教立場和方向，一方面讓信徒透過教會羅馬字，直接理解長老教會的教義、歷史和教導，相信也是現今研究者更深入探索早期長老教會傳教的重要史料。

關鍵詞：楊雲萍文庫、長老教會、羅馬字、白話字

一、前言

　　長老教會的傳教模式，其特色之一就是要求信徒直接閱讀聖經，強調聖經的重要性，白話字的形式更增加了讓所有信徒自己閱讀的可能性。早期臺灣長老教會的傳道四處傳教時，常隨身帶書，一邊講論道理一邊賣書或送書「（胡肇基）他還是常常帶著一些書，去到各地順便佈道。」[1]、「（趙爵祥）28歲有受公會派遣和豹兄（李豹）出門四處賣聖書。」[2] 其實除了聖經之外，長老教會還有許多其他的出版品，曾讓天主教道明會的神父頗為羨慕「若是我們有部小印刷機，那麼就能出版牧靈上所需要的書籍，一定可以幫助更多人認識信仰的真光。我很羨慕此地的基督教，他們有一部印刷機，每年印刷很可觀的書籍和傳單，散布全島各地。」[3] 所謂「很可觀的書籍」是指何種類型、哪些內容的書籍？更進一步問，晚清到日治時期的長老教會信徒，或者將對象擴大為懂得使用閩南語白話字的人，在當時究竟可以透過長老教會的出版品管道，獲得什麼樣的觀念？看到什麼樣的世界？接觸什麼樣的新知？針對這個問題，歷來關於教會報紙的綿密研究，已經給了許多肯定的答案。[4] 只是如果單就「書籍」這個形式的出版品而言，目前似尚闕如。因此筆者欲就臺大「楊雲萍文庫」中的白話字書籍進行整理研究，期能加以補足。

　　本文擬先依出版資訊，介紹楊雲萍教授收藏之長老教會白話字文獻，用表格整理呈現，接著依照書籍性質，分門別類分析討論，最後結語提出這批白話字文獻的特色和價值。

---

1 林絹熙，〈胡肇基的小傳〉，《臺灣教會報》，第358卷，1915年1月，頁3。
2 彭士藏，〈小傳趙爵祥〉，《臺灣教會報》，第399卷，1918年6月，頁3。
3 Fr. Pablo Fernandez O. P.著，黃德寬譯，《天主教在臺開教記》（臺北：光啟出版社，1996），頁157。
4 可以參考張妙娟，《開啟心眼——《臺灣府城教會報》與長老教會的基督徒教育》（臺南：人光出版社，2005）、陳慕真，《漢字之外：臺灣府城教會報Kap臺語白話字文獻中ê文明觀》（臺南：人光出版社，2007）。

二、文獻介紹──以表格爲形式

首先介紹楊雲萍教授（1906-2000）所藏，2001年起經由家屬捐贈，目前原件收藏於臺大「楊雲萍文庫」中之白話字文獻。[5] 該批文獻，經筆者仔細檢閱後，數量應有89小冊，多數版面長約20公分、寬約15公分，頁數都不多。除了《基督教問答》一書以漢文書寫之外，其餘皆以教會羅馬字書寫，包含閩南語羅馬字（82本）和客語羅馬字（6本）。著作編輯的人員、出版印刷的機構和書籍內容的性質，幾乎皆以教會人士、教會書局和長老教會傳教目的為主。可稽的出版年份，從早自1881年的《舊約的聖經──列王：下卷》，到1969年《白話字實用教科書》為止，時間範圍橫跨臺灣晚清、日治和戰後三個階段，其中以日治時期的出版品為最大宗。關於這批文獻的基本資訊，以下先以表 1 整理呈現[6]。

三、文獻分析

若探究、排列這批文獻，依其書籍的內容性質和出版目的，筆者約略先分做傳教相關、教育教材、宗教文學和雜項等四大類別，再從文體或語言，區分出其中的小類別。接下來就各個小類別討論其作者身分、大意形式和出版事項等，提出可能的研究課題和研究價值，或是已經出現的研究成果。礙於筆者個人的語言限制和學力不足，無法對每一個類別都進行深入分析，有的類別只能觀其表面、舉其大意，

---

5 參考網站「楊雲萍教授之生平年表」：http://www.lib.ntu.edu.tw/cg/manuscript/yangup/ information_002.htm。除了在臺灣大學圖書館的原件線裝書之外，另外在中央研究院人文社會科學聯合圖書館，也有一套複印本，但是冊數的部分，筆者目前只找到77冊。

6 這個表格，筆者是在翻閱過所有收藏書籍之後，以個別書籍的成書目的和內容性質，再佐以出版年月的早晚，來做簡單的分類排序。其中的「著者／編者」、「出版項」，有些與臺大圖書館網站或其他網路資料不同之處，筆者係以所見，再三確認過。若有書籍資料不足處，該表格處即以空白呈現。有些作者的中文譯名目前還無法確認，故筆者先行自譯，並加上問號以表明。另外，關於分類的方式和某些書籍的屬性，得益受教於論文評論人張妙娟教授甚多，深為銘謝。

表1：臺大楊雲萍文庫中之白話字文獻

編號	書名	著者／編者	出版項	成書目的／性質
(一) 傳教相關				
1.問答體				
1	真道問答			
2	廟祝問答		臺南：聚珍堂，1914	
3	經言問答		廈門：閩南聖教書局，1919	
4	談論道理	梅甘霧（Campbell Naismith Moody）	臺南：新樓書房，1920	
5	基督教問答	陳清義譯	基隆：昭明社圖書部，1934再版	「此冊問答，記載有五十條，無非示人悟道之要旨。因日本基督教會，是此冊最能振聵發聾，有三五名士，參稽酌量，以合本邦目下之適用，而刊行之。余觀夫臺灣基督教會，現時尚缺此佳本，不揣固陋，謹取和文翻譯漢文，刊印成冊，聊以補吾教之不逮云爾。」[7]；以漢文書寫。
6	真道問答		鼓浪嶼：閩南聖教書局，1934	

---

7 陳清義，〈基督教問答序〉，收錄於氏譯《基督教問答》（基隆：昭明社圖書部，1934再版），頁1-2。

2. 聖詩聖歌				
7	孩童聖歌	Hô An-lin（胡安鈴？）編輯	廈門：萃經堂，1922	「如今我重印此書，希望能有益於許多主日學學校和基督教家庭。」[8]
8	聖詩琴譜	臺灣基督長老教會大會聖詩編輯部編	臺南：新樓書房，1926	
9	聖歌	連瑪玉（Marjorie Learner）編	臺南：臺灣教會公報社，1934	
10	基督徒軍歌：讚美主	雪峰逸嵐（張春榮）編	高雄：ハレルヤ堂書店，1934	「現時臺灣及閩南各教會所用者，大都是聖詩及養心神詩而已，但是多不足供主日學及聖歌隊之用。……故編《軍歌讚美主》一冊，甚有活潑勇敢之氣，更合兒童心理，又可充聖歌隊及佈道之用，足可供全屬主之兄姊參考……。」[9]
11	聖詩	臺灣基督長老教會大會編	臺南：臺灣教會公報社，1941第二版	
12	傳道奮興歌			

---

8 Hô An-lin（胡安鈴？）編輯，《孩童聖歌》（廈門：萃經堂，1922），〈preface〉。

9 嚴祝三，〈序〉，收錄於雪峰逸嵐編，《基督徒軍歌：讚美主》（高雄：ハレルヤ堂書店，1934），頁1。

3.教義教理與研經註釋			
13	舊約的聖經——列王：下卷		聖書公會，1881	
14	論聖神的功夫		廈門鼓浪嶼：萃經堂，1892	
15	先知的教示	K. R. Green	廈門：萃經堂，1920	
16	救主受審遂被釘死的事		廈門：閩南聖教書局，1924	譯自 *The Trial and Death of Jesus Christ*，作者為 James Stalker。
17	主耶穌史略		廈門：閩南聖教書局	
18	耶穌基督的來歷			
19	救主的來歷	趙𡉏編	臺南：新樓書房，1930	「這本書是傳道師趙𡉏先生，在善化在職時，遇到祝聖誕，寫來講給眾人聽。」[10]
20	路加福音傳研究（第二本）			
21	四傳研究的要錄			
22	使徒信的摘問			
23	羅馬人書的研究			
24	舊約年歷紀要			「這本是要幫助人能照順序排列舊約所記載的好幾項要緊事。」[11]
25	聖書的記錄（第四本）		廈門：閩南聖教書局，1927	

---

10 趙𡉏編，《救主的來歷》（臺南：新樓書房，1930），〈小序〉。

11 不著撰人，《舊約年歷紀要》（出版地、出版年月不詳），〈頭序〉。

26	天路指明	廉德烈（A. B. Nielson）譯輯	臺南：新樓書房，1927	原書作者為楊格非（Griffith John）牧師「（《天路指明》）從發行至今，六十多年，救濟迷路的人，實在不少，幫贊傳道的工也是很大。總是所印的，都是漢文，對於認識羅馬字的白話的還未普及，所以這次才翻譯來印。」[12]
27	聖經內要緊道理	安義理姑娘（Miss Lily Adair）	臺南：新樓書房，1929	
28	舊約選錄		廈門：閩南聖教書局，1933	
29	通俗羅馬書（保羅書翰）	劉主安編	臺南：臺灣教會公報社，1942	
30	聖經選錄（第二本）	高金聲編修	臺南：臺灣教會公報社，1951	
31	聖經選錄（第三本）	高金聲編修	臺南：臺灣教會公報社，1951	
32	聖經選錄（第四本）	高金聲編修	臺南：臺灣教會公報社，1951	
33	聖經選錄（第五本）	高金聲編修	臺南：臺灣教會公報社，1951	

---

12 廉德烈（A. B. Nielson）、陳延齡，〈緣起〉，收錄於廉德烈譯輯，《天路指明》（臺南：新樓書房，1927）。

34	巴拿巴派好幾項的錯誤	孫雅各（James Dickson）	臺南：新樓書局，1930	「今日我們做為基督徒應該要責備那種用不合聖經和常識的方法來宣傳的假先生。我現在所要講起的，特別要，指這一派，就是近來在我們臺灣攪亂我們許多處教會的那個真耶穌教！」[13]
35	錢？——新約聖經的經濟倫理	陳泗治	臺南：臺灣教會公報社，1951	
4. 教牧相關				
36	備辦心守晚餐			
37	引人得救成聖			「出這本書本意是要幫贊做個人工的人，照順序說明救人的道理。又傳道先生若用這14課的問題來照順序，每個禮拜慢慢解說，一定也能利益很多人。」[14]
38	臺灣基督長老教會的典禮		臺南：聚珍堂，1919	「這本書就是大會在1918年的年錄第35、36條所議定的，遂准施行。」[15]
39	進教須知	廉德烈編輯	臺南：新樓書房，1930再版	
40	教會的典禮	臺灣基督長老教會大會編	臺南：新樓書房，1931	
41	臺灣北部基督長老教會憲法規則及條例	北部臺灣基督長老教會憲法部會編	臺北：北部臺灣基督長老教會憲法部會，1934	

---

13 孫雅各（James Dickson），〈頭序〉，收錄於氏著《巴拿巴派好幾項的錯誤》（臺南：新樓書房，1930）。

14 不著撰人，《引人得救成聖》（出版地、出版年月不詳），〈頭序〉。

15 不著撰人，《臺灣基督長老教會的典禮》（臺南：聚珍堂，1919），〈頭序〉。

5. 教會歷史			
42	北部臺灣基督長老教會的歷史	禧年紀念部編	臺北：北部臺灣基督長老教會傳道局，1923	「因為設教在臺灣北部50年，很多人非常欣慕想知道早年教會的事情。」[16]
43	教會歸正的歷史	巴克禮（Thomas Barclay）編	臺南：新樓書房，1925	
44	長老會的歷史	劉忠堅（Duncan Macleod）編	臺南：新樓書房，1927	「……著這本書讓列位知道臺灣的教會所承認的教派是什麼款式。論長老會的源由、歷史，以及種種的條規，臺灣的會友還不十分明白。」[17]
45	南臺教會的歷史	楊士養編輯	臺南：臺灣教會公報社，1953	
6. 客語羅馬字文獻			
46	請主神示	Ńg-Kin-Fù（黃金富？）	1906	以客語羅馬字書寫。
47	頌主新詩	Ńg-Kin-Fù	1906	以客語羅馬字書寫。
48	聖道問答	Ńg-Kin-Fù	禮拜堂印書館，1909	以客語羅馬字書寫。
49	詩篇採集		汕頭：Fûng-siet-hien印書館，1923	以客語羅馬字書寫。
50	真道問答		1926	以客語羅馬字書寫。
51	天路歷程tshîen-shu		汕頭：Fûng-siet-hien印書館，1927	以客語羅馬字書寫。

---

16 北部基督長老教會傳道局編輯，《北部臺灣基督長老教會的歷史》（臺北：北部臺灣基督長老教會傳道局，1923），〈頭序〉。

17 劉忠堅編，《長老會的歷史》（臺南：新樓書房，1927），〈頭序〉。

1.閩南語白話字教材

52	字母課本		廈門：閩南聖教書局，1931	
53	六百字編羅馬字註解	廉德烈編輯	臺南：臺灣教會公報社，1932第二版	「因為文字淺顯，應用又很寬廣，雖然只有六百字而已，若能將字音、解釋讀到很熟，就能夠變化來利用。這樣，就無論寫信或是作文，無不自由自在……總是懂羅馬字的人要學漢文，或是懂漢文的人要學羅馬字，都可以互相幫助。」[18]
54	白話字母		廈門：閩南聖教書局，1935	
55	白話字實用教科書	許有成編著	臺南：臺灣教會公報社，1969第23版	

---

18 廉德烈（A. B. Nielson）、陳延齡，〈頭序〉，收錄於廉德烈編輯，《六百字編羅馬字註解》（臺南：臺灣教會公報社，1932，第二版）。

2. 童蒙教材與教案書				
56	訓蒙淺說			內容與編號61，1903年出版的《訓蒙淺說》相同。
57	訓蒙淺說		鼓浪嶼：萃經堂，1903	
58	訓蒙淺說（第二本）		廈門：閩南聖教書局，1911	
59	幼稚課本（第二本）		1920	
60	幼稚課本（第一本）		1925	
61	幼稚課本（第二本）		1925	與編號63，1920年出版之幼稚課本（第二本）內容相同。
62	主日學中心之問題	潘道榮	臺南：新樓書房，1926	「不才在想，到這時還未有人用白話字來寫關係到主日學的書，所以順應這個機會，寫這本《主日學中心之問題》，敬獻給熱心同樣琢磨於主日學的好朋友做參考。」[19]
63	養心諭言		廈門，1931	19則伊索寓言。
64	日曜學校教案：基督徒生活的標準	臺灣教會公報社編輯	臺南：臺灣教會公報社，1942	
3. 地理教科書				
65	地理教科書（卷二）			
66	地理教科書（卷三）			
67	地理教科書（卷四）			

---

19 潘道榮，《主日學中心之問題》（臺南：新樓書房，1926），〈自序〉。

（三）宗教文學				
1. 證道故事				
68	新聞的雜錄		廈門：閩南聖教書局，1915	
69	有求必應	朱約安姑娘（Miss Joan Stuart）譯	臺南：聚珍堂，1917	「翻譯這本書的意思是要讓人更知道祈禱的大路用，因為所記載的事每項都是真實，人已經有這麼經歷過，果然上帝有允准他們的祈禱，成為干證。」[20]
70	招路指南：從死入活（下卷）		1921	
71	十個故事	文安姑娘（Miss Annie E. Butler）、朱約安姑娘譯	廈門：閩南聖教書局，1923	
72	女界名人	文安姑娘、萬真珠姑娘（Miss Margaret Barnett）譯著	臺南：新樓書房，1923	「這本書所記的，都是屬信主的女徒，不嫌折磨，不顧自己，獨獨要引領人就近耶穌，脫離罪惡，來作她們的責任，這樣所行的好，可以作我們的模範，所以取名為『女界名人』。」[21]
73	益智錄（卷二）		1929	

---

20 朱約安姑娘（Miss Joan Stuart）譯，《有求必應》（臺南：聚珍堂，1917），〈頭序〉。

21 文安姑娘（Miss Annie E. Butler）、萬真珠姑娘（Miss Margaret Barnett）譯著，《女界名人》（臺南：新樓書房，1923），〈頭序〉。

2. 宗教小說				
74	長遠兩友相論	J. Watson譯	廈門：閩南聖教書局，1914	原名 *The Two Friends*，又有翻為「張遠兩友相論」，作者為米憐（William Milne），1819 年於馬六甲首次刊行，號稱中國第一部基督教小說。[22]
75	眠夢中的人客	Maria Talmage[23]		
76	天路歷程的大意	廉德烈	臺南：聚珍堂，1915	
77	仰望地	H. C. Kip編輯	廈門：萃經堂，1917	原名*Expectation Corner*，作者為Emily Steele Elliott。
78	泰迪的鈕釦	H. C. Kip譯	廈門：閩南聖教書局，1917	原名 *Teddy's Button*，為 Amy Le Feuvre 在 1896 年出版之基督教兒童故事。
79	艾瑞克的福音	Mrs. Kin譯		原名*Eric's good news*，作者Amy Le Feuvre。
80	銀冰鞋			原名*The Silver Skates*，作者Mary Mapes Dodge。
81	希蘭的目的			
82	聖誕故事			
83	欣慕義親像飫嘴乾			

---

22 吳淳邦，〈19世紀90年代中國基督教小說在韓國的傳播與翻譯〉，《東華人文學報》，第9期（花蓮：國立東華大學人文社會科學學院，2006.7），頁218-219。
23 作者可能為打馬字（John Van Nest Talmage）牧師娘。

	（四）雜項			
84	內訓（大明仁孝皇后內訓）	明朝仁孝皇后著、林殷碧霞譯	廈門，1918	
85	經書合聖道	廉德烈編輯	臺南：新樓書房，1925	「這本書前已經印上臺灣教會報，是將四書五經的書句，摘出有合於聖道的。」[24]
86	成語集	林祥雲記、廉德烈編輯	臺南：新樓書房，1928	「這近日廉德烈牧師因為要回去英國，在整理行李的時候，忽然找出 20 年前，已經過世那個林祥雲先生所寫的成語和俗語百餘條。看完後不忍廢棄，所以貼錢下去印成這一小本書，用這樣來紀念他早時的先生。」[25]
87	身體理的總論		鼓浪嶼：萃經堂，1908	「論到人的身軀怎樣活，怎樣成長，有多項奧妙，人總不明白知道……如果備辦這本，不過是說一點比較淺的事，是要讓孩子能學點大概而已……讓他知道怎樣慎重，一世人勇（健）心命。」[26]
88	論偶像			韻文
89	淡水女學院同窗會會錄（第十三回）	私立淡水女學院同窗會	臺南：臺灣教會公報社，1934	

---

24 廉德烈、陳延齡，〈頭序〉，收錄於廉德烈編輯，《經書合聖道》（臺南：新樓書房，1925）。

25 陳延齡，〈頭序〉，收錄在廉德烈編輯，《成語集》（臺南：新樓書房，1928）。

26 不著撰人，《身體理的總論》（鼓浪嶼：萃經堂，1908），頁1-2。

祈請見諒。

（一）傳教相關

在這個範圍裡的書籍，主要就是包含長老教會的宣教媒介、信徒提升自身靈命的工具書、教會典禮和組織的須知以及教會發展的歷史過程，通稱為傳教相關類型。

1. 問答體

第一個小類別筆者稱之為「問答體」，因為這種類型的書籍，寫作型態是以一問一答為主，藉由兩個虛擬角色之間的對答，比方說傳道先生與廟祝，或者更簡單地直接模擬一般未信者可能會有的疑惑，透過一個問題和一個回答，解釋基督教的名詞概念，表達基督教和其他宗教的不同之處。基本上這是一種比較直接表達，敘述簡潔，口吻肯定，閱讀容易的宣教文字，對於剛有興趣於基督教者、初信者或兒童，都可以當作簡易的宗教入門書。另外，問答的體例，也利於讓負責傳教工作的傳道、牧師等人，揣摩宣講道理時可能面對的疑問，練習快速初步的應對。表格中，編號1到編號6，以及編號48和編號50，都是屬於這種類型。從各種問答體文獻的出版年月，以及印製的語言版本，除了閩南語羅馬字以外，還有以客語羅馬字書寫的《聖道問答》、《真道問答》，以及翻譯自日文、再以漢文書寫的《基督教問答》，可以看出這個類型應該是一種長期發行且廣泛使用的宣教書籍。[27]

---

[27] 除了楊雲萍文庫所藏之外，閩南語白話字書寫的問答體書籍，目前還有「淡水中學白話字史料」收的不著撰人，《聖冊的問答》（廈門：南福建倫敦聖教會，1915）、A. L. Warnshuis翻譯改寫，《習道問答》（廈門：閩南聖教書局，1918）二本。參考網站「臺灣白話字文獻館」：http://www.tcll.ntnu.edu.tw/pojbh/script/artical-12234.htm、http://www.tcll.ntnu.edu.tw/pojbh/script/artical-12233.htm。陳清忠也以問答體為體例寫文過，參見陳清忠，〈信仰的問答──論活基督〉，《芥菜子》，第12號，1927年1月，頁8-9。

2. 聖詩聖歌

　　第二個小類別即是在舉行禮拜、主日學教育或聖歌隊時，極為重要的聖詩和聖歌。從編號7的《孩童聖歌》到編號12的《傳道奮興歌》，皆是這個類別。有關於臺灣聖詩聖歌的歷史研究，目前已有相當專業的學術成果。[28] 在此，筆者想特意提出的，是《基督徒軍歌：讚美主》的編輯者——本地信徒張春榮，又名張亨寅，筆名雪峰逸嵐。他自述編《基督徒軍歌：讚美主》的原因有二：「（一）因十數年來於數教會主日學，充無名雜差，頗覺缺乏合於兒童心理之詩歌，故思須有此類發刊之必要。（二）同時於數教會組織聖歌隊，所有原稿未甘放棄，故為收拾，以供多數兄姊為參考。」[29] 可知他的教會服務多在主日學和聖歌隊，其實，日治時期他在教會報紙《芥菜子》、《臺灣教會公報》上，以筆名雪峰逸嵐曾發表過為數不少的文章，特別是在1920年代，即以兒童信徒為主體對象，傳達他想教導兒童的種種道理：

> 在這號的「芥菜子」，我要專門跟同屬主的孩子兄、孩子姊，一起講話。你們如果不會看，叫你們的阿娘、阿姊，讀給你們聽，你們一定會很歡喜。我也是很歡喜，因為我也曾當過孩子，我也有孩子，所以很愛和孩子講話。[30]

　　像這樣的選擇對象和文句寫法，在日治時期堪稱特殊，他的背景和文章，是否能呈現當時教會人士對於兒童的看法觀感和關心重點，值得一探究竟。

3. 教義教理與研經註釋

　　第三個小類別是輔助信徒研讀聖經的註釋書和聖經歷史。眾所周

---

28 江玉玲，《聖詩歌：臺灣第一本教會聖詩的歷史溯源》（臺北縣：臺灣基督教文藝，2004）。

29 張亨寅，〈自序〉，收錄於氏編《基督徒軍歌：讚美主》（高雄：ハレルヤ堂書店，1934），頁3。

30 雪峰逸嵐，〈智識的源頭〉，《芥菜子》，第10號，1926年11月，頁10。

知，長老教會十分鼓勵信徒直接閱讀聖經「要詳細知道耶穌的事情，得要從聖書；人若讀，就像親眼見到他。這樣聖書實在是人人所應該有的要緊書。」[31] 但是一般信徒在剛開始接觸聖經時，不僅內容浩瀚，還有文化相異的障礙和歷史背景的不足，往往茫然不得其道，甚或曲解原意，「雖然偶而遇到難以解說的句子，還是要趕緊講究 [研究] 到明白，千萬不能放棄……假設真的不知道這個意思，去請教牧師也不要緊；也要求聖神指示看完之後會透徹，才能說是確實有講究。要緊的是不要固執自己的意見來勉強解說，當作是得到它的意思，這樣的陷害不是小事。」[32] 請教牧師之餘，也因而產生這一類工具書的需求，在此排列在表格裡的編號13到編號35。

其中值得注意的，像是為了慶祝聖誕節而編寫《救主的來歷》的本地傳道趙匹，關於他的事蹟，目前僅知他儒名承箕，在嘉義的半天厝教會（下半天）和臺南的新市教會任職甚久，1908年入臺南神學院，中間停學一年，1913年畢業。他為人勤勉好學「傳道者有的畢業後不再讀書，在學校成績雖然很好，十餘年後就變做落伍者，有人畢業後繼續研究，趙匹先生他對四書五經實在有造就。」[33] 像這類沒沒無名的地方傳道，原來在1930年即有其著作出版，不僅為其個人履歷補上一筆文字事工，後來的研究者，也可以透過其著作，進一步去了解日治時期長老教會傳道的信仰水平和神學素養。另外，像孫雅各（James Dickson）牧師的《巴拿巴派好幾項的錯誤》，也是在研究日治時期真耶穌教會傳入臺灣後，與長老教會互爭信徒那段歷史的重要資料。

4. 教牧相關

這類書籍，是載明信教之後，個人應該要遵守的教條、教會的規章和組織的運作方式等，也包含了教會典禮的形式和教會憲法的規定。

---

31 高金聲，〈聖冊公會的報告〉，《臺南府城教會報》，第294卷，1909年9月，頁76。

32 Chhoà Jiók-san（蔡若山），〈論讀聖冊〉，《臺南府城教會報》，第141卷，1896年12月，頁91。

33 王占魁，〈我所尊敬懷念的師友〉，《臺灣教會公報》，第914期，1963年7月15日，頁14-16。

5. 教會歷史

　　從這七本書籍的資料來看，從日治時期開始，北部長老教會和南部長老教會都已經著手編纂記錄教會發展的歷史，另外，外籍宣教士也有針對宗教改革和長老會的歷史由來留下著作。

6. 客語羅馬字文獻

　　客語羅馬字的宣教文獻，是在客家地區傳教的必備，楊雲萍文庫中收有六本。其中《詩篇採集》和《天路歷程tshîen-shu》確定是在汕頭印刷出版，而長老教會在北部客家庄傳教的先驅鍾亞妹，即在赴任傳道前一年，被派往汕頭的長老教會見習一年，[34] 可見作為長老教會傳教中心之一的汕頭，在提供客家人傳教資源和經驗上的重要地位。研究者日後若想了解基督教的客家傳教史，尋訪汕頭等教會書局的客語羅馬字出版品，或許也是一種可行的研究方式。

(二) 教育教材

　　教育是基督新教傳教時一個重要的努力方向，也帶來不容小覷的影響。楊雲萍文庫中即收有學習閩南語白話字和啟蒙兒童的教科書。

1. 閩南語白話字教材

　　學習白話字的必要和必須、好處和功用，一直是長老教會特意著重、宣傳的部分，最直接的目的當然是要求信徒能夠自己閱讀聖經，但是白話字還有許多其他功用，「這個白話字不是說有趁 [聽從、服膺] 道理的人才能學，沒趁道理的人來學也是好。因為路用真開闊，記什麼事情都可以，跟漢文沒兩樣。不論是要記國家的事情，還是生意人要報行情，或是做小說，或是做論說，還是書信來往以及雜路用，都很合適。」[35] 為了推廣白話字的學習，適合的基礎教材理所應

---

34 鍾謙順，《煉獄餘生錄—臺獨大前輩坐獄二十七年回憶錄》（臺北：前衛出版社，1999），頁3。
35 〈教育的好法〉，《臺南府城教會報》，第314卷，1911年5月，頁38。

備。從編號52到編號55的四本教科書中，可以看到，除了直接以基本的字母、音調、例句的白話字練習教材之外，還有像是《六百字編羅馬字註解》這類運用白話字和漢字雙向學習的教材模式。像這樣子的學習教材，除了給未受過漢文教育、只受過白話字教育的信徒一個自學漢文的機會之外，也給了先受過漢文教育的人學習白話字的便利管道，應用範圍和使用對象可以更為擴大，就如同《六百字編羅馬字註解》曾在林獻堂家族和一新義塾發揮的作用。[36]

2. 童蒙教材與教案書

這個類別裡的九本書，包括了給幼童上課用的主日學教材《幼稚課本》系列，字數較多、難度較高的《訓蒙淺說》系列，翻譯伊索寓言的兒童讀物《養心諭言》，以及《主日學中心之問題》、《日曜學校教案：基督徒生活的標準》這二本討論主日學教授的師資、課程、管理、安排等，給主日學老師使用的教案書。當然這些書籍並非只有兒童能夠閱讀，就像其中的《幼稚課本》和《養心諭言》與問答體中的《真道問答》，在臺灣都列為主日學的初級白話字教材。[37] 只是就其書名訂定、書籍內容和篇幅字數等方面來看，其設計為教育兒童的目的應無庸置疑，因此通稱為童蒙教材。

臺灣基督長老教會的兒童教育，是從主日學和教會小學開始，作為傳教工作的一環。[38] 針對小學、主日學的設立目的和發展過程等，已有學者為文論證。[39] 只是基督教的兒童教材和課程內容，其實質為何？教會學校想要灌輸給孩子，是哪些知識和觀念？若一個生在日治

---

36 黃子寧，〈林獻堂與基督教（1927-1945）〉，收錄於許雪姬總編輯，《日記與臺灣史研究：林獻堂先生逝世50週年紀念論文集》下冊（臺北：中研院臺史所，2008），頁713-714。

37 潘道榮，《主日學中心之問題》，頁63。

38 張妙娟，《開啟心眼─《臺灣府城教會報》與長老教會的基督徒教育》，頁182。

39 張妙娟，〈日治時期臺灣南部長老教會的主日學教育（1895-1926）〉，《興大歷史學報》，第22期（臺中：國立中興大學歷史學系，2010.2），頁79-103。盧啟明，〈日曜學校與皇民化運動──以臺灣基督長老教會的主日學教育為中心（1937-1945）〉，《臺灣學研究》，第11期（臺北：國立中央圖書館臺灣分館，2011.6），頁33-57。

時期臺灣信徒家庭的小孩,在他既不擅長閱讀傳統漢文,也還不熟悉標準日文的時候,透過白話字他到底可以得到哪些書本上的智識?研究上述這些童蒙教材,或許可以給我們一些答案。《幼稚課本》有二本,第一本分為21課,內容各自獨立,最長的一課約有120個語詞、兩頁。[40] 大部分單元都只有一頁內容,也多附筆觸簡單的插畫。各單元標題如表2:

表2:《幼稚課本》第一本各課標題

第1課	論下雨	第12課	論天父
第2課	歌(數字)	第13課	論祈禱
第3課	論錢	第14課	論相疼
第4課	論嬰兒	第15課	論不貪心
第5課	論嬰兒滿月	第16課	論老實
第6課	論新娘	第17課	時鐘歌
第7課	論年尾	第18課	蜜蜂歌
第8課	論正月	第19課	聖詩
第9課	論讀書	第20課	論遊戲
第10課	歌(小鳥)	第21課	來禮拜
第11課	聖詩		

　　課程主題範圍,涵蓋兒童的日常生活(論錢、論遊戲)、弟妹手足(論嬰兒、論讀書)、年節儀式(論嬰兒滿月、論新娘、論年尾、論正月)、天氣時間(論下雨、時鐘歌)、動物昆蟲(蜜蜂歌、歌(小鳥))、品行品德(論不貪心、論老實),以及宗教教育(論天父、論祈禱、論相疼、來禮拜、聖詩)。整本課本的設定氛圍,主人

40　〈第21課 來禮拜〉,收錄在不著撰人,《幼稚課本》第一本(出版地不詳,1925),頁21-22。

翁就是一個大約6、7歲，出身信徒家庭，有上教會學校的孩童。這樣的主題重心和主角設定，在《幼稚課本》第二本再度呈現。

第二本變成一個長篇故事，描述一個名叫仁竹（Jîn-tek）的5歲男孩，隨阿媽回鄉下一個月度假的趣事。分為12節，每一節的字數約有200個語詞、兩頁左右。字數較第一本略增，故事的形式也讓可讀性增高。內容一樣提到親人、手足、好朋友、小動物和新奇的經驗（例如坐船、親近動物）等小孩子比較熟悉、有興趣的對象，也有阿媽帶他去做禮拜、好朋友在家拜床頭公等宗教教育場面。另外，比第一本更細膩的地方，在描寫孩子的心理層面，以及大人怎麼用宗教來安慰引導小孩的情緒。像仁竹要離家時捨不得妹妹，他就學媽媽說話，說：「小妹你要乖乖，不要吵人，你還不會祈禱，阿兄會替你祈禱。」[41] 母羊失去小羊，叫聲悲傷，仁竹看了很難過，阿媽就順勢教他：「耶穌很疼你，你是祂的小羊，你知道嗎？」[42] 還有像是仁竹異想天開，幫母雞孵蛋；去做禮拜時東問西問、靜不下來。基本上，《幼稚課本》第二本，對於小孩所喜歡好奇的事物，以及小孩敏感脆弱、淘氣好動的天性，其觀察和描摹都極為生動，如果不當成宗教教育的課本或是白話字學習的教材，而用現今的兒童讀物標準來看的話，也是很優秀的兒童作品。

《訓蒙淺說》也有兩本，楊雲萍文庫中所見的版本，出版年月較《幼稚課本》更早，曾經確實應用在什麼樣的學校系統或課程科目上，目前筆者尚未查到確定的輔證資料。因此，這裡只能單就書籍本身內容獲得並推測一些相關資訊。首先，《訓蒙淺說》第一本和第二本，一樣都有30課的獨立單元，第一本每一課的語詞數，少的約有120個語詞，多的則有280個語詞左右。第二本的話，短的單元約有150個語詞，長的單元則高達740個語詞。《訓蒙淺說》第一本的序中有提到：

---

41 不著撰人，《幼稚課本》第二本（出版單位、出版地不詳，1925），頁3。

42 不著撰人，《幼稚課本》第二本，頁21。

備辦這本書，要緊的意思是要開孩子的靈竅。先生不要讓學生連著讀很多；一日讀一課，就足夠了。

讀完先生要問意思，看孩子有明白否，還要舉圖畫（為例）。[43]

確實很多課，尤其是介紹動物、昆蟲的課程，都有附上一幅精美複雜的插圖。從序文、圖畫品質、課數和內容語詞數量的增加，足證《訓蒙淺說》確是教會的童蒙教材，而學習對象的年齡，想必比《幼稚課本》的設定再大一些。以下，表3和表4分別列出《訓蒙淺說》第一、二本的各課標題：

課程包括幾大類特色主題：

(1) 聖經教育：論上帝創萬物、論書

(2) 品格德行：不要懶惰、鶴母疼子、孩子的好模樣、孩子的心、論老實、惡有善報、名不合、求福氣

(3) 喻道故事：孩子的花種、蜘蛛絲救人、尾蝶的比喻、尾蝶的比喻II、金城在哪裡、賊改變的事、買魚不用錢

(4) 寓言故事：印度國的故事、會講究所看、憐憫遇得憐憫

(5) 動物相關：論鯨魚、論豺狼、論狗會救人、論象、論獅、捕象的方法、論駱駝、論貓、論猴、論豹、白熊、論花條馬、深海奇怪的生物

(6) 昆蟲：蜂蛾（燈蛾）、蜜蜂、虎頭蜂、草蜢、論蚯蚓、蜘蛛、論花會吃生物

(7) 地球環境：論地球、論海

(8) 自然現象：龍絞水、論空氣

(9) 中國名景、歷史故事：萬里長城、孔子的來歷、孟子的母親

(10) 世界大城：巴黎、馬尼拉、麥加、柏林、小呂宋、華盛頓

(11) 現代器具實業：論金、論船、論筆、論燈塔、論針、論摘海茸、論火燻車、印書

---

43 不著撰人，〈頭序〉，《訓蒙淺說》第一本（出版單位、出版地不詳，1903），頁（1）。

表 3：《訓蒙淺說》第一本各課標題

第1課	論上帝創萬物	第16課	論老實
第2課	不要懶惰	第17課	論獅
第3課	論地球	第18課	孩子的花種
第4課	論書	第19課	論火燻車[44]
第5課	論海	第20課	捕象的方法
第6課	論金	第21課	論駱駝
第7課	鶴母疼子	第22課	論貓
第8課	孟子的母親	第23課	孩子的心
第9課	論船	第24課	蜂蜙（燈蛾）[45]
第10課	論筆	第25課	論花會吃生物
第11課	論燈塔	第26課	龍絞水[46]
第12課	孩子的好模樣	第27課	論空氣
第13課	論象	第28課	論猴
第14課	蜜蜂，虎頭蜂	第29課	蜘蛛絲救人
第15課	論狗會救人	第30課	印書

　　這幾大類主題中，聖經教育類，講述萬物的由來和聖經的重要；品格德行類，是教導學生基督教徒應具備的好品行，像勤勞、孝順、疼惜別人、為別人想和脾氣溫和等；喻道故事類，是比較簡單一點的證道故事，藉著故事來強調信仰。這三類宗教意味濃厚，屬於宗教教育的層面。寓言故事裡的這三個故事，〈印度國的故事〉，講人放了虎，虎反而要吃人；〈會講究所看〉，講一個小孩用手指堵住堤防的洞，以免大水灌入；〈憐憫遇得憐憫〉，講一個奴隸幫獅子拔除腳上的刺，日後獅子報恩。其實筆者小時候也都曾讀過類似的版本，可見這是像伊索寓言一般，流傳甚久、含意深遠的經典故事。中國名景和

---

44 火燻車：火車。

45 蜂蜙（燈蛾）：飛蛾。

46 龍絞水：龍捲風。

表 4：《訓蒙淺說》第二本各課標題

第1課	惡有善報	第16課	論摘海茸
第2課	論鯨魚	第17課	柏林
第3課	孔子的來歷	第18課	論花條馬[47]
第4課	名不合	第19課	尾蝶[48] 的比喻
第5課	萬里長城	第20課	尾蝶的比喻 II
第6課	論豺狼	第21課	華盛頓
第7課	論針	第22課	深海奇怪的生物
第8課	小呂宋	第23課	金城在哪裡？
第9課	印度國的故事	第24課	草蜢
第10課	論豹	第25課	賊改變的事
第11課	會講究所看	第26課	論蚯蚓
第12課	馬尼拉	第27課	巴黎
第13課	麥加	第28課	買魚不用錢
第14課	白熊	第29課	蜘蛛
第15課	求福氣	第30課	憐憫遇得憐憫

中國歷史故事，可能是考量學生的文化背景而立。動物相關、昆蟲、地球環境、自然現象、世界大城和現代器具實業，所佔篇幅比例極重，其教導內容就是「格致學」，也就是所謂的「西學」、「新學」──外國傳教士在中國不僅是宣傳基督教，連帶地也帶入西方的整套知識體系、學問系統，並成立新式的教育學校和學制。關於西學流傳或教會學校影響的學術成果，洋洋灑灑，不勝枚舉，《訓蒙淺說》的出現，倒是為這個領域的研究路線，指出向下延伸的可能路徑，另外，也為中國、臺灣等地的童蒙教材研究，開出一條旁支的、帶著西方色彩的探索取向。

---

47 花條馬：斑馬。
48 尾蝶：蝴蝶。

3. 地理教科書

　　《地理教科書》的使用場所，可能是教會的小學，當時的上課科目有「國語、算數、漢文、修身、理科、地理、作文、習字、唱歌、繪圖、羅馬字這些」[49] 卷二講歐洲地理，卷三講中國地理，卷四講北美洲，內容極為簡要，需配合地圖，因此編者鼓勵每位讀者，或至少教師要準備地圖讓學生看。[50]

（三）宗教文學

1. 證道故事

　　所謂的基督教證道故事，就是藉著一篇篇故事的敘說形式，先講故事，最後再加上作者的感想，有的文末還會加上問題，向閱讀者提問，看看讀者是否真的了解故事意義。這種故事型的文體，從篇幅字數和直附作者評論來看，它比問答體的閱讀性更強，但又不像小說那麼意在言外，算是介於兩者之間。寫作目的，包括表達基督宗教的真正內涵，見證信仰上帝的真實利益，強調祈禱的重要性，或表彰殉教者等，希望帶領讀者思考，並進而砥礪自身，提升自我的信仰素質。不論哪種宗教，從古至今，這應該都是一種普遍可見的宗教文字體裁。

　　楊雲萍文庫裡收藏的證道故事，故事來源就遍及中外，倒是作者（或改寫者）方面，有一個有趣的現象，可以看到幾個日治時期的長老教會女宣教士頗致力於證道故事的書寫，包括文安姑娘（Miss Annie E. Butler）、朱約安姑娘（Miss Joan Stuart）和萬真珠姑娘（Miss Margaret Barnett）。《有求必應》、《十個故事》和《女界名人》都是她們的作品，除此之外，教會報紙上也有她們所寫的單篇證

---

49 胡紹芳，〈彰化小學告白〉，《臺灣教會報》，第365卷，1915年8月，頁10。
50 不著撰人，〈頭序〉，《地理教科書》卷二（出版地、出版年月不詳）。

道故事，像萬真珠姑娘的〈浪蕩子〉[51]、〈流傳的故事〉[52]，朱約安姑娘的〈乞丐〉[53]，文安姑娘的〈王的看護婦〉[54] 等。對於這三位女宣教士的事工，一般咸認為在教導女學、婦學，巡視教會、對外佈道等，[55] 其實從以上的資料來看，翻譯、改寫或創作證道故事，也是她們所注重的事工，其背景、原因和影響應該亦有細究空間。《女界名人》這本書，更是專門選擇女性模範信徒為書寫對象，預定的讀者群也是女性信徒，不知道是否是為了她們當時任教婦學、女學所需？或許可以當作研究日治時期長老教會的外籍女宣教士，甚至是整個長老教會在當時所抱持的女性觀史料之一。

2.宗教小說

以小說體裁承載宗教意涵，傳達基督教的思想和道理，在楊雲萍文庫的白話字文獻收藏中，這個類型多是翻譯小說，將當時歐美流行的、影響深遠的基督教小說、基督教故事，翻譯成閩南語羅馬字刊行，除了這裡的十本之外，廣為人知的《天路歷程》[56]、《安樂家》[57] 等，也都屬於這個類別。舉凡證道故事或宗教小說，都會牽涉到中西文化的接觸交流，語言文字的翻譯轉換，文類文體的流傳影響，思想觀念的遞嬗變化等，因此在比較文學、宗教文學和中西交流

---

51 萬（真珠）姑娘的〈浪蕩子〉，在《臺南府城教會報》連載，從1900年8月的第185卷，到1901年5月的第194卷。

52 萬（真珠）姑娘，〈流傳的故事〉，《臺南府城教會報》，第302卷，1910年5月，頁38。

53 朱（約安）姑娘，〈乞丐〉，《臺灣教會報》，第398卷，1918年5月，頁3。

54 文（安）姑娘，〈王的看護婦〉，在《臺灣教會報》連載，從1918年6月的第399卷，到1918年8月的第401卷。

55 羅仁愛，〈故萬姑娘的來歷〉，《臺灣教會公報》，第578卷，1933年5月；〈朱姑娘與文姑娘〉，參考網站「賴永祥長老史料庫」：http://www.laijohn.com/archives/pm/Stuart,J/biog/Ko,Kseng/Lim,Choa.htm。

56 《天路歷程》，原名*Pilgrim's Progess*，作者為John Buyan，為基督教寓言文學名著。最早的閩南語白話字版本，是由打馬字牧師（John Van Nest Talmage）在1853年印行。目前能看到的最早版本，是由廈門閩南聖教書局在1931年出版。參考賴永祥，〈紀念賓威廉〉，收錄於氏著《教會史話》第一輯，參考網站「賴永祥長老史料庫」（http://www.laijohn.com/index.htm）、網站「臺語文記憶」（http://210.240.194.97/memory/tgb/mowt.asp）上的掃描本。

57 《安樂家》，原名*Christie's Old Organ: or, Home Sweet Home*，作者O. F. Walton, Mrs.，是19世紀膾炙人口的基督教兒童小說，閩南語白話字版在1915年時有再版，每本價錢1角半。參見〈安樂家〉，《臺灣教會報》，第366卷，1915年9月，頁12。

史等學術領域裡極具研究價值。[58] 特別是宗教小說的文學性，讓其讀者比較不受限於信徒，受歡迎的宗教小說，其傳播的時間長度和範圍廣度，以及最重要的——讀者受感動的程度，遠超乎想像，即使到今日，像《泰迪的鈕釦》、《天路歷程》和《銀冰鞋》等，也都還在繼續出版。正如同研究晚清基督教文學的學者指出：「研究基督教敘事文學在很大程度上能豐富我們對晚清基督教史的認識」[59]，這些翻譯成白話字的宗教小說，對於日治時期的讀者和教會產生什麼樣的作用，不論是在文學創作或者宗教宣傳等方面，相信都會豐厚我們對這段時期歷史的認知。

（四）雜項

除了以上三個大分類之外，最後一類，是收入筆者覺得比較無法歸納出其性質取向的書籍，茲以「雜項」姑且名之，以下姑舉幾例，討論其內容大要和研究可能。《內訓（大明仁孝皇后內訓）》、《經書合聖道》和《成語集》三本，有其共同點，在於都與中國文化古典有關。《內訓（大明仁孝皇后內訓）》的譯者林殷碧霞，是曾任廈門大學校長的華僑林文慶之妻，[60] 兩人都是當地的著名教徒。她認為當時的中國人一切都想學外國，卻放棄了中國自身原有的好東西，「我們都沒有想到我們中國幾千年來是出名被稱為禮儀之邦，中間經過許多代的聖賢繼承、修正；關係一切日用家常的規矩，款待內、接應外的禮數，是真正昭備，足夠讓國內的女孩子去學去行。」[61] 所以出版明朝仁孝皇后的訓示，以供中國女子學習楷模。這其實寓含著一種想法——即使是信仰基督宗教的人，也還是要不忘本，需記取祖先的古

58 研究成果如李奭學，《中國晚明與歐洲文學——明末耶穌會古典型證道故事考銓》（臺北：中央研究院、聯經，2005）、吳淳邦，〈19世紀90年代中國基督教小說在韓國的傳播與翻譯〉，頁215-250、宋莉華，《傳教士漢文小說研究》（上海：上海古籍，2010）等。

59 黎子鵬，〈導論〉，收入氏編注，《晚清基督教敘事文學選粹》（新北市：橄欖，2012）。頁xlvi-ii。

60 陳育崧，《林文慶傳》（出版地、出版年月不詳，林文慶博士誕生百年紀念刊），頁46。

61 林殷碧霞，〈頭序〉，收錄於明朝仁孝皇后著、林殷碧霞譯，《內訓（大明仁孝皇后內訓）》（廈門：出版單位不詳，1918），頁1-2。

老教訓和智慧，而這跟《經書合聖道》的成書目的相比，頗堪玩味。《經書合聖道》是擷取四書五經中，與聖經道理能互相呼應的章句，有一種藉由接納引述中國文化，向傳統讀書人示好以宣教的氣味，但是編者又明指「經書合道理的話語是很多，可以知道早日的聖賢在教示人，仍然得趁上帝的道理，沒有離開聖經的範圍。」[62] 一語道破基督教的最高地位。一種是教訓已信者不要遺棄自身固有的優良傳統，一種是告訴未信者漢文化與基督教文化本有相通之處，但基督教文化更深更廣也更值得追隨，雖然，《內訓（大明仁孝皇后內訓）》是出版於民國7年（1918）的中國廈門，而《經書合聖道》則在大正14年（1925）的臺灣出版，其時臺灣已被日本殖民三十年，兩地基督教身處的時代背景、面臨的環境壓力的確有所不同，但是這些白話字書籍皆會在閩南、臺灣等地區互相流通，我們或許能夠想像漢文化的基督教徒可能會感受到的矛盾情結和複雜況味。

《成語集》就沒有什麼傳教意味，其中收錄了111條的成語和俗語，主要是讓讀者從白話字去理解漢文成語和慣用俗語的正確意思，學習之後，在作文方面應頗有助益，所以也可以當作寫作的參考書。其撰寫範式如下：

3. ＊ 人死留名，虎死留皮
人死，得留名聲讓人流傳，虎若死有留皮讓人利用。
這是說，不要做人還不如畜生。[63]

104. 借橋行路，借刀殺人
「殺人（*sat-jîn*）」是殺人（*thâi lâng*）。
這兩句話是說，人藉由別人的勢力來利益自己，陷害別人。[64]

---

62 廉德烈、陳延齡，〈頭序〉，收錄於廉德烈編輯，《經書合聖道》。
63 林祥雲記、廉德烈編輯，《成語集》，頁1。
64 同前註，頁22。

第一行粗體字是編號和條目，「＊」代表這句是成語，無則代表是俗語，第二句是直解，第三句是實質意義。對想研究日治時期，以閩南語發音的成語和俗語用法，或者是閩南語的文言念法等，這無疑是一本珍貴的史料。另外，《成語集》、《經書合聖道》和《六百字編羅馬字註解》，書末版權頁的編輯者都是宣教士廉德烈，但在本文前的序言，可以看到不是廉德烈和陳延齡同記，就是陳延齡單獨寫序，陳延齡是長老教中學的漢文教師，其漢文底子在以上這三本跟漢文有關的白話字書籍，應有所發揮。而他所參與的其他白話字書籍，還有戴仁壽醫生的《內外科看護學》[65]、J. Paterson Smyth原著，高德章翻譯的《平民的基督傳》[66]，主要幫助白話字的譯文部分，可見他的漢文和白話字素養都很不錯。賴永祥曾寫過一位本地信徒陳大鑼，因為他是好幾本白話字名著的幕後功臣，[67]陳延齡應該也因他對白話字書籍的貢獻，以及其在漢文與白話字之間的文字轉換功力，值得研究者日後為文一書。

　　《身體理的總論》是一本簡單的醫學書籍，以西醫的概念介紹人體器官構造和一些保健急救方法。長老教會在臺灣，醫療宣教和醫療事工是傳教的利器也是發展的特色，對於佈教的助力和信徒的影響，已有相當的學術論述。[68]透過接受西式的醫療方法，吸收新的衛生和防疫觀念，當時的信徒究竟對疾病和衛生的想法認知為何？1910年，牧師高金聲曾說生病是「敗壞時日的蟲」[69]，要如何剿滅這隻害蟲：

　　　　要調養身軀。聖經說，調養身軀，那個利益小，敬虔服待主，

---

65 賴永祥，〈《內外科看護學》成書ê經過〉，參考網站「賴永祥講書」：http://www.laijohn.com/works/kangsu/14.htm。

66 賴永祥，〈《平民ê基督傳》〉，參考網站「賴永祥講書」：http://www.laijohn.com/works/kangsu/13.htm。

67 賴永祥，〈書序有名陳大鑼〉，收錄在氏著《教會史話》第一輯，參考網站「賴永祥長老史料庫」：http://www.laijohn.com/BOOK1/033.htm。

68 如吳學明，《從依賴到自立——終戰前臺灣南部基督長老教會研究》（臺南：人光出版社，2003），頁120-158。傅大為，《亞細亞的新身體：性別、醫療與近代臺灣》（臺北：群學，2005）。

69 高金聲，〈敗壞時日的蟲〉，《臺南府城教會報》，第307卷，1910年10月，頁78。

那個利益大。雖然這樣，身體不照顧，來說性命天注定，導致衰微，怎麼能做工。拖過年月，這樣有合上帝的意思嗎？[70]

牧師郭水龍也說：

現在若論衛生的事，基督教的就比較贏世俗人。有看過身體若不弄清淨，又怎麼用清淨的心神來服侍聖潔的上帝？[71]

可見他們把保健身體、注重衛生與信仰連結起來，更進一步，連結了「文明」和「優良」的觀點，所以才會「比較贏世俗人」。那除了透過閱報、看西醫、服西藥來得到西方醫學知識外，閱讀《身體理的總論》這類的醫學書籍，也是一個來源管道。醫療史、身體史或疫病史等研究者更可以經由這類書籍的內容，更精準地掌握當時信徒對於所謂「醫學知識」、「衛生觀念」的實質理解。

四、結語——臺大楊雲萍文庫所藏之長老教會白話字文獻的價值

以上經過文獻介紹與分析之後，筆者認為，這批教會文獻因其書本的形式，本本是史料，處處皆題目。僅從大略的分類中，每一類就都有值得開發或補充前人研究的課題價值，個別的單書也有個別的研究題目可作，而且並不侷限於長老教會史的領域。

再從文獻整體來看，它們分別由臺灣、廈門和汕頭等地的教會出版，流通並使用在整個閩南地區，使得不同地方的信徒，可能擁有共同的閱讀和受教經驗，即使進入日治時代，臺灣長老教會的信徒也還是有機會透過出版品，接收了解中國教會的訊息。過去研究臺灣長老

---

70 高金聲，〈敗壞時日的蟲〉，《臺南府城教會報》，第308卷，1910年11月，頁89。
71 郭水龍，〈斯文和衛生〉，《臺灣教會報》，第356卷，1914年11月，頁8。

教會所受到的中國影響，多集中在真耶穌教會的傳入和宋尚節來臺佈教兩者，或許從出版品的交流角度來切入，也是可行的方向。當然這也足證研究日治時期臺灣長老教會的複雜程度，除了本地的教會發展之外，還需要考慮當時他們與日本教會、中國教會之間的互動往來。

以白話字為主要的出版文字，寫作者以貼近口語的寫法翻譯、改寫或創作，讓被設定為讀者的信徒，或學過白話字的人，不分男女老幼，也不分種族，都有漢文和日文選擇以外的閱讀機會。這一點對於長老教會的信徒，不管是社會邊緣、出身底層，被視為「靠番仔勢」的初代信徒，或是沒有能力接受日治時期高等教育的貧困信徒來說，教會的出版品的確為他們點了一盞求知的燈，他們也很珍惜，就像傳道洪金說過：

> 書房若有發賣羅馬字的書，我就買，現有的，每本我都有。[72]

光楊雲萍文庫中的白話字文獻，已經能夠分成11種類，像洪金這樣的在地信徒，除了傳道書籍外，他還有可能看到並讀懂歐美文學作品、中國古典作品、地理書、醫學書籍和世界各地的故事。白話字書籍能夠為信徒展開的，想必是一個驚人的、遼闊的、想像不到的知識世界。研究者如果親身了解被研究者曾經讀過的東西，相信能更貼近被研究者的心靈世界，也能做出更符合史實的歷史研究。舉一個簡單的例子，廣為人知的蘭醫生娘連瑪玉（Marjorie Learner），1928年移植自己的皮膚以救人的「切膚之愛」事蹟，常會連帶提到小病人周金耀在住院期間，蘭醫生娘常去看他，會教他讀《聖經》、《真道問答》、《訓蒙淺說》、《幼稚課本》等以排遣無聊。[73] 當我們實際了解《真道問答》、《訓蒙淺說》、《幼稚課本》的內容之後，就知道這幾本書原來是基督教的入門書籍兼童蒙教材，才完全明白為何蘭醫

---

72 楊天豪，〈洪金先生的天路歷程〉，《臺灣教會公報》，第731期，1949年11月，頁16。
73 參考網站「彰化基督教醫院院史文物館」：http://www2.cch.org.tw/history/page.aspx?oid=13。

生娘選擇這些書來教導13歲的孩子。

出版品，尤其是書籍，它能夠更完整的、仔細的、系統的表達作者想說的、想分享的、想教授的和想宣傳的東西。所以讀者在閱讀書籍之後，可能就像上述所說，會產生豐富心靈、充實知識的效果，更進一步的，還可能會生出創作文字、留下作品的想法。由讀者變成作者或翻譯者，由知識的接收者變成知識的創造者或再製者，像上述提過《救主的來歷》的作者趙爬、《平民的基督傳》的譯者高德章等人，那麼日治時期的本地信徒，在經過長老教會的培育和影響後，他們曾經得到哪些讀物薰陶，進而創造出哪些作品，從作品又反映出他們有哪些關懷重點，這也是我們定義、評價、研究所謂基督徒知識份子的重要層面。

最後，楊雲萍文庫的白話字文獻，還有一個對於研究者最重要的特色，就是便於利用。所藏的89小冊，幾乎都能透過臺大圖書館網站，在網路上看到原件的掃描檔案，也能印出使用。除此之外，網路上也還能找到部分文獻的漢羅翻譯，對於不擅使用閩南語白話字的研究者而言，確能縮短一點語言文字上的限制。目前楊雲萍文庫最被廣泛利用的收藏是歌仔冊，期待白話字文獻的利用也能與日俱進。另外，楊雲萍文庫的性質，究竟是個人的私人收藏，當然難以收集完全，若想要齊全所有長老教會出版的白話字書籍，應該還是需要教會、信徒個人和私人收藏庫等的協力合作，若能如此，對研究者和長老教會歷史來說，將是一大福音。[74]

---

74 根據與會學者張妙娟教授和盧啟明告知，在長榮中學校史館和臺灣神學院圖書館，也有收藏許多長老教會的白話字文獻，特此感謝。

【四・個案史料研究】

Politics, Society, and Culture in Taiwan: Some Observations of English Presbyterian Missionaries, 1865-1940

Rolf Gerhard Tiedemann

Center for Boxer Movement Studies

Shandong University, China

Abstract

The first missionaries of the Presbyterian Church of England (PCE) arrived in Taiwan in 1865 and were active on the island until the outbreak of the Second Sino-Japanese War. The Taiwan work was resumed in the late 1940s. Their surviving letters and reports are preserved in the PCE archival collection at the School of Oriental and African Studies in London. It is also available on microfiche from IDC Publications. In addition, the personal papers of Dr. James Laidlaw Maxwell (1836-1921) can be consulted at the University of Birmingham. It is also possible that certain missionaries sent reports on conditions in their respective areas to the British consular officials at Tamsui/ Tainan, to be included in the quarterly consular intelligence reports during the pre-Japanese and Japanese periods. The consular material is found in The National Archives in London.

Keywords: Presbyterian Church of England (PCE), The National Archives in London, Taiwan

During the second half of the nineteenth century, the island of Taiwan was still a raw frontier area administered until 1887 as part of Fujian province. Both early Protestant missionaries and British consular personnel found the place extremely challenging. As one writer has observed: "Much of the mountainous interior was the home of unsubjugated aboriginal tribes outside Chinese control. Fever abounded, and the island became notorious among foreigners for unhealthiness."[1] Yet the decades before 1895 were also a time when Western consuls, traders and travellers lived on or visited the island, attracted by its exotic environment, its fauna and flora, its original human inhabitants, as well as its natural resources. As a consequence, a sizeable body of literature concerning Taiwan and its people has accumulated.[2] The following is a brief overview – with selected examples – of the English Presbyterian missionaries' textual representations of what they called Formosa during the last decades of Qing rule and the Japanese colonial period.

Presbyterian missionaries were among the earliest Western residents in nineteenth-century Taiwan. The Presbyterian Church of England was established in 1844, and its Foreign Missions Committee appointed in the same year to "institute foreign missions in connection with this Church as speedily as possible". The Women's Missionary Association of the Presbyterian Church of England was set up as a supporting society in 1878. It functioned as an independent unit within the overall framework of the Presbyterian Church of England until 1925, when a union between the two missionary

---

1 P. D. Coates, *The China Consuls: British Consular Officers, 1843-1943* (Hongkong: Oxford University Press, 1988), p. 139.

2 The website of Reed College in the United States hosts a very substantial bibliography: *19th-Century European & North American Encounters with Taiwan: A Selective Bibliography*, compiled by Douglas Fix (Reed College) and John Shufelt (Tunghai University), http://academic.reed.edu/formosa/texts/EuroAmTaiwanBib . See also the bibliography of French and German-language articles, with substantial annotations in English: http://academic.reed.edu/formosa/texts/FrenchTexts.html ; and http://academic.reed.edu/formosa/texts/GermanTexts.html .

bodies was ratified. The missionaries were mainly of Scottish extraction, as the English Presbyterian Church had Scottish immigrants as its major social constituency. They had generally achieved a high educational level, as the men were usually graduates of Glasgow or Edinburgh University. "Like many Scots, they often manifested a scientific and historical curiosity about their surroundings which set them apart from many of their English contemporaries in the mission field."[3] Following an exploratory visit by two English Presbyterian missionaries from their mission base at Xiamen [Amoy] to the island in the early 1860s, the newly arrived medical missionary Dr. James Laidlaw Maxwell 馬雅各 (1836-1921) attempted to open mission work in Taiwanfu (now Tainan) in June 1865. However, a hostile Chinese crowd having driven him from that city, he was able to rent mission premises in Takow 打狗, where a British consul was already established. Thus began the English Presbyterian missionary enterprise on the island.

Resources for the Study of the English Presbyterian Mission

A variety of published and unpublished sources are available for the study of the English Presbyterian missionary enterprise in Taiwan. The Archive of the Presbyterian Church of England Foreign Missions Committee is the most significant collection of unpublished material. It has been deposited in The Library, School of Oriental and African Studies, University of London, Thornhaugh Street, London, WC1H 0XG, UNITED KINGDOM.

For further details, see Rosemary Seton, *Guide to the Archive of the Overseas Mission of the Presbyterian Church of England.* http://www.soas.ac.uk/library/ archives/news/file55128.pdf

---

3 A. Hamish Ion, *The Cross and the Rising Sun. Vol. 2: The British Protestant Missionary Movement in Japan, Korea, and Taiwan, 1865-1945* (Waterloo, Ontario: Wilfrid Laurier University Press, 1993), p. 19.

It should be noted, though, that during the Second World War the offices of the Presbyterian Church of England in London were damaged and much of the nineteenth-century material was destroyed. However, as the online SOAS hand list for the Presbyterian Church of England Archive indicates, a substantial amount of Taiwan material has survived: "Taiwan/Formosa: general correspondence, minutes and reports", Ref. No. PCE/FMC/6/01; "Taiwan/Formosa: individual files", Ref. No. PCE/FMC/6/02; "Taiwan/Formosa: miscellaneous and printed materials", PCE/FMC/6/03. "Women's Missionary Association: Taiwan/Formosa", PCE/WMA/05. These records have been published on microfiche by IDC Publishers; the guide to this collection can be consulted online: URL http://www.idc.nl/pdf/141_guide.pdf .

For image representations of Taiwan in the English Presbyterian archives, see "Taiwan/Formosa: Photographs, individual and group portraits, buildings, general views, post cards: 1875-1968. Ref. No. PCE/FMC/6/12".

The papers of the Presbyterian Church of England pioneer medical missionary to Taiwan, James Laidlaw Maxwell, Ref. No. XDA26, have been deposited in the Special Collections, Cadbury Research Library, Muirhead Tower, University of Birmingham, Edgbaston, Birmingham B15 2TT, UNITED KINGDOM.

Although the material in the archives of the English Presbyterian Mission may contain useful references to missionary activities, incidents and observations in Taiwan, such information – unless specifically intended for publication – would be accessible only to the members of the home board and therefore not available to inform the general public about conditions in Taiwan. Richer and more accessible textual representations of Taiwan are found in the missionary periodical literature:

Minutes of the Synod. 1836- . Presbyterian Church of England Foreign Missions *Annual Report*, 1841- .

The English Presbyterian Messenger (London), 1845-1867; continued by: *Messenger and Missionary Record of the Presbyterian Church in England,* 1868-1891; continued by: *Monthly Messenger of the Presbyterian Church of England,* 1891-1907; continued as: *Presbyterian Messenger,* 1908-1966. The Foreign Mission Committee began in 1878 to reprint China material as a monthly *Gospel in China* with a circulation of about 4000.

Our Sisters in Other Lands (London), 1879-1937; continued as: *Far Horizons: A Quarterly Magazine of the Overseas Missionary Work of the Presbyterian Church of England,* 1938-1966.

Women's Missionary Association of the Presbyterian Church of England – *Annual Report* (London), 1879- .

Besides regular reports and letters from the Taiwan mission field in missionary periodicals, a considerable amount of information can also be gleaned from monographs authored by the missionaries. The mission histories by Band and MacMillan not only set a framework in terms of chronology, personnel and activities for the study of the Presbyterian missionary enterprise, they provide useful additional information on the human and physical environment of the island.

Edward Band, *Working His Purpose Out: The History of the English Presbyterian Mission, 1847-1947* (London: Presbyterian Church of England, 1948).

Hugh MacMillan, *Then Till Now in Formosa*, ([Taiwan]: English and Canadian Presbyterian Missions in Formosa, 1953). iv, 102 pp.

2nd ed.: *First Century in Formosa* (Taipei : China Sunday School Association, 1963). iv, 136 pp. Chapters 1-6 are reprinted from the first edition.

It should, however, be noted that especially the representations of the 'Other' in the missionary periodical or monograph literature are not necessarily always objective. Although the Presbyterian missionaries were mostly university graduates, they were nevertheless expected to narrate their activities in terms of conversion successes in a hostile, 'superstitious' and 'devil-worshipping' environment. As Robert McClellan has observed,

> One of the greatest needs for the mission worker as well as the minister at home with regard to the missionary effort was to justify the expense in life and money of an evangelism reaching halfway around the world. Since the first requirement for a conversion experience was the presence of a sufficiently depraved subject, missionaries frequently described the moral condition of the Chinese in the blackest possible terms.[4]

A few Taiwan missionaries occasionally published in learned journals, but they were primarily targeting pious readers back home in order to encourage them to support their evangelistic endeavours. To this end, they transmitted edifying stories as well as tales of adventure and missionary heroism in exotic and faraway places, to be published in mission periodicals and popular monographs.[5] The mission historian is interested in accurate and specific detail, including the names of Chinese and aboriginal persons and places, preferably with Chinese characters. This kind of detailed local information that the Taiwan expert is nowadays seeking would, however, be wasted on ordinary readers in late-nineteenth and early twentieth-century England and Scotland. Hence it should not surprise modern scholars that such specific

---

4 Robert F. McClellan, "Missionary Influence on American Attitudes toward China at the Turn of This Century", *Church History* 38.4 (December 1969), p. 476, cited in Eric Reinders, "The Chinese Macabre in Missionary Publications and Horror Fiction", in Anthony E. Clark, ed., *Beating Devils and Burning Their Books: Views of China, Japan, and the West* (Ann Arbor, Mich.: Association for Asian Studies, 2010), p. 16.

5 Note, for example, Marjorie Ellen Learner Landsborough, *In Beautiful Formosa: Being a Personally-conducted Tour of Boys and Girls to View the People, the Scenery, and the Work of the Missionaries in Strange and Lovely Places* (London: R.T.S., 1922).

data is often absent in missionary publications. It is more likely to be found in the surviving material from the Presbyterian mission station archives and local publications in Taiwan.

The consular and legation records at The National Archives, Kew, Richmond, Surrey, TW9 4DU, United Kingdom, contain many files relating to British missionaries and their observations in various parts of mainland China, including reports from the English Presbyterian mission in eastern Guangdong and southern Fujian.[6] A preliminary consultation of selected volumes in series FO46, FO228, FO262 and FO371 has, however, yielded surprisingly little information concerning Taiwan and its inhabitants. It is, of course, possible that a more intensive search may yet reveal meaningful textual representations of the island by the missionaries of the Presbyterian Church of England.

One final comment concerning the transmission of knowledge from Taiwan to Europe in the nineteenth century. Most Western travellers who visited the island had to rely in one way or another on the missionaries' expertise, guidance and advice. Note, for instance, Arthur Corner's acknowledgement of "the assistance received from the Rev. W. Campbell..., without whose kind aid many difficulties of travel would have occurred".[7] As Yeh Er-jian has pointed out, "most of the travelling routes made by Western explorers were suggested, even dominated, by the European and North American missionaries. It was apparently impossible to undertake unaccompanied or casual overland journeys in Formosa because of a lack of familiarity among outsiders and the many restrictions they encountered."[8] It

6 For a recent academic study of the English Presbyterian Mission in nineteenth-century eastern Guangdong, see Joseph Tse-Hei Lee, *The Bible and the Gun: Christianity in South China, 1860-1900* (New York & London: Routledge, 2003). For the Chinese version, 見李榭熙，《聖經與槍炮：基督教與潮州社會（1860-1900）》（北京：社會科學文獻出版社，2010）。

7 Arthur Corner, "A Journey in Formosa," *The Chinese Recorder and Missionary Journal* 7.2 (1876), p. 117.

8 On the link between Western travellers and missionaries in nineteenth-century Taiwan, see Yeh Er-jian, "Territorialising

stands to reason that at least some of the information contained in the outsiders' writings was knowledge that they had acquired from the missionaries.

Early Encounters with Chinese Society

Maxwell's experience at Taiwanfu in 1865 is indicative of the difficult and at times violent encounter with Chinese society. The most serious case occurred in 1868 when a Presbyterian peaching station at Pithau in Fengshan district 鳳山縣埤頭 was destroyed by an angry crowd and a Chinese Christian was murdered. The case was complicated by the fact that a Roman Catholic chapel had also been burned down. Apparently the riot was caused by a rumour that the converts had been bewitched by poisoned water. Maxwell then appealed to the British consul for help in gaining redress for the destruction of the preaching station and the punishment of the murderers of the Chinese Christian. Unfortunately John Gibson 吉必勳 (d. 1869), the controversial British vice-consul, combined the missionary cases with the conflict between British merchants and the Chinese authorities over the camphor trade. This affair culminated in the so-called Camphor War and the attack on the Anping fort guarding the port of Taiwanfu by a British naval contingent.[9]

Colonial Environments: A Comparison of Colonial Sciences on Land Demarcation in Japanese Taiwan and British Malaya", Ph.D. diss., Durham University, 2011, pp. 60-66, with the routes of travel indicated on the map on p. 63. Available at Durham E-Theses Online: http://etheses.dur.ac.uk/3199/

9 For details, see Edward Band, *Working His Purpose Out: The History of the English Presbyterian Mission 1847-1947* (London: Presbyterian Church of England Publishing Office, 1948), pp. 78-81; Shih-shan Henry Tsai, *Maritime Taiwan: Historical Encounters with the East and the West* (Armonk, NY: M. E. Sharpe, 2009), pp. 75-85; Coates, pp. 322-327. See also Ku Wei-ying, "Conflict, Confusion and Control: Some Observations on the Missionary Cases in Nineteenth Century Taiwan," in Koen De Ridder, ed., *Footsteps in Deserted Valleys: Missionary Cases, Strategies and Practices in Qing China* (Leuven: Leuven University Press, 2000), pp. 11-38. On the involvement of Spanish Dominicans in this affair, see also John R. Shepherd, "From Barbarians to Sinners: Conversion Among Plains Aborigines in Qing Taiwan, 1859-1895," in Daniel H. Bays, ed., *Christianity in China: From the Eighteenth Century to the Present* (Stan-

These incidents were similar to those on the Chinese mainland and set the tone in the future encounters between the missionaries and the Chinese official-scholar class. At the same time, early Presbyterian missionaries tended to view the religious life of the Chinese in Taiwan as idolatrous and heathen. In 1907 Campbell Naismith Moody 梅甘霧 (1866-1940) noted that Taiwanese:

> bow down before Buddhist and Taoist idols indiscriminately, while they recite the teachings of Confucius, who scarcely taught of any divinity but God and Heaven, and did not worship idols at all. They worship obscure local deities, or make pilgrimages to distant shrines, paying attention to any and all who seem to promise effectual aid, and transferring their allegiance to the end in view, as we go to different shops for different goods, or according to the rise and fall of the idol's celebrity, just as we forsake one shop for another which offer better value.[10]

Nevertheless, the missionaries recognized the importance of ancestral tablets and their worship to the Chinese. "They understood that it was regarded as unfilial behaviour for the Chinese to neglect these duties. As a result, Presbyterian missionaries in Taiwan allowed Christian enquirers to retain their ancestral tablets."[11] Part of the prejudice which missionaries in Taiwan had against the Chinese authorities was the result of harsh experiences. Many early missionaries, like Maxwell, had been roughed up by crowds who were thought to have been incited by the literati. One missionary later wrote that:

---

ford: Stanford University Press, 1996), pp. 124-127.

10 Campbell N. Moody, *The Heathen Heart: An Account of the Reception of the Gospel among the Chinese of Formosa* (Edinburgh; London: Oliphant, Anderson & Ferrier, 1907), pp. 99-100.

11 Ion, *The British Protestant Missionary Movement*, p. 79.

Chinese officialdom in Formosa had evoked little confidence or respect. The influence of the Confucian literati also had been reactionary and anti-foreign. In their pride of learning they tended to despise the ignorant, and few scholars were found among church members. The prevailing atmosphere had not encouraged the reception of the Gospel. Baulked by a dull impassive resistance from the heathen, the Church seemed to have become spiritually stagnant during this last decade of Chinese rule.[12]

Understandably, after some initial apprehensions, all missionaries welcomed the Japanese occupation of the island because this would drastically reduce the power of the Chinese literati class.

Missionary Encounters with the Aborigines

While the English Presbyterians failed to attract large numbers of converts from among the Han Chinese settlers, they were more successful among some of the aboriginal peoples on the island. "To these marginal groups the missionary and his religion represented a potential source of status and power waiting to be tapped."[13] Broadly speaking, the Chinese had divided the various Austronesian ethno-linguistic groups that inhabited the island before Han settlement into two major categories: (1) those groups that lived in the western coastal plains and had come under Chinese control, thereby undergoing varying degrees of assimilation; (2) those aborigines that inhabited Taiwan's east coast and the high mountains and remained beyond government control until the early twentieth century. Employing rather

---

12 Band, *Working His Purpose Out*, p. 123.
13 Shepherd, p. 121.

pejorative terminology, the Chinese distinguished between 'raw savages' (*chhenn-hoan* 生番), i.e. 'uncivilized' aborigines, and 'cooked savages' (*sekhoan* 熟番), i.e. 'civilized' aborigines. As the Qing scholar-official Lan Dingyuan (藍鼎元, 1680-1733) observed during his sojourn on the island:

> Among the native savages of Taiwan there are two kinds: raw and cooked. Those who live deep in the mountains and who have not submitted to civilization are raw savages.... Those who live on the plains mixed [among the Han Chinese], who obey the law, and who perform corvée are the cooked savages. They are contented at farming with plow and hoe, no different from the [Chinese] subjects.[14]

In the second half of the nineteenth century, the English Presbyterians adopted the 'savage' label, at least as far as the mountain aborigines were concerned.[15]

It was not long before the missionaries were received by some of the 'plains aborigines' (*pepohoan* 平埔番). Under the growing pressure of the dominant Chinese, they had to a greater or lesser extent been sinicized. Hence they were known as 'cooked barbarians' (*sekhoan* 熟番), i.e. 'civilized' aborigines. Although the terms *pepohoan* and *sekhoan* seem to have generally been used interchangeably, the newly-arrived missionary William Campbell 甘為霖 (1841-1921), who evangelized extensively among the ethnic minorities, reserved the label *sekhoan* for the less sinicized inhabitants of the northern part of Chiang-hoa county 彰化縣, while employing *pepohoan* in

---

14 Quotation in Emma Jinhua Teng, *Taiwan's Imagined Geography: Chinese Colonial Travel Writing and Pictures, 1683-1895* (Cambridge, Mass.: Harvard University Asia Center: Distributed by Harvard University Press, 2004), p. 130. See also Emma J. Teng, *From "raw savage" and "cooked savage" to "mountain aborigines" and "plains aborigines": Images of Taiwan's Indigenous People in Qing Literature and Illustrations* (Taibei : Zhongyang yanjiu yuan, 2000).

15 See for example William Campbell, "Aboriginal Savages of Formosa," *Ocean Highways: The Geographical Review* n.s. 1 (1874), pp. 410-412.

connection with the aborigines in the Tainan area (i.e. the people now known as *Siraya* 西拉雅), who had a better command of Chinese.[16] He felt that these marginal groups were attracted to Christianity because the foreigners "were quite as influential and far more sympathizing than the Chinese around them".[17]

Campbell and other early Presbyterian missionaries became quite well acquainted with the people in the aboriginal villages on the plains and commented on their lives, habits and customs. These indigenous inhabitants were in certain respects still quite different from the Chinese – and hence of interest to readers in Britain. "The chief features of those who make up the civilized tribes of Formosa (the Sek-hwan and the Pi-po-hwan) are the narrowness of their lives in being poor crofters or hired cultivators of the soil, their illiteracy, and the laxity of their customs as regards marriage and divorce.... It is no uncommon thing to meet with young girls who have had three, or even four husbands; for when any little tiff or trouble arises, they at once begin to pair off with other partners."[18] He concluded that "all their adults have much less stability of character, shrewdness, and plodding perseverance than the Chinese. Consequently, owing to idle habits, tippling, and borrowing money at exorbitant interest on the title-deeds of their land, the Chinese have gradually encroached till the poor Hwan have been driven away from their productive rice-fields to the cultivation of little potato-patches on the hill-sides."[19]

Of considerably greater interest to readers in Britain and elsewhere were

---

16 William Campbell, *Sketches from Formosa* (London: Marshall Brothers, 1913) , pp. 33-34.

17 Ibid., p. 36.

18 Ibid., pp. 248-249. In his paper on the aborigines of Taiwan, Thomas Barclay also commented on their lax marriage notions. Thomas Barclay, "The Aboriginal Tribes of Formosa," in *Records of the General Conference of the Protestant Missionaries of China, held at Shanghai, May 7-20, 1890* (Shanghai: American Presbyterian Mission Press, 1890), p. 670.

19 Campbell, *Sketches from Formosa*, p. 249.

the inhabitants of the 'savage land' beyond the pale of Chinese civilization. While the missionaries' primary objective was to determine the conversion potential of the 'raw savages', their reports from the relatively inaccessible high mountains afforded the readers rare glimpses of an exotic and dangerous part of the island. Moreover, these accounts helped transmit knowledge about the hitherto hidden physical and human geography of the region, aspects that were of interest to those who wanted to exploit the potential forest and mineral resources in the interior.[20] However, it surely was the violent and murderous behaviour of the 'raw savages', especially their notorious practice of headhunting that excited the readers.

William Campbell caught his first glimpse of 'raw savages' during a visit in November 1872 to the newly converted 'acculturated' plains aborigines who had established a colony in the Po-li-sia 埔裏社 or Po-sia 埔社 settlement (the area is now called the Puli 埔里 basin) within the mountains. More specifically, the converts belonged to the Pazeh (巴則海).[21] While in the Po-sia settlement, Campbell and his companion Dr. Matthew Dickson 德馬太 came upon a group of 'wild' aborigines known as Bu-hoan 霧番 who were on friendly terms with the Pazeh *sekhoan*. "In many respects, they are a very fine race, tall, muscular, self-possessed, and not by any means so degraded as one might have expected them to be."[22] At the end of 1873, Campbell was able to make his pioneer visit to the Bu-hoan settlement 霧番社 because their chief Arek requested medical help. The missionary left a detailed account of his visit, introducing his readers to the dark world of 'raw savages'.

Rising early next morning I ventured out to look at the place. The

---

20 For a more detailed discussion, see Yeh, pp. 66-72.

21 The conversion of the Pazeh is discussed in Shepherd, pp. 127-130.

22 Campbell, *Sketches from Formosa*, p. 43.

first thing that arrested my attention was a string of skulls fastened up against the end of the chief's house. They were nearly all cloven in, and not a few had still some flesh adhering to them, as if they had been severed from the body only a month or two before. The majority of the other houses were similarly ornamented. I counted thirty-nine skulls on one hut, thirty-two on another, twenty-one on a third, and so on. I was told that they were the trophies of victorious clan fights, and of successful raids on the inhabitants on the western side of the mountains. The poor Chey-hoan sees his certain fall in the face of the encroachments of the swarming Chinese, and in his sullen despair his hand is against every man. I was informed that not a year passes without from ten to twenty of the Po-sia people being killed in these raids. When I re-entered the large cabin, I saw further evidence of the degradation of these savages. Many suspicious-looking implements were lying about, and there could be no doubt that the thick mass of long hair which dangled from one of the rafters, consisted of the pigtails of the murdered Sek-hoan and Chinamen whose skulls were bleaching outside. I believe that many of the Chey-hoan are cannibals.[23]

Needless to say, Campbell was rather appalled by the 'wild savages', their cruel practices and the "low, wretched charnel-houses in which they live".[24]

From time to time the desirability of missionary work among the mountain aborigines was discussed. Mr George Ede 余饒理 (1854-1908), an educational missionary of the English Presbyterian Mission, set out in

---

23 William Campbell, "Aboriginal Savages of Formosa," *Ocean Highways: The Geographical Review* n.s. 1 (1874): 410-412; quotation on p. 411. Note that these and other details are reprinted in *Sketches from Formosa*, pp. 60-66, a book dedicated "To the Boys and Girls of the Presbyterian Church of England".

24 Campbell, *Sketches from Formosa*, p. 66.

December 1890 on a two-months' journey into the dangerous and less often visited area of eastern Formosa. Readers of the *Presbyterian Messenger* were thus given another detailed account of the hazards of travel and life in aboriginal villages.[25] But no concrete steps were taken to initiate evangelistic work among the unacculturated peoples of eastern Taiwan.[26] After the Japanese occupation, the indigenous peoples in the mountains became less accessible and do not feature much in missionary accounts. Propagation of any religion (other than state Shinto) to the 'savages' was illegal. Nor is their often harsh treatment by the Japanese rulers mentioned in the Presbyterian publications.

Coping with Japanese Colonialism

Under the Treaty of Shimonoseki (1895), the Qing Empire was required to cede Taiwan to Japan. Initially, the advancing forces of occupation encountered resistance from anti-Japanese elements on the island. When Japanese troops approached Tainan, the local Presbyterian missionaries Thomas Barclay 巴克禮 (1849-1935) and Duncan Ferguson 宋忠堅 (1860-1923) became involved in surrender discussions with Liu Yongfu 劉永福 (1837-1917), leader of the Black Flag Army and the second and last leader of the short-lived Republic of Formosa. After Liu had fled to the Chinese mainland, it was hoped that in the absence of authority the Japanese would soon arrive to prevent a "rabble" forming. As Barclay informed the British consul Richard Willett Hurst (1849-1924), local deputations asked the

---

25 George Ede, "A Tour Through Eastern Formosa," *Presbyterian Messenger* (1 Oct 1890), pp. 6-9; (1Nov 1890), pp. 4-7; (1 Dec 1890), pp. 6-10; (1 Feb 1891), pp. 5-6; (1 Mar 1891), pp. 2-3; (1 Apr 1891), pp. 3-5, 8-10; (1 May 1891), pp. 12-14; (1 Jun 1891), pp. 11-14. Note also James Laidlaw Maxwell, *Savages, Sick and Sound: The Journal of a Month's Medical Missionary Tour among the Chinese and Amis of South and East Formosa* (T. French Downie, 1915).

26 Band, *Working His Purpose Out*, pp. 160-161.

missionaries to meet the Japanese and inform them of the surrender of the city. In spite of the prevailing anti-Christian climate on the island at this time[27], Barclay and Ferguson, carrying petitions with about one hundred "chops", approached the Japanese forces and had an interview with General Nogi Maresuke 乃木希典 (1849-1912). On 21 October Tainan surrendered peacefully to the Japanese.[28]

In light of the experiences of the thirty years before 1895, when relations with the Chinese ruling class were anything but cordial, the English Presbyterian missionaries were hopeful that Japanese colonial rule would promote modernization and eliminate the existing obstacles to the propagation of Christianity. Nevertheless, in the immediate aftermath of the conflict, as guerrilla warfare continued for some time, the initial missionary reaction to the harsh Japanese treatment of the Chinese was not entirely uncritical. As Thomas Barclay observed with regard to the 'bandit' suppression campaigns:

> Instead however of going to the hills to arrest the robbers, they began by burning down the villages in the surrounding plain, and continued to do so until some thirty villages were wiped out. Not only were houses and property burnt to the ground but hundreds of unoffending and unarmed villagers were shot in cold blood. The Japanese said it was necessary because the villages were hiding places

---

27 The English Presbyterians blamed the Roman Catholics for the hostility, on account of their "tactical mistake" during the Japanese advance. "They went out in procession to meet and welcome the Japanese, hoping in this way to gain favour with the new rulers. When the Japanese retired [because of the start of the rainy season], however, they were left behind to face an angry mob, who accused them of being in alliance with the Japanese. Their chapel in Tau-Lak [斗六] was destroyed, although our building in the same town was untouched." Band, *Barclay of Formosa*, p. 88.

28 Barclay to Hurst, Tainan, 22 October 1895, FO228/1199 (1895). These events connected with the occupation of Taiwan have been recorded in some detail in Edward Band, *Barclay of Formosa* (Tokyo: Christian Literature Society, 1936), especially in Chapters 8 & 9.

of the robbers, and the people manifestly were accomplices, because they did not come to inform the authorities![29]

Although Barclay was "sorely disappointed with some aspects of the new regime, and indignant at the brutality of some of the troops"[30], he also envisaged a more hopeful future under the Japanese.

> I am sometimes inclined rather to regard them with compassion. They have spent much blood and treasure on the island, with the only result of injuring their reputation and getting themselves into a mess.... We must not forget the kindness of many officials to ourselves, the happy intercourse with [Japanese] Christian officials, the issue of proclamations for the protection of our chapels, the improvement of roads, the currency, the telegraph and postal service, the efforts to put down bribery etc.[31]

In other words, the English Presbyterians were looking forward to an improved environment in which to work, better relations with officials and a more tolerant attitude toward Christianity. It is Thomas Barclay once more who expresses these sentiments most clearly:

> When the Japanese rule was set up it became at once evident that we were entering a new era in our relation to the authorities. During the first month of their occupation we had more intercourse with the officials than we had had with the Chinese magistrates during the thirty years of our residence in the island. The Japanese Government

---

29 Quotation in Band, *Barclay of Formosa*, pp. 119-120.

30 Band, in ibid., p. 120.

31 Quotation in ibid., pp. 120-121.

is impartial in its treatment of religions, but individual officials were on the whole more favourably inclined towards the Christian religion than towards idolatry. They knew it to be the religion of civilised nations, and to make, on the whole, for good order among the people. They also... recognised the better morality of the professing Christians.[32]

Still, Barclay felt in 1895 that it was "still too soon to attempt an estimate of the probable loss or gain to our work from the new regime". He concluded in his annual report for that year:

After six months we shall know more definitely what the Japanese intentions are. Their purpose, according to one of their statements, is to make the population of the island – body, soul, and spirit – Japanese. The next generation of missionaries will require to learn Japanese and the aspect of our mission work generally will be much changed. In the meantime there seem to be some advantages to be hoped for. The destruction of the Mandarinate and perhaps still more that of the literary class as a body, involving the discrediting of Confucianism, will remove more obstacles out of our way.... We are looking forward with much interest and hopefulness to the new year's work.[33]

Barclay's biographer, the English Presbyterian educational missionary Edward Band 萬榮華 (1886-1971), observed many years later:

---

32 Quotation in ibid., p. 117.

33 Thomas Barclay, *The Church in Formosa in 1895: The War, Mission Work, the Outlook* (London: Publications Committee 1896), p. 3; in the Presbyterian Church of England Archives, Microfiche No. 153, School of Oriental and African Studies. Reproduced in Band, *Barclay of Formosa*, pp. 109-110.

Gradually, however, as Japanese rule became more firmly established, peaceful conditions were restored. Under the Governor-Generalship of Nogi a change for the better became manifest in the treatment of the people. The Church settled down to the new regime with a growing confidence that if the Christians proved themselves law-abiding subjects, they would be treated favourably, or at least impartially, by their new rulers.[34]

Once guerrilla resistance had been overcome, the colonial masters set out indeed to 'civilize' the island. Itō Hirobumi 伊藤博文 (1841-1909) stated in a speech in 1896, entitled "Administration following the Sino-Japanese War", that because Taiwan was a "half uncivilized" area whose residents were "ruffians from Guangzhou province and Fujian" and 'aborigines', the Japanese military should impose effective control.[35] Although some felt that the military had been "needlessly cruel and severe"[36], on the whole the missionaries were satisfied with developments during the period 1895-1905. The Church progressed remarkably, which, according to Edward Band, was partly attributable to the influence of the new regime.[37] For one thing, the Japanese military had brought law and order to Taiwan and stamped out armed robbery. A stable and peaceful environment was presumed to be essential to the successful operation of the missionary enterprise.

Certain Chinese Christians, too, expected beneficial changes from the

---

34 Edward Band, *Working His Purpose Out*, p. 127.

35 For further details, see Komagome Takeshi, "Japanese Colonial Rule and Modernity: Successive Layers of Violence," in Meaghan Morris & Brett de Bary, eds., "'Race' Panic and the Memory of Migration," *Traces: A Multilingual Journal of Cultural Theory and Translation* 2 (Hongkong: Hong Kong University Press, 2001), pp. 207-258; Itō's comments on pp. 213-214.

36 Frederick R. Johnson 費仁純 to W. Dale, December 29, 1902, Presbyterian Church of England, Formosa Box 4 File 5, URC Archives, cited in Ion, *The British Protestant Missionary*, pp. 79-80.

37 Edward Band, *Working His Purpose Out*, p. 127.

Japanese presence on the island. Two prominent examples are Li Chunsheng 李春生 (1838-1924) and Lim Bo-seng 林茂生 (1887-1947). Li Chunsheng 李春生 (1838-1924) became a Christian in Xiamen, Fujian, and subsequently acted as comprador for Elles & Co. and other foreign firms. As a result of the Small Sword uprising in Xiamen in the early 1860s, Li moved to Daidaocheng 大稻埕 [or Twatutia] in Taibei and prospered in the tea trade. "Rather than resisting the modern transformation of East Asia, he was one who actively rode the waves of change. When Japan began its colonial administration, Li was among its active supporters, and in 1896 he was decorated by the Japanese government."[38] As Kabayama Sukenori 樺山資紀 (1837-1922), the first governor-general of Taiwan, pointed out to Itō:

> We haven't had the time to gain a complete knowledge of the feelings, customs, etc., of the indigenous people, but even though we find administration here extremely difficult, it is fortunate that a wealthy merchant [Li Chunsheng] and others have established a Bureau for Preserving Peace and order, and we have communicated our views on it, with the result that both colonial government and Japanese people rely upon it.[39]

Whereas Li had a rather humble background and was isolated both from intellectuals who strove to preserve Chinese civilization, Lim Bo-seng's father Lim Ian-Sin 林宴臣 (1859-1944), also known as 林燕臣, was a *xiucai* 秀才 degree-holder who, as the Taiwanese language teacher of the English Presbyterian missionaries at Tainan, had converted to Christianity and in time was ordained a minister. Lim thus grew up in a Christian environment,

---

38 Komagome, "Japanese Colonial Rule," p. 215. He was also known as Lee Chun-Sun, the "father of the Taiwan tea industry".

39 Report dated 3 July 1895, quoted in Komagome, "Japanese Colonial Rule," p. 223.

studied at the Tainan Presbyterian Middle School and afterwards went to Japan to study at Tokyo Imperial University. Having assumed the directorship of the board of managers of the Tainan Presbyterian Middle School in 1930, he subsequently had to endure harsh attacks from the Japanese which ultimately led to his banishment from the school. According to Komagome, the British missionaries were collaborating with the Japanese and betrayed him.[40]

This is, of course, not the place to discuss the delicate issue of the relationship between Formosan (i.e. Han Chinese) Christians and the Japanese authorities or the general history of Japanese colonialism in Taiwan. A substantial body of literature on the Japanese period has emerged in recent decades. But I would like to draw attention to the existence of Chinese language sources concerning the Presbyterian missions and church. We should, for instance, note the *Tâi-oân Kàu-hoē Kong-pò* (台灣教會公報 Taiwan Church News), a publication of the Presbyterian Church in Taiwan. It was first published in 1885 as the *Tâi-oân-hú-siâⁿ Kàu-hōe-pò* (台灣府城教會報) and printed in romanised Taiwanese using the *Peéh-ōe-jī* orthography. Another useful resource is the online archive created by John Lai 賴永祥, a librarian, scholar, and elder in the Taiwanese Christian community. In addition to historical accounts, he has collected biographical sketches of Chinese Christians and Western missionaries involved in the Christianization of Taiwan. For further information, see Elder John Lai's Archive 賴永祥長老史料庫 at http://www.laijohn.com/English/Home.htm.

---

40 See Komagome Takeshi, "Colonial Modernity for an Elite Taiwanese, Lim Bo-seng: The Labyrinth of Cosmopolitanism," in Liao Ping-hui & David Der-wei Wang, eds., *Taiwan under Japanese Colonial Rule, 1895-1945: History, Culture, Memory* (New York: Columbia University Press, 2006), pp. 141-159.

Educational Developments and the Shrine Question

Throughout the first three decades of the twentieth century, English Presbyterian missionaries made few criticisms of the Japanese colonial administration in Taiwan. One rare early voice was that of Dr. Peter Anderson 安彼得, a medical missionary at Takow 打狗. Concerning the excessive number of opium licenses issued by the Government-General, he reported that, "I do hear often enough of their hunting up those who have ceased to smoke (temporarily at least), with a view to their renewing their licenses", and "the local authorities are under great temptation to [employ] almost any methods that will bring in revenue".[41]

One area that gave rise to missionary concerns was in modern education. When Taiwan was under Chinese control, missionaries were the pioneers in the new education. This changed with the arrival of the Japanese. In particular, the establishment of government schools make life difficult for the smaller church schools. Still, Edward Band was able to put a positive gloss on the situation. "Though the Japanese educational authorities insisted on the use of the Japanese language in all day schools, they did not interfere with the teaching of the Bible in the Formosan Romanized edition which was used in the Sunday Schools. It was, therefore, possible for every child to be taught the Bible in the mother tongue."[42] Moreover, although the Japanese authorities opened the Taihoku Medical College 臺北醫學專門學校 as an essential Japanese language training facility for medical students, or other government secondary schools were established for Formosans during the first twenty years of Japanese rule.[43]

By 1929 a more critical note was creeping into Band's assessment. He

---

41 "Takow," *The Monthly Messenger* 709 (April 1905), quoted in Komagome, "Japanese Colonial Rule," p. 231.
42 Band, *Working His Purpose Out*, p. 141.
43 Ibid., pp. 141-142.

asked what the mission could do "in this island colony of Japan, one of the leading powers of the world, with an extensive, progressive and wonderfully efficient educational system.... Can we as a Mission with our small resources make any worthy contribution to the life of the island? Now that the Japanese government is developing and controlling education in Formosa, are we justified in carrying on?"[44] Yet he noted that there was "the same zeal for education among Formosans as among Japanese, but unfortunately there are not enough schools to meet the growing demand for education.... The Formosans complain that in the Government schools and colleges the authorities give undue preference to Japanese applicants to the exclusion of Formosans."[45] In the same report, Band raises the issue of the Shinto shrine worship.

> The main political and educational problem of the Government lies in assimilating the Formosans and winning them over to be loyal subjects of the Emperor. Mission schools in which foreigners are associated require to be specially careful to conform to this colonial policy.... Unfortunately as a sign of loyalty the Government has emphasized, more than in Japan proper, the attendance of all school pupils at the Shinto shrines on national holidays. We have always regarded this compulsory attendance as a breach of religious liberty and so have refused to take out pupils to perform obeisance. At the same time we have always observed such occasions in school by a special Christian service with prayers for the Emperor and a suitable address on loyalty.... There are other ways of fostering loyalty. Merely to satisfy a few over zealous Shintoist officials, it would be a mistake

---

44 Edward Band, "The Educational Situation in Formosa," in *The Japan Mission Year Book* (Tokyo, 1929), p. 267.
45 Ibid., pp. 270-271.

in colonial policy to impose unduly a Shintoist cult upon the Formosan people. To demand the attendance of pupils at the shrines ... would be religious tyranny, subtle and refined, but none the less cruel.[46]

While the English Presbyterian mission was still enjoying a period of steady growth in the early 1930s, after the Manchurian Incident in 1931 significant problems were gradually emerging. The Presbyterian Mission had to make concessions on account of the Japanese language issue, in spite of the fact that it had in Edward Band an educational missionary who was fluent in both Japanese and Chinese. In 1934, the Presbyterians appointed Kato Chotaro, an ex-commander in the Japanese navy, to be principal of the Tainan Middle School. Yet this did not stop the "deliberate campaign to bring an end to their educational work and eventually to their missionary work.... Because relations between Japanese and missionaries in Taiwan had generally been good since 1895", Hamish Ion concludes that "the tenacity of the Japanese campaign must have caught most of the missionaries by surprise."[47]

Edward Band, having returned from furlough in April 1938, sent a confidential report to "Dear Friends" three months later. Among other things, he observed:

A question which greatly concerns the Formosan Church is the spread of the Japanese language. For many years it has been the tradition of the Church, vigorously championed by Dr. Barclay all his lifetime, to give the people the Bible in their mother tongue. Naturally the Government aim is to foster the spread of Japanese and to make the

---

46 Ibid., p. 273, 274.

47 A. Hamish Ion, *The Cross in the Dark Valley: The Canadian Protestant Missionary Movement in the Japanese Empire, 1931-1945* (Waterloo, Ontario: Wilfrid Laurier University Press, 1999), p. 111.

people forget they ever belonged to China. For this reason the Church is regarded as a serious obstacle to the progress of Japanese culture in that it remains a formidable stronghold holding public meetings in the Formosan language which the authorities desire to suppress.[48]

By the late summer of 1939 anti-British feeling was running high and missionary wives and children were advised to leave the island. The men followed a year later and the English Presbyterian mission in southern Taiwan was closed on 22 November 1940. Afterwards the British consul informed the embassy in Tokyo:

The two old-established missionary organisations, the English Presbyterian Mission in South Formosa and the Canadian Presbyterian Mission in the north, both decided to withdraw following official advice. This advice was, however, merely the last straw. For at least six years past they had found their activities continually being more and more circumscribed. The movement for exclusion from educational work had its first big success in 1934, and by 1940 there was little left to lose. Evangelical work also was more and more restricted, not by regulations alone, such as limitations on the use of the Formosan language, but by the missionaries' own reluctance to expose their converts to the more and more tiresome

---

48 Band to 'My dear Friends' (Private and Confidential), Presbyterian Middle School, Tainan, July 1938, in Elder John Lai's Archive. Here it should be noted that the English Presbyterian missionaries in Taiwan, anxious that their mostly illiterate converts should learn to read and write, were convinced that the Romanized script (i.e. *Peéh-ōe-jī* 白話字) was easier to learn than Chinese characters. The printing of Romanized texts thus helped preserve the Taiwanese dialect well into the twentieth century. For further details, see Ann Heylen, "Missionary Linguistics on Taiwan. Romanizing Taiwanese: Codification and Standardization of Dictionaries in Southern Min (1837-1923)," in Ku Wei-ying & Koen De Ridder, eds., *Authentic Chinese Christianity: Preludes to Its Development (Nineteenth and Twentieth Centuries)* (Leuven: Leuven University Press, 2001), pp. 135-174.

inquisitions by the police which followed their visits.[49]

For much of the period since 1895, the English Presbyterian missionaries were on relatively good terms with the Japanese authorities, but when problems began to mount in the course of the 1930s, obliging them eventually to depart, there were no Protestant missionaries left to report on the deteriorating situation on the island during the Pacific War. It was not until 21 July 1946 that the Rev. Walter Ernest Montgomery 滿雄才 (1882-1968) and wife arrived to resume their missionary work under rather changed conditions.

Conclusion

The published and unpublished material generated by Presbyterian Church of England personnel in Taiwan is quite substantial, for some of the missionaries were prolific writers. It is, however, important to recognize that their primary concern was the evangelization of Taiwan. Transmitting knowledge about Taiwan to their British readers, while it had a valuable promotional function, was always of secondary importance. Understandably, although not lacking in academic ability, the missionaries tended to write from their own religious perspective. In common with their Presbyterian colleagues on the Chinese mainland, they often presented a negative picture of Chinese society during the last years of the Qing dynasty. They were critical of the Chinese ruling class as well as popular religious beliefs and practices. In view of the widespread Chinese opposition to the propagation of Christianity, the early missionaries paid greater attention to the acculturated indigenous

---

49 Clement Hugh Archer to Sir Robert Craigie, Tamsui, 22 January 1941, No. 13 Most Confidential 3133/23, FO371/28013 (Japan 1941).

inhabitants on the plains, but also showed an interest in the aborigines living in the eastern half of the island, beyond Qing control. Consequently, as the above examples show, their reports afforded readers rare glimpses into a world beyond the dominant Chinese settler society. At the same time, their linguistic work helped preserve the South Fujian dialect and made it available to later researchers. Similarly, knowledge was transmitted in connection with the introduction of Western concepts of health care and educational work.[50] During the colonial period, the missionaries initially welcomed the Japanese presence, but by the 1930s the relationship between the missionaries and the authorities began to deteriorate. Overall, there are few comments to be found in the Presbyterian sources that were openly critical of Japanese activities. In conclusion, then, based on the examples outlined in this paper, we can say that the published and unpublished material generated by the Presbyterian missionaries, in spite of certain inherent limitations, contributes to our understanding of Taiwan during the second half of the nineteenth and first half of the twentieth centuries.

---

50 Because of the specialist nature of the subjects, this paper does not include examples of missionary comments on prevailing health issues, especially infectious diseases and sanitary conditions in Taiwan, nor their attitudes toward Chinese traditional medicine or the changing nature of education during the Qing and Japanese periods.

Appendix

English Presbyterian Missionaries in Taiwan 1864~1950

Ministerial Missionaries (Ordained)				
Ritchie, Hugh 李庥		M[a]	1867-1879 †	Takow 打狗; Tainan 臺南
Campbell, William 甘為霖	D.D.	M	1871-1918	Tainan
Barclay, Thomas 巴克禮	M.A., D.D.	M	1874-1935 †	Tainan
Smith, David 施大闢		—	1875-1883	Tainan
Thow, William 涂為霖	M.A.	—	1880-1894 †	Tainan
Main, James 買雅各	M.A.		1882-1884	Tainan
Thompson, W. R. 佟	M.A.	M	1882-1887	Tainan
Ferguson, Duncan 宋忠堅	M.A.	M	1889-1923	Tainan
Moody, Campbell Naismith 梅甘霧	M.A., D.D.	M[b]	1895-1931	Chiang-hoa [Shoka] 彰化
Nielson, Andrew Bonar 廉德烈	M.A.	—	1895-1928	Tainan
Moncrieff, Hope 何希仁	M.A.	—	1909-1915	Chiang-hoa
Davies, A. E. 戴美斯	B.A.	—	1907-1909	Tainan
Montgomery, Walter Ernest 滿雄才	M.A., B.D.	M	1909-1950	Tainan
Band, Edward 萬榮華	M.A.	M[c]	1912-1940	Tainan
Jones, D. P. 曹恩賜	B.A.	—	1917-1919	Tainan
MacLeod, Duncan 劉忠堅 (CPM)	D.D.	M	1928-1965	Tainan; Chiang-hoa
Marshall, David Fraser 馬大闢 (CPM)	B.A., B.D.	M	1928-1937	Tainan
Copland, Edward Bruce 高瑞士 (UCC)		M	1929-1931	Tainan
Healey, Francis George 希禮智	M.A.	M	1930-1941	Tainan
Anderson, Boris 安慕理		M	1948-1965	Tainan
Beeby, H. Daniel 彌迪理		M	1950-1972	Tainan
Medical Missionaries				
Maxwell, James Laidlaw 馬雅各	M.A., M.D.	M	1864-1885	Takow; Tainan
Dickson, Matthew 德馬太	M.D.	—	1871-1876	Tainan

Anderson, Peter 安彼得	MRCS, LRCP	M	1878-1910	Tainan; Takow
Lang, John 萊約翰	M.D.	—	1885-1887	Tainan
Russell, Gavin 盧嘉敏	M.B., C.M.	—	1888-1892 †	?
Cairns, William Murray 金	M.D., C.M.	M	1893-1895	Tainan
Landsborough, David 蘭大衛	M.A., M.B.	M[d]	1895-1939	Chiang-hoa
Maxwell, James Laidlaw, Jr. 馬雅各二世	M.D.	M	1900-1923	Tainan
Gushue-Taylor, George 戴仁壽 (CPM)	M.D.	M	1911-1918	Tainan
Cheal, Percival 周惠霖 (a Quaker)	MRCS, LRCP	M	1919-1932	Tainan
Smith, Dansey 鐘寶能	MRCS, LRCP	M	1923-1926	Tainan
Mumford, Robert Harold 文甫道	M.B.	M[e]	1925-1933	Chiang-hoa
Little, John Llewellyn 李約翰 (UCC)	B.Sc., M.D.	M[f]	1931-1936	Tainan
Graham Cumming, George 甘堯理	M.B.	M	1933-1937	Chiang-hoa

Educational Missionaries

Ede, George 余饒理		M	1883-1896	Tainan
Johnson, Frederick R. 費仁純		M	1900-1908	Tainan
Singleton, Leslie 沈毅敦	B.Sc.	M	1921-1956	Tainan
Weighton, Robert Grant Pitts 衛清榮	B.Sc.	—	1933-1947	Tainan

Women's Missionary Association of the Presbyterian Church of England

Ritchie, Eliza Caroline 李麻牧師娘	Mrs	M[a]	1880-1884	Tainan
Murray, Elizabeth 馬	Miss 姑娘		1880-1884	Tainan
Stuart, Joan 朱約安	Miss		1885-1918	Tainan; Chiang-hoa
Butler, Annie E. 文安	Miss		1885-1925	Tainan; Chiang-hoa
Barnett, Margaret 萬真珠	Miss		1888-1926	Tainan
Lloyd, Jeanie A. 盧仁愛	Miss		1903-1933 †	Tainan
Benning, Annie 孟	Miss, nurse		1909-1910	Tainan
Learner, Marjorie Ellen 連馬玉	Miss	M[d]	1909-1912	Tainan
Fullerton, Alice J. 富	Miss, nurse		1911-1916	Tainan
Reive, Agnes Dickson 李御娜	Miss	M[c]	1913-1919	Tainan
Livingston, Ann Armstrong 林安	Miss		1913-1940	Chiang-hoa, Tainan

Mackintosh, Sabine Elizabeth 杜雪雲	Miss		1916-1940	Chiang-hoa
Arthur, Margaret Christian 'Peggy' 洪伯祺	Miss, nurse	M[b]	1919-1921	Chiang-hoa
Anderson Scott, Marjorie D. 蘇	Miss		1922-1925	Chiang-hoa
Galt, Jessie W. 吳礫志	Miss		1922-1936	Tainan
Connan, Jessie Murray 高若西	Miss, SRN		1925-1926	Chiang-hoa
Cullen, Sarah Gladys 連雅麗	Miss		1926-1947	Tainan
Nicol, Agnes 尼	Miss	M[e]	1926-1928	Chiang-hoa
Elliott, Isabel 烈以利（CPM）	Miss, RN		1927-1941	Chiang-hoa
Adair, Lily 安義理（CPM）	Miss		1928-1940	Chiang-hoa
Connell, Helen 高哈拿（CPM）	Miss		1930-1931 †	Tainan
Little, Flora Millicent 吳花密 （CPM）	Mrs, M.D.	M[f]	1931-1937	Tainan
Gauld, Gretta 吳阿玉（UCC）	Miss, RN		1931-1939	Tainan
Beattie, Margaret W. 米真珠	Miss, M.A.		1933-1949	Tainan
Brooking, Marjorie 巫瑪玉	Miss, SRN		1933-1934 †	Chiang-hoa
MacLeod, Ruth 劉路得（1955-71UCC）	Miss		1934-1955	Chiang-hoa
Moody, Kathleen E. M. 梅佳蓮	Miss		1948-1985	Tainan
Holmes, Christina Sybil 賀恩惠	Miss, nurse		1950-1976	Chiang-hoa

† died in Taiwan

M indicates married missionary

M[a] = Hugh Ritchie married Eliza Caroline Cooke on 1 July 1867 in Scotland

M[b] = Peggy Arthur became the second Mrs. Campbell N. Moody. The first Mrs. Moody, Margaret Rintoul Findlay, was the daughter of Dr. William Findlay.

M[c] = Edward Band married Agnes D. Reive

M[d] = David Landsborough married Marjorie Learner

M[e] = R. H. Mumford married Agnes Nicol in 1928

M[f] = Flora Millicent Gauld married John Llewellyn Little on 4 Apr 1927 in York, Canada. She was the daughter of William Gauld 吳威廉 and Margaret [Gretta] Ann Mellis, CPM missionaries in northern Taiwan.

Gretta Gauld of The Women's Missionary Society of The United Church of Canada offered for missionary service in Formosa [Taiwan] in 1946.

看似尋常最奇崛，成如容易卻艱辛：
張靜愚日記中有關中原大學創校史料的探討

李宜涯

中原大學通識中心教授

摘要

　　五十八年前中原大學在三股力量合作下興辦，這三股力量分別代表著傳教士、中國基督徒與桃園地方士紳，他們願意為百廢待舉的臺灣在高等教育上貢獻一份心力。然而這三股力量在學校成立後卻難以繼續合作，最後傳教士賈嘉美牧師（Rev. James R. Graham）離開中原大學董事會，另外在關渡建立基督書院，而中原大學也經歷了一段人事糾紛的時期。

　　近年來在此公案的相關史料上有了重大的突破，就是張靜愚的日記被其家屬捐贈給中原大學。張靜愚是中原大學創辦人之一，是創校三股力量中的中國基督徒一方，也曾經擔任過中原大學董事長，在政界、教會界與社會上都受到敬重。故他的日記可以說是中原大學早期發展的重要史料，顯示出當時建校人士的觀點、中原大學草創時期的困難、三方合作的情況，以及一位中國基督徒對建校艱難的內心感受。換個角度來說，這份珍貴的史料呈現了戰後臺灣高等教育發展的困難所在，故其不僅具備著中原大學校史的重要性，還有著教會歷史的意義，更蘊含教會與社會的互動關係。

關鍵詞：中原大學、張靜愚日記、賈嘉美（James R. Graham）、基督教高等教育

一、前言

在中華民國高等教育發展史中，1955年是很特別的一年。當時，臺灣僅有公立大專學校四所（分別是國立臺灣大學、臺南工學院、臺中農學院及省立師範學院），主要原因是在中華民國政府遷臺以後，國家預算極為拮据，能撥到高教的經費更是有限，致使儘管有大批學人、學子從大陸來臺，但是臺灣的大學院校發展仍是受到限制。[1] 這種情況一直到1954年才有轉機。二年之內分別成立了三所公立大學與四所私立高校，成為臺灣高等教育史的轉捩點。[2] 在這些風雲並起的私立大學中，以1955年同時創辦的兩間私立大學：中原大學[3] 與東海大學最引人注目。

然而這兩所同年成立的基督教大學，在創建初期的境遇卻有天壤之別。東海有若天之驕子，集當年差會在華建立高等學府的資源於一身，「美國在華基督教大學聯合董事會」（The United Board for Christian Colleges in China, UBCCC，以後簡稱「聯董會」）無法在華繼續辦學，遂將原先在大陸十三所教會大學的經費全部用在東海大學，使東海大學「學生少、教授多、待遇高……一枝獨秀，大師群集大度山」。[4]

反觀中原大學，與東海大學的發展截然不同。她沒有任何教會的

---

1 陳舜芬，〈光復後臺灣地區高等教育設校政策之探討〉，收於賴澤涵、黃俊傑編，《光復後臺灣地區發展經驗》，頁208-209。

2 當張其昀在1954年5月接掌教育部後，即首先著手於大陸原有大學及學術機關的恢復，於是政治大學、清華大學及交通大學先後在二年內分別復校。私立大學當時也應運而生，私立東海大學、東吳大學、中原理工學院及中國醫藥學院分別在他任內成立，張部長更在一個拜中核定了實踐專、銘傳商專設校。見周祝瑛，〈20世紀臺灣教育〉，收於顧明遠編，《中國教育大系》（湖北：湖北教育出版社，2004），頁3370-3739。

3 由於中原大學的校名從「基督教中壢農工學院」、「私立中原理工學院」、「私立中原大學」有不同階段的變化，為求行文方便，本文概以中原大學稱呼。

4 東海大學校長梅可望曾表示：「當本校創辦初期，美國聯董會把大陸十三所教會大學的經費全部用在東海。第一任校長曾約農先生，更是雄心萬丈，創行新制，建立大學教育的理想，一時之間，校譽鵲起。那時本校學生少、教授多、待遇高，整個臺灣不過只有四所大學，東海一枝獨秀，大師群集大度山。」見梅可望，〈東海與我──「東海三十年」代序〉，古鴻廷等編，《東海三十年特刊》（臺中：私立東海大學，1985年11月2日），頁2。

奧援，更無雄厚有力的金主在背後支持。其創立是由外國傳教士、中國基督徒與臺灣地方士紳，三股背景截然不同的力量合作所致。由於經費不足，再加上人事紛擾，致使在初期經歷過一段慘澹經營，十分艱辛的過程。對於其中紛擾可稍見端倪的是，早期中原老師與校友，只要提起這段創建歷程，莫不搖頭嘆息，但對其中內因卻莫衷一是。且中原大學的官方網頁對於中原建校期間的資訊，亦是非常隱諱。

在中原大學的官方網頁中，只能看到從民國42年6月15日開始倡議設校：

> 由篤信基督，熱心教育人士張靜愚先生、郭克悌先生、美籍賈嘉美牧師及桃園中壢地方士紳吳鴻森先生、徐崇德先生等會商，決定在中壢埔頂設立一所農工學院。由張靜愚、郭克悌、陳維屏、瞿荊洲、柯里培、賈嘉美先生等組成「基督教中壢農工學院籌備委員會」。與地方人士吳鴻麟、張富、林添奎先生等組成之促進委員會訂約，並由徐崇德縣長，省政府吳鴻森委員，中壢鎮民代表會主席李天生先生等為見證人。會同辦理中壢鎮公所提供校產交割事宜。[5]

可是後來三股力量為何無法同心合作卻未見提及。

至於創校經費的籌措與人事遞嬗的原由，亦均未有詳細的說明。如在中原建校史前兩年中佔有重要地位的美籍傳教士賈嘉美（Rev. James Graham, 1898-1982），在1955年結束後，就再也不見其身影；與他同時身為中原副董事長，後為代董事長的中原第一任代院（校）長郭克悌，於1956年5月17日宣布辭職，但原因為何，一字不提。這與大事紀對於日後每任校長的去留均有說明大不相同。這段時間，中原到底在人事上發生什麼樣的問題？慘澹經營的中原又是如何處理捉襟見肘的財務？均是校史記載中未曾解決的問題。

---

5 中原大學的官方網頁：http://ann.cycu.edu.tw/kcy/index.jsp，網頁登錄時間：2011年11月23日。

在中原大學校史的記載上，近年有了重大的突破。當年參與創校的重要人物，也就是中原大學第二任董事長張靜愚（1895-1984）的日記出土，由其家屬捐贈給中原大學圖書館，使得當年紛擾的過程得到有力的物證，同時也見證了當年中原創校的艱辛。本文即是以中原大學創校董事兼董事長張靜愚的私人日記為主，輔以董事會會議記錄，再參酌相關文獻與出版，來呈現中原當年創校的問題。

二、張靜愚其人其事

本名張保的張靜愚，字精一，山東高唐人，清光緒21年（西元1895年）5月5日生。其10歲失怙，由母親仲太夫人教養成人。張靜愚的受教歷程正如清末民初的發展歷程一般，充滿傳統私塾與西方教育交替的洗禮。張靜愚未入小學以前，就由其父親傳授四書、《易經》等中國傳統典籍。而在小學畢業後，即離鄉背井，前往濟南就讀「省立濟南農林學堂」（今大陸山東農業大學前身），但同時由「庚子賠款」成立的「清華留美預備學堂」亦在北京開辦招生，張靜愚遂放棄全公費的省立學校，全心準備留美預備學堂的考試，在16歲時，順利考取該校。

但張靜愚進入「清華留美預備學堂」後並未沉浸於安逸的求學生活。其一，是因時值歐戰戰火炙熱之時，就讀高等科二年級的張靜愚與同校同學張邦永、吳澤湘結伴考取歐戰華工翻譯。儘管戰場無情，但擔任華工翻譯不僅吃穿無虞，更可藉機遊歷歐洲各地，這對於莘莘學子而言，無疑是夢寐以求的求知之旅。1917年8月，張靜愚便與其他華工翻譯啟程前往英國利物浦。其二，也就在歐戰結束後，張靜愚並未依原先「清華留美預備學堂」的規劃，前往美國深造，而是在1919年攻讀英國利物浦工業學院機械工程系。這一番求學歷程的轉變，深深影響張靜愚日後的發展。

前唐榮鋼鐵董事長吳嵩慶（1901-1991）曾將張靜愚的一生概分

三個階段：武職、文職、基督教聖工。[6] 前兩個階段皆與民國政治發展有密切的關係。實際上從張靜愚就讀利物浦工業學院後，其便與中國政局產生了聯繫。1921年，張靜愚被孫中山選派為中國國民黨利物浦支部負責人，在其學成歸國後，又於1924年任職國民黨中央黨部秘書。至此，張靜愚開始涉入民國時期多變的政局，其角色更因時局的演變而充滿多樣性。同年夏季，擔任甫成立的黃埔軍校第二團黨代表，並隨軍出征，此也為張靜愚武職身分的開端。

值得注意的是，張靜愚的軍旅生涯和當時初創的廣州空軍密不可分。其先後出任大元帥府航空局長、國民革命軍總司令部航空處長（1926年）、北伐軍航空司令（1928年）。後任軍政部航空署副署長、署長，期間奉令於南京成立航空班（1929年1月），是為中國空軍的濫觴，亦為今空軍官校的前身。北伐結束後，轉任黃埔軍校外語文總教官。[7]

民國邁入全國統一之後，張靜愚的角色也出現變化，武職的身分退而文職起，且其職務性質多屬於經濟實務。1932年，出任軍事委員會訓練總監部政治訓練處長，位處全國中學軍訓教育的重要地位；任河南省政府建設廳長，積極建設電訊、水利、公路工程等地方重要基礎建設；1938年，任財政部川康兩省禁煙督察處處長；1940年，再任財政部全國稅務署署長，完成稅法與稅務改革，對於此時因抗戰軍費耗損嚴重的國府而言，有著重要的貢獻。抗戰勝利後，張靜愚任國民大會代表，參與制憲工作，又於1948年擔任立法委員。來臺後，張靜愚改任經濟部次長；1954年出任臺灣鋁業公司董事長；1967年又任臺灣機械公司董事長。[8] 此為張靜愚在政府部門出任要職之梗概。

張靜愚在其後半生則致力於臺灣高等教育的建設。1955年與外國

---

6 吳嵩慶，〈懷念張靜公〉，《張靜愚先生追思紀念集：一束思念》（臺北，家屬自行出版，1987），頁44。

7 張光正整理，〈張靜愚先生事略〉；鄭彥棻，〈懷念張靜愚兄〉，《張靜愚先生追思紀念集：一束思念》，頁38。

8 張光正整理，〈張靜愚先生事略〉。

傳教士、中國基督教徒、地方士紳合力創建中原大學，並任董事長
（共28年）；1957年，出任私立東海大學董事長（共3年）。除了擘
畫與籌建基督教在臺教育機構外，身為虔誠基督教徒的張靜愚亦積極
獻身於基督教現世教化的工作上，更甚者，是在聯繫海內外基督徒捍
衛基督信仰。1962年，為對抗共產主義無神論的高漲，張靜愚號召國
內外基督徒創立「亞洲基督教護教反共聯合會」，並於1969年後擴大
成為「世界基督教護教反共聯合會」。1966年協助中華學術院成立研
究所、籌建禮拜堂與教堂，並成立以印贈聖經為主要工作的「國際基
甸會中華民國分會」及「國際基督教從業人員協會中華民國總會」，
致力推廣臺灣的基督教信仰。[9]

　　1984年3月，張靜愚因病逝世於三軍總醫院，享年91歲。

三、中原創校爭執之疑問

　　中原大學創校起源始於1951年，最初是由中壢地方士紳、外國傳
教士與中國基督徒三者結合與努力的成果。但若與成立時擁有雄厚教
會與社會資源支援的私立東海大學相比，中原大學的創建過程顯得渺
小與低調。[10]

　　中原大學創校之問題歷來備受討論。但若回顧其建校時之時代背
景，似可找尋到部分的解答。歷來爭議之話題主要在於宗教教育在臺
灣高等教育的適法性，其原因歸因於我國高等教育法規明文規定私立
學校不得以宗教科目為必修課、不得在校內傳教、不得強迫學生參加
宗教儀式等相關限制性條文，簡言之，就是在我國高等教育內達到
「去宗教化」的目的，也由於這些先天性的限制，最後導致中原大學

---

9 張光正整理，〈張靜愚先生事略〉；尹士豪，〈張靜愚先生傳略〉，《張靜愚先生追思紀念集：一束思
　念》，頁122。

10 東海大學的校園設計由名建築師貝聿銘（1917- ）操刀，建校破土典禮甚至邀請時任美國副總
　統的尼克森（Richard Nixon, 1913-1994）參加。

的奠基者之一的美國傳教士賈嘉美憤而離開中原大學。[11]

　　但在王成勉的文章之中，我們卻可以看到中原大學建校時所面臨的難題，即董事會成員之間的傾軋。上文已經提到，中原大學得以建校乃拜三股力量聯合所致，分別是外國傳教士（賈嘉美）、中國基督徒（經濟部次長張靜愚、工礦公司董事長郭克悌）、中壢地方士紳（桃園縣長徐崇德〔1900-1985〕、省府委員吳鴻森〔1897-1991〕）。而發起建校活動的動機，一則是因地方士紳有感於中壢人口雖日漸增加，但卻苦無高等學府，以至於該地子弟必須遷就他地大學，因此在中壢地區籌建一所高等學府，勢可一舉解決當地的教育需求，於是便開始向教育當局反映此一地方需求。而另一方面，也是因當時臺灣大學實在太少，相對而言也壓縮臺灣虔誠基督徒接受更高層次的專業教育，因此部分的基督徒家屬便開始向傳教士表達，希望能在臺灣建立一所以傳授基督教義為主的高等學府。而這兩股力量，再加上擁有顯著政經地位的中國基督教徒，此便是中原大學建校的大致雛形。[12]

　　依照這三股力量的屬性，中壢士紳協助建校所需的土地需求，並統籌相關的地方資源與行政手續；賈嘉美負責向海外籌措建校資金，號召有意願與能力的傳教士協助建校或任教；最後則由中國基督徒運用其在政經地位上的聲望，爭取政府立案與取得政府相關部門的配合與襄助。然而這樣的搭配卻未能使中原大學的建校工作順利開展。

　　除了硬體上的缺乏以外，例如土地取得遭遇來自軍方的阻礙，軍方遲遲未能釋出全部土地讓其辦校，使得中原大學即便在1955年開學時仍有部分軍隊駐留；而開辦學校最重要的經費問題，則因地方士紳與賈嘉美都未能籌措到足夠財源，讓中原大學的校園建設始終未能逐

---

11 阮若荷，《中國心·宣教情》（臺北：基督書院，2001），頁129；林本炫，〈我國私立大學的設立、經營和合併問題〉，《教育與社會研究》，第10期（2006年1月），頁72-73。賈嘉美牧師與中國的基督教育淵源深厚，其在出生後六個月就隨父母來華，後任江蘇淮美中學校長，長期在華從事宣教活動，來臺後曾在美創建自由中國基督大學協會、參與籌設中原理工學院；而在離開中原理工學院後，便在淡水關渡創建基督書院，後者並未在教育部立案，從而避免了《大學法》禁止在我國大學內從事宗教教育、活動的限制。

12 王成勉，〈臺灣基督教大學教育的檢討〉，《佛光學刊》，第1期（1996），頁86。

步到位，是故，簡陋校舍與貧瘠設備乃成為該校開學後難以迴避的艱困局面。[13] 然而，中原建校初期所面對最嚴重的問題，實為董事會內部的人事爭執。

依過去的相關研究顯示，中原建校是在全無章法的摸索中成立的，其中影響最深者應為爭執不休的董事會。原先預定的董事長鈕永建（1870-1955，時任國民黨中央評議委員）於1953年因病赴美就醫，空缺下來的位子即由郭克悌代理；校長人選則到了1954年底向教育部呈報立案時，仍然懸而未決，只能讓郭克悌繼續暫代。也由於主管校務的高層人選遲遲未能決定，連帶使得建校之初的人事制度亦不完備，造成學校師資人才的聘用僅能依賴董事之間的推薦與介紹，遂造成管理上的諸多問題。董事會內部的爭議最後遂引發代理董事長兼校長郭克悌的辭職。[14]

郭克悌請辭後，中原大學董事長改由張靜愚接任（1956年3月上任），校長人選則由對學術生態較為熟悉的謝明山接任（1956年5月上任，任職時間1955-1969），董事會爭議暫告一階段後，賈嘉美也於相近時間內辭去中原大學副董事的職位，卸下主導校務的重要角色。[15]

就時間點來看，從1953年8月第一次董事會開議之後，直至1956年5月郭克悌請辭職務，新任董事長與校長上任後，董事會問題才暫告落幕，顯然董事會對於應該由何人來主持校務始終未有一個確切的人選，以致於郭克悌長期代理兩個重要職務，但卻在校務起步階段決意辭職；從另一個角度來看，中原大學建校後不到幾年的光景就有兩位重要的奠基者（郭克悌與賈嘉美）相繼離開，尤其賈嘉美在離開後另建新校，創立一個更符合他理想中的教會學校，更可見董事會的內部問題並不單純。

---

13 同前註，頁86-87。
14 王成勉，〈臺灣基督教大學教育的檢討〉，《佛光學刊》，頁87、91。
15 同前註，頁91。

四、最後一張拼圖——張靜愚日記中的中原創校經過

相較於同一時期的東海大學，中原大學的創校歷程似乎較少為人所知。東海大學由於有聯董會的有力支援，故其創校過程有一脈絡可循，[16] 亦可從相關人物的追憶中尋覓部分事蹟。[17]

反觀中原建校初期之情況，現今似未留下詳盡的文字資料或是直指相關問題的史料，反倒是詳述賈嘉美一生的代表性著作《中國心‧宣教情》，在描述中原大學建校初期這段關鍵時刻時，僅是以「賈嘉美堅決主張辦教育的目的首在宣教，如果不能達成宣教的目標，寧可不辦校……便在情勢被迫之下離開了〔中原〕，僅居董事會中的董事席位。〔中原〕的經歷他不再對外提起，但是親近他的學生，則對他不只一次提及這段往事時的難過與氣憤印象深刻。」[18] 身為中原創校的奠基者，賈嘉美不可能不知當時《大學法》相關條例的規範，甚至中原大學從草擬的「基督教中壢農工學院」，到了立案時必須依據《大學法》規定更名為「私立中原理工學院」，這期間所遭遇的現實阻礙，賈嘉美勢必有所了解，因此，他辭去中原副董事長職位，到關渡另建一所宗教學院（關渡基督書院）的因素，不太可能僅是為了無法實現其校園宣教的理想；是否仍有其他更為嚴峻，乃至現實利益的問題「迫使」他另謀他算？而身為中原大學董事會重要成員，賈嘉美是否在問題重重的董事會活動中遭遇到了難以言明的困難？

由於賈嘉美並未留下確切而完整的記錄，本文的研究途徑便是以張靜愚所留下的私人日記中，尋找相關蛛絲馬跡。

---

16 「篳路藍縷」，http://www.thu.edu.tw/1_chinese/1_about/2_history/1_rough.html，網頁登錄時間：2011年11月23日。

17 張振義，〈東海大學創校經過〉，《傳記文學》，第36卷6期（1980年6月），頁29-32；李爾康，〈東海大學創校經過補遺〉，《傳記文學》，第37卷1期（1980年7月），頁39-41。

18 阮若荷，《中國心‧宣教情》，頁128。

（一）張靜愚日記的史料價值

作為私人的文字記錄，日記通常可以反映出一個人物對於私人領域乃至公眾人物、事務的記錄與感觸。而就本文主角——張靜愚的日記而言，其性質很大一部分可視為其每日的工作記錄，亦是摘錄其生活與周遭人事物相當多元化的筆記。

現今留下的張靜愚日記主要集中在政府遷臺以後，且集中於1950年代（缺1950、1958、1959年），其餘則為1961、1963、1964、1965、1967、1971年之日記。目前皆典藏於中原大學張靜愚紀念圖書館。除了私人日記以外，另有兩年的工作筆記（1951、1952年），其內容是以其參加的各政府部會之會議記錄為主，未有工作以外之記事。

身為一位宗教信仰非常深厚的基督徒，張靜愚日記以相當虔誠的態度記錄下每日的個人、家庭與周圍基督徒的宗教活動，包含每日的經文抄寫、家庭讀經、團體禮拜、個人的信仰啟發等，在在都顯示出張靜愚對於基督信仰的堅實信念，甚至在其晚年輕度中風後，仍以左手編寫《耶穌是誰》中英文對照一冊。此可作為檢視其宗教信仰一個相當鮮明的角度。

而在樸實內斂的宗教信仰之外，張靜愚日記最引人注目的即是其每日條列、精簡的工作記錄。於是乎，我們可以看到日記主人在其日記之中除了求得身心靈滿足的內心信仰世界之外，便是記錄下平時認真勞動的繁雜俗世工作。由於張靜愚此時已是經濟部次長的身分，就其日記記錄，除了得面對重要的美援業務，其中包含各式各樣種類繁雜、內容多樣的援助事宜，亦得處理部內各項經常業務。由於此時中華民國政府才開始接受美援，而自身的經濟與財經改革也正如火如荼地進行，因此可以看到這位日記主人的每日行程經常是各部會間的工作會議，以及南北奔波的業務考察。很難想像在這樣如此忙碌、高壓的工作環境之中，張靜愚仍舊可以忠實而不間斷地寫下其工作歷程，並且還能為其篤信的宗教信仰留下令人深刻的註記。

因此在這樣的寫作習慣之下，關於中原大學的建校事蹟同樣也被記錄在張靜愚的日記中。但如同其日常工作一般，有關中原大學的建校活動記錄亦是簡短，且未帶太多個人的評論或是雜感，因此必須在其日積月累的記事條目之中，細究端倪才能發掘中原大學的相關記錄。

（二）張靜愚筆下的中原大學建校

張靜愚日記中最早關於中原大學的建校記錄出現在1951年。

> 余陪賈嘉美牧師往訪廣播電臺總經理董顯光，談籌辦教會學校事，擬請董將來擔任籌備指導委員。[19]

如同上文有關中原大學建校歷程之討論一般，中原大學創校之始源於一群有心於臺灣高等教育的中外人士，張靜愚日記當中亦可以看到賈嘉美對於建立一所新宗教大學的期望與熱情，許多籌備討論皆是由賈嘉美發起與召集，更多的則是日記主人與賈嘉美兩人私下的討論。

不過，在張靜愚於1953年的日記裡，隱約可看出幾項日後出現的問題。首先，張靜愚甚早表明，由於自身工作關係，恐難以在此重大議題上貢獻太多心力，但他也相當憂心對於建校工作非常熱心的賈嘉美，似乎過於躁進而無完全準備，甚至張靜愚還曾因擔憂建校諸事繁雜，婉謝擔任董事會董事：

> 下午赴賈嘉美寓，因商談中壢基督教學院 [指中原大學] 事，余主張先由籌備委員會呈報有關教育機關，余因無時間及見于不易進行，不居名義，只從旁盡力協助其成功，賈牧師對此無經驗，且其步伐太亂，急于求成，而無準備。[20]

---

19 張靜愚日記，1951年9月24日記事。文中所指教會學校即指中原大學。此記事雖言及董顯光（1887-1971，時任中國廣播公司總經理），但之後建校事宜並未有其參與。

20 張靜愚日記，1953年5月4日記事。

> 賈嘉美牧師擬創辦中壢基督教會工業科學校 [指中原大學]，
> 來部洽余參加為董事，余因其情形複雜，婉謝。[21]

其次，賈嘉美多次承諾赴美進行建校款項之籌募，但卻遲遲未見相關資金到位，甚至僅募集到兩成資金：

> 下午訪賈嘉美牧師，郭克悌在座，商基督教中壢農工學院 [指中原大學] 董事會立案事，主要關鍵在基金尚未籌足，賈已函美友人募捐，一時當不能立案，函與基金需籌2萬美金。[22]
> 上午賈嘉美牧師來談，他為中壢農工學院籌款現僅有23萬臺幣，至少須有100萬臺幣，將可向教部呈請備案設立。[23]

最初命名為「基督教中壢農工學院」之校名，其「基督教」之名稱遭到時任教育部長的程天放（1899-1967）否決，程態度強硬，毫不通融：

> 下午賈嘉美牧師來談，他由曹某介紹見程天放談中壢學院事，程堅持應省基督，不得加以基督教字樣于學院之上，決不通融。[24]

不過，儘管高層事務諸多不順，但校舍興建尚稱順利，張靜愚也多次親赴中壢監督工程，與吳鴻森、吳鴻麟（1898-1995）等當地士紳聚會，實際經手建校事宜甚多。

> 上午偕夫人及郭克悌夫婦早上八時赴賈嘉美牧師寓早餐，赴桃

---

21 張靜愚日記，1953年6月24日記事。
22 張靜愚日記，1953年8月25日記事。
23 張靜愚日記，1953年9月15日記事。
24 張靜愚日記，1953年8月31日記事。

園縣政府由□主任秘書及黃秘書陪同，赴中壢鎮邀同吳委員鴻
森及縣議會議長吳鴻麟等赴農工學院校舍視察，其工程須尚有
一月以上時間將可完工，又視察原建學生宿舍四合房間，校本
部係二層樓房，□□面積每層四百坪，共八百坪，宿舍約一千
坪，下午三時返臺北。[25]

臺糖公司農業工程處工程師梁藝來見，商為中壢農工學院鑿井
事。[26]

下午楊家瑜教授來寓將所擬中壢農工學院工科四年課程帶
來。[27]

　　在籌辦中原大學建校的同時，張靜愚亦參與私立東海大學的開辦
工作，然而在其日記裡，對於其紛爭不休、日益對立的校長人事傾軋
感到厭煩與無奈。

下午二時參加東海大學董事會，杭立武主席，杭講話一篇牢
騷，與聯合董事會衝突頗大，恐將不久於斯職，討論聯董會來
文□□該會與東海大學董事會關係時，意見複雜，余主張接受
不必修改，遂全數通過，余離會後，人事問題、校長問題，推
舉陳錫恩代表代理。[28]

上午九時參加東海大學董事會，選舉陳錫恩為校長11：2，陳
表示不滿，因討論時間過久，並有多人不主張在徵詢教育部同
意前報票，惟□□□+□□□堅決即行報票，結果陳雖當選，
故仍感不快，且不肯與道賀之董事長握手，會中并推杭立武蔡
培火與□報告教育部；下午董事會繼續開會，選舉蔡一□為校
務委員會主席，下午四時半杭董事長立武接到張部長其昀電

---

25 張靜愚日記，1953年9月19日記事。
26 張靜愚日記，1953年10月12日記事。
27 張靜愚日記，1953年10月23日記事。
28 張靜愚日記，1954年5月8日記事。

話，表示不贊成陳為校長，杭當場報告，多數董事失望；晚董事會在圓山飯店歡迎陳錫恩代表舉行晚餐，陳向余密談，對杭極不滿意，我認為陳、杭都不智也。[29]

　　於是在其將心力大量投注在排解東海大學校長人事之糾紛時，中原大學的建校事務便成為一段段簡要的活動片段，此為1954年日記大半之情形。直至東海大學校長人選爭議告一段落後，從該年11月開始，中原大學的建校活動又逐漸活躍在日記主人的每日行程中。

> 上午偕郭克悌陪教育部周督學視察中原理工學院房舍，並與桃園縣政府、中壢鎮公所負責人講話，午餐後返臺北。[30]
> 上午十時偕賈嘉美牧師赴教育部訪張部長其昀，為創辦中原理工學院事，經余紹介後，相談甚為融洽，張送賈書籍五六種，並送賈至部大門外，俟車行後始返，其對賈禮貌之隆，很少見也；中午郭克悌應周督學之請與吳委員鴻森及余見面，郭邀在吉萬午餐，商談關於中原理工學院視察報告，他表示願為贊助成立。[31]
> 上午十一時參加中原理工學院董事會，報告工程進度及註冊情形，並決定明春 [1955年，實際招生時間是下半年] 開學招生120名，分三班或四班上課，推郭克悌代理校長，通過。[32]

　　在此後階段，張靜愚除了多次前往中壢視察校舍興建進度、安排各科系課程外，董事會會議也成為日記記述的重點。不過此時潛藏的人事衝突也逐漸浮上檯面，尤其是賈嘉美與郭克悌之間的矛盾與衝

---

29 張靜愚日記，1954年8月16日記事。東海大學校長爭議主要是因該校董事會推舉的校長陳錫恩，除因其具有雙重國籍身分外，更被懷疑曾傳播共產思想，因此才會有教育部長張其昀（1901-1985）以電話通知否決一事。此校長人選前後爭論多時，張靜愚也因身為董事，多次涉入這項人事爭議之中。
30 張靜愚日記，1954年11月17日記事。
31 張靜愚日記，1954年11月23日記事。
32 張靜愚日記，1954年12月3日記事。

突。從1956年開始，賈嘉美在與張靜愚的晤談之中，多次表達他對郭克悌的個人意見，儘管張靜愚並未記錄其中之言論，但從後來的發展來看，賈嘉美對郭克悌的看法顯然是負面的。

> a. m. Dr. J. Graham [賈嘉美] came to my office & told me about Mr. Kuo Keh-ti [郭克悌] .[33]
>
> a. m. & p. m.... 。Dr. J. Graham came to see and talked about Mr. Kuo Keh-ti.[34]
>
> Mr. & Mrs. Kuo Keh-ti came to see me about Chung Yuan College troubles between him & Dr. Graham.[35]

至此之後，賈嘉美甚至向張靜愚表明要求郭克悌辭去與中原大學相關的職務。

> a. m. Being at Dr. Gramam's house, he proposed to asked Mr. Kuo Keh-ti to resign his post as the president of Chung Yuan College. [36]

賈嘉美甚至利用其與中央政府高層的良好關係，向張群（1889-1990，時任總統府秘書長）、甚至是蔣中正總統（1887-1975）告狀，其指控郭克悌的罪狀是極為嚴重的傳播共產思想。

> a. m. arrived Taipei at 7:50 a. m. Attend with S. T. [張靜愚夫人陳秀德女士英文簡稱] the Shih Lin Church, Pres. Chiang (蔣中正總統) prsent, Chou Lian Hwa [周聯華牧師] preached. General Chang

---

33 張靜愚日記，1956年2月20日記事。

34 張靜愚日記，1956年3月5日記事。

35 張靜愚日記，1956年3月6日記事。

36 張靜愚日記，1956年3月27日記事。郭克悌已於該日主動請辭董事長一職，並由張靜愚代理（此人選亦由賈嘉美推舉）。

Chun [張群將軍] had words with me about Dr. Graham's attitude toward Chung Yuan College. Min. Chang [張其昀] too.[37]

p. m. Minister Chang Chih-yun told me that someone told Pres. Chiang that Kuo K. T. encouraged Communist in the Chung Yuan College, so Kuo must leave. This is from James Graham's accusation.[38]

在龐大的壓力之下,郭克悌最終在5月15日主動請辭校長,兩天後改由謝明山擔任。

在高層人事風波告一段落後,張靜愚的生活彷彿回到過往的忙碌與平靜,關於中原大學的記錄僅止於一些校務的籌備與執行。

(三)董事會記錄下的人事風波

關於中原大學創校初期的疑議,張靜愚日記雖然提供一條清晰的發展脈絡,但因其記事風格極其簡短,細節部分難以釐清,故勢必得由其他史料加以佐證、補充其說法。是故,此關鍵史料即為中原大學的董事會開會記錄。

依據1955年12月29日與1956年1月24日第26、27次董事會記錄,賈嘉美告知董事會,由於與國軍協調相當不順,導致校地內的駐軍遲遲不撤出。迫於學校已經招生開學,董事會遂決議,以向華南銀行貸款購買私人土地的方式,解決校地空間不足的問題。針對此一問題,賈嘉美甚至告知董事會,其已請求蔣中正總統協助,向國防部交涉土地問題。

賈牧師報告:關於本院駐軍遷讓事宜,本人曾不斷與顧問團洽商,但因第三戰鬥團為非受軍援單位,致顧問團無法直接協助,經數度商洽已經聯勤供應司令部召集各有關單位開會決

---

37 張靜愚日記,1956年4月22日記事。
38 張靜愚日記,1956年5月4日記事。

定。本院駐軍最遲於四十五年六月底以前可以遷出，並在未遷出以前，本院可以先行修建房屋及利用土地。[39]

賈牧師報告：關於本院駐軍遷移問題，軍方意見須由地方當局撥地十五甲，始能遷讓，惟據徐縣長謂該縣所有公有土地均撥交國防部使用，地方已無餘存，現擬請徐縣長將撥交國防部公地名冊抄錄一份，以便向軍方再行交涉。……[討論事項] 賈牧師提議地方為本院購置私地一案，據謂已議妥每坪10.50元，並已決定照購，惟現款一時無法籌足，請求本會代洽華南銀行借款新臺幣五、六萬元（約56,000）以便照購校地，並允於舊曆二月間收到稅款後，即行償清，是否可辦，請討論案……。決議，為本院校地迅速解決起見，可以同意，並請吳董事代表本會辦理。[40]

賈牧師報告：關於學校駐軍謙讓事宜，曾盡力催辦並請MAAG [美國軍事顧問團] 協助。蔣總統且已通知國防部核辦。[41]

　　然而，校地問題與建校經費有著密不可分的關係，因此帳務問題遂直接引爆賈嘉美與代理董事長兼院長的郭克悌之間的衝突。

　　由於賈嘉美認定郭克悌未能妥善處理帳務，導致諸多款項不清，遂於3月27日第29次董事會開議前一天，向郭克悌遞交一封措詞強烈的信件，引發郭克悌的極度不滿。郭克悌遂於當次會議中辭去董事長，甚至主動請辭院長一辭：

郭代董事長兼院長提議：本人就任後院長係由本會正式通過聘請，並經教育部批准有案，欣見學校成立近年，漸有軌道可循，原擬於本學年終了辭去院長辭務，昨忽接賈牧師來信對本人既多誤會復欠禮貌，深感遺憾，乃向各位董事提出辭去院長

39 中原大學董事會開會記錄，1955年12月29日第26次。
40 中原大學董事會開會記錄，1956年1月24日第27次。
41 中原大學董事會開會記錄，1956年2月21日第28次。

職務，請即予照准案。[42]

　　儘管包含吳鴻森等多位董事極力緩頰，並請求郭克悌還是等到學年終了再辭院長一職，但兩人的衝突已然在董事會中造成極大的風波：

> 吳鴻森董事：本人代表地方人士企待兩點，1. 教育應無分國際，為最高事業。2. 中美應密切合作，在學校事情上應充分表現出來，現本校正值學期當中，大家均應相愛相處意見一致，若有不一致之處，亦應盡量使之一致。[43]

　　賈嘉美的舉措不僅導致郭克悌的請辭風波，更在校園內引發學生間的非議。由於學生間盛傳由於賈嘉美的包庇，使得該校總務長張遠南恣意妄為，逾越職務干預校務，早已對兩人有所不滿；甚至當郭克悌請辭董事長不久，便有美籍教師闖入校長室，以嘲弄的語氣向郭克悌施以握手禮「歡送」其離職。學生在目睹此一荒謬行為後群起鼓譟罷課，並有學生代表向張靜愚遞交「全體學生」的抗議信：

> ……校政大權，操於美籍賈嘉美之手，賈牧師雖虛懷若谷，可惜錯信總務長張遠南，張先生總攬採購，收支帳目混沌不清，且欲上下其手，校務、訓導各方面均加干涉，使教務長賈伯里博士，徒有教務長之名，而訓導處亦有其勢力存在，故今形成舉校員生均仰總務長鼻息，而總務長更到處製造謠言，挑撥是非，使學校日呈混亂，生等均一一收入眼底……不料最近賈嘉美牧師竟迫郭院長辭職，而九日下午更有美籍教授數人湧入院長辦公室干涉院長，形同威脅，態度極其傲慢，生等既痛失良

---

42 中原大學董事會開會記錄，1956年3月27日第29次。
43 中原大學董事會開會記錄，1956年3月27日第29次。

師，復感校務黑暗至此，學校前途至感失望，忍無可忍……[44]

然而，學生引燃的校園風潮卻被賈嘉美視為由郭克悌動員學生的「學潮」，雖然之後教育部介入調查後認定並非嚴重的校園問題，但顯然此事已被賈嘉美渲染成郭克悌意圖在校園傳播共產思想的行徑。[45]

而在4月24日第30次的董事會中，董事之一的方子衛，以調停人的姿態向董事會報告，他在與賈嘉美多次晤談後，認為賈嘉美的行為，主要在反映出校務多由郭克悌主導而不滿，賈嘉美身為建校資金的籌措者，理應對於校務規劃與執行擁有更多的發言權：

> 方子衛董事：……其後一月廿七日董事會前一天，賈牧師約我談話，他說：「郭某人豈有此理，我捐來的錢他花」，當時我勸他不必如此急，但賈牧師說非如此做不可……[46]

賈嘉美甚至發言指出，有人惡意散播他染指從美國募集而來的資金，並暗示郭克悌鼓動學潮，坦言已無法和其共事；如果郭克悌再不辭去院長一職，則他將離開中原大學的董事會。

> 賈嘉美董事：我們應該有妥善的辦法挽救這事，本人已捐到132萬元用在學校。關於郭院長，上次董事會，我們已決議留他，郭先生自己說他專管教務的事，可是本人去菲一星期期

---

44 〈陳情書〉，未標明時間，置於第29次董事會開會記錄中。信中所謂「美籍教授數人湧入院長辦公室干涉院長」一事，張靜愚於4月9日記事中記載 "p. m. Mr. Kuo Keh-ti told me American Prof. K. A. W. insulted him by demanding." ；在日後的董事會記錄中，董事方子衛更明白寫出事件經過：「……至星期一，郭院長與校領例會，下午院務會議，郭院長說明其辭職原因，會中一切照常，會後兩個外國教授至院長室，說：『我們很高興你走，現在歡送握手！』態度極欠禮貌，學生所見，氣憤不已。」中原大學董事會開會記錄，1956年4月24日第30次。

45 張靜愚日記，1956年5月4日記事。

46 中原大學董事會開會記錄，1956年4月24日第30次。

間，四月九日那天學校起了很大的學潮，並聽說學生有人吃菸喝酒的事，最好學校先選舉五位董事照顧，我情願完全不辦學校的事，學生既對我如此，我一輩子不到學校去，實在學校鬧的學潮很大……聽說學校有人罵我是騙子，由美國捐來很多錢都入腰包，我很灰心，本人退出，我不曉得有什麼結果，大家要我退，我就退出，教育的事我感覺失敗，郭先生要在，我就退出，若郭院長再做下去，無法擔保是否再鬧。[47]

換言之，其餘董事必須對兩人的誰去誰留作出決議。不久，郭克悌親筆向董事會表明，由於賈嘉美與美籍教師對他不尊重，他決定在學期未結束之前，辭去院長一職。

查在三月廿七日董事會席上，克悌曾懇辭本院院長職務後，經董事會請本人繼續負責院長職務至本學期終了，當允勉予照辦，惟在四月廿四日董事會席上，有Nelson及賈嘉美董事提議要求本人仍辭院長職，似此先後出爾反爾，形同兒戲，且有歪曲事實，語涉侮辱本人者，該董事既無君子之風，更無基督徒之精神，本人忍無可忍，茲特提出再辭本院院長職務，並望即日另選院長前來交接為荷。[48]

將近半年的高層人事風波，由於郭克悌的主動請辭而暫告一段落。

五、傳教士的心態──賈嘉美的手段與堅持

不管從張靜愚的私人日記或是中原大學的董事會開會記錄，都可

47 中原大學董事會開會記錄，1956年4月24日第30次。
48 郭克悌親筆辭職信，1956年5月12日。

看到中原大學的創辦人之一——賈嘉美的顯著身影。身為一位長年在中國與臺灣傳教的外籍傳教士，其對於中國的基督教育發展有著無可抹煞的功勞。然而就如同其剛烈、直率、不輕言放棄的性情，讓其在創辦中原大學時難以避免地和理念不合者產生衝突。

賈嘉美曾自撰其對於開辦基督教育的理念，從其中可以感受到其堅守西方傳統基督教育精神與宗旨，甚至對於現代科學精神與社會思想的極端排斥。在〈創辦基督書院的目的〉一文中，賈嘉美明白表示，當代西方的諸多思想，包含達爾文的物種進化論、馬克思的共產主義、杜威的實證主義，在在都衝擊了傳統西方文明發展中以上帝、聖經為核心的教育理念、重視家庭與社會功能的核心價值乃至源遠流長的經驗主義。賈嘉美認定美國早已被這些現代化的俗世觀污染、毒化（故其非常排斥學生留美），當世的戰爭、犯罪、性別與家庭問題，都因這些「邪惡」的思想所影響。因此，其對於學校教育的屬性，應是重返已逐漸逝去的基督精神來規劃，重視學生的靈性、道德教育，以宗教教義來啟迪學生的心靈與性情，以宗教活動來塑造學生對於基督精神的崇拜與實現。[49]

以此精神，可以看出賈嘉美十分堅持基督教育的獨立性，甚至可以說與西方近世的科學精神保持距離。但這樣的理念不一定為其他中原大學的董事所認同。如上文所討論到，中原大學的建立有一部分的需求在於解決中壢學子對於高等教育的需求，這一部分的考量忠實地反映在中原首次招生考試時，還特地設置禮遇中壢子弟的保送條款，顯然解決當時高等教育的不足也是中原建校的考量，甚至發生入學考試落榜者公開毀謗該校的考試歧視中壢當地子弟；[50] 而從校名的易迭也可看出，賈嘉美的基督學校宗旨一開始便無法相容於臺灣的教育政策。

不過賈嘉美並非未經歷過教會學校與中國現世教育體系的衝突，

---

49 阮若荷，《中國心‧宣教情》，頁161-170、174-178。

50 除了優待中壢子弟外，依照當時的教育政策，中原大學的入學考試同樣也得優待革命功勳子弟以及華僑。中原大學董事會開會記錄，1955年9月22日第25次、12月26日第26次。

早在1920年代其便已面臨中國教育界「收回教育權」的浪潮，教會學校的主導權不僅被中國人所掌控，學校的教學計畫更貼近現時教育需求。故賈嘉美並非首次面對其教育理念遭到干預的景況，而其試圖重新掌握中原大學的方式即控制校務經費的來源。為了捍衛中原大學作為教會學校的獨立性，賈嘉美曾於董事會中強調中原建校之緣起乃是由其與另一位董事柯理培（Rev. C. L. Culpepper）向中壢士紳提議才得以進行，而其建校理念係來自美國基督教教育（Christian Education），故為了維持教會學校的獨立性，學校基金應多由教會負責籌募，減低教會以外的捐獻：

> 本院創辦之初衷係鑒於美國Wheaton College之辦理基督徒教育之成功，是故在創辦以前，本人與柯理培博士等，曾兩度與地方人士開會並曾說明以創辦基督教育大學之宗旨，地方人士亦均無異議，於是地方捐贈校地廿甲大樓一棟後，陸續收到美國捐款，至目前為止，總計40,000元，始有今日之規模。本院自始至今，均維持基督教育，至以後捐款盼由教會而來，否則校外捐款若佔了多數，則對本院基督教育恐有影響，不能不注意也。[51]

雖然賈嘉美此舉乃基於維持校務發展的獨立性，降低外界的干預，但此言論無異於清理門戶，除了針對學校帳務不清一事外，更有貶抑中壢士紳僅提供校地之貢獻。此言論遂引起其他董事的微辭，也興起一波波清查帳務的行動。[52]

除此之外，上文曾提及方子衛董事曾試圖與賈嘉美溝通，以求化解董事會爭議。方氏向其強調，今日臺灣的教育政策不同於中國時期，政府貫徹政令的態度比過往更加堅決；方子衛更提醒賈嘉美，其

---

51 中原大學董事會開會記錄，1956年2月21日第28次。
52 中原大學董事會開會記錄，1956年3月27日第29次。

從未提出確切的捐款人名冊，亦未交代美金與新臺幣匯兌之方式，遲早會遭到教育部調查。

> ……本人曾在去年十一月間即已料到 [指郭、賈衝突導火線的帳務問題]，當時曾與賈牧師談兩小時之久，並曾告訴賈牧師說，臺灣今日與大陸時期不同，大陸教育失敗，因為有許多政府法令行不通，今日臺灣則一切政令均須推行，賈牧師在美代本校捐款，本會幾次決議函謝捐款人，賈牧師均未交出名單，又如何將美金變成臺幣，凡此種種，將來教育都要過問……[53]

其後，賈嘉美更直截了當地向方子衛抱怨道，「郭某人 [指郭克悌] 豈有此理，我捐來的錢他花」、「我的意思請郭董事長辭職，我們不能跟他合作」，甚至賈嘉美也無視方子衛警惕他引發學潮的危險：

> 本人 [方子衛] 說：「你不怕會鬧學潮嗎？」賈說：「不管」，後來幾經勸說，算是說服，但仍不決定……[54]

在逼退郭克悌後，中原大學的部分董事也紛紛辭去董事職務，惟為顧及董事會的整體發展，多主動請辭，以免引發更多的爭執。[55]

儘管賈嘉美對於基督教育理念的堅持和創辦教會學校的熱情，並非有意地中傷其他人，但阮若荷在其專著中言明，賈嘉美過度直率的急性子，經常引起共事者的不滿與誤會。[56] 在中原大學董事會的記錄之中，顯見這樣的描述更切中了其爭議的源頭。

---

53 中原大學董事會開會記錄，1956年4月24日第30次。
54 中原大學董事會開會記錄，1956年4月24日第30次。
55 中原大學董事會開會記錄，1956年5月15日第31次。在此次董事會中，郝益民、海牟登、杭克安皆已提出辭呈，海牟登更提議討論如學校因故停辦後教職員的薪資發放問題。
56 阮若荷，《中國心‧宣教情》，頁187-189。

六、結論

　　中原大學是臺灣在1950年代私人興學的典範，在沒有外界奧援的情況下，由外國傳教士、民間士紳、以及中國基督徒，克服萬難、通力合作下的成功範例。在歷經多年的經營後，該校已成為臺灣數一數二的私立大學。然而與其他同時期的學校相比，該校創辦歷程的艱辛，實非外人所能想像；創辦的歷程亦始終難為外人所熟知，除了三方合作以外，便再也未有更多的詳情披露，而第三方的研究亦因資料的欠缺而難以解釋何以該校的高層異動之問題根源所在。

　　本文利用曾任中原大學董事長的張靜愚撰寫的私人日記，並試圖解讀在其工作記事當中蒐羅關於該校創立時所遭遇的問題。張靜愚的日記寫作方式相當精簡，儘管每日都能記下其禮拜、讀經、工作、聚會等生活常態，但字句簡潔，亦未帶太多個人的評論或是感想。儘管如此，由於張靜愚的寫作風格平緩，又具有一定的規律性，故若有重要事件或是個人經驗，非常容易從其日記內容得到相關發現。

　　這樣的寫作風格亦有助於後人釐清關於中原大學董事會爭執的相關經過。在和董事會會議記錄比對之後，日記中的記錄帶出更加清晰的時序性。而從別的角度來看，作為中原大學的創校董事之一，張靜愚與郭克悌、賈嘉美的私人接觸恐怕大於其他董事，再加上其具有一定的社會地位，因此郭、嘉兩人的爭執一起，張靜愚擁有更多的資訊來了解這些爭執的根源，甚至賈嘉美更希望利用張靜愚來替代郭克悌成為中原大學的董事長。

　　此外，由於賈嘉美向來堅持基督教育的理念與教會學校的獨立性，是故造成其對單一管道的經費來源極度要求，遂造成與其他董事的摩擦。這意味著傳教士所寄望的傳統教會學校，在政府當時嚴守「去宗教化」的高等教育政策下，其實是難以深植於臺灣。而後賈嘉美離開中原，設立一間未立案的基督書院，或者才是其期望的教會學校的真正實現。

　　王安石有一首〈題張司業詩〉，詩云：「蘇州司業詩名老，樂府皆言妙入神，看似尋常最奇崛，成如容易卻艱辛。」雖是頌讚他人的詩文，但最後兩句如果用來描述張靜愚的日記與中原大學初期建校的情況，卻有相當程度的貼切：看似普通尋常的東西，卻是最奇特不凡的；看似容易成功的，實際上的經過卻困難重重，暗藏艱辛。這兩句詩真可謂是張靜愚日記與中原大學建校的最佳註腳。

論長老教會地方教會議事錄應用於學術研究之現況與未來展望：輔以淡水教會議事錄爲例

鄭睦群

中國文化大學史學研究所博士

馬偕醫護管理專科學校通識中心兼任講師

摘要

　　長老教會在臺灣擁有近一個半世紀的歷史，信徒與地方教會數量皆十分眾多，是目前臺灣教勢最大的基督宗派。而該教派許多地方教會的議事錄長久以來不間斷的記錄著教會內部的大小事務，訴說著一間教會的成長與對時代的回應，具有一定程度的史料價值。不過由於隱私以及缺乏相關法規配套等問題，在學術研究的應用上受到了很大的限制，使長老教會坐擁龐大的資料庫卻無法應用，殊為可惜。本文介紹淡水長老教會議事錄以及分析近十年來學位論文應用地方教會議事錄的概況，並且提出關於利用地方教會議事錄的建議與展望，期待長老教會能夠更積極開發這個史料區塊，發揮應有的研究價值。

關鍵詞：淡水長老教會、小會議事錄、長執會議事錄、任職會議事錄

一、前言

　　1999年，時任長老教會歷史委員會主委的鄭仰恩牧師在第2477期的《臺灣教會公報》公開呼籲，臺灣教會的史料長久以來遺失損毀的情況非常嚴重，應加強史料的保存與蒐集工作。[1] 這份呼籲迄今（2011年）已過了十二年，臺灣神學院史料中心（成立於1994年）經過多年的努力，目前已成為完備的史料蒐集與保管機構。史料中心收集早期教會的文獻與出版品為主，其中包含了歷屆總會、大會、中會的議事錄，嘉惠了許多研究者，但是關於地方教會議事錄的收集卻是心有餘而力不足。目前地方教會議事錄被應用於歷史或宗教研究的機會相當有限，也沒有一套完整的保存或引用辦法，被引用過的地方教會議事錄與長老教會的教會數量完全不成比例。

　　長老教會的地方教會議事錄通常有小會議事錄、長執會議事錄與任職會議事錄三種。小會是長老教會在治理教會上最基礎的單位，早期也被稱為督會或是長老督會，由牧師與長老組成，掌理事項甚多，如辦理會員籍、決定牧師的聘任、管理教會附屬機構、主持聖餐以及信徒洗禮等等。長執會是由小會成員加上所有執事與傳道師所組成的會議，主要任務為辦理庶務及小會委辦的事項，可以說是教會事工的協調與執行單位。[2] 另外長執會也可以邀請教會所設組織之負責人列席，例如主日學校長、團契會長等等，上述會議則稱為「任職會」。

　　總而言之，小會是一間教會的最高決策單位，長執會或任職會則包含較多的執行層面，這些單位都留下了數量與時間長短不一的議事錄。這些會議記錄不但是教會的基礎資料庫，也反映了特定教會的歷史、政策、觀點、討論及決定。[3] 淡水教會的議事錄始於1915年，等於是從旁觀察了臺灣社會近百年來的變化。其中皇民化運動、戰後與

---

1 《臺灣教會公報》，第2477期（1999年8月22日），第2版「教會要聞」。

2 臺灣基督長老教會總會法規委員會編，《臺灣基督長老教會教會法規》（臺南：教會公報出版社，2004年），頁9-12。

3 王成勉，《教會、文化與國家：對基督教史研究的思索與案例》（臺北：宇宙光，2006），頁224。

二二八事件、美國救濟物資援臺、長老教會倍加運動等重要的歷史過程，都可以在其議事錄中找到與時代的回應。

本文主旨擬分為三個部分。介紹淡水教會小會與任職會議事錄，其次是對近二十年來使用地方教會議事錄之學位論文進行分析，最後對議事錄史料功能的限制與如何確實應用於研究上提出建議。

二、淡水教會與其議事錄概述[4]

1860年開港後的臺灣成為基督教於十九世紀大宣教運動的一部分，基督教開始深耕這塊土地。[5] 加拿大長老教會的偕叡理牧師（George Leslie Mackay, 1944-1901，即馬偕博士）於1872年以淡水為據點，展開他在臺灣北部的宣教事工。淡水教會是偕叡理設立的第一間教會，其歷史可以回溯至1872年3月9日，至今已一百三十九年（2011年），目前仍是淡水區最大的基督教會之一。[6]

淡水教會升格為獨立堂且開始有了小會記錄是在1915年1月31日，以下簡述1915年至1984年共八冊議事錄。該教會小會的議事錄主要記錄了牧者的聘任、信徒的領洗、聚會的人數、信徒會籍的移出與移入、重要活動的舉辦，以及會友紛爭的調解等事項。

（一）第一冊小會議事錄

淡水教會第一冊小會議事錄的起迄日期是1915年1月31日至1930年5月30日，十五年半中共記錄了118回的小會記錄（含會員和會）。在1928年3月4日之前，會議記錄全由羅馬拼音的白話字寫成，1928年3月4日之後則是白話字與漢文並行，也就是在記錄中分別有白話字與漢文翻譯。第一回小會記錄會出現在1915年的原因在於淡水教會在該

---

4 以下議事錄分析與表格，皆為筆者整理自淡水教會小會與任職會議事錄。

5 賴永祥著，《教會史話》第一輯（臺南：人光出版社，2000），頁6。

6 關於淡水教會的歷史參見蘇文魁主編，《滬尾江河：淡水教會設教120週年紀念冊》（臺北：淡水基督長老教會，1992），頁26-33。

年升格為堂會。

　　在起先尚未聘牧的四年內，淡水教會小會的議長則由中會派宣教師負責，他們也是北部長老教會早期重要的人物。例如第一回的小會淡水教會出席人員為長老偕叡廉（George W. Mackay，偕叡理獨子）、蕭安居牧師，其中蕭安居擔任會議記錄，而負責主理的牧師則是吳威廉牧師（William Gauld），他也是北部中會第一任的議長。[7] 吳威廉從1915年1月31日至1916年6月18日一共主持了4回的小會，而1917年7月2日至1919年2月19日的14回小會則是由劉忠堅牧師（Duncan MacLeod）主理，這段時間劉忠堅曾任北部中會傳局長，並且擔任未獨立教會的小會議長。[8] 由此可以看出本地牧師之不足與宣教士依舊主導教會的運作，因此當時北部教會離完全自立尚有一段距離。之後淡水教會的牧師是鍾天枝牧師，他也是淡水教會第一任獨立聘牧的牧師，任期為1919年3月1日至1935年3月。鍾天枝就任後，小會議長就由他來擔任（偶爾告假不論），會議記錄則一直都是蕭安居。

（二）第二冊小會議事錄

　　第二冊小會議事錄的記錄起迄時間為1930年6月1日至1938年11月13日，在這七年半中一共有113回的小會（含和會），開會次數比起上一冊多了約一倍。在記錄方式上仍舊延續上一冊的風格，至1936年2月18日之前，每回都是白話字加上漢文翻譯，因此在閱讀上較為方便。1936年2月18日之後便只有白話字的記錄，詳細原因不得而知。由於鍾天枝的任期到1935年3月，直到1937年4月15日第二任牧師汪宗程牧師就任之前，淡水教會小會代理議長有兩位，分別是偉彼得牧師

---

7 吳威廉牧師（Dr. William Gauld, 1986-1923），英屬加拿大人，1892年來臺與馬偕博士共同經營北臺灣的宣教，馬偕博士逝世後組織北部中會，並鼓勵地方教會自立自養。參見楊士養編著，《信仰偉人列傳》（臺南：人光出版社，1989），頁95-98。

8 劉忠堅牧師（Rev. Duncan MacLeod, 1872-1957），蘇格蘭人，1907年來臺，曾任臺南神學院院長。參見楊士養編著，《信仰偉人列傳》，頁155-158。

表1：《淡水教會小會議事錄第一冊》保存概況表

冊別	小會議事錄第一冊。
記錄時間	1915年1月至1930年5月。
尺寸	長23公分，寬16.5公分。
封面提示	以粉筆標明為1915至1930，月份難辨識。
外部材質	厚紙板，線裝。封面材質為黑色細布，破損嚴重。書背有橫金紋裝飾。
內部材質	一般印刷用紙。
內部樣式	橫式書寫，內容標線首條為紅線，以下為藍色分隔線，間距約0.8公分。
頁碼	無。
用筆用色	黑色鋼筆。
用印用色	起始議長與書記皆為紅色，1923年12月2日起書記改用藍色。
附錄	1. 1909年至1924年淡水教會小會成員。 2. 1919年至1930年淡水小會設立之長執一覽。

表2：《淡水教會小會議事錄第二冊》保存概況表

冊別	小會議事錄第二冊。
記錄時間	1930年6月至1938年11月。
尺寸	長27公分，寬19.5公分。
封面提示	以粉筆標明1930至1938，月份難辨識。
外部材質	厚紙板，線裝。封面材質為黑色細布，破損嚴重。書背包裝已損壞遺失。
內部材質	一般印刷用紙。
內部樣式	1. 橫式書寫，日期標線為雙紅線，內容標線首條為紅線，以下為藍色分隔線，間距約0.8公分。 2. 內頁首頁與末頁皆有淡綠色廣告頁，並有商標兩種，一為菱形內寫橫寫T.O.字樣，一為圓形內有獅馬共推直式TO樣式。
頁碼	頁碼頁共200頁，藍色印刷，右頁標於右上角，左頁標於左上角。
用筆用色	黑色鋼筆。
用印用色	1. 1930年6月1日至1930年12月7日議長為紅色，書記為藍色（頁1-9）。 2. 1931年6月6日至1934年2月11日議長與書記皆為藍色（頁11-71）。 3. 1934年5月4日至1934年6月3日議長為紅色，書記為藍色（頁72-77）。 4. 1934年7月13日至1938年11月3日議長與書記皆為藍色（頁78-200）。
附錄	1930年至1938年淡水小會設立之長執一覽。

（J. D. Wilkie）與明有德牧師（Hugh MacMillan）。偉彼得牧師代理時間為1935年3月17日至1936年1月18日，明有德牧師代理時間為1936年2月18日至1937年3月14日，純以白話字記錄就是自明有德牧師代理議長開始，一直到該冊記錄末了。[9] 汪宗程就任後小會就由他來主持，從此便無外籍宣教士主理淡水教會小會；會議記錄在汪牧師未就任之前以蕭安居與陳瓊琚長老為主，就任後主要則是由柯設偕負責。[10]

（三）第三冊小會議事錄

第三冊小會議事錄起迄時間為1938年12月4日至1956年1月11日，大約十七年，共召開134回（含和會），平均次數較前一冊為少，時代也從日治時期進入到戰後。從1938年12月4日到1941年6月8日的記錄方式皆為白話字而無漢文翻譯，到了1941年12月7日開始便改成以漢文記錄，從此白話字記錄便不再出現於淡水教會的小會議事錄中。汪宗程的任期為1937年4月15日至1966年8月17日，也是淡水教會史中任期最長的牧師。此外從汪牧師的簽名與用印可以得知，他在殖民時期的最後幾年當中曾經改名為「文田宗義」，這或許與當時日本政府的政策有關。

（四）第四冊小會議事錄

第四冊小會議事錄起迄時間為1956年2月16日至1964年12月13日，前後將近九年，共127回（含和會），平均次數與第二冊相當，議長與書記依舊是汪宗程與柯設偕。該冊的特色為記錄了相當多關於該教會或外界舉辦培靈、佈道會的事務與消息，與長老教會「倍加運動」推行的年代是相符合的。

---

9 明有德牧師（Rev. Hugh MacMillan, M.A., Ph.D, 1892-1970），英屬加拿大人，1924年抵臺，曾任臺灣神學院院長、淡水中學校長、馬偕醫院董事長。參見鄭仰恩，〈開創新時代的普世宣教者——明有德牧師小傳〉，《新使者雜誌》，第31期（臺北：新使者雜誌社，2003），頁26-29。

10 柯設偕（1900-1990），偕叡理外孫，畢業於臺北帝國大學，曾任淡江中學教師並二度代理該校校長。參見蘇文魁主編，《滬尾江河》，頁276-269。

表 3： 《淡水教會小會議事錄第三冊》保存概況表

冊別	小會議事錄第三冊。
記錄時間	1938 年 12 月至 1956 年 1 月。
尺寸	長 27 公分，寬 19.5 公分。
封面提示	以粉筆標明 1938 至 1956，月份難辨識。
外部材質	厚紙板，線裝。封面材質為黑色細布，破損嚴重。書背包裝已損壞遺失。
內部材質	一般印刷用紙。
內部樣式	橫式書寫，日期標線為雙紅線，內容標線首條為紅線，以下為藍色分隔線，間距約 0.8 公分。
頁碼	頁碼頁共 200 頁，黑色印刷，右頁標於右上角，左頁標於左上角。
用筆用色	黑色與藍色鋼筆。
用印用色	全冊皆為紅色。
附錄	無。

表 4： 《淡水教會小會議事錄第四冊》保存概況表

冊別	小會議事錄第四冊。
記錄時間	1956 年 12 月至 1962 年 12 月。
尺寸	長 26 公分，寬 17.5 公分。
封面提示	以粉筆標明 1938 12 至 1956 12，尚可辨識。
外部材質	厚紙板，線裝。封面材質為墨綠粗紙，書背為褐色間花紋，並印有「補助簿」字樣。
內部材質	一般印刷用紙。
內部樣式	1. 橫式書寫，日期標線為雙紅線，內容標線首條為紅線，以下為藍色分隔線，間距約 0.8 公分。 2. 內頁首頁與末頁為褐色廣告頁並印有「模範牌」商標。 3. 頁首印有目錄與末頁印有帳冊範例。
頁碼	頁碼頁共 200 頁，黑色印刷，右頁標於右上角，左頁標於左上角。
用筆用色	黑色與藍色鋼筆。
用印用色	全冊皆為紅色。
附錄	無。

（五）第五冊小會議事錄

第五冊小會議事錄起迄時間為1965年2月5日至1972年9月10日，前後大約為七年半的時間，共開132回（含和會），平均開會次數創下新高。淡水教會小會於1967年11月19日的臨時和會中通過了汪宗程退休一事，並且成為淡水教會的名譽牧師。汪牧師退休後繼續代理了14回的小會議長，並且在下一任牧師郭東榮牧師尚未就任之前（1969年8月17日就任），與當時臺北中會前後任議長李鏡智、李長裕以及副議長郭應啟共同代理淡水教會小會議長。

該冊還有一個特別之處，在議事冊的最前面附有以白話字完成的「議事錄紀錄樣式」，說明議事的流程與樣式，也表示當時出現了長老教會官編樣式的議事冊。

表5：《淡水教會小會議事錄第五冊》保存概況表

冊別	小會議事錄第五冊。
記錄時間	1963年2月至1972年9月。
尺寸	長26公分，寬17.5公分。
封面提示	封面下方貼有長12.4公分，寬7.2公分之白色紙張，印有「臺灣基督長老教會＿＿＿＿＿議事錄」，並在空格處填上「淡水」二字。
外部材質	1. 厚紙板，線裝。封面材質為墨綠色粗紙，上方印有金色圓形商標，圖案為一顆樹，字樣為「NEC TAMEN CONSUMEBATUR」。 2. 書背為白色細布，印有「臺灣基督長老教會議事錄」字樣。
內部材質	一般印刷用紙。
內部樣式	1. 首頁印有目錄，並有白話字「議事錄紀錄樣式」規則流程。 2. 橫式書寫，日期標線為雙紅線，內容標線首條紅線，以下為藍色分　隔線，間距約0.8公分。每行前2.5公分處皆有紅色縱線。
頁碼	頁碼頁共200頁，黑色印刷，右頁標於右上角，左頁標於左上角。
用筆用色	黑色鋼筆與藍色原子筆。
用印用色	全冊皆為紅色。
附錄	1.淡水教會沿革。 2.歷代傳道師一覽。 3.1954年至1973年淡水教會長執一覽。

（六）第六冊小會議事錄

第六冊小會議事錄起迄時間為1972年12月10日至1984年4月15日，前後大約是十一年半的時間，共開135回（含和會），開會次數較上一冊略少。郭東榮牧師於1977年離任，並暫代淡水教會議長，但在會議記錄的最末端並沒有蓋印（1977年2月27日至11月6日），其原因不得而知。之後一直到1979年11月6日淡水教會第四任牧師趙信愿就任之前，由吳憶清與莊經顯牧師代理小會議長，記錄多由連易宗長老負責。另外該冊的特色在於收附許多原始稿件，例如與臺北中會的往來信件、洗禮報名單、若干特別禮拜的程序單與週報等等。這樣的特點在第五冊後段時就已經開始出現，主要是在郭東榮牧師就任後，因此可能與牧師個人的想法或是堅持有關。

表6：《淡水教會小會議事錄第六冊》保存概況表

冊別	小會議事錄第六冊。
記錄時間	1972年12月至1984年4月。
尺寸	長26公分，寬17.5公分。
封面提示	印有金色「臺灣基督長老教會議事錄」字樣。
外部材質	1. 厚紙板，線裝。封面材質為墨綠色粗紙，上方印有金色圓形商標，圖案為一顆樹，字樣為「NEC TAMEN CONSUMEBATUR」。 2. 書背為白色細布，印有「臺灣基督長老教會議事錄」字樣。
內部材質	一般印刷用紙。
內部樣式	1. 首頁印有目錄，並有白話字「議事錄紀錄樣式」規則流程。 2. 橫式書寫，日期標線為雙紅線，內容標線首條紅線，以下為藍色分隔線，間距約0.8公分。每行前2.5公分處皆有紅色縱線。
頁碼	頁碼頁共200頁，黑色印刷，右頁標於右上角，左頁標於左上角。
用筆用色	黑色、藍色鋼筆與藍色原子筆。
用印用色	全冊皆為紅色。
附錄	小基隆偕叡廉紀念教會與新竹圍教會沿革。

（七）第一冊任職會議事錄

第一冊起迄時間為1915年5月2日至1949年1月25日，一共有165回的任職會，年代橫跨大正、昭和與戰後。而時間前後約三十四年，因此可知任職會並不常召開。該冊至1941年10月5日之前皆以白話字記錄，若干關鍵字如人名再標以漢字，當中僅有兩回有特殊情況而出現漢字記錄。[11] 自1942年1月2日至1948年7月10日間的29回記錄，出現以全漢文方式記錄的情形，1948年9月8日起又回到了白話字的記錄方式。該冊議事錄記錄了教會的財務與大小庶務之運作狀況，以及土地所有權之登記事項與教會相關買賣事宜等，並且經歷淡水教會建堂的歷史，可以了解建堂過程；另外因為有對外捐款及房舍與器物之外借，因此也可以了解淡水教會與社區或是地方上互動之關係。

表7：《淡水教會任職會議事錄第一冊》保存概況表

冊別	任職會議事錄第一冊。
記錄時間	1915年5月至1949年1月。
尺寸	長26公分，寬19.5公分。
封面提示	以粉筆標明，但年月皆難辨識。
外部材質	厚紙板，線裝。封面材質為黑色細布，破損嚴重。書背為褐色並有橫金紋裝飾。
內部材質	一般印刷用紙。
內部樣式	橫式書寫，內容標線首條為紅線，以下為藍色分隔線，間距約0.8公分。
頁碼	頁碼頁共200頁，黑色印刷，右頁標於右上角，左頁標於左上角。
用筆用色	黑色鋼筆。
用印用色	起始議長與書記皆為紅色，大部分無蓋印。
附錄	1. 1924年至1941年執事的任命日期。 2. 洗禮證明等。

---

11 一回是1933年7月18日，淡水教會要立碑因此需要以漢文確定碑文；另一回是淡水教會行文北部臺灣基督長老教會說明土地事宜，會議記錄中以漢文抄錄該信內容。

（八）第二冊任職會議事錄

第二冊起迄時間為1949年5月30日至1967年6月4日，前後約十八年，共召開132回，較上冊略多。全本以白話字記錄，若干名辭、人名或關鍵字同樣會用漢文表示。本冊詳細記錄了淡水教會收到美援物資的數量與分配方式，相當具有歷史價值，另外也統計了若干年度的信徒奉獻表，對了解教會發展有很大的幫助。

表8：《淡水教會任職會議事錄第二冊》保存概況表

冊別	任職會議事錄第二冊。
記錄時間	1949年3月至1967年6月。
尺寸	長26公分，寬19.5公分。
封面提示	無。
外部材質	厚紙板，線裝。封面材質為黑色細布，破損嚴重。
內部材質	一般印刷用紙。
內部樣式	橫式書寫，內容標線首條為紅線，以下為藍色分隔線，間距約0.8公分。
頁碼	頁碼頁共200頁，黑色印刷，右頁標於右上角，左頁標於左上角。
用筆用色	黑色鋼筆與藍色原子筆。
用印用色	大部分無蓋印。
附錄	數年信徒奉獻表等。

自1915年1月31日至1984年4月15日，淡水教會一共開了約757回的小會；而任職會從1915年5月2日到1967年6月4日，淡水教會的任職會大約召開了297回，因此其研究價值應是無庸置疑的。但這類史料目前在歷史或相關研究上的應用程度如何？或是使用上有什麼樣的限制？這類較為實際的問題則是接下來討論的重點。

三、地方教會議事錄與學位論文

（一）近十年來使用議事錄的學位論文

　　儘管議事錄被認為是相當重要的史料，但是由於議事錄是相當私密的教會文件，要取得並不容易，所以使用議事錄作為研究素材的論文並不多見。若以「小會」、「長執會」、「任職會」、「會議記錄」、「議事錄」等關鍵字在「臺灣博碩士論文加值系統」中的「參考文獻」中搜尋與交叉比對，會發現近年來將地方教會議事錄放入參考書目的學位論文約只有9篇，其中8篇為碩士論文，1篇是博士論文。

　　將這些論文按照出版先後順序排列，分別為2000年吳學明〈臺灣基督長老教會的傳教與三自運動：以南部教會為中心〉，使用拔馬長老教會議事錄；[12] 2003年謝秀伶〈左鎮地區新港社群之社會變遷（1845-1945年）——以親屬結構與宗教信仰為例〉，使用山豹教會（現澄山教會）與拔馬教會（現左鎮教會）的小會議事錄。[13] 2003年蔡重陽〈新興都會區教會研究——以高雄市「新興基督長老教會」之傳道與社會服務為例1938-2000〉，使用新興長老教會小會與長執會的議事錄；[14] 2003年黃招榮〈巴克禮在臺灣的傳教研究〉，使用拔馬教會小會議事錄；[15] 2005年張綺雅〈臺南市臨安基督長老教會的發展〉，使用臨安長老教會小會與長執會的議事錄；[16] 2007年葉天文〈澎湖七美基督長老教會之研究〉，使用七美長老教會小會與長執會

12　吳學明，〈臺灣基督長老教會的傳教與三自運動：以南部教會為中心〉。臺北：臺灣師範大學歷史研究所博士論文，2000年。

13　謝秀伶，〈左鎮地區新港社群之社會變遷（1845-1945年）——以親屬結構與宗教信仰為例〉。臺南：臺南大學鄉土研究所碩士論文，2003年。

14　蔡重陽，〈新興都會區教會研究——以高雄市「新興基督長老教會」之傳道與社會服務為例1938-2000〉。臺南：臺南師範學院鄉土文化研究所碩士論文，2003年。

15　黃招榮，〈巴克禮在臺灣的傳教研究〉。臺南：臺南師範學院鄉土文化研究所碩士論文，2003年。

16　張綺雅，〈臺南市臨安基督長老教會的發展〉。臺南：臺南大學臺灣文化研究所碩士論文，2005年。

的議事錄；[17] 2008年陳子仁〈從金門後浦堂會議事錄看教會懲戒——一個教會史料的探究〉，使用金門基督教會的小會與長執會議事錄；[18] 2008年鄭睦群〈淡水基督長老教會對時代的因應——以「二二八事件」與「美援時代」為研究中心〉，使用淡水長老教會小會與長執會的議事錄；[19] 2011年邱秋香〈基督教在客庄教會歷史的探討——以新埔基督長老教會為例〉，則在參考書目中出現了新埔長老教會小會議事錄。[20]

上述論文雖來自於歷史研究所、文化研究所與宗教研究所，但就論文內容未必受限於畢業的系所。如果從研究對象來看，研究者多以單一教會做為研究主體，其中吳學明、謝秀伶與黃招榮例外。吳學明研究南部長老教會的傳教與自立，謝秀伶則是以左鎮地區的新港社群為研究對象，黃招榮則將重點放在巴克禮在臺灣的傳教活動。

至於以單一教會做為研究主體的論文大致上又可分為兩種，一種較偏向撰寫教會的整體發展史，例如蔡重陽、張綺雅、葉天文、邱秋香的論文大致上皆屬此類。此外，陳子仁與鄭睦群則集中探討教會的某些議題。陳子仁以金門後浦堂會議事錄中的案例分析該教會的懲戒方式與其信仰意涵，鄭睦群則討論了淡水教會處理美援救濟物資的過程與其面對二二八事件的轉折，其研究對象雖然同樣是單一教會，但已具有較明確的研究主題。

（二）曾被引用過的議事錄

因此從前述論文的參考文獻來看，目前被使用過的議事錄分別為拔馬教會小會議事錄（現左鎮教會）、山豹教會小會議事錄（現澄山

---

17 葉天文，〈澎湖七美基督長老教會之研究〉。臺北：臺灣師範大學歷史研究所碩士論文，2007年。
18 陳子仁，〈從金門後浦堂會議事錄看教會懲戒——一個教會史料的探究〉。臺北：政治大學宗教研究所碩士論文，2008年。
19 鄭睦群，〈淡水基督長老教會對時代的因應——以「二二八事件」與「美援時代」為研究中心〉。臺北：淡江大學歷史研究所碩士論文，2008年。
20 邱秋香，〈基督教在客庄教會歷史的探討——以新埔基督長老教會為例〉。桃園：中原大學宗教研究所碩士論文，2011年。

教會）、新興教會小會與長執會議事錄、臨安教會小會與長執會議事錄、七美教會小會與長執會議事錄、金門基督教會小會與長執會議事錄、淡水教會小會與長執會議事錄、新埔教會小會議事錄。所以一共有八間教會的議事錄應用於學術界，其中只有拔馬教會小會議事錄有重複被引用的情況，共有吳學明、謝秀伶、黃招榮等三篇論文。吳學明對該議事錄使用得最早（2000），其來源應該就是左鎮教會。謝秀伶與黃招榮分別在參考文獻與註釋中說明該史料為吳學明提供。[21] 因此除了拔馬小會議事錄，其他教會的議事錄則為其研究者所獨自引用。另外前述議事錄在參考文獻出現之時的格式都不太一樣，有些同時標明了議事錄的冊別與年份（陳子仁、鄭睦群）、有些只有年份而無冊別（蔡重陽、張綺雅、葉天文、邱秋香），也有無冊別也無年份的情況（吳學明、謝秀伶、黃招榮）。

　　因此以有在參考文獻中清楚標明記錄起迄年代的議事錄（不分小會與長執或任職會）依照年代順序先後排列，分別是金門基督教會議事錄（1900-1999）、淡水教會議事錄（1915-1984）、新興教會議事錄（1943-2000）、新埔教會議事錄（1965-2004）、七美教會議事錄（1966-2006）、臨安教會議事錄（1984-2003）。其中年代最久遠也最連貫的是金門基督教會議事錄，時間長達近一百年，最短的則是臨安教會議事錄。另外雖然拔馬教會與山豹教會的議事錄無法就參考文獻上清楚判斷其年代，但從謝秀伶文中的關於信徒領洗與領聖餐的表格大致上可以知道，拔馬教會小會議事錄與山豹教會小會議事錄分別始於1896年與1918年。[22]

---

21 謝秀伶，〈左鎮地區新港社群之社會變遷（1845-1945年）──以親屬結構與宗教信仰為例〉，頁104；黃招榮，〈巴克禮在臺灣的傳教研究〉，頁40-41。

22 謝秀伶，〈左鎮地區新港社群之社會變遷（1845-1945年）──以親屬結構與宗教信仰為例〉，頁89-90。

表 9：近十年使用議事錄之學位論文表

作者	論文題目	出版單位與學位別	出版時間	使用議事錄
吳學明	臺灣基督長老教會的傳教與三自運動：以南部教會為中心	臺灣師範大學歷史研究所博士論文	2000 年	拔馬教會小會議事錄
謝秀伶	左鎮地區新港社群之社會變遷（1845-1945年）——以親屬結構與宗教信仰為例	臺南大學鄉土研究所碩士論文	2003 年	拔馬教會小會議事錄、山豹教會小會議事錄
蔡重陽	新興都會區教會研究——以高雄市「新興基督長老教會」之傳道與社會服務為例 1938-2000	臺南師範學院鄉土文化研究所碩士論文	2003 年	新興教會小會與長執會議事錄
黃招榮	巴克禮在臺灣的傳教研究	臺南師範學院鄉土文化研究所碩士論文	2003 年	拔馬教會小會議事錄
張綺雅	臺南市臨安基督長老教會的發展	臺南大學臺灣文化研究所碩士論文	2005 年	臨安教會小會與長執會議事錄
葉天文	澎湖七美基督長老教會之研究	臺灣師範大學歷史研究所碩士論文	2007 年	七美教會小會與長執會議事錄
陳子仁	從金門後浦堂會議事錄看教會懲戒——一個教會史料的探究	政治大學宗教研究所碩士論文	2008 年	金門基督教會小會與長執會議事錄
鄭睦群	淡水基督長老教會對時代的因應——以「二二八事件」與「美援時代」為研究中心	淡江大學歷史研究所碩士論文	2008 年	淡水教會小會與長執會議事錄
邱秋香	基督教在客庄教會歷史的探討——以新埔基督長老教會為例	中原大學宗教研究所碩士論文	2011 年	新埔教會小會議事錄

四、論文中議事錄的引用情形

在初步了解近年將議事錄列於參考書目的學位論文與其所使用的議事錄之後，現在要深入歸納這些議事錄在論文中應用的情形，例如引用的次數多寡以及在什麼情況下最常被引徵。由於並不是每篇論文的研究取向都相同，而這也會影響議事錄在當中的使用情況，因此筆者暫且將這幾篇論文歸納為單一教會整體研究、單一教會主題研究與非單一教會研究三種研究取向，期待能更加清楚的分析議事錄在不同類型研究中的重要性。

（一）單一教會整體研究

以單一教會的整體發展為研究重心的有蔡重陽〈新興都會區教會研究——以高雄市「新興基督長老教會」之傳道與社會服務為例1938-2000〉、張綺雅〈臺南市臨安基督長老教會的發展〉、葉天文〈澎湖七美基督長老教會之研究〉、邱秋香〈基督教在客庄教會歷史的探討——以新埔基督長老教會為例〉等四篇，每篇引用議事錄的次數都不太相同。

蔡重陽大量的使用了新興教會的小會與長執會的議事錄，引用的年代橫跨了新興教會自1943年創立至2000年的歲月。全文對小會與長執會議事錄的引用約90次（含圖表），且這尚不包括引用該會其他單位的議事錄（如新興教會社會館議事錄等），可說將議事錄運用得十分透徹。引用之處除了信徒與受洗人數等數據之外，也有各項與教會歷史相關的議決與瑣事。另外值得一提的是，雖然該論文是以單一研究做為對象，但是蔡重陽卻用議事錄說明了新興教會對時代的回應。例如倍加運動時教會的各項努力、高雄中會的分裂等等，都可以在小會或長執會的議事錄中找到記錄，儘管敘述的篇幅並不大。因此不管就議事錄的使用程度或對時代的敏感度，該論文應是運用議事錄撰寫教會發展史的佳作，將議事錄中看似不起眼的瑣事編寫成新興教會的歷史故事。

張綺雅這篇論文所使用的議事錄與其他論文相比，在記錄時間方面相對上是比較短的，因此自然也限制了使用的力度。全篇論文應僅用了1次長執會的記錄，將1984年至1999年中教會招募牧師與傳道的歷年記錄整理成表。[23] 由於該教會的資料多數均已遺失，因此也只能使用紀念冊與口述方法來完成論文的撰寫。[24] 由此可知議事錄的使用程度也要看教會的保存狀況。

葉天文約引用了21次（含圖表）的小會與長執會的記錄，使用情形為引徵年代、信徒受洗名單等數據統計、開會次數統計、各式議決等等。該論文完整的論述七美教會的歷史發展與現況，議事錄的運用在各章節尚屬平均，也發揮了史料的作用。

邱秋香在序論中說明其整理了新埔教會的會議記錄，另外在參考書目也列上了新埔教會的小會議事錄，但是在文中卻沒有引用該教會的小會議事錄，算是一個比較特別的例子。[25]

（二）單一教會主題研究

陳子仁與鄭睦群同樣以單一教會作為研究主體，但與前述論文不同的地方在於，其研究重點並非以單一教會的整體發展或成長為主，而是將研究重心鎖定於該教會的某些主題。

陳子仁〈從金門後浦堂會議事錄看教會懲戒———一個教會史料的探究〉以「教會懲戒」為中心，並以金門後浦堂會的議事錄為舉證的主要史料。由於該文註解的用法與歷史學稍顯不同，因此較難從中認定引用了幾次議事錄的史料。不過根據陳子仁統計，後浦堂會議事錄中有95項關於懲戒的記錄，成為該文相當重要的史料基礎。由於史料豐富與主題明確，加上陳子仁以宗教學的背景論述了教會在懲戒上的信仰依據，這篇學位論文應是運用地方教會議事錄的另一佳作。

鄭睦群〈淡水基督長老教會對時代的因應———以「二二八事件」

---

23 張綺雅，〈臺南市臨安基督長老教會的發展〉，頁54。

24 同前註，頁98。

25 邱秋香，〈基督教在客庄教會歷史的探討——以新埔基督長老教會為例〉，頁3。

與「美援時代」為研究中心〉則是將焦點放在淡水教會對於美援救濟物資的發放與分析對教會的影響。也因為淡水教會有三位二二八事件的受難者，因此該教會如何處理與面對二二八事件是另一個論述重心。該論文直接引用淡水教會的議事錄共25次（含圖表，但不含歷年受洗與陪餐人數統計），其中鄭睦群整理了1956至1962這七年間淡水教會所收到的美援救濟物資，記錄了該教會如何發放救濟物資以及討論發放物資對教會的影響，可以讓學界了解長老教會地方教會對美援救濟物資的處理過程。[26]

此外，陳子仁與鄭睦群論文有兩個共通點。其一是將論述集中於某一主題之外，其次為將所運用的議事錄做了較為完整的介紹，例如介紹每一冊議事錄記錄的起迄時間、用印與記錄的形式、開會的次數等等，這是其他論文所沒有的。

（三）非單一教會研究

由於使用地方教會議事錄的論文多為研究單一教會，因此研究單一教會以外作為研究主旨的論文，筆者暫且盡歸一類。

吳學明〈臺灣基督長老教會的傳教與三自運動：以南部教會為中心〉引用了5次拔馬教會的小會議事錄，並且集中於第一章〈南部教會傳教的阻力與對策〉的第二節「教會傳教的阻力」。該節敘述南部長老教會如何處理信徒在民間習慣、社會陋俗與教會規範之間的拉扯的情況，拔馬小會議事錄的使用是舉例說明該教會小會在清末與日治時期勸戒會友等情事。[27] 由於該論文主要論述對象並非單一教會，此處也僅僅只是引徵拔馬教會的案例，因此對其小會的議事錄使用有限。

謝秀伶〈左鎮地區新港社群之社會變遷（1845-1945年）——以親屬結構與宗教信仰為例〉引用2次拔馬教會小會議事錄與1次的山豹教會小會議事錄，主要是說明1896年至1945年（拔馬教會）與1918年

---

26 鄭睦群，〈淡水基督長老教會對時代的因應—以「二二八事件」與「美援時代」為研究中心〉，頁85-93。

27 吳學明，〈臺灣基督長老教會的傳教與三自運動：以南部教會為中心〉，頁94、112。

至1945年（山豹教會）的受洗、聽道理、禁晚餐與再就晚餐的人數，以及1896年到1940年拔馬教會禁晚餐的原因。[28] 這三次引用都集中在第四章〈左鎮地區新港社群的宗教變遷〉的第二節「左鎮地區新港社群的宗教信仰的改變」。與吳學明運用小會議事錄的情況相同，受到論文主旨的影響，小會議事錄的引用並不頻繁。

黃招榮的論文旨在研究巴克禮牧師在臺灣的傳教情況，引用了1次拔馬教會小會的議事錄，將拔馬教會被禁聖餐的原因統計成表格，並且在註釋中感謝吳學明對史料的提供以及謝秀伶表格的製作。[29]

五、影響前述論文引用議事錄的因素與其分析

因此儘管上述每一篇論文的參考書目裡都放有地方教會的議事錄，但應用的情形卻有很大的落差，這一點值得再深入探討。由於大部分的議事錄筆者皆無緣親見，因此其推論僅為筆者的淺見，以下就四點加以分析。

（一）論文題目與地方教會的關連性

論文的研究對象會影響目前地方教會議事錄在研究上的使用。吳學明以南部長老教會的自立為研究主題，研究範圍十分廣泛，史料的選取自然不會侷限於單一教會的檔案。因此教會方面的史料引用較多的是教會公報與中會、大會層級的議事錄，拔馬教會的小會議事錄只是做部分的引徵，謝秀伶與黃招榮的情況也有些類似。例如謝秀伶研究左鎮區新港社群的宗教信仰轉變，拔馬教會與山豹教會小會議事錄能給予的幫助相對有限，這與議事錄的功能無關，基本上取決於研究者的研究題目是否需要議事錄的支撐。

---

28 謝秀伶，〈左鎮地區新港社群之社會變遷（1845-1945年）──以親屬結構與宗教信仰為例〉，頁89、90、94。

29 黃招榮，〈巴克禮在臺灣的傳教研究〉，頁40-41。

（二）地方教會對議事錄的保存與其記錄特色

張綺雅曾在結論中表示臨安教會過去未認識保存史料的重要性，因此許多資料均已遺失，甚至連週報與歷年和會手冊亦遺漏許多，許多地方要靠著口述方法來補其不足。[30] 由此可見如果以單一教會做為研究對象，不管是整體研究還是主題研究，議事錄若是保存狀況不佳，甚至是短缺，即便是巧婦也難為無米之炊。但是除了保存狀況之外，議事錄本身記錄的內容也會有所影響，因為每一間教會都有自己的故事與特色，並非所有的議題都能在議事錄中找到相關的佐證。例如陳子仁曾經借閱左鎮與文林基督教會的議事錄，卻發現只有左鎮教會有懲戒的相關記錄。[31] 淡水教會小會議事錄雖有懲戒或信徒紛爭調解的記錄，但遠不及後浦堂會來得多。

所以就算同樣是小會或長執會的議事錄，同樣是歷史悠久的教會，但每一間教會的生命歷程皆有所不同，議事錄的內容自然也會不一樣。

（三）紀念刊物、週報、和會手冊與議事錄的史料功能重疊

筆者認為這是議事錄史料功能最為受限之處。以邱秋香的論文為例，該論文雖未引用新埔教會小會的議事錄，但是仍舊使用該教會的紀念刊物與口述方法完整的撰寫新埔教會的歷史，而張綺雅也使用和會手冊來完成多項的數據統計。事實上，當一間教會的紀念刊物、週報合訂本、和會手冊愈齊全，同樣的也會擠壓到議事錄的使用空間。因為小會與長執會並不常召開，而且儘管會議可能很精彩（熱切討論或是失控吵架等情事），但是會議記錄在內容上卻往往只有結論。相較之下，週報的資訊則非常即時，包含每週的聚會人數、內容，教界消息或代禱事項也能夠反映當時的時事。會員和會則為一年一度的大事，幾乎所有重要的數據如財務狀況、受洗名單、教會聚會人數都會

---

30 張綺雅，〈臺南市臨安基督長老教會的發展〉，頁98。
31 陳子仁，〈從金門後浦堂會議事錄看教會懲戒——一個教會史料的探究〉，頁106。

做出年度的統計，這也算是研究者的福氣。因此如果就數據功能而言，議事錄對於某些教會撰寫早期歷史上確實具有史料功能，但隨著年代愈晚近或是該教會相關刊物愈完備，這樣的功能也隨之降低。

　　紀念刊物可說是教會對自身歷史回顧的好機會，目前編寫類似的紀念刊物的風氣也十分普遍，臺灣神學院的史料中心就收藏了453冊長老教會地方教會的紀念冊。但每間教會史料保存與應用的狀況不一，因此在歷史研究上能夠呈現的效果也會有所差異，有些甚至變成以信徒見證為主的刊物，這一點也有學者提出類似的看法。[32] 但是不管紀念刊物的內容是否豐富，在實際的研究工作上，教會紀念刊物中的歷史沿革與大事年表等依舊是研究者必須依賴的資料，因為不僅方便且仍然有一定程度的正確性。所以當一位研究者要去回顧某教會歷史的時候，紀念刊物的便利性遠遠大於議事錄。

　　當然紀念刊物在編輯的時候也有可能使用議事錄的資料，那麼研究者也算是間接使用了議事錄。例如前哈佛大學燕京圖書館副館長賴永祥教授編輯的和平教會十週年紀念刊《和平之聲》，就使用了大量的長執會記錄、教會日誌與週報。[33] 但是這些歷史沿革或大事記通常並未註明出處，因此紀念刊物與議事錄之間很難找到明確的關連，這或許只有當初編輯的人才會曉得。而且如果其歷史沿革與各項早期發展數據皆引自議事錄，那對日後的研究者來說，也就更不用費心的去翻閱議事錄了，可能又更降低了研究者使用議事錄的意願。

（四）研究者的個人因素

　　議事錄的使用也牽涉到研究者個人的選材能力與意願。例如有可能議事錄中確實有某些重要的相關記錄，但研究者並不這麼認為，或者是根本就沒有注意到；也有可能即便研究者意識到某些資料有其重

---

32 王成勉，〈臺灣基督教史料之研究〉，收於林治平主編，《臺灣基督教史——史料與研究回顧國際學術研討會論文集》（臺北：宇宙光，1998），頁255。

33 賴永祥，〈臺灣教會史——史料研究回顧與展望〉，收於林治平主編，《臺灣基督教史——史料與研究回顧國際學術研討會論文集》，頁11。

要性，但基於研究題目的不同或某些個人因素而不加以選取。

六、議事錄史料功能的再發揮

照上述的分析，議事錄的史料功能某種程度上受到週報、和會手冊、紀念刊物的排擠，降低了研究者對議事錄的需求。因此假設議事錄的功能只剩下單一教會沿革的撰寫與補充，或是提供領洗人數等統計數據，而這些功能又逐漸被週報等刊物給取代了，那麼議事錄的史料功能該如何發揮？

這裡並不是說歷史沿革或各項數據不重要，但是更可以試著將單一教會的歷史、數據與時代的脈動或議題相呼應，賦予歷史沿革與眾多數據新的生命。淡水教會小會與任職會議事錄中的部分記錄或許可以作為拋磚引玉的參考。

（一）二二八事件的應對

二二八事件的苦難曾親自臨到淡水教會，使教會失去了兩名會友，其中陳能通執事在該事件中遇難，至今仍找不到屍骨。事件發生後，參照北部大會與淡水小會的議事錄可以得知該教會對二二八事件的回應。

1949年3月10日上午十點，第四屆北部臺灣基督長老教會大會召開於當時位於中山北路的臺灣神學院大禮堂。3月10日下午六點開始第二堂會議，第十條為「書記朗讀書信及各中會提案」[34]，在朗讀書信與中會提案內皆有淡水教會對於「二二八事件」的反應，大會朗讀的書信共有三件如下：

1. 書信
（1）美國基督教會會議邀請本大會派員參加之書信。

---

34 書記為吳清鎰牧師。

（2）陳蕭美德哭訴書。

（3）黃何長妹哭訴書。[35]

第（2）及（3）件皆為淡水教會「二二八事件」受難者遺孀的哭訴
書，陳蕭美德是淡水中學校長陳能通的妻子，黃何長妹則是淡水中學
訓導主任黃阿統的妻子。這兩封哭訴書的內容至今仍不得而知，應該
是由作為妻子的立場對家庭遭逢如此巨變向北部大會求助。另外在議
案第（22）之處，淡水小會提案「黃陳兩先生家族慰問之件」，希望
北部大會討論如何慰問這兩個家庭。

　　北部大會對於淡水教會提出的書信與提案在3月12日下午的第六
堂會議中有了結果，第62條議決如下：

> 第二十二號議案，淡江中學陳、黃兩先生家族慰問之件，大會
> 議決對陳能通、黃阿統、林茂生、盧園四位先生之家族，各中
> 會負責捐募六十萬元以上寄交財務局，託常委分配設法。[36]

另外淡水教會也在1949年11月20日的小會記錄上首次出現對陳能通家
族伸出援手的記錄：

> （10）小會議決關於恤貧事，自以前有補助安順姆外，增加補
> 助陳丁然（以上兩名每月補助米），及一時補助蕭美德五十萬
> 元（新臺幣十二元五角）可與主日學補助她合之。（此項方針
> 通知任職會）[37]

淡水教會小會以「恤貧」為由，對陳能通遺孀蕭美德給予新臺幣12元

---

35 黃六點主編，《臺灣基督長老教會北部大會大觀》，〈第四屆北部臺灣基督長老教會大會議事錄〉（臺
　　北：臺灣基督長老教會北部大會出版，1971），頁145。

36 貨幣單位是舊臺幣。

37 「一時補助」的意思為補助一次，《淡水教會小會議事錄第五冊》，頁101。

5角的補助，並交由任職會執行，記錄中所謂的「一時補助」就是補助一次的意思。至於對於黃家人的補助，則沒有進一步的資料說明。因此淡水教會小會轉交北部大會一份陳能通遺孀陳蕭美德的「哭訴書」給第四屆的北部長老大會，讓北部大會討論對受難者家屬的補助。另外淡水教會小會也透過恤貧的名義給予金錢上的支持，用實質的行動幫助自己的會友。如果也能在其他的教會議事錄中找到相關的記錄，就可以比較出各教會在面對二二八事件時的差異。

（二）美援救濟物資的發放

1956年，美國政府議決透過臺灣的天主教福利會與基督教福利會為窗口，撥贈四八〇號公法第三章項下大量剩餘農產品分發給臺灣以及外島居民，臺灣基督福利會將這些農產品與先前美國基督徒所捐贈的金錢物資根據該公法分成三種。第一種為"Tittle 1"，使用範圍是幫助政府建設；第二種是"Tittle 2"或是稱為"Community Development Program"，用來幫助社會發展之用；最後是"Tittle 3"或是"Family Feeding Program"，是為救濟貧民之用。[38]

淡水教會自1956至1962年之間與基督教福利會合作，一共收到了32次的美援救濟物資（見表10），也為此開了32次的任職會來決定如何分配這些物資，儼然成為淡水地區美援救濟物資的發放中心。

基督教福利會在當時委託全臺長老教會所屬的400多間教會作為救濟物資發放中心，淡水教會只是其中一間。[39] 前總會總幹事黃武東曾在回憶錄中表示，當時地方教會在發放救濟物資時曾有弊端的產生，例如徇私先給自己的會友、轉賣物資等情事，給予社會負面的觀感。[40] 但是從淡水教會的任職會議事錄可以得知，該教會清楚認知自

---

38 行政院美援運用委員會編，《中美合作經援發展概況》（臺北：行政院美援運用委員會，1957），頁2-4。

39 黃六點等編，《臺灣基督長老教會百年史》（臺南：臺灣教會公報社，1984），頁339-340。

40 黃武東，《黃武東回憶錄》（臺北：前衛出版社，1988），頁312-314。

表 10：淡水教會收到救濟物資總數一覽

物品名稱	數量	物品名稱	數量
奶粉	149 包與 822 箱	脫脂奶粉	822 箱
麵粉	759 包與 214 袋	包穀粉（玉米粉）	579 包
食用油	148 箱	奶油	94 箱
黃油	24 箱	大豆	48 包
花豆	43 袋	罐頭（未註明）	312 罐
棉被	大小共 50 件	營養麥	76 包
衣物	約 150 包	碗盤與杯子	共 156 件

己只是轉送的窗口，並沒有將救濟物資當成教會的私產，在分配之際尚屬公平。因此假設能夠找到其他曾經參與發放工作教會的議事錄記錄，就能更全面的了解長老教會在處理美援救濟物資時的整體概況。

以淡水教會首次關於救濟物資的會議記錄為例，該教會收到救濟物資之初要決定發放的對象與發放的數量。因此在收到救濟物資後便先放在牧師館的樓下，然後再召開任職會決定如何分配物資，發放的工作則交由自己的會友來執行，搬運等工作多由年輕人負責。[41]

淡水教會1956年6月21日任職會第一次救濟物資的會議節錄如下：

（3）從Mr.Wiskson收到基督教國際救助會臺灣分會
脫脂奶粉130箱
奶油 10箱
議決禮拜天分脫脂奶粉50箱，奶油10箱，交王名山先生去分配。

---

41 牧師館即為教會提供給牧師的宿舍，位於淡水教會旁。

（4）議決交鎮公所所報貧民

淡水鎮內291戶，291罐

小基隆307戶，307罐

會內小基隆教會182罐　共780罐 [42]

淡水教會在收到第一次救濟物資時即由鎮公所調查貧民發通知單，淡水教會再從中配合，這便是初次發放的基本模式，之後的發放工作同樣經由任職會來決定。淡水教會陳穎奇長老回憶當時的情況為由鎮公所發與有資格領取的鎮民通知單，鎮民再憑通知單前往教會領取，發放的時間則由教會自己決定。[43]

（三）倍加運動的回應

倍加運動是長老教會為了紀念宣教百週年而推行的福音事工，歷時約十一年，達到了教會數目倍增的目標。[44] 關於倍加運動的相關研究不在少數，多半是以恢弘的角度俯視長老教會在這段期間內的整體作為，較少從議事錄中觀察地方教會對倍加運動的回應。

淡水教會在這段時間舉辦了不少的佈道會、靈修會，甚至在運動結束後依舊不減，有教會獨立舉辦或邀請講員，有的則是對前來淡水舉辦佈道會的人士予以協助。例如1956年2月16日小會議決該年3月4日到3月7日每晚七點半舉行連續四天的佈道會。同時也決議長老與執事協助5月初至5月中花翹奇牧師在淡水警局後方廣場所舉辦的福音會幕；[45] 1963年5月4日，小會決定於該年舉辦數次佈道會，並且每天早上六點在教堂都有以這些佈道會為中心的早晨祈禱會。[46] 而佈道會的型態也不僅止於講道，1966年8月19日，小會議決9月12日至14日連續

---

42 淡水教會任職會，《淡水教會任職會議事錄第二冊》，頁33。

43 陳穎奇長老訪談，2008年2月26日，陳長老自宅。

44 黃六點等編，《臺灣基督長老教會百年史》，頁342-352。

45 《淡水教會小會議事錄第四冊》，頁1。

46 同前註，頁147。

三天晚上舉行電影佈道會，邀請視聽聯合會的陳光輝牧師主持。[47]

　　另外有個耐人尋味的地方，即淡水教會雖然在這段期間舉辦了不少佈道會，但是小會記錄並沒有正式提到倍加運動（PKU）這一名詞，這或許也是長老教會北部與南部對該運動的認同差異。

（四）懲戒與紛爭的調解

　　教會是由人組成的團體，自然也會有屬世的紛爭，淡水教會小會要如何處理這些事務？比起陳子仁研究的金門後浦堂會，淡水教會關於懲戒的記錄相對要少，較多的是調解信徒紛爭的案例，議事錄通常記錄調解的事項、過程與最後結果。

　　最引人側目的案例記錄於1935年3月17日小會議事錄中，該教會兩位女性（簡稱A與B）發生嚴重的肢體衝突事件，兩人的夫婿在教會皆任有公職。兩人先是發生口角，接著A推B去撞牆，B則咬住A的手指，最後雙雙掛彩。事件發生後教會召開小會，請兩位當事人與另一位目擊者分述事件經過，並在歸納三人的敘述內容後，決定B是較為理虧的一方。小會最後決議與B細談，請她勿再惡語傷人。[48] 除了該案例之外，小會也會為了處理信徒之間的紛爭奔走於兩造當事人之間，由此可以觀察教會在信徒的生活中不只是信仰的中心，並用實例了解小會調解信徒紛爭的方法。

七、關於議事錄收集、保存與使用的相關建議

　　所以只要能夠將議事錄的內容放在時代的脈絡下討論，或是集中於某項議題研究，其史料功能就能夠再次的被發揮出來。但不管是二二八事件、發放美援救濟物資、倍加運動還是紛爭調解等研究方向，都會遇到議事錄取得不易的問題，不僅無法做出比較，有些議題更因

---

47 《淡水教會小會議事錄第五冊》，頁38。

48 《淡水教會小會議事錄第二冊》，頁121。

史料不足而根本無法研究。

　　地方教會的議事錄屬於私密性較高的文件，記錄的範圍十分廣泛，包含人事、收支與紛爭處理等等，關乎教會或是信徒隱私。如果研究者無法得到該教會的信任與首肯，儘管研究者知道長老教會有這麼多的議事錄可以研究，但卻只能放棄這類的史料。另外雖然長老教會的中會規定要定期的審閱地方教會的議事錄，不過卻沒有訂定對地方教會保存審閱過後的議事錄的相關辦法，因此地方教會保存這些議事錄情況並不一定。

　　例如多年前淡水教會在大掃除的時候，清出了許多不要的物品，其中竟然包含了三本教會最初的小會議事錄與任職會議事錄。幸好當時該教會一位長老將這三本議事錄從垃圾堆中撿了回來，否則對研究臺灣長老教會的歷史又少了三本史料。所以地方教會的議事錄是否有保存有時也要碰碰運氣，希望這些史料就算教會本身不在意，但也能安全的放在教會的某個角落。因此在重視歷史的長老教會中，地方教會議事錄的保存程度不佳以及無法大量加以運用，可以說是相當遺憾的事情。

　　關於地方教會史料的分析與統計，以王成勉在1992年到1997年之間所做的調查最為完整，一共訪查了1,048間的教會。其中討論了許多教會排拒史料訪查的原因，歸納出受過去政教不合的影響、教會的保守心態、神學與教會立場分歧等等三個因素。至於教會會議記錄方面，由於牽涉到教會內部的問題，開放上格外嚴謹。[49] 目前臺灣神學院史料中心已有一定規模，但受限於整體的現實環境，仍舊無法蒐集地方教會的議事錄。因此應從制度面著手，透過總會或中會層級的立法來推動地方教會對議事錄的重視，進而制定保存、複製與使用等辦法。中央大學王成勉教授亦認為教會應該將目前的史料有系統的分類和整理，另外訂出一套管理與儲存辦法，若限於經費或空間，則可

---

49 王成勉，〈臺灣基督教史料之研究〉，收於林治平主編，《臺灣基督教史─史料與研究回顧國際學術研討會論文集》，頁244-249。

與大學或史料單位合作。[50]

　　臺神史料中心主任鄭仰恩表示確實應從制度面來解決這些問題，地方教會通常強調議事錄的私密性，但連國家檔案也都有解密的年限，教會的檔案何嘗不能仿效。[51] 例如我國《檔案法》第二章〈應用〉第二十二條規定：「國家檔案至遲應於三十年內開放應用，有其特殊情形者，得經立法院同意，延長期限。」[52] 而加拿大長老教會檔案館對小會議事錄亦有自己的開放原則，其年限是五十年內除了自己教會的小會員以外，不得對外開放。[53] 這都是長老教會可以參考的。但鄭仰恩也提到，就目前長老教會地方教會的文化面而言，就算總會或中會通過了相關的規定，地方教會也未必會遵行，這又是另一個棘手的難題了。曾經參與史料中心史料收集的林昌華對此也提出了同樣的看法，認為地方教會是否配合才是關鍵。[54] 因此除了立法之外，推動與遊說地方教會進行議事錄的整理與開放必須同步進行，否則便可能徒為具文。

八、結論與展望

　　賴永祥曾在1998年由中原大學舉辦的「臺灣基督教史：史料與研究回顧」國際學術研討會時表示，各地教會的資料同樣需要注意，因為這些資料是以前很少人使用的，其中包括教會裡的小會記錄。[55] 十多年前賴永祥認為這些史料「很少人用」，但是如今一樣仍然「很少人用」，這實在是相當可惜的事。以近十餘年的學位論文來看，只有

---

50 同前註，頁256。

51 鄭仰恩訪談，2011年10月18日，臺灣神學院教會史料中心。

52 參閱檔案管理局網站：http://www.archives.gov.tw/Chinese_archival/Publish.aspx?cnid=247。

53 Kim Arnold, Sharon P. Larade演講，林昌華記錄翻譯，〈歷史資料如何整理，收藏和保存〉，收於鄭仰恩主編，《臺灣基督長老教會歷史教育手冊》（臺北：使徒出版社，2010），頁223。

54 鄭仰恩訪談，2011年10月18日，臺灣神學院教會史料中心；林昌華訪談，2011年10月19日，電話訪問。

55 賴永祥，〈臺灣教會史——史料研究回顧與展望〉，收於林治平主編，《臺灣基督教史——史料與研究回顧國際學術研討會論文集》，頁14-15。

9篇在參考文獻上列上了地方教會的議事錄，其篇數不可謂多。或許僅以學位論文做為參考很可能低估了地方教會議事錄在學術研究上的使用情形，但大致上還是能夠反應出這份史料目前被應用之現況尚存龐大的開發空間。

此外，這些學位論文對議事錄的引用情形又會因為保存狀況、研究題目或個人因素而有所不同，引用的次數自然也有很大的差異。特別是當議事錄的史料功能與紀念冊、和會手冊、週報重疊時，就必須要找到另一條出路，議事錄的史料價值才能跳脫出單一教會歷史沿革或各項統計數據，賦予它新的生命，呈現歷史的另一個面相。

長老教會入臺已將屆滿一百五十年，教會數量為1,205間（2009年統計數據），是目前臺灣歷史最悠久、教會數量最多的教派。[56] 每一間地方教會就像一台不關機的駐點攝影機，用自己的角度連續記錄著這片土地的故事，然後把一部分的檔案存放在議事錄裡。而長老教會所屬的駐點攝影機遍布全臺灣，留下了豐富的資料庫。持平而論，淡水教會的議事錄本身並沒有太特殊之處，不過就是記錄了一間教會所發生的故事，但是如果能夠把長老教會眾多的地方教會議事錄做有系統的整理與保存，就能夠將長老教會散布於臺灣的「點」連成一個「面」，勾勒出一幅完整的圖像。如此一來，地方教會議事錄對不管是與時代的互動還是議題的研究，都將更深刻的見證長老教會在臺灣所走過的痕跡。

---

56 資料來源為臺灣基督長老教會總會教勢統計網站：http://churchstat.pct.org.tw/。

此次舉辦「臺灣教會史料國際學術研討會」
以及後續出版事宜承蒙

國科會

中央大學研發處

中央大學文學院

中央大學出版中心

中央大學歷史研究所

中原大學通識教育中心

臺灣基督教史學會

等單位撥款贊助，謹此致謝

附錄：臺灣教會史料國際學術研討會議程

主辦單位：中央大學歷史研究所
協辦單位：臺灣基督教史學會、中原大學通識教育中心、行政院國家
　　　　　科學委員會
會議地點：國立中央大學文學院文學一館國際會議廳

2011年12月2日（星期五）

09:00-09:20　報到		
09:20-09:30　開幕式		
09:30-10:00 主題演講	狄剛（前天主教臺北總教區總主教）	
10:00-10:15　拍攝團體照		
10:15-10:35　茶敘		
第一場 10:35-12:00 （主持人） 李宜涯	Martha L. Smalley（司馬倫） 　Documenting the Church in Taiwan: the 　Perspective from Yale University Rolf G. Tiedemann（狄德滿） 　Politics, Society, and Culture of Taiwan: 　Observations of English Presbyterian 　Missionaries, 1865-1953	（評論人） 王成勉 梁唯真
12:00-13:40　午餐		
第二場 13:40-15:10 （主持人） 古鴻廷	古偉瀛 　臺灣天主教主要史料：《教友生活周刊》 　之研究 王政文 　十九世紀臺灣基督徒研究與史料探討 黃子寧 　臺大楊雲萍文庫之長老教會白話字文獻 　研究	陳聰銘 張妙娟 張妙娟

15:10-15:30　茶敘			
第三場 15:30-17:00 （主持人） 古偉瀛	Jonathan Benda（班達）使用預錄影音 e-file 發表 　A New Perspective on the Christian University in Taiwan: Seeing Tunghai University through the Records of the Oberlin Shansi Memorial Association in the Oberlin College Archives, 1955-1979	古鴻廷	
	Yuki Takai-Heller（高井由紀） 　Articles about Taiwanese Churches that Appeared in News Periodicals of Churches in Japan during Japanese Colonial Rule of Taiwan: A Point of Contact between Japanese and Taiwanese Christianities	查忻	
	陳世榮 　日治時期臺灣官文書中所見教會資料之研究	查忻	

2011年12月3日（星期六）

08:45-09:00 報到		
第四場 09:00-10:30 （主持人） 吳蕙芳	王成勉 　臺灣教會史料分布與典藏之研究	（評論人） 吳昆財
	張妙娟 　「臺灣基督長老教會歷史資料館」館藏 　史料之研究	鄭仰恩
	鄭睦群 　淡水基督長老教會議事錄介紹：兼論地 　方教會議事錄之史料價值、限制與應用 　展望	鄭仰恩
10:30-10:45 茶敘		
第五場 10:45-12:15 （主持人） 張光正	梁唯真 　尋本溯源：太平境馬雅各紀念教會史料 　與歷史撰述之分析研究	洪健榮
	李宜涯 　張靜愚日記中有關中原大學史料的探 　討	張光正
	蔡蕙光 　教會聚會所典藏資料分析：以聚會所在 　臺灣的初期福音開展為中心（1949- 　1962）	周琇環
12:15-13:40 午餐（臺灣基督教史學會年會）		
第六場 圓桌論壇 13:40-16:50 （主持人） 鄭仰恩	13:40-14:15 專題演講	黃淑薇（香港浸會大學圖書館資深助理館 　長） 中國基督教史料蒐集的機遇與合作
	14:15-15:00 論壇Ⅰ	查時傑（基督教臺灣浸會神學院教授） 陳方中（輔仁大學天主教史料研究中心主 　任） 盧啟明（臺灣神學院史料中心研究助理）
	15:00-15:20 茶敘	
	15:20-16:50 論壇Ⅱ	林哲宗（臺北市中華基督教青年會幹事） 尹　遜（臺灣基督教青年會協會秘書） 陳志宏（臺灣信義會監督） 莊秀禎（中華福音神學院圖書館館長）
16:50-17:00 閉幕式		

國家圖書館出版品預行編目（CIP）資料

臺灣教會史料論集 / 王成勉主編 . -- 初版 .
-- 桃園縣中壢市：中央大學出版中心；
臺北市：遠流, 2013.12
　面；　公分
部分內容為英文
ISBN 978-986-03-9171-8（平裝）

1. 教會 2. 史料 3. 臺灣

247.0933　　　　　　　　　　102024208

臺灣教會史料論集

主編：王成勉
執行編輯：許家泰
編輯協力：黃薰儀

出版單位：國立中央大學出版中心
　　　　　桃園縣中壢市中大路 300 號 國鼎圖書資料館 3 樓
　　　　　遠流出版事業股份有限公司
　　　　　台北市南昌路二段 81 號 6 樓

發行單位／展售處：遠流出版事業股份有限公司
地址：台北市南昌路二段 81 號 6 樓
電話：(02) 23926899　傳真：(02) 23926658
劃撥帳號：0189456-1

著作權顧問：蕭雄淋律師
法律顧問：董安丹律師

2013 年 12 月 初版一刷
行政院新聞局局版台業字第 1295 號
售價：新台幣 420 元

遠流博識網 http://www.ylib.com E-mail: ylib@ylib.com